THE SLAYING OF MEGHANADA

THE SLAYING OF MEGHANADA

A Ramayana from Colonial Bengal

Michael Madhusudan Datta

TRANSLATED WITH AN INTRODUCTION BY

Clinton B. Seely

OXFORD
UNIVERSITY PRESS

2004

OXFORD
UNIVERSITY PRESS

Oxford New York
Auckland Bangkok Buenos Aires Cape Town Chennai
Dar es Salaam Delhi Hong Kong Istanbul Karachi Kolkata
Kuala Lumpur Madrid Melbourne Mexico City Mumbai
Nairobi São Paulo Shanghai Taipei Tokyo Toronto

Published by Oxford University Press, Inc.
198 Madison Avenue, New York, New York 10016

www.oup.com

Library of Congress Cataloging-in-Publication Data
Dutt, Michael Madhusudan, 1824–1873.
[Meghanadabadha kabya. English]
The slaying of Meghanada: a Ramayana from colonial Bengal /
Michael Madhusudan
Datta; translated with an introduction by Clinton B. Seely.
p. cm.
"This poem is a retelling of an episode about the character
Meghanada from the Ramayana."
ISBN 978-0-19-516799-3
I. Seely, Clinton B. II. Title.

PK1718.D74M413 2004
891.4'44—dc21 2003049889

Printed in the United States of America
on acid-free paper

for Gwen,

who has lived with
and loved Michael
as long as I have

PREFACE

It began, as so many intellectual pursuits begin for an academic, out of necessity. One had to be prepared to go into the classroom and teach, sometimes teach a text or materials relatively new and unfamiliar. Back in the early 1970s when I joined the faculty of the University of Chicago, I teamed up with my own professor, Edward C. Dimock, Jr., to offer a two-quarter survey course on the cultural and literary history of Bengal. His interests centered primarily in the premodern period around the figure of Sri Caitanya and the Vaishnava poets and theologians associated with this Bengali saint. It was left to me to cover the modern period, which meant, roughly, the nineteenth and twentieth centuries. I had been working on a dissertation that focused upon one of the premier poets of the twentieth century, Jibanananda Das, and so felt comfortable with the more modern material. The nineteenth century, however, seemed somewhat of an enigma. I had to prepare myself. And what better place to begin than with Michael Madhusudan Datta, identified by the literary historians as the man who began the modern age, literarily, and a man who wrote during the heart of the nineteenth century? His magnum opus, "The Slaying of Meghanada," was not available in an English translation. I had to struggle through this very erudite poet's rich but linguistically complex text. The experience proved rewarding, so much so that I have kept on reading and translating and rereading and retranslating his epic poem ever since. As my erstwhile colleague, a fine poet and translator of poetry, A. K. Ramanujan used to be fond of saying, one never really finishes the translation of a poem, one simply at some point must abandon it. I have come to that point and now abandon my translation of Datta's epic, a translation, as with all translations, still in progress.

But, of course, I shall not really abandon my translation, for I'll continue to teach this text to undergraduates and grad students alike, as I have off and on over the last three decades. And it is to the students I have had during those years that I must express my warmest thanks. Their responses to Datta's poem were for the most part gratifying, though I could not convince all of them of its charm. I wish also to thank my colleagues for their encouragement in this project, particularly Dipesh Chakrabarty here in my department at Chicago, and also Rachel Fell McDermott at Barnard College, who read the manuscript with a helpful eye and who herself has taught this text through my translation in her own classes.

Without a publisher, Datta's poem, originally in Bangla, would have remained relatively unknown to those who cannot read that language. I am truly grateful to Oxford University Press and specifically to Theodore Calderara, Associate Editor, for agreeing to at least look at the manuscript. Not all presses were so generous. And I am more thankful still that Oxford has seen fit to publish Datta's marvelous work. I am obliged to Margaret Case, who, as copy-editor, has spared me from committing any number of typographical errors and infelicitous locutions. Those that remain—it goes without saying—are all my doing, or undoing, as the case may be. Writing a book is one thing; actually producing the physical object is quite another. Rebecca Johns-Danes, production editor, saw to that end with a sure hand, which I appreciate. My sincere thanks also go to Janel M. Mueller, Dean of the Division of the Humanities, and to the Pritzker Endowment for South Asian Studies here at the University of Chicago for their generous moral and financial support of this publication.

Finally and emphatically, I thank my companion, my critic, my confidante, my Gwendolyn, my wife, a truly lovely person. It is she who has sustained me over these many years. And it was she who set a fine example of how to translate great literature with her rendition of the ornate Sanskrit prose narrative *Kadambari* by Banabhatta. Now Datta's *The Slaying of Meghanada* will take its place side by side with Bana's *Kadambari* on our bookshelf at home, as it should be. Michael, I'm sure, would be pleased.

CONTENTS

DRAMATIS PERSONAE
(also see Glossary)

Rākṣasas of the isle of Laṅkā

Citrāṅgadā, a wife of Rāvaṇa and mother of fallen Vīrabāhu
Mandodarī, main wife of Rāvaṇa and mother of Meghanāda
Meghanāda, eldest son of Rāvaṇa; also: *Indrajit, Rāvaṇi, Vāsavajit*
Pramīlā, wife of Meghanāda
Rāvaṇa, patriarch of the Rākṣasas; also: *Daśānana, Naikaṣeya, Paulastya*
Saramā, wife of Vibhīṣaṇa
Sūrpaṇakhā, sister of Rāvaṇa
Vibhīṣaṇa, a brother of Rāvaṇa and defector to Rāma's side; also: *Rāvaṇānuja*

Rāma, some of his family and his allies from the Indian mainland

Daśaratha, father of Rāma and Lakṣmaṇa
Hanumān, son of Pavana/Prabhañjana and a major southern warrior
Lakṣmaṇa, brother of Rāma; also: *Rāghavānuja, Rāmānuja, Saumitri*
Rāma, also: *Dāśarathi, Rāghava, Rāghavacandra, Rāghavendra, Rāmabhadra, Rāmacandra*
Sītā, wife of Rāma; also: *Jānakī, Maithilī, Vaidehī*
Sugrīva, new monarch of the southern kingdom of Kiṣkindhyā
Sumitrā, mother of Lakṣmaṇa and one of Daśaratha's three wives
Ūrmilā, wife of Lakṣmaṇa

Goddesses

Durgā, the supreme goddess and wife of Śiva; also: *Abhayā, Ambikā, Annadā, Bhagavatī, Bhairavī, Bhavānī, Bhaveśvarī, Bhīmā, Cāmuṇḍā, Caṇḍī, Gaurī, Haimavatī, Īśānī, Īśvarī, Jagadambā, Kātyāyanī, Kṣemaṅkarī, Mahāśakti, Maheśī, Maheśvarī, Nistāriṇī, Pārvatī, Śakti, Śaṅkarī, Śaśāṅkadhāriṇī, Satī, Tāriṇī, Ugracaṇḍā, Umā*
Lakṣmī, goddess of good fortune; also: *Indirā, Kamalā, Rājalakṣmī, Ramā, Śrī*
Māyā, a goddess, "illusion" deified

Rati, wife of Kāma; also: *Varānanā*

Śacī, wife of Indra; also: *Indrāṇī, Paulomī*

Sarasvatī, goddess of speech, the arts, and learning; also: *Bhāratī, Varadā*

Vāruṇī, wife of the god of the sea, Varuṇa/Pracetas/Pāśī

Gods

Agni, god of fire and Meghanāda's personal deity; also: *Hutāśana, Sarvabhuk, Sarvaśuci, Vaiśvānara, Vibhāvasu, Vītihotra*

Indra, known as lord of the gods, lord of the skies; also: *Āditeya, Ākhaṇḍala, Devendra, Jiṣṇu, Kuliśī, Mahendra, Meghavāhana, Purandara, Sahasrākṣa, Śakra, Sunāsīra, Vajrapāṇi, Vajrī, Vāsava*

Kāma, god of love; also: *Anaṅga, Kandarpa, Kusumeṣu, Madana, Manasija, Manmatha, Mīnadhvaja, Pañcaśara, Phuladhanu, Smara*

Kārttikeya, general of the gods; also: *Kumāra, Ṣaḍānana, Śaktidhara, Śikhidhvaja, Skanda, Tārakāri*

Kṛṣṇa, see Viṣṇu; also: *Śyāma*

Pavana, god of the wind; father of Hanumān; also: *Prabhañjana*

Pracetas, god of the sea; also: *Pāśī*

Śiva, the supreme god and husband of Durgā; also: *Āśutoṣa, Bhairava, Bhava, Bhaveśa, Bhīma, Candracūḍa, Dhūrjaṭi, Digambara, Girīśa, Hara, Īśāna, Jaṭādhara, Kapardī, Maheśa, Mohana, Mṛtyuñjaya, Nīlakaṇṭha, Pañcamukha, Paśupati, Pinākī, Rudra, Sadānanda, Śambhu, Śaṅkara, Sthāṇu, Śūlapāṇi, Śūlī, Tāpasendra, Tripurāri, Triśūlī, Tryambaka, Vāma, Virūpākṣa, Viśvanātha, Vṛṣabhadhvaja, Vṛṣadhvaja, Vyomakeśa, Yogīndra*

Viṣṇu, a major god with ten avatars, including Kṛṣṇa; husband of Lakṣmī; also: *Caturbhuja, Cintāmaṇi, Gadādhara, Hari, Hṛṣīkeśa, Keśava, Kṛṣṇa, Mādhava, Murāri, Pītāmbara, Puṇḍarīkākṣa, Sauri, Upendra*

Yama, god of death; also: *Daṇḍadhara, Kṛtānta, Śamana*

THE SLAYING OF MEGHANADA

INTRODUCTION

Michael Madhusudan Datta (1824–73 C.E.), exceptional as poet and playwright in both English and Bangla (also known as Bengali), in many ways typified educated Bengalis of his day when East and West met constantly in Calcutta, the administrative capital of Britain's East Indian colony. His name itself, one part Christian-European (Michael) and two parts Hindu-Indian (Madhusudan Datta),[1] calls attention to the clash as well as the accommodation of cultures that took place in South Asia at the height of the two hundred years of her colonial period, a period that would end upon the stroke of midnight dividing the 14th from the 15th of August 1947, with the concomitant partitioning of British India into the independent nation-states of India and Pakistan. Datta's magnum opus, *Meghanadavadha kavya* (The slaying of Meghanada) (1861), needs be seen, very much like its author, as simultaneously extraordinary and representative. It is an extraordinary piece of literature, a sophisticated verse narrative in nine cantos; it is utterly representative of the cosmopolitan culture of mid-nineteenth-century India.

Bengali literary historians even today mark with his text and its year of publication the divide between the so-called premodern and modern eras in Bangla literature. From the vantage point of the twenty-first century, it may seem strange to refer to a time in the nineteenth century as modern. It remains, however, the way that moment is viewed from within Bangla cultural history, and justifiably so, particularly today, when "modern" can imply passé in a here-and-now world self-characterized as postmodern. But modern contrasts with traditional, and it is this meaning of modern that pertains to Datta's poem. His narrative does not deny, negate, or ignore the traditional. It does, though, contrast with what preceded it. Datta's *Meghanada* marks a major shift in imaginative writing, a shift in the Bangla literary sensibilities of its day. Bengal during the nineteenth century and on into the beginnings of the twentieth century took the lead on many fronts. It was said then that what Bengal thinks today, the rest of India thinks tomorrow. Similarly, what happened in Bengal as exemplified in the works of Datta would happen later throughout India. Modernity in the literatures of South Asia began in 1861, and began with Michael Madhusudan Datta.

Background

Call it a fluke of history, but Kolkata (then known as Calcutta)—not Mumbai (Bombay), not Chennai (Madras), not the Asian banking hub of Hong Kong—became the Second City of the British Empire.[2] Chartered in the year 1600 by Queen Elizabeth, when Shakespeare strode the English stage, the East India Company later that same century chose the Bengal area of the Indian subcontinent for its commercial headquarters. Calcutta did not exist before the British merchants, Job Charnock prominent among them, set up shop along the banks of the Hooghly just north of the mouth of that river that empties into the Bay of Bengal. In the year 1990, Calcutta officially and with panache celebrated its 300th anniversary. Back in its infancy, business, as it is wont to do, turned to politics. And after Robert Clive had defeated in 1757 the Nawab of Bengal, Sirajuddaula, in the Battle of Plassey north of Calcutta, the Company sued for and got the *dewani* or revenue-collecting authority for the region. The Company was, so to speak, now really in business. It would remain so throughout the eighteenth century and through much of the nineteenth, until the latter half of that century when, following the Sepoy Rebellion of 1857—seen from another angle as the first Indian War of Independence—the crown assumed authority, dissolving the East India Company and taking unto itself India, figuratively its crown jewel.

The nineteenth century had begun in Calcutta with a hotly contested colonial debate temporarily resolved, a debate that pitted Orientalists against Anglicists. Both designations referred to the British colonial administrators, not to the indigenous Indian population. The label Orientalist at the beginning of the 1800s meant something far different from the connotations that same term has assumed since the publication of Edward Said's *Orientalism* (1978). Said's book changed forever the way we look at other cultures, other peoples. Orientalism, since Said's perspicacious study, refers to the political acts—whether intended by the actors as political or not is immaterial—by which the West has defined and thereby created the Orient, and created it as its own other, nowadays capitalized and nominalized into "the Other." Orientalism now refers to an attitude, a view of the Orient held by the West, the Occident. Orientalism is expressed through words as well as representation via other media, through books and reports, through drawings and paintings, through museums of various sorts. Overt military conquest and even economic conquest are quite another matter. Orientalism points to what might best be called a narrative conquest, as opposed to a physical conquest. Orientalism, in the post-Saidian sense, had deprived and still does deprive the non-Western cultures of agency in the making of their own identity. That is to say, these cultures were and are defined by the West for the West's own purpose, which is fundamentally, in Saidian terms, imperialistic even today. From the Saidian perspective, both the Orientalists and the Anglicists of 1800 were Orientalists. Both contributed to the British colonial enterprise and particularly to the justification for colonialism. Both saw India in need of British tutelage in order for the people of that land to become something other than, better than, what they were. In Calcutta of the early nineteenth century, however, the so-called Orientalists (in a pre-Saidian sense) were those who argued in favor of both the classical as well as the vernacular languages of India. They were those who, in many cases, studied these languages and valued the literatures written in them. The Anglicists, on the other hand, tended to see little merit in the indigenous texts and indigenous knowledge systems, though they would concede the utility of learning native tongues as a means by which to rule the colony. Anglicists felt that the English language itself and the literature and the culture and the knowledge conveyed through English were superior to anything found in India.

At the start of the nineteenth century, the Orientalists among the British colonialists had won the day temporarily. Lord Wellesley, then governor-general, the chief executive officer in India of the John Bull Company, as it was sometimes called, proved sympathetic to the Orientalists' view of how to administer the colony and of what value to place upon the languages of India. It was Wellesley who established in 1800 a college at Fort William, said fort being the British military stronghold in Calcutta and the symbol of colonial power. Fort William College, which began instruction the following year, in 1801, came into being for the express purpose of training young British administrators so that they could better perform their duties in the colony. The college provided instruction in several of the languages of India, languages that would serve this new administrative cadre well. It was an institution—the Asiatic Society of Bengal, established in 1784 being another—where the languages of India and at least some of the texts in those languages were taken seriously. How seriously and in what sense the Orientalists took these South Asian languages seriously can be glimpsed somewhat through the subjects for "Public Disputations and Declamations" staged during the initial decade or so of the college's existence. For the first of these public displays of the linguistic competence of the Company servants, in 1802, topics were proposed for three of the languages taught at the college: Persian, Hindustani, and Bengali. Bengali's topic, pejorative as well as paternalistic in the extreme, was the following: "The Asiatics are capable of as high a degree of civilization as the Europeans."

And, two years later, the topic for disputation in Bengali by the college's students reveals more clearly the Orientalists' position vis-à-vis South Asian languages per se: "The translation of the best works in the Sanskrit into popular languages of India would promote the extension of science and civilization."[3] Orientalists would say yea; Anglicists would say nay, arguing that there was nothing in those ancient texts that could advance science and civilization.

In 1813, the British parliament passed a renewal of the East India Company's charter, reaffirming the Company's right to operate in India but at the same time redefining and refining the Company's responsibilities in terms of Britain's then currently envisioned colonial mission. The Charter of 1813 recognized education of the colonial subjects as a major principle upon which the colonial enterprise should be based. Gauri Viswanathan shows how and how well this new commitment to the education of the natives fit with the overarching efforts of the British to consolidate power in their colony.[4] The commitment to education, however, could hardly be considered one-sided and the concern of the imperialists only. In 1816 a group of the leading Hindu gentlemen of Calcutta established Hindoo (the older spelling of Hindu) College "to instruct the sons of the Hindoos in the European and Asiatic languages and sciences."[5] Hindoo College survives today as Presidency College, the premier institution of its sort in the state of West Bengal and undoubtedly one of the finest colleges in all of India. There were then and had been long before the advent of the British the *tol*, a traditional school for the learning of Sanskrit, and the *madrasah*, a school for Islamic education. The Company had even financed the establishment of two educational institutions, the Hindu College in Benaras and the Calcutta Madrassah, its version, albeit in imperial garb, of those more traditional schools. But here was a college (the "junior division" of which being what is now called a "school") that disseminated learning of both the European and Asiatic sort—its curriculum and its medium of instruction eventually becoming decidedly more European than Asiatic.

A decade after its founding, Hindoo College had increased considerably the importance ascribed to English. Of Hindoo College, cultural historian Sushil Kumar De writes: "The institution was meant to supply liberal education in English, but prominence was given to the study of English language and literature, and from 1826 [carried into effect in 1827] all lectures were delivered in English. For the first time English language was cultivated in this college, not as done before to the slight extent necessary to carry on business with Europeans, but as the most convenient channel through which access was to be obtained to the literature of the West."[6]

At this very point in time, an amazingly charismatic and brilliant young man joined the faculty of Hindoo College, in March of 1826, a month shy of his seventeenth birthday. His name was Henry Louis Vivian Derozio. Though born in India, he had Portuguese blood in his ancestry, as the name might indicate. Derozio took his schooling at the Dhurmtollah Academy in Calcutta, run by a "freethinking" Scotsman, and the young Henry likewise developed into a freethinker, a questioner of religion. He was also a poet, among the first Indians to write poetry in English, and quite patriotic Indian poetry to boot. The most famous of his compositions, a sonnet, begins, "My country! in thy day of glory past." Derozio's country was India, and he was proud of it.[7]

Hindoo College appointed the soon-to-be-seventeen Henry Derozio to teach English literature and history, which he did passionately. His syllabus—strictly speaking, the college's syllabus for "the first three classes"—from which he taught, in 1828, reads like a course in Western Civilization: Oliver Goldsmith's histories of Rome and England; William Robertson's *The History of the Reign of the Emperor Charles V with a View of the Progress of Society in Europe, from the Subversion of the Roman Empire, to the Beginning of the Sixteenth Century*; William Russell's *The History of Modern Europe: With an Account of the Decline and Fall of the Roman Empire; and a View of the Progress of Society, from the Rise of the Modern Kingdoms to the Peace of Paris in 1763, in a Series of Letters from a Nobleman to His Son*; John Gay's fables; Alexander Pope's translations of the *Iliad* and *Odyssey*; John Dryden's *The Works of Virgil*; John Milton's *Paradise Lost*; and one of Shakespeare's tragedies.[8] But Derozio did far more than just teach in the classroom. Around him gathered a coterie of Hindoo College students, by upbringing Hindus, but nonetheless attracted to this smart, charming, young, questioning, atheistically inclined teacher. Derozio's residence in Calcutta developed into the gathering spot for many of these students, who collectively came to be known as Young Bengal. These collegegoing intellectuals were eager to assimilate many of the more progressive ideas to which they had been exposed, were equally eager (some of them) to explore their own cultural past and willing (some of them) to speak out against British abuses of power in India as well as to denounce what they viewed as superstitious, obscurant practices among their fellow Hindus, including parents. Their outward acts of defiance against orthodoxy included, most notably, eating beef and imbibing alcohol—both taboo among good Hindus of the day.

Derozio and the atmosphere of Hindoo College were not the only forces to challenge Hindu orthodoxy. The Charter of 1813 had granted Christian missionaries, long held at bay by official Company policy, greater access to India. But even prior to that, the Bengali Hindu community felt the sting of sanctimonious Christian criticism. In part in response to such criticism of, among other things, idolatry and the myriad gods and goddesses of the Hindus, Ram Mohun Roy (1772–1833) and associates established in 1828 the Brahmo Sabha (The assembly of Brahma), subsequently recast and renamed the Brahmo Samaj (The society of Brahma). Purified Hinduism, of Ram Mohun Roy's creation, consisted of a monotheistic religion, devoid of any anthropomorphic deity. The "Brahma" here is not the god that is part of what is sometimes referred to as the triumvirate of Brahma-Vishnu-Shiva, but instead the abstract principle of "brahman," ethereal divinity pure and simple. This reenvisioned Hinduism, grounded upon the ancient Hindu sacred texts known as the Upanishads, formed the basis for the Brahmo Samaj's theology. Brahmoism was still Hinduism, but it looked very much like a form of Christianity without Christ. Though from one viewpoint still Hinduism, the Brahmo Samaj became seen by orthodox Hindus as apostasy. And Hindus, in many cases, rejected Brahmos, even their own blood relatives, as outcastes.

During that same year of 1828 the tide had begun to turn within the colonial administration against the Orientalists and in favor of the Anglicists. William Bentinck took up the mantle of governor-general in 1828. During his tenure, the College of Fort William closed its doors.[9] Other institutions of learning, catering to the cultivation of South Asian languages and knowledge systems, suffered from a lack of official colonial administrative support. Bentinck was the first of the truly anti-Orientalist, pro-Anglicist governors-general. And it was while he governed that the Orientalist-Anglicist controversy solidified into just that, a real controversy. In the words of one of the Anglicists, Charles Trevelyan, the Orientalists' objective "was to educate Europeans in the languages and cultures of the East" whereas the Anglicists sought "to educate Asiatics in the sciences of the West."[10] Trevelyan's pronouncement came out in a publication entitled *A Series of Papers on the Application of the Roman Alphabet to All the Oriental Languages*, issued from Serampore's Mission Press in 1834. The title itself makes evidently clear the thrust of the Anglicists. They even wanted to Anglicize the Bangla alphabet. Serampore, a village north of but close to Calcutta, was headquarters for the Baptist missionaries, William Carey prominent among them. Carey had been and continued to be a champion of the Bangla language, not just for the language qua language but also for its utility as a proselytizing vehicle. He had served as the first and most prominent professor of Bangla in the Fort William College. But, as David Kopf notes in his richly documented history of this period, even Serampore College, feeling the pressure from the Anglicists during the Bentinck period, Anglicized its curriculum and thereby "lost its attractiveness to Indians."[11]

The Indians' reaction, in general, to Anglicizing curricula may not have been as obvious or as negative as Kopf's statement implies. It should be kept in mind that the Hindu gentlemen who founded Hindoo College in 1816 intended its curriculum to include prominently "European . . . languages and sciences." What did bother a number of guardians of students who attended Hindoo College was not the curriculum per se but the extracurricular activities and growing influence of the college's star instructor, Henry Derozio. These Hindu parents and guardians feared this charismatic teacher might cause their children—his students—to reject the Hinduism of their forefathers and convert to Christianity or join the Brahmo Samaj, both equally sacrilegious moves.

Throughout the nineteenth century but particularly in the first half of it in the intellectual crucible of Calcutta, Christianity represented not just a religion but also an intellectual, even civilizational, tradition. Christianity stood for the European Enlightenment. It stood for Western Civilization. Christianity subsumed within it the literature of Milton, to be sure, but also that of Shakespeare and that of Virgil and Homer—however incongruent with Christianity these latter pagans might seem—and all the other texts included in the Hindoo College syllabus from which Derozio and his colleagues taught. As Datta would put it in an essay written toward the middle of the century, in 1854, Christianity, the British, and the English language itself were all three civilizing forces and should be brought to bear on India. Quite spectacularly, albeit bombastically, Datta employs in that essay the Virgilian conceit of Aeneas approaching Carthage, having left Troy behind on his destined journey to Italy and empire. India, "this queenly Hindustan," as he styles her, is Dido. Britain, particularly the British imperial advent into India, is a fair-haired, virile Aeneas. Datta begins this essay of his entitled "The Anglo-Saxon and the Hindu" with an epigraph in Latin from the Aeneid (Bk IV)—*Quis novus hic nostris successit sedibus hospes*?—which he translates: "Who is the stranger that has come to our dwelling?" The answer: It is the Anglo-Saxon. It is the Anglo-Saxon, who brings with him his language: "I acknowledge to you, and I need not blush to do so—that I love the language of the Anglo-Saxon. Yes—I *love* the language,—the glorious language of the Anglo-Saxon! My imagination visions forth before me the language of the Anglo-Saxon in all its radiant beauty; and I feel silenced and abashed."[12] And this Anglo-Saxon, in the course of Datta's essay, becomes transformed from Aeneas into the Crusader. But unlike Aeneas—who leaves Dido, who in turn, distraught, commits suicide—Datta's Crusader has a mission to perform in that land to which he ventures. "It is the glorious mission, I repeat, of the Anglo-Saxon to renovate, to regenerate, or—in one word, to Christianize the Hindu."[13]

Though Datta was himself a Christian convert, he had clearly less concern for the theological side of Christianity in this essay than with Christianity as a civilizing force. Derozio, in many ways an atheist and accused of being such—he denied it—represented and had preached that same civilizational Christianity to his students, inside and outside the classroom. And some within the Hindu elite community were sorely afraid for their sons. One of Derozio's students, Krishna Mohan Banerjee, who would convert to Christianity and become the Reverend K. M. Banerjee, the most prominent Bengali Christian cleric of his age, described the tenor of some of the discourse associated with Derozio and his students, at Derozio's own quarters and at a debating club known as the Academic Association: "The authority of the Hindu religion was questioned, its sanctions impeached, its doctrines ridiculed, its philosophy despised, its ceremonies accounted fooleries, its injunctions openly violated and its priesthood defied as an assembly of fools, hypocrites and fanatics."[14]

Anxiety within the Hindu community ran high. Rumors circulated disparaging Derozio, impugning his moral character. On April 23, 1831, Hindoo College's managing committee called for Derozio's dismissal from the faculty, a decision taken by the Hindus alone, for the British members had recused themselves from this matter that concerned Hindus and Hinduism fundamentally. In his letter of resignation dated April 25, solicited by and addressed to H. H. Wilson, who was officially known as the Visitor of the College but was in fact the person in charge of the college administratively, Derozio denied the allegations made against him and decried the managing committee's refusal to allow him to testify in person before it. Wilson, feeling obliged to abide by the wishes of the committee, accepted Derozio's resignation. By quirk of fate, eight months later, in December of 1831, the twenty-two-year-old Henry Louis Vivian Derozio died of cholera. His legacy, however, lived on palpably and profoundly, in those labeled Young Bengal. Nearly six years after Derozio's death, Madhusudan Datta would be admitted to this college's junior department (school), starting in 1837, when he was thirteen years old. He would remain at Hindoo College, both junior and senior divisions, for the next five years, five truly formative years of his life. If biographer Suresh Chandra Maitra is correct, these five years were not just formative but literally transformative of Datta, who had been, writes Maitra, a tongue-tied, shy youth.[15] By the time he left that college, Datta had become a boldly expressive, utterly confident young man.[16]

Two years earlier, in 1835, Thomas Babington Macaulay had issued his famous (or infamous, depending upon one's perspective) minute on education. Macaulay, a committed Benthamite Utilitarian, as were many in Britain at this time, had come to India only the year before and had been made presiding officer of the Committee on Public Instruction. The title itself calls attention to the importance placed upon education, a desideratum-cum-justification of Britain's colonial enterprise. It was the committee's charge to select, in the interest of improving the education of Indians, the language through which Company-funded schools would give instruction. The question itself, whether English or one of the South Asian languages should become the sanctioned medium of instruction, formed the very crux of that ongoing Orientalist-Anglicist controversy. From Macaulay's minute, one can infer that the committee was unanimous in rejecting any of the Indian vernaculars, Bangla among them. Even Persian seems not to have been considered seriously. Only Sanskrit, Arabic, and English remained in contention, and the committee split down the middle on Sanskrit and/or Arabic versus English. Macaulay opted for English. In his minute he asserted:

> I have no knowledge of either Sanscrit or Arabic. But I have done what I could to form a correct estimate of their value. I have read translations of the most celebrated Arabic and Sanscrit works. I have conversed both here and at home with men distinguished by their proficiency in the Eastern tongues. I am quite ready to take the Oriental learning at the valuation of the Orientalists themselves. I have never found one among them who could deny that a single shelf of a good European library was worth the whole native literature of India and Arabia. The intrinsic superiority of the Western literature is, indeed, fully admitted by those members of the committee who support the Oriental plan of education.[17]

Hindoo College, already an English-medium institution, was unaffected by the pronouncement, but such a statement reaffirmed the correctness of their position for those who attended the college or supported its educational philosophy. The essence of Macaulay's decision had been urged by a number of the educated Bengali elite including such a notable figure as Ram Mohun Roy. Roy had argued in a letter to the governor-general more than a decade earlier against Sanskrit both as a medium of instruction and as a purveyor of (worthwhile) knowledge: "The Sanscrit language, so difficult that almost a lifetime is necessary for its acquisition, is well known to have been for ages a lamentable check to the diffusion of knowledge, and the learning concealed under this almost impervious veil is far from sufficient to reward the labor of acquiring it."[18] And no matter how insulting Macaulay's 1835 minute might appear to be, it was meant less as a snub of India's cultural heritage than as an endorsement of English as a medium through which all knowledge, of India's heritage as well as of European arts and sciences, should be transmitted to the educable Indian population. The way Macaulay saw it, "Within the last hundred and twenty years, a nation which has previously been in a state as barbarous as that in which our ancestors were before the Crusades, has gradually emerged from the ignorance in which it was sunk, and has taken its place among civilized communities. I speak of Russia. . . . The languages of Western Europe civilized Russia. I cannot doubt that they will do for the Hindoo what they have done for the Tartar."[19] But education, specifically education in and through English, was not for everyone, Macaulay conceded. So what should be the goal of the Company's educational policy? Macaulay is clear about his objectives:

> In one point I fully agree with the gentlemen to whose general views I am opposed. I feel with them, that it is impossible for us, with our limited means, to attempt to educate the body of the people. We must at present do our best to form a class who may be interpreters between us and the millions whom we govern; a class of persons, Indian in blood and colour, but English in taste, in opinions, in morals, and in intellect. To that class we may leave it to refine the vernacular dialects of the country, to enrich those dialects with terms of science borrowed from the Western nomenclature, and to render them by degrees fit vehicles for conveying knowledge to the great mass of the population.[20]

As outrageous as Macaulay's statement on the goals of education might appear ("to form a class . . . of persons, Indian in blood and colour, but English in taste, in opinions, in morals, and in intellect"), the Company's educational policy proved, to a degree, successful. Hindoo College, in a sense, had preempted Macaulay's minute. It was already producing those persons described by Macaulay. Michael Madhusudan Datta epitomizes the perfect Macaulayan product, acculturated to English tastes, notably in literature. Little wonder, then, that Datta began his literary career writing in English.

Michael Madhusudan Datta

He was born January 25, 1824, of the Common Era—the year 1230 by the Bangla calendar. His father Raj Narain and mother Jahnabi were then residents of the village of Sagardari in the district of Jessore, which now lies within the borders of Bangladesh. At the *nama-karana* or "name-giving" ceremony, his parents called him Madhusudan or literally "the slaying of the demon Madhu," a feat accomplished by Vishnu and thus one of that god's many epithets, besides being a rather common Hindu name at the time. Madhusudan was the first issue of this couple. They had two other children, boys who both died young, leaving Madhusudan for all practical purposes an only child.

The family was not poor. Datta's father practiced law. As was necessary for anyone in the legal profession in those days, Raj Narain spoke Persian, the language of the law courts, a legacy from the Moghul Empire perpetuated by the British East India Company until 1837, when English replaced Persian in the colonial legal system. Calcutta, as opposed to a village in the hinterland, would naturally be the place to practice law. It was to Kidderpore, a neighborhood (then little more than a village) near Calcutta's harbor that he moved his wife and son, when Datta had reached the age of eight. Raj Narain plied his profession in the colonial courts of Calcutta, the Sudder Dewani Adalat (chief civil court), attaining considerable renown and the wealth that often goes with reputation. He has been described as "one among the three best-known and highest-paid lawyers" at this time.[21] The other two, moreover, appear to have been formidable rivals: Ramaprasad Roy, Ram Mohun Roy's son, and Prasanna Kumar Tagore, a cousin of Rabindranath's grandfather, Dwarkanath Tagore.[22] However, Datta's most recent as well as thorough biographer, Ghulam Murshid, dismisses such statements about the elevated status of lawyer Raj Narain as pure fabrication.[23] Be that as it may, the family seems to have lived quite comfortably, at least through Datta's student days.

Whether from his father or not, Datta had learned Persian, as is evident from his ability to recite Persian *ghazal* verse, entertaining fellow Hindoo College students with such recitations. His primary languages, though, were Bangla and English, Bangla being his mother tongue. And from his mother, we are told by his biographers, he heard—in Bangla, naturally—the *Ramayana* and the *Mahabharata,* Hindu India's two great epics. English, not Bangla, may have been his first language, if not chronologically, at least with respect to his command of it. By the time he became a young adult, he had attained a phenomenal command of the Queen's English. He flourished and felt comfortable in an English-medium environment. He read literature in English, much of it English literature or European literature in English translation. An excerpt from the first essay that we have of his, entitled "On Poetry Etc." and in English, shows his precocity:

> It is the misfortune of the modern Muse to be loaded with ornaments which too often veil her native charms:—To illustrate this, we need not go very far: The works of a famous living poet—

> "Anacreon Moore" will serve our purpose:—Beautiful as the poetry of this writer is, where is the reader who does not feel a sort of sickening refinement in many passages—a collocation of epithets and expressions which often prove destructive of that effect which naked simplicity would produce—Tom Moore, lavish as he is in his similes of "flowers" and "stars", "breezes" and "Zephyrs", has never written a better line of poetry or given a sweeter description of a flower than Spenser. When the latter sweetly warbles of the—
>
> "Lily, ladie of the flowering field"
>
> Fairy Queene.[24]

Another essay, written in 1842 after he had been at Hindoo College for a number of years, garnered a prize, a gold medal, presented to him with great fanfare at a public meeting. Following the simple title of "An Essay," that prose piece bore the lengthy subtitle of "On the importance of educating Hindoo Females, with reference to the improvement which it may be expected to produce on the education of children, in their early years, and the happiness it would generally confer on domestic life."[25] English was clearly his forte.

Thanks to Gour Dass Bysack (also spelled a number of different ways, including Gour Dos Bysac, by Datta himself), his best friend at Hindoo College and one to whom he dedicated a number of his poems, we have examples of his college poesy, including an acrostic based on Bysack's name:

AN ACROSTIC

G-o! simple lay! And tell that fair,
O-h! 'tis for her, her lover dies!
U-ndone by her, his heart sincere
R-esolves itself thus into sighs!
D-ear cruel maid! tho' ne'er doth she
O-nce think, for her thus breaks my heart
S-ad fate! oh! yet must I love thee,
B-e thou unkind, till life doth part!
Y-oung Peri of the East! thou maid divine!
S-weet one! oh! let me not thus die:
A-ll kind, to these fond arms of mine
C-ome! and let me no longer sigh![26]

Poetry was his passion, but Hindoo College, as its charter declared, attended to education in both the arts and the sciences. And Datta, through one of his poems, acknowledges that other branch of a college education:

Oh! how my heart exulteth while I see
These future flow'rs, to deck my country's brow,
Thus kindly nurtured in this nursery!—
Perchance, unmark'd some here are budding now,
Whose temples shall with laureate-wreaths be crown'd
Twined by the Sisters Nine: whose angel-tongues
Shall charm the world with their enchanting songs.
And time shall waft the echo of each sound
To distant ages:—some, perchance, here are,
Who, with a Newton's glance, shall nobly trace
The course mysterious of each wandering star;
And, like a God, unveil the hidden face
Of many a planet to man's wondering eyes,
And give their names to immortality.[27]

The "future flowers" are, of course, his fellow students in the Hindoo College "nursery," some of whom would be likely to blossom into prominence in their adult careers. For those successful in the arts, there will come fame, indicated here by the very European image of the nine Greek muses and the laurel they twist into crowns. Nowhere is there mentioned Sarasvati, the Hindu goddess of the arts and learning; Datta had yet to find his Indian roots. And there are those among his colleagues who would make their mark in the sciences, who would develop the perceptive eye of a Sir Isaac Newton, and go on to reveal something of the mysteries of the heavenly bodies and by so doing become famous. The arts—narratively speaking in this sonnet and in Datta's estimation generally—come before the sciences in many ways. After all, he contended elsewhere, Shakespeare, with some schooling, could learn what Newton knew, but Newton, without the native talent of a Shakespeare, could never learn to write like him.[28]

Datta would introduce sonnets, of which the above is a somewhat idiosyncratic example with its rhyme scheme of abab cddc efef gg, into Bangla literature when later in his career he turned to writing in his mother tongue. There are precious few notable Bengali poets from the time of Datta to the present who have not composed Bangla sonnets. That poetic form remains to this day extremely productive in Bangla literature. After its introduction into Bangla, it migrated to Marathi poetry and to various other South Asian literatures. The history of the sonnet in South Asia, in languages other than English, dates from 1860 when Datta wrote to a friend, "I want to introduce the sonnet into our language," and then included his Bangla sonnet entitled

Kabi-matribhasha (The poet's mother tongue), subsequently revised and renamed *Bangabhasha* (The language of Bengal).[29] Beneath his poem he asked rhetorically, "What say you to this my good friend!" And he adds, "In my humble opinion, if cultivated by men of genius, our sonnet in time would rival the Italian."[30] Five years later, in 1865 while living in Versailles, France, Datta would send Victor Emanuel a sonnet on Dante, "a little oriental flower," as he called it, composed in Bangla with both an Italian and a French translation done by himself, on the occasion of that poet's 600th birth anniversary.[31]

True to his love and esteem of poetry, Datta aspired from his Hindoo College days to become a poet. He ardently wished to be physically a part of England and English-cum-European culture. That sentiment is articulated again and again during this time in his life:

> I sigh for Albion's distant shore
> Its valleys green, its mountains high;
> Tho' friends, relations, I have none
> In that far clime, yet, oh! I sigh
> To cross the vast Atlantic wave
> For glory, or a nameless grave!
>
> My father, mother, sister, all
> Do love me and I love them too,
> Yet oft the tear-drops rush and fall
> From my sad eyes like winter's dew,
> And, oh! I sigh for Albion's strand
> As if she were my native-land![32]

No matter that he was an only child and had no sister, the sentiments expressed were heartfelt. It was as if he had two native lands, England and Bengal, emotionally as well as intellectually, though to date he had never left Bengal. Datta wrote the poem in 1841. It would take him a score of years and some dramatic changes in his life before he would actually sail off to England in 1862 to study for the bar at Gray's Inn. But his poetry could, and would, precede him. Possibly emboldened by his receipt of the gold medal for that essay, as noted above, he sent off in October of 1842 some of his poetry to a couple of British journals, informing his friend of this in a feigned offhanded yet typically effervescent manner, in English, of course, the language of all his letters: "Good Heavens—what a thing have I forgotten to inform you of—I sent my poems to the Editor of the *Blackwood's* Tuesday last: I haven't dedicated them to you as I intended, but to William Wordsworth, the Poet. My dedication runs thus: 'These Poems are most respectfully dedicated to William Wordsworth Esq, the Poet, by a foreign admirer of his genius—the author.' Oh! to what a painful state have I committed myself. Now, I think the Editor will receive them graciously, now I think he will reject them."[33] In that same month he wrote to the editor of *Bentley's Miscellany*, London: "It is not without much fear that I send you the accompanying productions of my juvenile Muse, as contribution to your Periodical." He identified himself thus: "I am a Hindoo—a native of Bengal—and study English at the Hindoo College in Calcutta. I am now in my eighteenth year,—'a child'—to use the language of a poet of your land, Cowley, 'in learning but not in age.' "[34]

The Irish poet Thomas Moore had published in 1830 his biography of George Gordon Lord Bryon (1788–1824), who, coincidentally, happens to have died the same year Datta was born. We get a sense of the intellectual excitement felt by Hindoo College students as we learn of Datta and Bysack reading that same biography, one lending it to the other, and of Datta's exuberance upon reading it. And then he, in one of his typically confident assertions, writes to Bysack in November of 1842, "I am reading Tom Moore's Life of my favourite Byron—a splendid book, upon my word! Oh! how should I like to see you write my 'Life' if I happen to be a great poet—which I am almost sure I shall be, if I can go to England."[35] The poems mentioned in the letters, though they got to England by post, were never published. For the time being, he could "sigh for Albion's distant shore," and he could revel in the intellectual ferment that went with being a student at Hindoo College. But that was about to change, dramatically.

Toward the end of 1842, Datta's father decided it was high time his eighteen-year-old son wed. Datta reacted with abhorrence to the very idea of marriage at this moment in his life, and specifically to the type of bride his father had chosen for him. A spate of letters to Bysack, four in three days at the very end of November, reveals something of Datta's state of mind at that moment:

> I wish (Oh! I really wish) that somebody would hang me! At the expiration of three months from hence I am to be married;—dreadful thoughts! It harrows up my blood and makes my hair stand like quills on the fretful porcupine! My betrothed is the daughter of a rich zemindar;—poor girl! What a deal of misery is in store for her in the ever inexplorable womb of Futurity! You know my desire for leaving this country is too firmly rooted to be removed. The sun may forget to rise, but I cannot remove it from

> my heart. Depend upon it—in the course of a year or two more, I must either be in England or cease "to be" at all—*one of these must be done*![36]

"At the expiration of three months from hence I am to be married;—dreadful thoughts!" So dreadful to him were those thoughts and so strong were his desires to go to England that Datta made a momentous decision well before the expiration of that three-month period. He opted to convert to Christianity. It might have been his father's plan to get him married that precipitated Datta's conversion leading to, or so he fervently hoped, a passage to England.

There were Hindoo College students who had fallen away from Hinduism and either joined the relatively new Brahmo Samaj or converted to some form of Christianity. The Rev. K. M. Banerjee can be pointed to as just such a former Hindoo College student, and Rev. Banerjee in 1842 was the most prominent Bengali Christian convert in Calcutta, in all of British India, for that matter. And it was to Rev. Banerjee that Datta went to discuss his contemplated conversion. In his reminiscences, Rev. Banerjee confirms what the epistolary evidence has already hinted at: Datta evinced little genuine interest of any sort in Christianity, certainly not the fervor of a committed convert-to-be. Writes Rev. Banerjee, "I was impressed with the belief that his desire of becoming a Christian was, scarcely, greater than his desire of a voyage to England. I was unwilling to mix up the two questions; and while I conversed with him on the first, I candidly told him that I could lend him no help as regarded the second question. He seemed disheartened and came to me less frequently after that."[37]

Datta's father opposed his son's plan completely and seemed bent on thwarting him. He hired *lathials*, professional toughs, enforcers who wielded sticks or *lathis*. To ensure that their prize and future convert not be kidnapped by his own father and kept from them, the Christian authorities housed Datta in Calcutta's Fort William. And these same authorities allowed but few visitors to see the illustrious Hindoo College student who turned nineteen that January 1843. Bysack did get permission to meet once with his good friend, but the meeting was cut short by one of the British caretakers, "lest I should be," as Bysack put it in his reminiscences, "tampering with his new faith." It was a faith or "new light," Bysack recalled, the slightest glimmer of which had not been seen by any of Datta's college friends prior to that point.[38] Whatever might have been his real reason for converting, the baptism took place, on February 9.[39] Datta recited his own four-stanza poem, titled "Hymn," for the occasion.

Long sunk in Superstition's night,
By Sin and Satan driven,—
I saw not,—cared not for the light
That leads the blind to Heaven.

I sat in darkness,—Reason's eye
Was shut,—was closed in me;—
I hasten'd to Eternity
O'er Error's dreadful sea!

But now, at length thy grace, O Lord!
Bids all around me shine:
I drink thy sweet,—thy precious word,—
I kneel before thy shrine!—

I've broken Affection's tenderest ties
For my blest Savior's sake:—
All, all I love beneath the skies,
Lord, I for Thee forsake![40]

The consequences of Datta's conversion were in some cases predictable, in others not. The marriage his father had negotiated for him did not take place, a consequence Datta desired. He had to withdraw from Hindoo College, a consequence not anticipated. Some ten years later, he would have been allowed to stay enrolled there, even though not a Hindu. In 1843, however, Hindoo College did not abide a convert.[41] His newly acquired Christian co-religionists, Europeans primarily, so eager to have him join the church, on the whole cooled noticeably once he had become one of them. Nevertheless, Datta, ever the good student, seems to have applied himself to the study of Christian theology more conscientiously than anyone, Rev. Banerjee included, might have predicted. But probably the most coveted consequence of his conversion, a chance to go to England, failed to materialize, though the desire stayed strong.

After a hiatus of nearly two years, Datta returned to college in November of 1844, with financial help from his father, who though unhappy about the conversion had not disowned his only son. This time it was Bishop's College, however, just across the river from Calcutta and an institution, as the name implies, with a Christian orientation. He was officially a lay student and neither European nor Anglo-Indian, which put him in the minority on all counts. He remained a student there for three full years and took his classes seriously, as both the brevity and in some cases the content of his letters to Bysack indicated.

Bishop's College, 27th January 1845

My dear Friend,

It is a matter of regret to me that I haven't been able to answer your two *very* kind letters ere this; but if you were to know how my time is engaged here, I am sure you would excuse me. However, at anytime that is convenient to you, I should be extremely happy to see you as well as the friends you intend to bring with you. By the bye, you ought to address me in the following manner.

"M. Dutt Esqr. or Baboo" (if you please) Bishop's College; and nothing more. I must beg pardon for this short letter, but upon my word, I can't afford a minute more; so good-night.

Yours ever the same.[42]

The instructions on how to address him came after twice admonishing Bysack in previous short notes. The postscript for one of those read: "You write on the back of your letter 'To Christian M. S. Dutt from G.D.B.' *I do not like it.*" The last line of another declared: "I do not like 'My dear Christian Friend M. etc.' "[43] To be noted here and in the letter above are both his attitude and his name, or rather his initials. Concerning his attitude: The aversion to being labeled "Christian," as though such a rubric were an essential part of his identity, need not be taken to imply that Datta felt himself somehow less than a committed Christian. He may have had ulterior motives for converting, but, as Ghulam Murshid argues, he became a serious student and practitioner of the religion. At one point, possibly due to the influence of another student who had come to Bishop's College from Mauritius to prepare for a life of missionary work back home, Datta even considered becoming a Christian missionary.[44] Yet his Christianity was probably always more intellectual than emotional, more cerebral than visceral. A Christian he remained throughout his life, but his devotion would be first and foremost to literature.

Concerning his name: Datta did not become "Michael" upon his conversion to Christianity—was not given any new, baptismal, or Christian name at all—but remained simply Madhusudan. There is in fact no reason to expect a change of name or an additional name to be bestowed at the time of conversion. The Reverend Krishna Mohun Banerjee, Datta's senior and himself a

Bengali convert to Christianity, took no Christian or English name but remained Krishna Mohun (K. M.) Banerjee throughout his lifetime. Murshid includes in his biography a photocopy of the pertinent page from a baptismal registry where, under the column labeled "Child's Christian name," we find one word, "Modoosoodan." The following year, after Datta had enrolled in Bishop's College, his name appears on the college's registry as simply "Mudhoosooden Dutt," no "Michael."[45] Datta's admonitions to Bysack concerning the manner in which he should be addressed are all made while Datta is at Bishop's College. The "M" in "M. Dutt Esqr.," "Christian M. S. Dutt," and "My dear Christian Friend M." can only stand for Madhusudan, not Michael, for "M. S." perforce must be the abbreviation of Madhu Sudan. The name Michael becomes evident only after he has left Calcutta and is residing in Madras. It appears in full on a page of a marriage registry (1848); it appears as an initial only on the cover of Datta's first book, *The Captive Ladie* (1849), where the author is given as "M.M.S. Dutt."[46] The first "M" quite obviously stands for Michael. "Michael," then, turns out not to be any official baptismal name but rather Datta's assumed Christian-cum-Anglo-Indian moniker, adopted by him probably after his arrival in Madras but definitely before his marriage some seven months into his stay there. Precisely when and why he chose to prefix this particular English-Christian name to his—and not Matthew or Mark or the name of one of the other archangels such as Gabriel—we may never know, for he does not call attention to his new name or the circumstances surrounding his choice of it in any of his letters that we have.[47]

It was in 1847 that the course of Datta's life began to change again. His father, once one of Calcutta's most sought-after lawyers (he was what is known as a "vakil"), had fallen on relatively hard times.[48] Raj Narain's relationship with his only son became strained, even more so, it would seem, than following Datta's conversion. The specific causes and the depths of the emotional rift are hard to fathom with any certainty. Quite probably the father's new and reduced economic status affected the way he viewed his son, still a student in need of financial assistance at age twenty-three. Moreover, in what would appear to be an effort to obtain a Hindu (as opposed to a Christian) son both to perform his religiously sanctioned funeral rites and to carry on his lineage, the senior Dutt took a second wife—then a third wife, for his second wife died almost immediately after marriage. Datta's mother Jahnabi seems not to have been terribly upset with her new domestic situation.[49] For a Hindu gentleman of that day to have more than one wife was not uncommon, though a segment of the Bengali intellectuals protested strongly against polygamy. No issue, male or female, ever came of his father's other marriages. Whether the father's marital situation exacerbated the problem between father and son can merely be surmised.

The only direct evidence we have of Datta's mental state around that time comes in two forms: a short note to Bysack, the last such note to be written from Bishop's College, and a statement in a subsequent letter to Bysack, written more than a year and a half later. The initial sentence in the first of these, dated "Bp's Coll: 19th May, 47," reads: "Since I last heard from you I have been almost half dead with all manner of troubles."[50] The second letter, the very next communication from Datta to Bysack, begins as follows:

> Madras Male Orphan Asylum
> Black Town, 14th February, 1849
>
> My Dearest Friend,
>
> By my truth you wrong me! It is impossible for me to forget you—and you may rest assured that I have often and often thought of you with feelings of deeper love than many whom I know. When I left Calcutta, I was half mad with vexation and anxiety. Don't for a moment think that *you alone* did not receive a valedictory visit from me. I never communicated my intentions to more than 2 or 3 persons.[51]

On December 29, 1847, Datta, "half mad with vexation and anxiety," had boarded a ship for Madras, fleeing the city of his father, fleeing a father who quite possibly stood in need of financial help or emotional support or both. The son knew no one well in Madras, where his ship dropped anchor offshore on January 18.[52] It was through Christian connections, first established at Bishop's College among fellow students who hailed from Madras, that Datta found a place to live in the Black Town neighborhood, and soon thereafter a job as a teacher (the official title was "usher") in the Madras Male Orphan Asylum, also situated in Black Town. Calcutta likewise had its Black Town neighborhood, though the Dutts of Calcutta did not live there; Black Towns, for better or worse, formed part of the British colonial cityscape.

In the East India Company's India at this time, orphanages served the children of the Europeans. Just how European the child had to be was not necessarily relevant. The father would certainly be a European of some sort, for there has not been found a single recorded marriage between an Indian man and a European woman until that between Michael Moodiu Sooden Dutt and Rebecca Thompson McTavish, on July 31, 1848.[53] When Datta joined the orphan asylum staff, two months after landing in Madras, Rebecca was a student in the counterpart institution for girls, the Madras Female Orphan Asylum. Four months later, Michael, 24, and Rebecca, 17, wed in a church-solemnized ceremony, following the procedure known as the reading of the banns.[54] In the letter cited partially above, the return address for which is the orphanage, Datta continues to Bysack:

> Since my arrival here, I have had much to do in the way of procuring a standing place for myself,—no easy matter, I assure you,—especially, for a friendless stranger. However, thank God, my trials are, in a certain measure, at an end, and I now begin to look about me very much like a commander of a barque, just having dropped his anchors in a comparatively safe place, after a fearful gale!—Here's a smile for you, my boy!
>
> Your information with regard to my matrimonial doings is quite correct. Mrs. D. is of English parentage. Her father was an indigo-planter of this Presidency [Madras Presidency, one of three such administrative units in British India at this time—Calcutta Presidency and Bombay Presidency being the others]; I had great trouble in getting her. Her friends as you may imagine, were very much against the match. However, "all is well, that ends well!"[55]

Of Rebecca's "English parentage," we have learned, thanks to the diligent work of Ghulam Murshid, that her father Robert Thompson, whose occupation according to Rebecca's baptismal records was "horse artillery brigade gunner," had married Catherine Dyson, identified in those same records as "Indo-Britton" or, translated into other nomenclature, Anglo-Indian. Catherine's father had been English (accounting for the surname Dyson) and her mother South Asian, a father-mother combination possibly analogous to that of Rudyard Kipling's famous Kim, a lad born in India who could blend into the "native" population when he wanted to, a lad whose Irish father, Kimball O'Hara, had served with a military unit and later the railway in India and whose mother is, curiously, never mentioned by name.[56] Rebecca's father's name shows up as Dugald McTavish and hers as Rebecca Thompson McTavish in the Archdeaconry of Madras's marriage registry. Robert Thompson died in 1844, orphaning Rebecca and her siblings. Dugald McTavish, an employee on an indigo plantation but not the plantation owner, despite what Datta implies in his letter to Bysack, seems to have given refuge to the widow Catherine Thompson and possibly some of her children. In 1848, however, Rebecca was living in the Madras Female Orphan Asylum. Dugald McTavish played the role of her guardian. She paid her respects to him by using his surname as hers in the registry.[57]

In that same letter—it is a lengthy one, making up for better than a year of silence—Datta tells Bysack of the first book he is about to publish, at his own expense. Preceding that is almost an aside, responding to the announcement by Bysack of the death of his father. Datta's gesture at condolences represents the sum total of statements from him reflecting his religious self at this point in time. "I am sorry to hear of your severe loss, but, I trust, you have sense enough not to murmur against One whose wisdom is infinite and who is—merciful God!" There is Datta, the Christian, and his Christianity—understated, matter-of-fact, and almost perfunctory. He shows much more enthusiasm for his impending publication: "You will, I am sure, be surprised to hear that, though beset by all manner of troubles, I have managed to prepare a volume for the press. This will be my first regular effort as an author. The volume will consist of a tale in two cantos, yclept the 'Captive Ladie' and a short poem or two. I must give you a description of my 'Captive.' It contains about twelve hundred lines of good, bad and indifferent octo-syllabic verse and (truth, 'pon my honour!) was written in less than three weeks."[58]

The slim book, entitled *The Captive Ladie*, contained the title poem and a lesser verse narrative named "Visions of the Past." Those two, juxtaposed as they are, can be seen as indicative of things to come. The visions in "Visions of the Past" are Christian ones, of Adam and Eve and the Fall and the hope for divine grace, all presented in a very Miltonic meter:

> They wept—but not in dark despair—they wept
> As Guilt—all penitent—when, Mercy! thou
> Dost plead—nor plead in vain—in gentle strains
> To justice stern to win redeeming grace![59]

"The Captive Ladie," on the other hand, takes as its subject the elopement of Prithviraja, the raja of the Delhi region, and the princess of Kanauj, who is the captive of the first canto. The second and final canto concludes with the defeat, toward the end of the twelfth century, of Prithviraja at the hands of Muslim forces that had invaded Hindustan from the west, led by Muhammad Ghuri. It is historical; it is heroic; and it is Indian.[60] The meter of "Captive" is Byronic, octosyllabic, as Datta declares in his letter, but an octosyllabic that avoids as well as any of the English Romantics the "fatal facility" of saccharine singsong, which Bryon had warned against in his introduction to his poem "The Corsair." The events—couched in Byronic sensibilities also, somber and lush at the same time, tragic and romantic in tone—mark symbolically the fall of Hindu hegemony over north India.

> 'Tis morn:—along the Moslem line,
> Ten thousand spears all brightly shine,
> And many a flashing blade is bare,
> And voice of triumph on the air,
> As column'd warriors onward press,
> With all the haste of eagerness,
> When Vengeance sternly wings the feet,
> To rush where falchion'd foe-men meet;
> On—on they press,—'tis idlesse all,
> There stirs no foe on yonder wall,
> And wide the portals gape and far,—
> Deserted—lone—as if no War
> Rag'd round to crush—destroy and mar!—
> 'Tis noon—and from his car on high,
> The sun looks down, his burning eye,
> Now sees the Crescent's blood-red wave,
> Gild fall'n Husteena's lowly grave,[61]

Of significance in this pairing of two poems in Datta's first published book is the contrast in thematic focus between Eden, the Levant, and Christian concerns, in "Visions," and India and a South Asian setting in "The Captive Ladie"—Husteena (i.e., Hastina) being the name for the capital city associated with present-day Delhi. He had used Indian material before in his poetry. But the prominence given here to the South Asian thematic matter hints at a comparable change of priorities taking place in Datta himself, from aspiring to become a noted poet in English to that of devoting his creative energies to writing in his South Asian mother tongue. He is by no means turning his back on English literature. He is, though, looking more favorably toward Bangla at this point in his life. In February of 1849 prior to the publication of "Captive," Datta penned a letter to Bysack requesting copies of the Bangla retellings of both the *Ramayana* and the *Mahabharata*.[62] Later that same year, in August, he writes his college friend again, setting down his daily regimen of language study, which begins at 6 A.M. with Hebrew, ends at 10 P.M. with English, and includes Latin and Greek, as well as Tamil, Telugu, and Sanskrit. Datta asks rhetorically, self-assuredly: "Am I not preparing for the great object of embellishing the tongue of my fathers?"[63]

In the spring of 1849, Datta had copies of his "Captive" sent to Calcutta—to Bishop's College, to friends and respected Bengali acquaintances, to John Elliot Drinkwater Bethune, who was president of the Council of Education at the time, and to the most prominent periodical publication, the *Hurkaru*, in hopes of a favorable review. He tells Bysack toward the end of April that his book "is rising into popularity here [Madras]."[64] To Bhoodeb Mukherjee, a former Hindoo College classmate who became a leading Bengali intellectual of his day, Datta writes in May: "The Captive has met with a pretty fair reception here," prefacing that with "I have some intention of republishing it in London with my new Poem."[65] By June, however, the tide had turned. The *Hurkaru* deprecated the book. Datta tried to appear undaunted in a letter to Bysack at the beginning of that month: "I find that your 'Hurkaru' has been somewhat severe with me. Curse that rascal, his article reached me like a shaft which has spent its force in its progress. Know, O thou noble youth, that I have girt my loins to do battle manfully, even as a gallant knight, who seeks the loftiest guerdon on this earth—the Poet's crown of laurel-leaf! Methinks, that after the praises I have received from some whose claims to bestow them are indubitable, I can afford to stand a little abuse."[66] Bysack himself was less than enthusiastic. Datta counters, "You seem to consider the 'Captive' a failure, but I don't. For look you, it has opened the most splendid prospects for me, and has procured me the friendship of some whom it is an honour to know." In that same letter he adds, "Remember, my friend, that I published it for the sake of attracting some notice, in order to better my prospects and not exactly for Fame." And, he reasserts, "I tell you the 'Captive' has produced a favourable sensation here."[67]

Then came Bethune's patronizing appraisal of *The Captive Ladie*, sent not to Datta but to Bysack, who had presented Bethune with a copy of the book: "He might employ his time to better advantage than in writing English poetry. As an occasional exercise and proof of his proficiency in the language, such specimens may be allowed. But he could render far greater service to his country and have a better chance of achieving a lasting reputation for himself, if he will employ the taste and talents, which he has cultivated by the study of English, in improving the standard and adding to the stock of the poems of his own language, if poetry, at all events, he must write."[68] Bysack agreed completely with Bethune. In his letter to his friend, in which he paraphrased Bethune's letter, Bysack admonished Datta to do what the Englishman urged: "His advice is the best you can adopt. It is an advice that I have always given you and will din into your ears all my life. . . . We do not want another Byron or another Shelley in English; what we lack is a Byron or a Shelley in Bengali literature."[69]

Bethune would become a founding member of the Vernacular Literature Society the following year.[70] In a way, such a society might seem to be antithetical to the Anglicists' and Macaulay's desire in his minute of 1835 of producing "persons, Indian in blood and colour, but English in taste, in opinions, in morals, and in intellect." But times had changed, and so had the Company's educational goals. The colonial enterprise needed less the educated, sophisticated brown-skinned "Englishman" and more the capable bureaucrat, competent to function in offices throughout the colony, fit to handle the quotidian minutia of empire.[71] Datta, in many ways, epitomized the absolute success of Macaulay's and the Anglicists' original project. He was the equal of the English in taste and intellect. He and his kind may have become, in a certain sense, a threat, or at least credible competition. What better way to neutralize that competition than for Englishmen like Bethune to support a vernacular literary society?

As noted above, Datta had shown interest in Bangla texts, the Hindu epics of his childhood, even prior to the publication of his first book of poetry in English. Poor notices in the English-language press for *The Captive Ladie* combined with Bethune's and Bysack's frank directives may have encouraged Datta's move away from English and into the field of Bangla literature. It took ten more years, however, before the first of his Bangla pieces, a five-act play based upon an episode from the *Mahabharata*, appeared. Meanwhile, he continued to write in English. Besides carrying out his duties as a schoolteacher, Datta edited or assisted in the editing of several English-language journals: *Madras Circulator and General Chronicle, Athenaeum, Spectator*, and *Hindoo Chronicle*. Under the pseudonym of Timothy Penpoem, he also published a number of his own poems in these periodicals. And his reading of literature, in a number of languages including English, never ceased. The breadth of that reading cannot but impress. In his essay, "The Anglo-Saxon and the Hindu," which he wrote and delivered as a public lecture in 1854 or possibly somewhat before, he makes reference to Eva and Topsy from Harriet Beecher Stowe's *Uncle Tom's Cabin,* employing the disparity between the two of them to reinforce the disparity between the glorious Anglo-Saxon and, in Datta's colorful rhetoric, the degraded Hindu: "You now see before you, as it were, on a stage, two actors—the Anglo-Saxon and the Hindu. One of them is indeed well-graced, ravishing the eyes of the audience with his manly beauty—enchanting the ears of the audience with the dulcet tones of his voice! The other, I fear, is ill favoured, worn out by the ceaseless waves of time, hoarse and dissonant as an untuned harp, as an unstrung lute." And then the parallel pairings, Octavius–Brutus, Eva–Topsy, to emphasize the nature of the central pair, the Anglo-Saxon and the Hindu:

> Octavius feasting in the tent of the luxurious Antony, the golden goblet blushing and sparkly with the delicious blood of the vine of sunny Italy in his hand, the chaplet of dewy roses on his head; Brutus sternly watches the purple current of life, ebbing out from the ghastly wound inflicted by his own suicidal hands! Eva, with the transplanted rose of the West, blooming on her cheek, the blue heaven of her eyes beaming with cloudless sunlight; and poor Topsy—the degraded daughter of a degraded race, standing before her like a ghastly phantom, an unearthly vision! Flowering Youth, decaying age; radiant beauty, hideous deformity; exulting valour, pallid fear; sparkling diamond, dim crystal;—but why should I multiply such images? The contrast is indeed very great![72]

Stowe's book came out in 1852. A mere year or so later, in far-off Madras, Datta had obtained a copy and already read it.

Datta's father died in 1855. His mother had passed away several years before that. Bysack wrote his friend to inform him of his father's death and to tell him to return to Calcutta to ensure his inheritance. Datta replied in late December that year, saying, among other things, "Yes, dearest Gour, I have a fine English wife and four children."[73] He arrived in Calcutta in February 1856, alone. Rebecca and their four children never joined him. Instead, he took up with another European lady, Henrietta Sophia White, someone he had known in Madras who followed him to Calcutta. Michael Madhusudan Datta seems to have had no further contact with Rebecca. Henrietta would bear him a daughter and two sons—a fourth child was stillborn—and remain his lifelong companion, whether legal wife or not is to this day unconfirmed. No records of divorce or remarriage have yet been discovered. In 1862 he realized his dream, his overriding fixation, when he finally journeyed to England, to study law. Henrietta would eventually join him, but in Versailles to which he had repaired, for it was cheaper to live there than in London. Still then, in France they and their children passed their days in virtual penury. After having been called to the bar in London, he returned home to Calcutta in 1867. That same year, though not immediately, Datta was accepted as a barrister by Calcutta's High Court, but only after overcoming serious opposition to him on personal grounds from some of the local legal establishment who knew the flamboyant poet by reputation. Henrietta and children followed him back to India. There he practiced law intermittently and with limited success.

Though he continued to write, Datta's productive days as poet and playwright, for all intents and purposes, had come to an end. A volume of his Bangla sonnets appeared in 1866, while he and the family were still in Europe. In 1873, the year of his death, he managed to complete a play, though he never had the chance to polish it to his satisfaction. His prose version of the *Iliad*, entitled "The Slaying of Hector," remained half completed. Michael and Henrietta died within three days of each other in June of 1873 in Calcutta, suffering from what would appear to have been consumption, the quintessential Romantic's disease of the nineteenth century, though the cause of their deaths was never specifically identified as such. Bysack observed Datta during his last days, "gasping under the excruciating effects of his disease, blood oozing from his mouth, his wife lying in high fever on the floor."[74] Biographers have listed liver, spleen, and throat ailments, and also dropsy (edema) due to cirrhosis of the liver. Ghulam Murshid, the latest of those biographers, adds to that list heart disease.[75] Michael Madhusudan Datta was but forty-nine when he succumbed, and Henrietta, thirty-seven.

The period between 1858 and 1862—two years after he had returned from Madras and right up to when he went to England—was a time characterized by the editor of Datta's collected works as a veritable "festival of creativity." In this span of five years, Datta published five plays, three narrative poems (one of four cantos, one of nine, and the other eleven cantos long), and a sizeable collection of lyrics organized around the Radha-Krishna theme, all in Bangla. Along with all of this, he found time to translate three plays from Bangla into English—one, a Bangla rendition of a Sanskrit drama *Ratnavali*; another, his own original play *Sermista*, based upon an episode from the *Mahabharata*; and a third translation, that of *Nil Darpan* by Dinabandhu Mitra, a politically controversial piece that depicts cruelties inflicted upon the peasantry by British indigo planters in Bengal.

The first of these English translations, along with the Bangla version from which he did the translation, served as the impetus for Datta to begin his own career as a playwright and poet in Bangla. The incident concerning how Datta came to pen his very first piece of literature in Bangla—the Bangla original of his play *Sermista*—is related by Bysack in his essay of reminiscences. He had taken Datta to a rehearsal of Ramnarayan Tarkaratna's Bangla rendition of *Ratnavali*, the drama originally composed in Sanskrit by Harshavardhana (606–647 C.E.). Tarkaratna, an accomplished Sanskrit scholar and also one of the earliest playwrights in Bangla, had translated the Sanskrit drama into Bangla.

Tarkaratna's Bangla play was to be performed on the stage of the short-lived but highly influential Belgachia Theatre, a theater founded and supported by the brothers Pratap Chandra and Isvar Chandra Singh. As was the custom at the time, the local British elite would be invited to attend, and for their sake an English translation needed to be prepared. Bysack had persuaded the Singhs, who were known as the rajas of Paikpara, to engage Datta to do the translation, for Datta, Bysack well knew, was a master craftsman with the English language. After attending the first rehearsal and even before he had embarked upon the translation, Datta, according to Bysack, said to him, "What a pity the rajas should have spent such a lot of money on such a miserable play. I wish I had known of it before, as I could have given you a piece worthy of your theater."[76] Bysack writes that he laughed at the very idea of his friend, who had never before composed anything in Bangla, now implying that he could produce a play in Bangla. A week later Datta handed Bysack a draft of the first act of what would be a five-act play, utterly Shakespearean in formal characteristics, about the triangular relationship involving the king Yayati, his wife Devayani, and Sermista, daughter of the Asuras' monarch but also both servant to Devayani and mother, illicitly, of children by Yayati.

The first staging of *Sermista* took place in September of 1859. Even before that, the rajas of Paikpara had urged Datta to turn his hand to drama of another sort, the domestic farce, "just to show the public that we can act the sublime and the ridiculous both at the same time and with the same actors."[77] Midway through the nineteenth century, the originally high ideals of the Derozio-inspired Young Bengal group—an earnest, enlightened quest for knowledge coupled with a rejection of what they viewed as demeaning superstition—had been misinterpreted by some to mean aping the British and flouting social norms. In particular, patronizing dancing girls, eating meat, and drinking alcohol, along with speaking a modicum of English, came to symbolize, for some, their "enlightenment." One of two farces Datta penned during this period—commissioned for the Belgachia Theatre in 1859 but suppressed by the proprietors out of fear of protests coming from Young Bengal types—held these misguided libidinous, carnivorous, brandy-quaffing "liberals" up to ridicule by depicting members of a bogus *Jnanatarangini sabha* (River of knowledge society) as carousing with queans, all the while spewing catch phrases of social reform interlarded with pretentious exhortations to be free and enjoy oneself.[78] Such societies—real societies—had been a prominent feature of the Calcutta scene in the second quarter of the nineteenth century. Datta himself, if we have the right Modoosooden [*sic*] Dutt, had become a member of just such an organization, the Society for the Acquisition of Knowledge, while still a student at Hindoo College.[79] The subsequent pseudo Young Bengal mimic-men, however, whom Datta now satirized, convinced the rajas not to stage Datta's drama. The Belgachia Theatre, begun in 1858 with the performance of *Ratnavali*, for which Datta had made a translation into English, closed its doors for good in 1859, after staging *Sermista*, but without bringing Datta's satires to the boards.[80]

Failure to get his most recent plays performed did not curtail Datta's creative exuberance, though he later expressed some regret: "Mind you, you broke my wings once about the farces; if you play a similar trick this time, I shall forswear Bengali and write books in Hebrew and Chinese!"[81] The two farces were published in 1860, thanks to the financial support of the rajas, who no doubt felt embarrassment at having to scrap the actual staging. Datta had in 1859 already started a fourth drama, even before finishing the first. And he cast *Padmavati*, name of both the play and its heroine, entirely in Indian settings and with Indian characters, though its inspiration came from Greek mythology, a pattern for things to come. *The Slaying of Meghanada* is a riot of incorporations, from Milton, Tasso, Homer, Virgil, and Dante, cross-fertilized with the Hindu epics and much, much more from the Hindu tradition. He had, in fact, prepared himself, as he wrote from Madras to Bysack, "for the great object of embellishing the tongue of [his] fathers."

The Poem

The Slaying of Meghanada (Meghanadavadha kavya)—a poem *(kavya)* on the slaying *(vadha)* of Meghanada, the eldest son of Ravana, Rakshasa monarch—tells of Meghanada's third and final fight in defense of the Rakshasa clan, his demise, and finally his obsequies. Meghanada and the Rakshasas are characters drawn from a larger tale, the *Ramayana*. That epic—the name itself means the wanderings *(ayana)* of Rama—recounts the adventures of prince Rama while away from the kingdom of Ayodhya in a self-imposed fourteen-year exile in the forests to the south. During those wanderings, Ravana kidnaps Rama's wife Sita, who accompanied her husband into exile. It is this act that brings about a war on the island of Lanka, the epic's central event. Rama and his brother Lakshmana, together with an allied army of "southerners," identified as monkeys and bears in most texts, have invaded the island kingdom, there to confront the Rakshasa forces.

With respect to epic literature, the South Asian situation differs markedly from the European. Although Homeric tales are many, there is but one *Iliad* and one *Odyssey*. And if we look to the modern European languages—say,

English, French, and German—we find various epics but not standard English, French, or German versions of the classical epic narratives. There is no English *Iliad*, with an identifiable English poet or author. There are any number of English translations of Homer's *Iliad*—Chapman's, Pope's, Lattimore's, Graves's, Fagles's, and Lombardo's, to name a few. But these are translations and are so identified. In India, on the other hand, a number of modern languages have within their literary traditions a *Ramayana* or, in most cases, several *Ramayana*s that follow basically the Valmiki text but, at the same time, are in many ways original compositions. In Hindi literature, for instance, there is the Rama epic composed in the sixteenth century by Tulsidasa known as the *Ram Carit Manas* (The holy lake [*Manasa*] of the acts/character [*carita*] of Rama). Hindus in the Hindi-speaking areas of India look with pride to Tulsidasa's narrative as the authoritative *Ramayana*. I do not mean to say that Valmiki's Sanskrit version is unknown in that language area. But by and large it is through Tulsidasa's telling of the tale that the Hindi-speaking populace knows Rama's story. The situation is similar in other modern Indian languages. Bangla literature, for example, possesses what might be termed an authoritative or standard Bangla *Ramayana* composed by the poet Krittivasa, thought to have lived during the fourteenth/fifteenth century. Here, too, Krittivasa's *Ramayana* is viewed with pride as a Bangla original, not a Bangla rendering of the Sanskrit epic.[82]

Certainly the greatest difference, other than the language itself, between Valmiki's *Ramayana* and the later epics by Krittivasa and Tulsidasa is found in a particular aspect of the characterization of Rama, who in the older text was essentially a mortal prince, a young warrior. The first and last books of Valmiki—considered by scholars to be later additions to the text—speak of Rama as one of the incarnations of Vishnu. In contrast, Krittivasa's and Tulsidasa's Rama has become inextricably the god Vishnu. No longer is the fight between Ravana and Prince Rama a fight between mighty warriors with god-given weapons and extraordinary powers. It has changed radically, into a fight between good god and bad demon. The demons become even further transformed, in these vernacular Rama tales, into devotees of sorts of Vishnu, the very god whom they battle. A transformation—transformations can be seen as part and parcel of the *Ramayana* tradition—takes place in Datta's Rama tale as well, but in the opposite direction. Rama, the apotheosized prince of Krittivasa's premodern text, returns to his mostly mortal persona and becomes a nineteenth-century Rama, a creation of the colonial encounter.

The Slaying of Meghanada starts in medias res, with a knowing nod to the opening lines of Milton's *Paradise Lost*. It ends by evoking the cremation scene from the final book of the *Iliad* wherein are performed the obsequies for Troy's greatest warrior. The eighth canto of *Meghanada* has Rama, Datta's antagonist, proceeding to the netherworld—and these are Datta's own words—"like another Aeneas."[83] In this land-beyond-the-living, Rama passes through a gate emblazoned with the Dantean admonition: "By this path sinners go / to suffer constant sorrow in the realm of sorrows—you / who enter, give up all hope as you step inside this land!" (8: 207–9) The evident presences of Milton-Tasso-Homer-Virgil-Dante notwithstanding, Datta's epic remains throughout, and through and through, a partial embodiment of the *Ramayana*. In narrating this episode from the *Ramayana*—the slaying of Meghanada (resonant with, intentionally, the slaying of Priam's son Hector)—Datta shows sympathy for the traditionally opposing side, that of Lanka's King Ravana and his Rakshasa clan, in much the way Milton makes sympathetic his Satan. *Meghanada* is a text wherein East meets West, where literary traditions blend in Datta's adept hands to become the epitome of the cultural assimilation, selective as it was, taking place in the elite Bengali population of nineteenth-century Calcutta. The period has been labeled the Bengal Renaissance for its reinvigoration and reconfiguration of the Hindu past and for the florescence of the literary arts. (Muslim Bengali literary historians are apt to refer to the same period as the Hindu Renaissance rather than the Bengal Renaissance, for it had a very Hindu tone to much of it.) *Meghanada* and its author are, each in his own way, perfect metonyms for their times.

Literary Sleight of Hand

The Slaying of Meghanada has much to do with deception, an artful and literary sleight of hand. It is a slice of the *Ramayana* but also more than, and different from, that. Furthermore, the deception is not always concealed but trotted out boldly, proclaimed proudly. Datta writes in a letter to a friend, "People here grumble that the sympathy of the Poet in Meghanad is with the Rakshasas. And that is the real truth. I despise Ram and his rabble while the idea of Ravan elevates and kindles my imagination; he was a grand fellow."[84] There is no doubt that the poem itself conveys precisely those sentiments. Yet, when examined closely and contrasted with its most proximate and prominent literary source, the Bangla *Ramayana* of Krittivasa (fifteenth century C.E.), and even with the more distant but more pervasively influential text, the Sanskrit *Ramayana* of Valmiki, it becomes crystal clear that Datta has not altered the characters of Rama and Ravana. They are in *Meghanada* what they are in the more traditional *Ramayanas*. But the deception—and quite obviously Datta enjoys deceiving his reader—works.

Any number of critics could be cited who insist that Datta's Rama and Ravana become something other than what they are in the mainstream Hindu tradition. For instance, Rabindranath Tagore wrote that Datta created a Rama who was "more timid than a woman."[85] Ashis Nandy tells us, "As is well known, Meghnadvadh retells the *Ramayana*, turning the traditionally sacred figures of Rama and Lakshmana into weak-kneed, passive-aggressive, feminine villains and the demons Ravana and his son Meghnad into majestic, masculine, modern heroes."[86] But a comparison of the characterizations of Rama and Ravana in both Datta's text and Krittivasa's *Ramayana* calls Nandy's statement into question. Consider the following pairs of passages, when Rama takes the fallen Lakshmana upon his lap and weeps uncontrollably. First, from Krittivasa's older text:

> Having won the battle, Raghunatha [Rama] withdrew;
> Holding Lakshmana upon his lap, he cried profusely.
> "At what star-crossed moment did I leave Ayodhya?
> My father, Dasharatha, ruler of the realm, succumbed.
> Sita, daughter of King Janaka, the stunning beauty of my life,
> In broad daylight, Ravana kidnapped her, whisking her away.
> Now I've lost my fondest sibling, you, young brother Lakshmana;
> What need have you of kingdom's comforts? Let's back to the forest.
> Oh Lakshmana, the treasured son, the darling of Sumitra,
> What shall I say to her to stem the gushing of her tears?
> I brought away with me the treasure she'd held tied to her sari;
> Then upon the ocean's shore, Providence turned foul for me.
> At my misfortunes, Lakshmana, it's you who always sympathized,
> Why then now so heartless that you do not respond to me?
> Everyone will ask for news, if now I were to go back home,
> Where would I find the nerve to speak of your demise?
> For my sake, brother, do not die;
> I shall take you with me, go begging in some distant land.
> I have no need of royal wealth, nor have I need for Sita;
> I shall cast myself into the sea, grief-stricken over you.
> From dawn to dusk, throughout the whole wide world,
> Am I to be notorious, remembered for your death?
> Get up, brother Lakshmana, before you drown in blood,
> Why oh why did you accompany me to banishment?
> It is on account of Sita that you have lost your life,
> But you, my Lakshmana, I hold as equal to my life.

While bartering for gold, I used a gemstone as inducement;
Complicit in your death, I've stained our Raghu family name.
Why did I enter into warfare with the likes of Ravana?
What being stole the treasure-trove containing my life's breath?
The greatest among warriors, that Arjuna among the Pandavas,
Matched with him, you, Lakshmana, show an ocean of more skills.
Such a Lakshmana like this of mine that Rakshasa slew;
I can never more return back home, to the land of Ayodhya.
It was my father's orders that I obtain the royal parasol and sceptre;
But in this matter, stepmother Kaikeyi intervened amorally.
To keep my father honest, I went off into exile."
To which responded Providence, "Ah, all is lost, ruination!"
Then from the heavens came the call, from the assembled gods,
"Don't cry, weep not, O Rama, you'll have Lakshmana back again."
Rama heaved a heavy sigh, intoning, "Brother, O my brother."
And thus wrote Krittivasa of Rama's lamentation.[87]

Compare that passage from Krittivasa with the comparable scene in *Meghanada,* where Rama laments the seeming loss (he will be miraculously revived) of his brother Lakshmana:

Once their lord regained consciousness, he, grief-stricken, chided—
"When I renounced the kingdom and went to live in exile
in the forest, Lakṣmaṇa, as night set in, O expert
archer, bow in hand, you, at the door of our hut would stand
alert to guard me. Yet here today in the Rākṣasas'
enclave—this day, this very city of the Rākṣasas!—
I, among foes, here founder in these perilous waters.
Still then, O great-armed one, you forsake me, seeking respite
upon the ground? Who will rescue me today, please tell me?
Stand up, brave one! Since when do you not heed your brother's words?
But if by some ill luck of mine—I who am unlucky
always—if you have indeed abandoned me, then tell me
honestly, you who are to me much more than life, for I
must hear. What misdeed is hapless Jānakī at fault for,
in your opinion? Day and night she weeps as she, confined
by Rākṣasas, thinks of Lakṣmaṇa, her husband's brother.
How did you forget—Brother, how could you ever forget
this day the one who like a mother always cared for you
so warmly? O pinnacle of Raghu's clan, she, a clan

wife, shall she remain incarcerated by Paulastya?
Is it right that you should rest before you first destroy in
combat such a wicked thief—you who are invincible
in battle, bold as omnivorous fire? Arise, my fierce-
armed one, victory pennant of the Raghu clan! Minus
you I am helpless, a charioteer whose chariot
is missing wheels. With you supine on this bed, O hero,
Hanumān is powerless, a bow without its bowstring.
Aṅgada wails pitifully; friend Sugrīva, noble-
minded, is heartsick; good charioteer Vibhīṣaṇa,
Karbūra supreme, he too mourns; a host of heroes grieves.
Get up, console these eyes, my brother, by the gaze of yours.
"If, however, you have tired of this awful war, then,
O archer, let us go back to our forest home. Sītā's
rescue, fondest one, is not to be—that luckless woman.
It is not for us to vanquish Rākṣasas. But if you
do not accompany me, how shall I, Lakṣmaṇa, show
my face upon the Sarayū's far shore where Sumitrā,
your mother who so loves her son, laments? What shall I say
when she asks me, 'Where, O Rāmabhadra, is the object
of my love, your little brother?' How shall I answer to
your wife, Ūrmilā, and to the people of the city?
Stand up, dear child. Why do you turn a deaf ear today toward
this plea your brother makes, for love of whom you quit the realm
with its amenities and took to the forest? Out of
sympathy, you always used to cry whenever you would
see these eyes of mine moist with tears. Tenderly you dabbed those
teary rivulets. Now I am drenched with water from my
eyes, yet you, who are to me much more than life, will you not
so much as glance my way? Lakṣmaṇa, does such behavior
ever suit you, Brother (you who are renowned throughout the
world as one devoted to his brother!), you who are my
everlasting joy? All my life I held firm to *dharma*
and worshiped the gods—and is it this the gods have given
in return? O Night, compassion-filled, you who nightly make
the flowers, withered by the summer's heat, succulent with
drops of dew, revive this blossom. You who are a fount of
nectar, god of nectar rays, pour down your life-bestowing
juices, save Lakṣmaṇa—save beggar Rāghava, kind one."

The foe of Rākṣasas, forlorn, wailed upon the field of
battle, cradling his dearest younger brother. All about,
the warrior throng howled with sadness, just as howls a stand of
stately trees at midnight when winds blow deep in the forest. (8: 17–78)

If expressing one's emotions outwardly can be characterized as "weak-kneed" and "feminine," in Nandy's words, then Rama is that. But he is that in both Krittivasa's *Ramayana* and Datta's poem. There has been no fundamental alteration of Rama's character. Ravana, like Rama, expresses human emotions when confronted with the loss of his sons and does so in both the fifteenth-century sacred *Ramayana* and in the nineteenth-century secular *The Slaying of Meghanada*. How does one account for Nandy's and others' reading of Datta's text and their conclusion that Datta changed Rama into a weak-kneed, effeminate character? How does one account for the more general claim that Datta turned traditional heroes into villains and villains into heroes? A major part of the answer lies in the strategic deployment by Datta of subversive similes. Such similes embellish, as all similes do, but at the same time link incongruous actors or objects, thereby inviting homologation of characters where no similarity formerly existed.

Take, for instance, the scene early in *Meghanada*'s first canto, the sumptuous assembly hall in which Rakshasa monarch Ravana sits:

The umbrella bearer held the parasol;
ah, just as Kāma might have stood in Hara's anger's flame,
unburned, so he stood on the floor of that assembly hall,
as bearer of the royal parasol. Before its doors
paced the guard, a redoubtable figure, like god Rudra,
trident clutched, before the Pāṇḍavas' encampment's gateway!
Constant spring breezes delicately wafted scents, gaily
transporting waves of chirping, ah yes! enchanting as the
flute's melodic undulations in the pleasure groves of
Gokula! Compared to such an edifice, O Maya,
Dānava lord, how paltry was that jeweled court built at
Indraprastha with your own hands to please the Pauravas!

With this set of four similes, subversion has begun. Datta does not say that the umbrella bearer is Kama, which would imply that Ravana is god Shiva; nor that the assembly hall is either the Pandavas' camp or their Indraprastha assembly hall, which would imply that Ravana is Yudhishthira, eldest brother among the five Pandavas; nor that the surrounding gardens are the pleasure groves of Gokula wherein god Krishna acts out his divine love-play. He says that the assembly room is wonderful, and uses similes ostensibly to make more vivid the scene depicted. But the implications, however tenuous, are there. Juxtaposition of actors in the similes and main narrative invites homologation, or the indirect linking of Ravana with gods Shiva and Krishna and with the Pandavas, winners, after a fashion, and sympathetic heroes of the Mahabharata war.

Were this the only time such an association occurs between Ravana and the heroes of Hinduism, one might assume the connection inadvertent or even just an overly ambitious reading of a poetic conceit. However, these sorts of similes occur again and again and are built round three clusters of Hindu mythology: the *Mahabharata* epic (concerning the war between the Pandavas and their cousins, the Kauravas), Vaishnavism (concerning Krishna and the Gopis), and Shaktism (concerning the mother-goddess and Shiva). Another of the many examples is found in the seventh canto, containing Ravana's retribution for the slaying of Meghanada. Once Ravana has learned of his son's death, he summons the Rakshasa troops and readies himself for battle. A series of conceits describes the mustered army:

> As the Dānava-quelling Caṇḍī, born from the power
> of the gods, laughed jauntily while she, Satī, armed herself
> with godly weaponry, so in Laṅkā armed the corps of
> fearsome Rākṣasas—in war a wrathful Ugracaṇḍā.

After much fighting, Ravana fells Lakshmana. With his son's death avenged, Ravana retires with his army from the battlefield back to the walled city:

> The Rākṣasa
> legion marched into the city—as ferocious goddess
> Cāmuṇḍā, victorious in battle, having vanquished
> Raktabīja, returned shouting, dancing wildly, a smile
> upon her bloody lips, her body drenched in streams of gore!
> As the gods en masse sang Satī's praises, so the bards with
> joy extolled in victory songs the Rākṣasas' army!

Candi is not just a powerful, awesome being. She is *the* Hindu goddess. That the Rakshasas should be compared to her is ironic as well as subversive, for according to one myth the goddess was created from the combined power of the gods for the express purpose of destroying such god- and man-harassers.

Without question, one of the most intriguing features of Datta's epic continues to be his characterization of Rama (along with brother Lakshmana) and the Rakshasas, much of which lies under the surface in those wily subversive similes that are both traditional—using traditional mythic material—and modern. Such similes act subliminally, and the variety of reactions to Datta's achievement reveals how well he hid his persuaders. The final canto of *Meghanada* ends, somewhat as the entire work began, with intimations of Ravana's defeat by Rama—in keeping with the traditional *Ramayana.* But the subversive similes, among other narrative strategies, have skewed the reader's usual response to the tale so that we are now not quite sure whether to anticipate Ravana's death with culturally sanctioned joy or with disquieting, guilty sorrow.

Filial Piety

The Slaying of Meghanada has much to do with the father-son relationship. From the very inception of the story, we find Meghanada, Ravana's eldest son—and only remaining son, all the others having been killed in the war—enjoying a well-deserved retreat for rest and recreation. He had not merely overcome but actually killed in combat the main aggressor against his father and their insular kingdom of Lanka. As he lounges with his wife and her many fawning handmaidens, word comes to him through a goddess disguised as his childhood wet nurse that his father's supposedly slain nemesis, Rama, has somehow revived and threatens once again the island's walled city, also referred to as Lanka. The gods have intervened, justifying such action by a certain mythic logic: Inevitably, according to the *Ramayana* and Hindu mythology generally, Ravana must be destroyed by Rama, and Ravana cannot be destroyed until all of his able-bodied warrior sons have been defeated. It is also unseemly, by Hindu social etiquette and therefore by the etiquette of the gods, that a father should be put in jeopardy when he has an adult son to fend for him. Upon being notified by the goddess-cum-wet-nurse, Meghanada immediately ceases his sensual indulgences and rebukes himself for failing his father in this moment of great need. The scene with its fulsome luxury owes much to Torquato Tasso's *Geruselema Liberato*, a text Datta had been reading with delight at this precise time. (While working on the third canto, he wrote to a friend, "I am just now reading Tasso in the original—an Italian gentleman having presented me with a copy. Oh! what luscious poetry. If God spares me for some years yet, I shall write a poem, a Romantic one in the *Ottava Rima* or stanzas of eight lines like his.")[88] But Meghanada is no Rinaldo, the hedonistic, arrogant Christian Crusader who needs to be coaxed back into the fray. Nor is Meghanada an Achilles, proud but pouting over the poaching of his female companion by a fellow Achaian. Meghanada's emotions and motivation at this point—love of and duty toward father—have less in common with either Rinaldo of Tasso's tale or even the *Iliad's* Achilles than with Rama, his father's adversary and hero of the *Ramayana*.

Two very human and very male features drive the *Ramayana*: libido and filial piety. Rama is not forcibly exiled for fourteen years from his paternal kingdom of Ayodhya. Quite the contrary. His father, Dasharatha, begs him not to go. Dasharatha, in fact, dies of a broken heart, following the departure of his eldest son Rama. It is Rama who chooses exile, in order to preserve the integrity of his father, as Rama notes in the Krittivasa-composed lament cited above: "To keep my father honest, I went off into exile." Years earlier, Dasharatha, overcome by passion for his youngest of three wives, had promised Kaikeyi that their son, Bharata—as opposed to Rama, Dasharatha's eldest son by his first wife—would be installed upon the throne when he, Dasharatha, chose finally to abdicate. In addition, before allowing her husband to engage in sex with her, Kaikeyi demanded a second boon, which required her husband's eldest son to be sent into exile for fourteen years, thereby physically removing him from the kingdom and making less likely any challenge to her own son's rule. Dasharatha, at the moment addled by lust, assented. When it came time for Dasharatha to step down from the throne, he dearly wanted to install in his place his virtuous eldest son—not that the other three sons were unvirtuous. It was Rama who insisted that he go into exile and by so doing kept his father true to his promises. Bharata, son of Dasharatha by Kaikeyi and himself a paragon of virtue, refused to ascend the throne, instead agreeing only to caretake it in Rama's absence. He placed a pair of Rama's sandals on the throne in his stead.

Like Rama, Meghanada is his father's eldest son. Like Dasharatha, Ravana, motivated by sexual desire for a woman, has placed his son (and his entire kingdom) in jeopardy. Again like Rama, Meghanada comes to his father's aid willingly. Again like Dasharatha, Ravana, the loving father with true paternalistic instincts, wants not to place his son in harm's way. But it is the son, in both cases, who insists upon courting danger (exile, battle) and supporting his father over that very father's objections.

If the wanderings of Rama—the *Ramayana* narrative per se—can be seen as predicated upon Dasharatha's immoderate libido, then the attack upon Lanka by Rama and his forces needs to be understood in terms of Ravana's similarly immoderate sexual desire. It is Ravana's sister, Surpanakha, who creates the problem. While wandering in forests away from Lanka, Surpanakha spies Rama and his brother Lakshmana. She is smitten by the handsome Rama and makes amorous advances toward him. Rama, toying with her, sends her to Lakshmana, who mocks her and ends up harming her, cutting off her nose. Surpanakha returns to Lanka bent on getting her brother to avenge her humiliation. She motivates him through her description of Rama's wife Sita, inflaming Ravana with lust for the now fancied gorgeous woman. Ravana demands the assistance of a fellow Rakshasa by the name of Marica, who transforms himself into a golden stag and entices Sita, who in turn begs Rama to go capture the deer for her. Ravana, disguised as a holy mendicant, manages to kidnap Sita in Rama's (and Lakshmana's) absence and spirit her away back to the isle of Lanka. The justification for Rama and company to invade Lanka and attack Ravana and his Rakshasas is first and foremost to retrieve Sita. No matter what the reason for the war, whether it is caused by his paternal aunt or by his own father, Meghanada comes to that father's aid, the ever-dutiful son.

Reinforcing the theme of filial piety, Datta employs one of his many epic similes in the very first canto, alluding to yet another son who comes to his father's aid in time of need. As Ravana surveys the battlefield on which his last-but-one fallen son Virabahu lies:

> . . . Likewise Vīrabāhu—crown-gem of warriors—
> fell, crushing hostile heroes, as Ghaṭotkaca, raised in
> Hiḍimbā's loving nest, like a Garuḍa, had fallen
> at the time Karṇa, wielder of Kālapṛṣṭha, let fly
> his missile called Ekāghnī to preserve the Kauravas.

And here too, there is a suggestion of libido gone astray. Ghatotkaca, a warrior of tremendous size, was born from the illicit relationship between one of the Pandavas—heroes of that other Hindu Indian epic, the *Mahabharata*—and a Rakshasi by the name of Hidimba. Rakshasas (Rakshasi being the feminine of Rakshasa) in general are endowed with the power to assume various forms at will. Hidimba, in the guise of a voluptuous beauty, engaged in coitus with the Pandava Bhimasena. Following the birth of their son Ghatotkaca, Bhima, who along with his four brothers was already in a polyandrous marriage to Draupadi, abandoned both son and mother. But Ghatotkaca, steadfastly faithful, vowed to come to his father's aid whenever and wherever called to mind. It was during the main battle narrated in the *Mahabharata*, between the Pandavas and their cousins, the Kauravas, that Bhima thought of his son. Immediately Ghatotkaca appeared and fought effectively on the side of the Pandavas, killing many Kauravas before being slain himself by the projectile called Ekaghni (literally, "single-slayer," able to kill anyone, but only one), launched from the bow named Kalaprishtha (literally, "black-back") by the warrior Karna. Even when slain, Ghatotkaca, that mountainous being, was able to kill additional enemies merely by falling on them.

Meghanada ultimately is killed, as the title to the poem implies. In the ninth and final canto, he is cremated along with his still living wife (the two are seen transported to Shiva's heaven in the chariot of Fire—Agni's chariot). His father eulogizes him, and all the Rakshasas of Lanka mourn his passing. The battle will resume after the poem ends, for Ravana yet lives and must be vanquished—can be vanquished now[89]—by Rama, in keeping with the *Ramayana* from which comes Datta's elaborated episode. But the tale of loyal, selfless son Meghanada is now complete.

Datta tells us in one of his letters how it pained him to kill off Meghanada. "It was a struggle whether Meghanad will finish me or I finish him. Thank Heaven. I have triumphed. He is dead, that is to say, I have finished the VI Book in about 750 lines. It cost me many a tear to kill him."[90] Meghanada, after all, represents the ideal son, the son that Datta himself had failed to be. Rather than honor his father's wishes and marry, he had rebelled, going so far as to leave his father's cultural community and become a Christian. Rather than come to the aid of his father when his father's fortunes had taken a turn for the worse, Datta the son had fled Calcutta for Madras, returning briefly once following his mother's death and then coming back permanently—abandoning his wife and four children in Madras—to claim his patrimony only after his father had passed away. Meghanada gave his all for his father. Even Ghatotkaca sacrificed himself for the sake of his father. Rama, though faithful to his father, had in fact left him and gone south into self-imposed exile, thereby causing Dasharatha's premature death. It is Meghanada, not Rama, who served his father best. It is for Meghanada and, I submit, for himself as a failed Meghanada-like son that Datta is grieving, a cathartic sort of grieving.

Humanism

The Slaying of Meghanada has much to do with a mid-nineteenth-century, Bengali Hindoo-College-fostered humanism. It shows up prominently in the characterizations of the main combatants—Rama, Ravana, and the eponymous Meghanada. Though Hindu gods always have had their human aspect—to wit, Shiva as the marijuana-smoking irresponsible husband—they are also divine. Rama, considered to have been an actual, historical prince, has long since been apotheosized into one of the incarnations of the god Vishnu. As opposed to the *Mahabharata*, the *Ramayana* is a sacred text, the mere hearing of which confers religious merit. The *Ramayana*'s Rama, for all his foibles, is understood to be a god. Not so for Datta's Rama. This nineteenth-century Rama comes to us shorn of his divinity. Bengali Marxists in the middle of the twentieth century noted gleefully this humanizing of deified Rama by Datta and hailed the poet of *Meghanada*, however anachronistically, as a good Communist fellow traveler.[91] It is not just Rama who is humanized at the hands of Datta. Hanuman, the monkey god and ally of Rama, becomes in Datta's poem neither god nor monkey.

Datta had no problem making human both Rama and the opposing Rakshasas. Recasting Hanuman proved more difficult. Datta struggled initially with Hanuman's simian nature, as we see in his letters to Raj Narain Bose. In May 1860, while composing *Meghanada*, Datta writes: "I must tell you, my dear fellow, that though, as a jolly Christian youth, I don't care a pin's head for Hinduism, I love the grand mythology of our ancestors. It is full of poetry. A fellow with an inventive head can manufacture the most beautiful things out of it."[92]

The dilemma seems perfectly clear. For Datta, it was a matter of separating out the mythological from the religious in the *Ramayana*, something akin to the proverbial classical Indian goose that could sip the milk from a mixture of milk and water, leaving only the water. But the mythological so extracted included a flying monkey named Hanuman who could transport the mountain Gandhamadana. That sort of Hanuman seems to have been unacceptable to Datta, too godlike perhaps, too supermonkey, certainly. In the end, Datta has the mountain come to Lanka on its own rather than have Hanuman transport it from the mainland to Lanka. Before that, however, Datta humanizes Hanuman, but does so without making him explicitly into a man. In July of 1860 he writes:

> Excuse the rambling letter and let me hear what favour the glorious son of Ravana finds in your eyes. He was a noble fellow, and, but for that scoundrel Bivishan, would have kicked the monkey-army into the sea. By the bye, if the father of our Poetry had given Ram human companions, I could have made a regular *Iliad* of the death of Meghanad. As it is, you must not expect any battle scenes. A great pity! Adieu, praying God to bless you and yours,
>
> I am, dear R., ever yours affectionately,[93]

And several letters later: "I have resumed Meghanad and am working away at the Third Book. If spared, I intend to lengthen this poem to ten Books and make it as complete an epic as I can. The subject is truly heroic; only the Monkeys spoil the joke—but I shall look to them."[94] Datta did indeed "look to them," as he puts it, transforming what he clearly acknowledges as monkeys, in his letters, into something else in his poem.

Let us consider for a moment the imagined geography of the *Ramayana's* world. The tale of Rama's wanderings is, after all—despite its appeal throughout the South Asian subcontinent and Southeast Asia—a "north Indian," or what could be called "Aryan-centric," epic. Today one might even call it an "Orientalist" epic, in the Saidian sense of that term, for the *Ramayana* clearly makes those imagined characters living to the south into the Other, demonizing some, animalizing others. In particular, those living in the imagined southern portion of the subcontinent proper include monkeys as well as bears, animals all. And it is here that Datta resisted the influence from his *Ramayana*-poet predecessors. His southern warriors become just that, southern and warriors. It is left to the reader to infer a simian nature in them, or not, as he or she so chooses. No such nature is actually denoted.

Take, for instance, the occurrence of Hanuman and of Sugriva in the first canto, where Ravana surveys the opposing forces arrayed against him. Writes Datta:

> At the northern gate stood guard the king himself, Sugrīva,
> a lion of a hero. And Dāśarathi watched the
> western gate—alas, downcast without his Jānakī, like
> the lotus-pleasing moon without his moonlight!—backed up by
> Lakṣmaṇa; the wind's son, Hanumān; and best of comrades,
> Vibhīṣaṇa. The opposition ranks had surrounded
> golden Laṅkā, just as a hunting party deep within
> the densest jungle, cautiously with teamwork ensnares a
> lioness—whose form is charming to the eye, whose force is
> furious, like goddess Bhīmā!

Of note is the manner in which Sugriva and Hanuman are identified—by proper name with an accompanying epithet: "Sugrīva, a lion of a hero" and "the wind's son, Hanumān." This practice of employing proper names, sometimes with and sometimes without identifying epithets, is followed consistently throughout *Meghanada*. If the epithets conjure up a monkey god in the reader's mind, so be it. Never does Datta suggest as much. Never does he use any of the several terms for monkey in Bangla. On the other hand, never are Hanuman and company referred to explicitly as men, either.

In the third canto, there comes a time when Hanuman tries to impede the movement of Meghanada's wife, Pramila, as she and her attending entourage of women head for the Rakshasas' walled city of Lanka. Nrimundamalini, her maidservant, insults Hanuman by referring to him as all manner of animal. Writes Datta:

> The attending Nṛmuṇḍamālinī (that wrathful, hot-
> tempered woman) twanged her bow inflamed, shouting threateningly,
> "Barbarian, bring here at once that lord of Sītā! Who
> wants you, you wretched little beast! We, by choice, have not struck
> the likes of you with our weapons. Does the lioness pick
> a quarrel with a jackal? We spared your life, now scamper
> off, jungle-dweller! Simpleton, what is there to gain by
> killing you? Be off with you, call the lord of Sītā here,
> and your master Lakṣmaṇa, and call that blemish on the
> clan of Rākṣasas, that Vibhīṣaṇa! Foe-conquering
> Indrajit—his wife is pretty Pramīlā—that woman
> now will enter Laṅkā, by force of arms, to worship at
> her husband's feet! What man of arms, you fool, can block her way?"

The insults, of course, are rhetorical. Still, Datta has nicely associated Hanuman with his more traditional animal character without actually making him so. He, in a way, has his cake and eats it too. He lets someone from within the narrative call Hanuman an animal while he, the poet, does not.

When Datta refers to Rama's southern allies collectively, he does so not as monkeys but as "southerners" (*dakshinatya*), pure and simple, "those who dwell within the southern regions." In the seventh canto, Rama speaks to his supporters:

> "Save my clan, my honor,
> and my life, supporters of the Raghus, and rescue her,
> the Raghu wife, incarcerated by the wiles of that
> Rākṣasa. You have bought this Rāma with the coin of your
> affection; by conferring generosity, now bind
> firm with a noose of gratitude today the entire
> Raghu line, O *you who dwell within the southern regions.*"

In the ninth and final canto, Lakshmana has been revived. Rama's forces shout for joy. Ravana, distraught, having thought Lakshmana slain, is reported to by his minister as follows:

Hands cupped in deference, that best of ministers replied
with regret. "Who comprehends gods' *māyā* in this world of
māyā, Indra among kings? Gandhamādana, sovereign
among mountains and a god by nature, came himself last
night bearing a panacea and resuscitated
Lakṣmaṇa, O king. That is why their legions shout for joy.
As at winter's end a snake possesses twice the vigor,
likewise champion Saumitri shows a renewed spirit—now
intoxicated by the wine of valor. And so too,
with Sugrīva, *the southerners* are enlivened, like a
herd of elephants, my lord—one hears—with its lordly bull."

Though the southerners are here likened by simile to a herd of elephants, Lakshmana is compared to the herd's lordly bull. Neither part of the simile is anything but flattering. Nowhere are the southerners referred to as animals literally, neither as monkeys nor as any other sort of beast. To be noted is the absence of Hanuman as the transporter of mountain Gandhamadana. In Valmiki and Krittivasa, it is Hanuman who uproots the panacea-bearing mountain and flies it to Lanka. In *Meghanada*, it is the mountain itself to whom Datta attributes divine qualities, and we know that mountains in Hindu mythology once had wings and used to fly. Hanuman, by his very absence in this passage, is looking more and more the human warrior, less and less the flying monkey god of the traditional *Ramayana*.

Transformations from Canonical Texts

The Slaying of Meghanada has much to do with the internalizing of the Western literary canon taught and consumed at Hindoo College in the first half of the nineteenth century. Datta wrote his poem for his Bangla-speaking audience, but he expected them—the educated among them—to see and appreciate his incorporation within it of a rich sampling from the Western classics. Part of the beauty of the poem stems from perceiving the manner in which Datta folds text into text. To paraphrase and at the same time play with the wording of Macaulay's 1835 minute on education: *Meghanada* is a text that is utterly Indian in language and imagery but "Young-Bengal" Indian, "Bengal-Renaissance" Indian, "mid-nineteenth-century-educated-Bengali" Indian in taste, in morals, and in intellect. The educated Bengali Indian of that day knew his Shakespeare, had read his Homer. To his friend Raj Narain Bose, in 1860 upon finishing the first canto, Datta wrote: "It is my ambition to engraft the exquisite graces of the Greek mythology on our own; in the present poem, I mean to give free scope to my inventing powers (such as they are) and to borrow as little as I can from Valmiki. Do not let this startle you. You shan't have to complain again of the un-Hindu character of the Poem. I shall not borrow Greek stories but write, rather try to write, as a Greek would have done."[95] In the same letter, Datta adds ten lines of his own poetry, identifying them as the opening lines to the second canto of *Meghanada*, adding:

> You will at once see whom I imitate;
>
> "Who of the gods impelled them to contend?
> Latona's son and Jove's—" Cowper's Homer's Iliad.
>
> Milton has imitated this—
>
> "Who first seduced them to that foul revolt?
> The infernal serpent"—Book I

But in the following letter, he tells Raj Narain that he has reconsidered that "exordium" for the second canto, stating that it will be quite different. The very next letter came with a manuscript of the complete second canto. And a letter later, Datta tells Raj Narain: "As a reader of the Homeric Epos, you will, no doubt, be reminded of the Fourteenth Iliad, and I am not ashamed to say that I have intentionally imitated it—Juno's visit to Jupiter on Mount Ida. I only hope I have given the Episode as thorough a Hindoo air as possible."[96]

The appropriation of literary texts along with their transformation was by no means confined to works from the Western canon. Datta's primary source of inspiration is, of course, the *Ramayana*, a canonical Indian work of literature. Datta saw himself very much a part of the *Ramayana* tradition, as is obvious from the invocation that begins the fourth canto, an invocation that includes a litany of classical Sanskrit poets who composed literature of various sorts on the Rama tale, both poetry and dramas. He ends by including in his list of artistic ancestors the Bengali poet Krittivasa:

> I bow before you, guru among poets, before your
> lotus feet, Vālmīki. O crown-gem upon the head of
> Bhārata, I, your slave, humbly follow after you just
> as the wretched poor follow as camp followers of an
> Indra among kings when that king goes on a pilgrimage
> to a sacred spot. Meditating day and night on foot-
> prints you have left, how many pilgrims before me have gained
> entrance to fame's temple, by subduing world-subduing

Śamana—to become immortal. Śrī Bhartṛhari;
scholar Bhavabhūti, called Śrīkaṇṭha; a man of marked
mellifluence, Kālidāsa—known throughout Bhārata
as the favorite son of Bhāratī; most captivating
Murāri, epitome of his namesake's melodic
flute; and poet Kṛttivāsa, a repository of
achievements, ornament of this Bengal.—O forefather,
how am I to sport with regal geese upon the lake of
poetic *rasa* if you do not guide me? I shall string
anew a garland after plucking blossoms tenderly
from your literary garden. I strive to beautify
our language with divers decorations, but where shall I
(impoverished me!) obtain that gem cache, Ratnākara, if
you do not help? Show compassion, lord, to this needy one.

Valmiki is that poet, or collectively those poets, referred to as the *adi kavi* (first poet) to whom is attributed authorship of the authoritative Sanskrit *Ramayana.* Bharata stands for the Indian subcontinent. Death—one name for the god of death is Samana—subdues all the world but can, of course, be defeated by reputation when one's name lives on. Then comes a litany of real poets, Bhartrihari, Bhavabhuti, Kalidasa, and Murari, all composers of literary works in Sanskrit on the topic of Rama and his wanderings. The list of his "forefathers" ends with Krittivasa, author of the Bangla *Ramayana* so dear at this time to Datta's heart. Ratnakara, whose name quite literally means "gem mine" and who, through penance and devotion to the god Rama, became transubstantiated into the poet Valmiki himself, is asked by Datta in this apostrophe for assistance in his own poetic endeavor.

Though the *Ramayana* constitutes the primary South Asian text informing Datta's narrative, it is by no means the only one from that tradition to be blended into *Meghanada.* The *Mahabharata,* India's other major Hindu epic, shows up in a number of similes but also figures prominently in the eighth canto, where, in Datta's own words, "Mr. Ram is to be conducted through Hell to his father, Dasaratha, like another Aeneas."[97] There is no question but that the *Aeneid* provides much of the framework for Rama's descent into the netherworld, where we also find clearly traceable references to Dante's *Inferno* and Milton's *Paradise Lost.* During the descent, there is even an image, *agni sthambha* (pillar of fire), drawn verbatim from the Bangla translation of the Bible, an image of the fiery staff that goddess Maya takes with her to illuminate the nether regions. The hell Rama visits, however, is not that of the *Aeneid* or the *Inferno* or any other Western work of literature. The hell in *Meghanada,* with its four directional gates and its eighty-four punishment pits, some of them specifically named and all of them situated in the southern region, is that netherworld known as the city of Yama, Hindu god of the dead. It is the nether region as depicted in the Bangla *Mahabharata.*

That same *Mahabharata,* composed in Bangla by Kasiramadasa (seventeenth century), provides the name of and some of the personality of one of the new characters, Meghanada's wife Pramila, introduced into *Ramayana* lore by Datta. Literary scholars, knowing Datta's range of reading, have seen in Pramila—as she appears in canto 1 (the loving bride), canto 3 (the warrior woman), canto 5 (the loving wife again), and canto 9 (the faithful widow-cum-suttee)—aspects of not only Tasso's Armida but also his Clorinda, Virgil's Camilla, and Homer's Andromache. Datta, moreover, endows Meghanada's spouse with many of the qualities of an idealized Indian wife. But it is the Bangla *Mahabharata* source text that dominates, particularly for Pramila as Datta depicts her in the third canto. In the "Ashvamedha Parva" (horse-sacrifice book) of the *Mahabharata,* Pramila appears in her own queendom, a strong warrior sovereign who confronts Arjuna. It is after the great Bharata war between the Pandavas and Kauravas in which all Kauravas are killed. Yudhishthira, eldest of the Pandavas, suffers remorse, tries to commit suicide by starvation, but is admonished against such a sinful act by the sage Vyasa, who counsels him to perform a horse-sacrifice as expiation. In such a sacrifice, a horse is decked with silver and gold, allowed to wander at will for a year throughout the world, but must be protected by an accompanying escort from anyone who might seek to possess it. In effect, those into whose realm the horse wanders are expected to acknowledge the sacrificer's superior power. To the forehead of Yudhishthira's horse was affixed a shiny gold mirror, signed by Yudhishthira with a warning:

> This horse shall roam the earth at will.
> Should any warrior there impede
>   The sacrificial stallion,
> Him I shall best, by strength of arms,
> Shall free this equine, then complete
>   The *ashvamedha yajna.*[98]

At the completion of its wanderings, the horse is beheaded.

Yudhishthira and one of the Pandava twins remain in Hastina, while Arjuna and the others troop behind the free-roaming horse. In various kingdoms, it provokes crises or battles, all of which Arjuna somehow surmounts. At one point, the horse enters Pramila's queendom, a land inhabited solely by women warriors—this, the result of a curse. As Pramila, foremost of the warrior women, tells Arjuna, she was the son of a raja who while hunting one day chanced upon Shiva and Parvati making love in the forest. Parvati caught sight of the peeping monarch and, mortified with embarrassment, cursed him along with his army (among which was his son) to be women and remain in the woods. If a male child somehow were born to any of them, he would die after his twelfth year. Initially Pramila appears hostile to Arjuna, defying the great Pandava warrior. It is this aspect of her that, in some ways, defines her character. She is strong and confident, able to stand up to any man. No matter that in the end she agrees to relinquish the horse and requests Arjuna to wed her. She remains, symbolically, the defiant woman warrior.

Datta drew upon this lightly sketched character (the Pramila episode occupies only two of the more than a thousand pages in one printed version of the Bangla *Mahabharata*) for his own Pramila, who in canto 3 defies Rama and with her retinue of armed women enters the walled city of Lanka. We have confirmation, in one of the satirical farces Datta wrote the year before, that his Pramila has links to that character in the *Mahabharata.* As already mentioned, Datta had been commissioned by the Paikpara raja brothers to write two social satires. *Ekei ki bale sabhyata*? (Is this what's called civilization?) mocks those pseudo Young Bengal men who, without the benefit of schooling such as that which Hindoo College imparted to the likes of a Michael Madhusudan Datta, caroused and visited brothels and pretended to know English, all in the name of being cultured, Western, "civilized." The targets of the second of the two satires, *Bura salikera ghare rom* (Hair on the back of the old coot's neck), were those of the landowning class or zamindars who took advantage, sexually and otherwise, of the poor peasants living on their property. The latter work has as its main character the old lecher landowner by the name of Bhaktaprasad, who lewdly eyes one of the young peasant girls. To himself he muses, with comical bombast and an air of resignation, that he might not be able to have his way with her. "After conquering the entire world, oceans and all," says Bhakta in a theatrical aside, "was not Partha (Arjuna) in the end bested at the hands of Pramila?" (act 2, scene 1). This same Pramila of the Bangla *Mahabharata* will be fleshed out and transformed into Meghanada's wife in *Meghanada.*

The Meghanada character in Krittivasa's Bangla *Ramayana* does not have a named wife, though his wives, plural, are said to number nine thousand. Valmiki, in the Sanskrit *Ramayana,* gives Meghanada no wife at all. Meghanada, however, already had acquired a wife in two other South Asian texts to which Datta had access, though he does not list their authors in the litany of poets to whom he pays homage in the passage cited above. In neither of these other two texts is she named Pramila but rather Sulocana ("she of beautiful eyes") instead. One of the texts is a *Ramayana* written in Bangla some seventy years prior to *Meghanada*. Its authors were Jagata Rama and his son Rama Prasada, and their *Ramayana* became designated the Jagadrami *Ramayana*, from the prime author's name. The other texts are the various scripts for the Ramlila, literally, "the divine play [*lila*] of Rama."

Ramlila scripts come, if not verbatim at least in essence, from the *Ramayana*, most often the Hindi *Ramayana* by sixteenth-century poet Tulsidasa. Ramlila dramas are annual enactments of the mythic clash between Rama and Ravana, culminating in the defeat of the Rakshasa sovereign. They are usually staged outdoors, often but not always progressing from one location to another throughout the town or village in which the performance takes place. And they are performed throughout northern India.[99] Moreover, they were also performed in Calcutta during Datta's lifetime. We know this from one of the most significant works of Bangla literature of this period, *Hutoma pencara naksha* (Sketches by Hutom, the owl). In that book, the character Hutom, from his bird's-eye vantage point, draws verbal sketches illustrating buffoonery and the absurd among everyday people and common events in contemporary Calcutta. One of those sketches bears the title "Ramlila." Though Hutom shows the reader more of the characters on the periphery surrounding the performance, it is the Ramlila enactment, held in the garden of one of Calcutta's wealthy elite of that day, that serves as the central event and motivation for the actions sketched.

The Ramlila, no doubt, was at that time in the middle of the nineteenth century part and parcel of Calcutta culture. Furthermore, as evidence that Datta would have been acquainted with the Ramlila, we have the statement of his best friend, Bysack, indicating that he, and thus other cosmopolitan Bengalis, knew well this non-Bengali dramatic form: "The Hindustani Ram Jatra and Ram Lila are performed with great éclat mostly by professional people."[100] In the Ramlila scripts one finds Meghanada with wife—one and only one wife, who has the name Sulocana. Though Ramlila scripts vary in length, depending upon the number of days over which the drama is to be enacted, many of them contain the audience-pleasing scene of not just the slaying of Meghanada but also his cremation. In these Ramlilas, Sulocana mounts Meghanada's funeral pyre and becomes a "suttee," the common English spelling of the word *sati*, meaning "true wife." (Suttee had been banned as illegal by the British East India Company in 1829.) Datta concludes his epic in similar fashion, with Meghanada's wife Pramila becoming a suttee and being taken by the god of fire, Agni, up on high to Shiva and Durga's heaven.

The Jagadrami *Ramayana* (1790–91) likewise incorporates the cremation of Meghanada and has his wife, Sulocana, mount the funeral pyre and become a suttee. It seems quite probable that the Jagadrami *Ramayana*'s Sulocana herself as well as the cremation of both Meghanada and wife come directly from the Ramlila, or more precisely from Tulsidas's *Ramayana* mediated through the Ramlila. And, it is from the Jagadrami *Ramayana* or the Ramlila or a combination of the two that Datta takes a part of the character of his creation, Pramila. But Pramila and Sulocana are not the same person. Though Sulocana and her entourage of female attendants proceed both to Rama's encampment and to the walled city of Lanka, as do Pramila and her women in *Meghanada*, Sulocana and company do so not "like the Amazonians as described by Michael Madhusudana Datta, but as devotees of Rama," writes Dinesh Chandra Sen.[101] The Amazonian nature stems from the Bangla *Mahabharata*.[102]

The cremation proper is lavish; the symbolism, pointed. The pyre becomes like an altar for Durga, the form of the goddess most widely and warmly worshiped by Hindu Bengalis. What the Ramlila is to much of northern India, Durga Puja is to the Bengal region. These two Hindu religious events—Durga Puja and the Ramlila—take place simultaneously, in both real and mythic time. It is Durga's puja that gives rise each year to the largest public festival in the Hindu Bengali community. Symbolically, in the autumn Durga—also known as Parvati and by more than a hundred other names—returns home, just as married daughters everywhere in Bengal return home to their parents' household. She arrives on the sixth day of the waxing moon; stays for the seventh, eighth, and ninth days; and on the tenth day must return to her husband's house—to Shiva's home on Mount Kailasa. During her stay, during the Durga Puja festivities in Bengal, she is honored ritually with sacrifice. The tenth day, called *vijaya dasami* (the victorious tenth), is a bittersweet time for all Hindu Bengalis, since the goddess (the symbolic daughter) must depart for yet another year. The image of the goddess is on that day immersed in the Ganges whereby she (her spirit) travels upstream to the Himalayas and her husband's home. Left behind, once the water has washed away the clay, is "the empty / splendor of an idol's frame without its lifelike painted / image, at the end of an immersion ceremony"—so Datta depicts the wife of Meghanada on her way to the cremation pyre. And with that cremation, comparable to the immersion of the goddess, the ninth and final canto of *Meghanada* draws to a close. In Hindu mythic history, with all its many tales intertwined, Rama is said to slay Ravana on "the victorious tenth," the very day Parvati departs for Mount Kailasa. It is with the slaying of Ravana that Ramlilas, of no matter how many days' duration, end. By concluding his epic with a reference to that tenth day of

Durga Puja, Datta has effectively foreshadowed the inevitable demise of the Rakshasa king, in accordance with the traditional *Ramayana*.

There is yet another canonical text that informs part of the last canto of *Meghanada*, and that is the *Iliad*, the twenty-fourth and final book of that Homeric epic. Ravana's farewell address to his daughter-in-law and slain son recalls those of Andromache, Hekabe, and Helen to the corpse of Hector. Where Priam had extracted from Achilles a promise to cease hostilities for eleven days (nine to mourn, one for cremation and burial, and one to build a grave-barrow), Datta's Ravana requests seven. (In the Jagadrami *Ramayana*, hostilities cease for one day only.) *Shraddha*, or ceremonies honoring the dead, vary in length among Hindus from caste to caste. A week is not an uncommon period of time for such an activity. The Rakshasas weep for their beloved prince, "seven days and seven nights."

Épique à Clef

There has always been some question as to what if anything in political terms Datta meant by *Meghanada*. He composed and published the poem only a few years after the Sepoy Rebellion of 1857, but no mention of that ever appears in any of Datta's extant letters. Bengali intellectuals of this period seemed little concerned by that rather significant event in British colonial history. Datta clearly had a sense of history, however. His first published piece, "The Captive Ladie," took the defeat of the Hindu king Prithviraja and the symbolic start of Muslim hegemony in north India as the underlying subject matter for his romantically tragic tale of love and death. From his letters, we know that he was receptive to the idea, despite his false modesty, that he himself might write a national epic: "The subject you propose for a national epic is good—very good indeed. But I don't think I have as yet acquired sufficient mastery over the 'Art of poetry' to do it justice. So you must wait a few years more. In the meantime, I am going to celebrate the death of my favourite Indrajit."[103] Raj Narain Bose had suggested as subject matter Simhala Vijaya (Victory over Simhala [Sri Lanka]), which, Datta tells Bose rather nonchalantly, "I have forgotten the story and do not know in what work to find it; kindly enlighten me on the subject."[104] It happened to be a subject dear to Bose's heart and one about which he later wrote, while extolling the virtues of Bengalis as a people: "Prince Vijay Simha, who was banished from his homeland by his father and with several followers boarded an ocean-going vessel, proceeded to Simhala, and conquered that aforementioned island and by whose name, Simha, that Simhala island came to be known—he was a Bengali."[105] It would have been a national epic depicting the conquest of Sri Lanka by a Bengali, with the Bengali being the vanquishing hero. Instead, Datta wrote about almost the same topic, the conquest of Lanka, but with the hero, Prince Meghanada, the vanquished.

Datta mined what came to be the source book for another historical tradition, a work that captured the fancy of many Bengali intellectuals in the nineteenth century. James Tod's *Annals of Rajasthan* seemed somehow to provide Bengalis, Datta included, with a sense of the Indian heroic. Datta took the plot for his drama *Krishnakumari* from Tod. The Bengali novelist Bankim Chandra Chattopadhyay (1838–94), in his search for truly heroic Indian characters, would likewise follow Datta and others to the annals. Datta, as already noted, thought poorly of "Ram and his rabble," preferring the "grand fellow" Ravana. Chattopadhyay later in that same century would write equally disparagingly about the Bengali Krishna, so popular in the Radha-Krishna songs then and even now. Though he did not refer to the lover of Radha as rabble, Chattopadhyay rejected that Krishna completely while at the same time professing his admiration for a different Krishna—a grander fellow, so to speak—the Krishna of the *Mahabharata*, the Krishna who did not engage in (divine) erotic sport with Radha and the gopis but instead drove warrior Arjuna's chariot into battle and counseled killing one's enemies. First Datta, then later Chattopadhyay, would take this critical look at Bengali cultural heroes of the day and find them wanting. Each writer in his own way would try to discover the truly heroic, which in both cases meant reformulating one's own tradition slightly while at the same time looking outside the immediate confines of one's dominant popular culture.

The gestures by Datta toward Indian history and national epic, and his reformulation of the Indian heroic aside, the question remains as to the political significance, if any, of *Meghanada*. Does Datta's text in some way presage or encourage, as Chattopadhyay's writings would do, a nationalist consciousness among Indians and thus participate in the nationalist movement that was to emerge in the last quarter of the century? Can his poem be read sensibly as allegory? Is it in some meaningful way an épique à clef? The writer and critic Pramathanath Bishi thought so:

> Michael Madhusudan Datta's era was a time of not insignificant social change in Bengal. Such a minor revolution had not taken place in Bengali society for quite some time. It was not just that many of the English-educated Bengali elite of that day imbibed the foreigners' alcohol—British culture itself acted upon their minds like some

> sort of intoxicant. Each and every English book appeared in their eyes like a bottle of spirits. They forgot their mother tongue; they converted to Christianity in hopes of becoming pukka Western gentlemen and in furtherance of those aspirations even spelled their names in English in the most contorted of ways; and they nurtured fantasies of being able to dream in English. Disgust toward "Ram and his rabble," the sparking of one's imagination at the idea of Ravana and Meghanada—those attitudes were not peculiar to Datta. Many of his contemporaries had the very same feelings. What was native seemed despicable; what was English, grand and glorious. Such was the general temperament. Ravana and his son stood as the symbolic embodiments of such a scenario. Ravana's grandeur, Ravana's heroic nature, Ravana's golden Lanka, Ravana's animus toward Rama—all of these utterly captivated the educated elites. Though Datta may have written Lanka, he was thinking England. Blending the above-mentioned attitudes with the contemporary societal situations, Datta cast Ravana's character as representative of the English-educated segment of society. He built up Ravana to such proportions that none could be greater—hence, by comparison, Rama and Lakshmana appear diminutive.[106]

Read this way, *Meghanada* becomes all that much more tragic. The cultured, cosmopolitan Indians, the Hindoo-College-educated class, the Calcutta elite that had enriched themselves with the literature and science and philosophy coming from the West and in turn would enrich their own culture, as Datta is enriching his—those sorts of Indians were doomed to defeat at the hands of the traditionalists, the parochial, provincial but powerful majority who had tradition on their side. But tragic heroes are heroes nonetheless. In defeat, Meghanada becomes, by the rules of tragedy, the victor, capturing one's imagination. Likewise, it will be the vanquished elites who in many ways become the victors and, during the next decades, will contribute to the emerging nationalist debate.

A different interpretation of Meghanada comes from William Radice, who finds the key to this epic in a combination of xenophilia and xenophobia. The xenophilia need hardly be argued. It is patently clear in the liberal borrowings from Western literature. Datta and the Hindoo-College-educated elite could be said to love the foreign, epitomized by Western literary culture. On the other hand, the xenophobia, reasons Radice, has much to do with nationalism. "To trace the nationalist or xenophobic strain in Madhusudan requires subtlety and empathy: one must be prepared to read between the lines sometimes, to look for the deeper implications of his writing. But there is an upper layer, so to speak, which is obvious. Patriotism does not necessarily imply xenophobia, but it is xenophobia's *sine qua non*—and patriotism Madhusudan had in abundance."[107]

As part of his effort to "read between the lines," Radice "look[s] closely at Book VI, for evidence of implicit xenophobia—not so easy to detect as the xenophilia of the epic's Miltonic verse-form, Virgilian structure and Homeric tragic pathos."[108] It is in this canto, or book 6, that Lakshmana actually slays Meghanada.

Radice tells us something of the reading experience. Readers of Meghanada, he says, see Lanka as "home." The Rakshasas are "us," the "insiders"; Rama and his cohorts are "them," the "outsiders."[109] The "us" here corresponds to Hindu India whose surrogate becomes Meghanada, slain while performing a very Hindu sort of worship to the Hindu god Agni. "We have, in short, in Book VI of Madhusudan's masterpiece, an intense and impassioned projection of the shameful and humiliating defeat of the champion of the 'insiders' by the dastardly and immoral tactics of the 'outsiders'. Is it too far-fetched to suggest that this reflects the shameful subjugation of Hindu India by the alien, outcaste British?"[110]

"Ram and his rabble," in Radice's reading, take on the symbolic value of colonial power in opposition to traditional Hindu India. In Bishi's reading, Ram et al. serve symbolically as traditional Hindu India itself, countering and encumbering the Westernized educated, modern (vs. traditional) Indians of nineteenth-century Calcutta. Both of these allegorical, historicized readings, it should be noted, come from the twentieth century, not from an audience contemporary with Datta.

Reception, Assessment

Datta himself provides us, through his letters, with a number of reactions to his poem. All of them ring positive, which should hardly come as a surprise, given his self-confidence and ebullient personality. *Meghanada* was published in two installments, cantos 1–5 in January of 1861 and then cantos 6–9 in July of that same year. After bringing out the first installment, and having finished the sixth canto, he bragged to Raj Narain Bose: "The poem is rising into splendid popularity. Some say it is better than Milton—but that is all bosh—nothing can be better than Milton; many say it licks Kalidasa; I have no objection to that. I don't think it impossible to equal Virgil, Kalidasa and Tasso.

Though glorious, still they are mortal poets; Milton is divine."[111] And throughout that year, up to and beyond the publication of the second installment, he wrote that same Raj Narain, often including some mention of his cherished epic composition:

> On the whole the book is doing well. It has roused curiosity. Your friend Baboo Debendra Nath Tagore [Rabindranath's father], I hear, is quite taken up with it. S— told me the other day that he (Baboo D) is of opinion that few Hindu authors can "stand near this man," meaning your fat friend of No. 6 Lower Chitpore Road, and "that his imagination goes as far as imagination can go."[112]

> Some days ago I had occasion to go to the Chinabazar. I saw a man seated in a shop and deeply poring over Meghanad. I stepped in and asked him what he was reading. He said in very good English—"I am reading a new poem, Sir!" "A poem!" I said, "I thought there was no poetry in your language." He replied—"Why, sir, here is poetry that would make my nation proud."[113]

> I have not yet heard a single line in Meghanada's disfavour. The great Jotindra has only said that, he is sorry poor Lakshman is represented as killing Indrajit in cold blood and when unarmed. But I am sure the poem has many faults. What human production has not?[114]

In July of 1862, Datta finally reached England, the land of his dreams. The month before, he had written Raj Narain announcing his departure but also the republication of *Meghanada*: "Meghanad is going through a second edition with notes, and a real B.A. has written a long critical preface, echoing your verdict—namely, that it is the first poem in the language. A thousand copies of the work have been sold in twelve months."[115]

Lest we think the above epistolary evidence all puffery and self-congratulation, it should be noted that one of the leading Bengali authors and emerging intellectuals of the day, Kaliprasanna Simha (1840–70), felt so moved by Datta's literary accomplishment that he convened—in February of 1861, a month after the first installment of *Meghanada* appeared—a public assembly at which he honored the poet, with words of praise and a "silver claret jug"; at least that was the way Datta himself described the object in one of his letters. Simha came from a wealthy family and had both the time and the money to pursue matters that interested him. Much younger than Datta, he had at the tender age of thirteen founded one of the societies for the acquisition of knowledge that were popular at the time, his being called the *Vidyotsahini sabha* (Society for encouraging learning). Simha studied at Hindoo College but completed his education at home. In his teens he had composed several dramas. He took an active part in the current social reform movements, such as promoting widow remarriage and opposing both polygamy and prostitution. Between 1862 and 1864, he published his popular and genre-breaking social commentary, *Sketches by Hutom, the Owl,* in which, as noted above, there is reference to the Ramlila performances in Calcutta at this time. With help from Sanskrit scholars, Simha translated the entire Sanskrit *Mahabharata* into Bangla, no mean feat. It was this Kaliprasanna Simha who personally presented Datta with that expensive token of his—and the like-minded Bengali intelligentsia's—sincere appreciation for Datta's extraordinary artistic accomplishment. He and his fellow Bengalis recognized that the piece by Datta was something the likes of which had never before been seen in the Bangla literary world. A new era had begun, and they wished to acknowledge the event properly.

The Slaying of Meghanada went through six editions during Datta's lifetime, testimony in itself of the poem's generally positive reception.[116] Following Datta's death in June of 1873, an obituary appeared in Bankim Chandra Chattopadhyay's journal *Bangadarshan,* the premier Bangla-language journal of the day. It was penned partially by Chattopadhyay himself and included two poetic tributes to Datta by other poets. For his part, Chattopadhyay began by saying that Bengal had now learned to cry, that Bengalis openly, unabashedly were weeping for a Bengali poet. He then lavished praise upon Datta, mentioning no specific work of his, not even *Meghanada*, but ranking Datta as one of the two finest poets Bengal had ever produced—Jayadeva, a Bengali of the twelfth century who wrote a single work and that in Sanskrit, the *Gitagovinda,* being the other poet of distinction.[117]

A number of years later, in 1881, a piece on *Meghanada* came out in that same journal, authored not by Chattopadhyay but by one of the staff writers, which the author of the article himself regrets, claiming that only Chattopadhyay could do justice to Datta's poem. Be that as it may, this author goes on to examine the Meghanada character in detail, citing passage after passage from the text proper. When it comes to Meghanada's noble and brave response to Lakshmana in Canto VI, in the slaying scene, the author says he deems it unnecessary to be specific, assuming that all of his readers know that part of the poem by heart: "Were I to be capable of conjuring up before you in its entirety that unprecedented scene of the temple of the Nikumbhila sacrifice, I would be able to convey to you the magnanimity of Meghanada's character.

But such is hardly necessary. We know full well, that particular section of the poem is imprinted in searing letters of fire upon the hearts of educated Bengalis."[118]

What drives the narrative, that is to say, what causes the death of Meghanada, the author concludes, is the truth of the axiom that the sins of the father are visited upon the son. "Due to the faults of the father, the son is destroyed; it is an ancient notion. This very truism, however, is the essence of *The Slaying of Meghanada.*"[119] It is his father, Ravana, who seals Meghanada's fate and causes his demise. But in a more generalized, abstracted sense, it is Fate itself that seals his fate, a fate beyond Meghanada's control. The "modern scientific fatalist," according to the author, says the same thing. *Meghanada,* our author declares, had been built upon the solid foundation of fatalism. The majority of the world's immortal poetry, he states forthrightly, has this philosophy as its unifying principle.[120] This "modern scientific fatalist" (*adhunika baijnanika adrstabadi*) aside—whatever our author might have had in mind when he wrote those words in 1881—to be noted here is his inclusion, by inference, of *Meghanada* among "the world's immortal poetry."

As one might expect, not everyone gave *Meghanada* unqualified praise. A certain young man destined to become the most celebrated Bengali writer of all time found Datta's poem lacking. Rabindranath Tagore (1861–1941), born the very year in which *Meghanada* appeared, declared straightforwardly and unequivocally that the work failed, that it was no epic at all. Tagore, twenty-one years young at this time, may even have been responding indirectly to the laudatory criticism of less than a year earlier in *Bangadarshan,* which he and almost all educated Bengalis read religiously. "In *mahakavyas* [literally, 'great poetry,' but also 'epic']," he wrote, "we want to see a grand personage; we want to see grand feats accomplished by that grand personage."[121] None of that do we find in *Meghanada,* concluded Tagore. Nothing as glorious as the defeat of the Trojans by the Greeks. Nothing immortal in the characters, not in Meghanada himself, certainly, not in Ravana nor Rama nor Lakshmana.

Tagore then spoke of a parallel world that we all inhabit, peopled by characters from myth and fiction, a world that is different for different cultures with different mythic and literary traditions. It is a world, unseen, whose inhabitants, without our consciously knowing it, affect our very thoughts and lives. We know these people. They are, in some sense, alive for us. Shakespeare's Hamlet frets and dithers, worries and wonders about his father, his mother, his uncle. Hamlet is "real," he "lives," Tagore would say, a permanent inhabitant of that world of immortal, memorable characters. What characters has Datta created with his *Meghanada* who now take up residence in that parallel universe of the imagination? The answer Tagore gives to his own rhetorical question is, none. Datta has added no lasting, living character to the Bengali reader's mind, not a new sort of Meghanada, not a Pramila, his wife, not a different Ravana, with personality and unforgettable character, to accompany us in life. "It is the task of the *mahakavi* [literally, 'great poet,' but also 'epic poet'] to create all those immortal companions. Now I ask you, how many new inhabitants has Michael [Madhusudan Datta] sent off to live in that all-pervasive poetic world that surrounds us? If he has sent not a one, then which of his writings are you going to call *mahakavya*?"[122] Obviously not *Meghanada*: "I have not dissected *The Slaying of Meghanada* limb by limb and examined each—I have critiqued its fundamental substance, the source of its very life's breath. And, I found it had no breath of life. I found it was no *mahakavya* at all."[123]

Tagore subsequently explained away his attack on Datta's text as just so much juvenile exuberance: "Previously, in the heat of youth's brash overconfidence, I had penned a harshly critical piece on *The Slaying of Meghanada.* The juice of the mango yet unripe is full of acid—likewise, immature criticism is acerbic. When other skills are found in short supply, that of poking-jabbing-clawing-scratching becomes finely honed. I, by drawing bared nails across this immortal poem, had been looking for the easiest way to elevate my name to immortality."[124] Youthful, misguided egotism, Tagore implied, propelled his actions. Harold Bloom a century later would identify this behavior as "the anxiety of influence."[125] Here was a genius, Tagore, encountering a genius of his previous generation as well as encountering a work of genius, *Meghanada.* He, Tagore, needed to "misunderstand," to "misperceive," in order to control and to avoid being controlled by it and by Datta. It is a classic Harold-Bloomian case of misprision, as Bloom calls it. It is the anxiety of influence acted out by the twenty-one-year-old Tagore, the Nobel-laureate-to-be.

Meghanada—Datta's *Meghanada*—has no doubt taken his place among those living in the parallel world of literary characters of which Tagore spoke. Pramila—not the Pramila of the Bangla *Mahabharata* but Datta's Pramila of *Meghanada*—is living there too. To simply aver that such is the case rings hollow. To prove the existence of particular characters in this mind-based world is nearly impossible without the testimony of some other member of the Bangla-speaking community who could say, "yes, they live in my parallel universe." We do have some evidence, albeit inconclusive, in the form of Bengali given names. Meghnad Saha, born in 1893, was to become a world-renowned nuclear physicist. His given name, the spelling of which reflects the Bangla pronunciation of Meghanada, has never been particularly common among Bengalis. I presume Meghnad Saha became the namesake of Datta's character. Meghanada is also known as Indrajit ("victorious [*jit*] over Indra"), and Indrajit, unlike Meghanada, has become a rather prevalent name among Hindus in Bengal. But Indrajit serves as an epithet for more than Meghanada. A number of gods defeated Indra, a Vedic god whose prowess in the later Hindu period had waned. Indrajit can stand for Vishnu. The prevalence of Indrajit as a Bengali man's given name does not necessarily tell us anything about the presence or absence of Datta's Indrajit in the parallel world of literary characters. Of real live Pramilas, there are two Bengali women about whom we know, one of them because of the fame of her husband, Kazi Nazrul Islam (1899–1976), a prolific poet, composer and singer of songs, political magazine editor, and all-around charismatic figure. Nazrul Islam, who married a young woman named Ashalata, actually renamed his wife Pramila, undoubtedly after Datta's dramatic heroine.[126] He knew *Meghanada* well, having some years earlier adapted Datta's epic poem to a dramatic folk genre called *letogan*.[127] And, there lived one Pramila Nag, whose birth date is unknown and who died in the Bangla year 1303 (1896–97 C.E.). We know little about her other than the fact that she was a poet.[128]

The more persuasive proof that Datta's characters had gained entry to the parallel literary universe of the mind comes in the form of a *Ramayana* told by one Dhan Gopal Mukerji (1890–1936). Mukerji was a Bengali, resident in the United States of America and one of the very few public intellectuals from India in the States during this period. He contributed to a book entitled *What Is Civilization?*, brought out in 1926, introduced by Hendrik Willem Van Loon (author of *The Story of Mankind*), which contained additional contributions by, among other notable personages, Maurice Maeterlinck (Belgian poet and philosopher, Nobel laureate in 1911, two years prior to Tagore) and W.E.B. Du Bois (leading African-American intellectual, editor of the mouthpiece journal of the NAACP). Two years earlier, in 1924, Mukerji had published a children's book, *Hari, the Jungle Lad*. He responded to Katherine Mayo's critical *Mother India* with his *A Son of Mother India Answers* (1928). And in 1930 there appeared his *Rama, the Hero of India: Valmiki's "Ramayana" Done into a Short English Version for Boys and Girls* (New York: E. P. Dutton). Of note is the claim in the title that the retold tale draws upon Valmiki's *Ramayana*. When it comes to the chapters named "Indrajit's Fall" and "Indrajit's Funeral," Mukerji's so-called Valmiki *Ramayana* transmogrifies into something based squarely upon Datta's

The Slaying of Meghanada. There is no funeral for Indrajit (Meghanada) in Valmiki's epic. There is in a Ramlila performance, but Mukerji's depiction of the funeral procession matches uncannily that described in *Meghanada.* And Mukerji mentions Meghanada's one and only wife—no name, just the designation "wife"—who emerges out of Datta's text, not from Valmiki's or even Krittivasa's *Ramayana.* That Datta's Meghanada and wife had so blatantly and effortlessly assumed their places in this retelling, by a Bengali, of the *Ramayana* belies Tagore's youthful assertion that no characters from *Meghanada* were meet to enter the immortal literary world. They were indeed meet, and they did enter.

Over the years, Tagore's proved to be not the only voice to negatively criticize Datta's poem. Pramatha Chaudhuri (1868–1946), editor of one of the most prestigious avant-garde literary magazines of the early decades of the twentieth century and himself a close friend of Tagore, disparaged *Meghanada* for being foreign, too foreign. It was not of the soil, so to speak, and therefore did not smell right—didn't smell at all, oddly enough. "Since the seeds of thought borne by winds from the Occident cannot take root firmly in our local soil, they either wither away or turn parasitic. It follows, then, that *The Slaying of Meghanada* is the bloom of a parasite. And though, like the orchid, its design is exquisite and its hue glorious, it is utterly devoid of any fragrance."[129]

Except in the eyes of Tagore, Pramatha Chaudhuri, and a few others, Datta's *The Slaying of Meghanada* has maintained its status from its time of publication to the present as a worthy piece, even a masterpiece of Bangla literature—and not just written literature but staged drama, too. It was dramatized by the great Bengali playwright Girish Chandra Ghosh in 1877 and performed on the boards of the National Theatre, which had come into existence during the decade of the 1870s.[130] Previous to that, there had been a staging of another dramatized version at the Bengal Theatre, in 1875; subsequently Haraprasad Sastri, literary scholar of great renown, did his own rendition, producing it in 1899.[131] And Kazi Nazrul Islam, as noted above, adapted *Meghanada* to the *letogan* dramatic folk genre. In his study of Tagore, which appeared in 1926, Edward Thompson had cause to mention Datta and his signature poem: "He [Datta] keeps an almost unbounded popularity, and there can be very few among Bengal's thousands of annual prize-givings where a recitation from his chief poem is not on the programme."[132] Moreover, still today *Meghanada* gets performed in the Kolkata theater to rave reviews and appreciative audiences, done by a cast of a single actor playing out the many parts. Datta's text lives on.

On Translation

Just a few words on my translation process: The meter I have adopted is a compromise between the original Bangla and the manner in which Datta suggests, in a personal letter, that his meter should be read:

> You want me to explain my system of versification for the conversion of your sceptical friends. I am sure there is very little in the system to explain; our language, as regards the doctrine of accent and quantity, is an "apostate", that is to say, it cares as much for them as I do for the blessing of our Family-Priest! If your friends know English, let them read the Paradise-Lost, and they will find how the verse, in which the Bengali poetaster writes, is constructed. The fact is, my dear fellow, that the prevalence of Blank-verse in this country, is simply a question of time. Let your friends guide their voices by the pause (as in English Blank-verse) and they will soon swear that this is the noblest measure in the Language. My advice is Read, Read, Read. Teach your ears the new tune and then you will find out what it is.[133]

The most common meter in premodern Bangla literature goes by the name of *payar,* which designates a scansion system—that is to say, a way of counting poetic feet—as well as a couplet structure. Traditional *payar* couplets display end rhyme. Each line of the couplet consists of fourteen syllables, generally divided in some sort of meaningful way with a caesura or break after the eighth syllable. The couplets tend to be semantically self-contained. What might be thought of as a sentence or a clause could spill over from one hemistich to the other, but not from one couplet into the following couplet. For example, from Krittivasa's *Ramayana:*

1	2	3	4	5	6	7	8	9	10	11	12	13	14
bhag-	*na-*	*du-*	*ta*	*ka-*	*he*	*gi-*	*ya*	*ra-*	*va-*	*na*	*go-*	*ca-*	*ra*

The bearer of bad tidings went to Ravana and said:

1	2	3	4	5	6	7	8	9	10	11	12	13	14
vi-	*ra-*	*ba-*	*hu*	*pa-*	*re*	*vart-*	*ta*	*su-*	*na*	*lan-*	*ke-*	*sva-*	*ra*

"Virabahu fell, now hear the news, O lord of Lanka."

1	2	3	4	5	6	7	8	9	10	11	12	13	14
so-	*ke-*	*ra*	*u-*	*pa-*	*re*	*so-*	*ka*	*ha-*	*i-*	*la*	*ta-*	*kha-*	*na*

On top of sorrows came more sorrow at that time;

1	2	3	4	5	6	7	8	9	10	11	12	13	14
sim-	*ha-*	*sa-*	*na*	*hai-*	*te*	*pa-*	*re*	*ra-*	*ja*	*da-*	*sa-*	*na-*	*na*

Raja Dasanana tumbled from his lion-throne.[134]

Note the end rhymes: *cara / svara* and *khana / nana*. Note too the self-contained nature of the lines, ending with a punctuation mark, at least in my literal English rendering.

Datta took that basic *payar* structure, retained the fourteen-syllable line, discarded end rhyming, and allowed for enjambment. That is to say, his poetic lines flow across the weak boundaries within a line, suppress the sense of a couplet structure altogether by not exhibiting couplet rhyming, and come to an end, meaningfully, anywhere within the line, not just at the end of one. He names his meter *amitraksara chanda* ("unfriendly letter meter," that is, unrhymed meter) or, in other words, the Bangla version of blank verse, a major innovation in Bangla prosody at the time. From a scene somewhat comparable to that narrated above from Krittivasa's *Ramayana*, Datta writes in *Meghanada*:

1	2	3	4	5	6	7	8	9	10	11	12	13	14
ni-	*sa-*	*ra*	*sva-*	*pa-*	*na-*	*sa-*	*ma*	*to-*	*ra*	*e*	*va-*	*ra-*	*ta,*

This news of yours is like a nightmare,

1	2	3	4	5	6	7	8	9	10	11	12	13	14
re	*du-*	*ta!*	*a-*	*ma-*	*ra-*	*vrin-*	*da*	*ya-*	*ra*	*bhu-*	*ja-*	*ba-*	*le*

Oh messenger! By whose strength of arms the immortals

1	2	3	4	5	6	7	8	9	10	11	12	13	14
ka-	*ta-*	*ra,*	*se*	*dha-*	*nurd-*	*dha-*	*re*	*ra-*	*gha-*	*va*	*bhi-*	*kha-*	*ri*

are harassed, that wielder of the bow the Raghava beggar

1	2	3	4	5	6	7	8	9	10	11	12	13	14
va-	*dhi-*	*la*	*sam-*	*mu-*	*kha*	*ra-*	*ne?*	*phu-*	*la-*	*da-*	*la*	*di-*	*ya*

has slain in face-to-face battle? With flower petals . . . .

The rhyming is gone. The second line runs into the third: "By whose strength of arms the immortals / are harassed." The fourth line completes one sentence and begins another, with only a prepositional phrase.

In my translation, I hold to the fourteen-syllable, unrhymed line displaying enjambment, though I make no effort to force my lines to be coterminous with the original. The four lines above I render as follows:

> This news of yours, messenger, is like a nightmare! Beggar
> Raghava in face-to-face battle slew the archer who,

> by his strength of arms, has harassed even the immortals?
> [Did Providence,] with flower petals, . . .

My lines of poetry are neither in Miltonic iambic pentameter nor are they equivalent in sound to Datta's. As Datta notes in his letter cited above, Bangla does not exhibit the "doctrine of accent and quantity." Put differently, Bangla does not have stressed and unstressed syllables. The iamb relies on stress patterns in English, specifically that of two syllables, one unstressed followed by one stressed, as in the snippet from *Paradise Lost* that Datta quotes in another letter:

> Who first seduc'd them to that fowl revolt?
> Th' infernal Serpent

Though I cannot and should not avoid stress within words, for that is natural to the English language, I have tried to avoid an iambic pattern, or any other pattern, of stress.

Bangla, as Datta tells us, cares as much for stress as he, a Christian, cares for the blessings of his natal family's Hindu *purohit*. Restated in terms of linguistics—and less colorfully, to be sure, than in Datta's metaphoric English—stress is not phonemic in Bangla. Stress is phonemic in English. Many words become almost unintelligible to the native English speaker if they are pronounced with the stress on the wrong syllable (the wrong *syl-LA-ble*, for instance). We differentiate in English between some pairs of words solely on the phonemic feature of stress. For example, there is the pair present/present, or *PRES-ent* and *pre-SENT*. The first is either a noun and means a gift, or an adjective indicating existing now. The second is a verb, meaning to bestow or give or display. Stress is found in Bangla, too, but there it is not phonemic. There are no such pairs of words in Bangla (like "present/present") that contrast only by differing accented syllables. Stress can be used in Bangla to convey emphasis, but normally all syllables within an individual word receive equal stress. One should keep this in mind when encountering the innumerable proper names in Datta's poem. The reader, of course, is free to pronounce—or mispronounce—them in any way whatsoever in English, but might want to try giving every syllable equal weight: *ME-GHA-NA-DA*. If any syllable is going to receive a slight stress—and this happens when a word is spoken in isolation from other words—then it should be the first: *ME-gha-na-da*, not *me-GHA-na-da* or *me-gha-NA-da* or *me-gha-na-DA*.

I have adhered to Datta's own paragraph divisions. He does indent, and so do I. In most cases I have reproduced his punctuation, also. All parentheses in my translation are to be found in his original. I must admit to diminishing slightly the number of exclamation marks, however. Datta, in his letters, in his poetry, and in life, is exuberantly exclamatory.

Datta's language is extremely rich, appropriate to the elevated style frequently found in art epics, or what are sometimes called secondary epics. I have made an attempt to reflect some of that grandeur with the lexicon upon which I draw. Datta liberally uses epithets as appellatives and modifiers. I chose not to double-translate those. That is to say, I have either let the epithet stand untranslated in the poem (but explained in the glossary) or rendered it into its literal meaning. For example, in the initial line we have "Virabahu," a character whose name means "he whose arms (*bahu*) are 'virile' (*vira*) or strong." I leave this appellative epithet as a proper name and do not double-translate it into "strong-armed Virabahu." Comparably, in the third line we have the goddess of ambrosial speech (*amrtabhasini*), an epithet for the goddess Sarasvati, also known as Bharati. I translate this literally but do not include the proper name, Amritabhasini, or add the word Sarasvati, which does not appear here in the text at all. When, in lines 7 and 8, the reader finds "the hope of Rakshasas" and "conqueror of Indra" and "Meghanada" (literally: "cloud [*megha*]-noise [*nada*]" or "thunder") all together, she or he can rest assured that all three epithets occur in the original text: *raksasabharasa / indrajit meghanade.* I treat two of these as adjectival ("the hope of Rakshasas"; "conqueror of Indra") and one, the final member of the series, as an appellative epithet ("Meghanada").

Datta employs his epithets as poetic ornamentations in several ways: their variety adds a lushness to the text, their tonal qualities often provide alliteration, and their literal meanings can transform these epithets into metaphors in their own right. In lines 16–19, for example, Datta plays off of the literal meanings for three epithets he places there. Mritunjaya, a name for Shiva, means "victorious over death"; the poet Valmiki also became victorious over death, by virtue of his "immortal" poem, the *Ramayana*. Varada, literally the "giver of boons" (here referring to goddess Sarasvati), is praised for the boon of hers that made Ratnakara (Valmiki's name before he became a poet)—"ratnakara" means both "mine (*akara*) of gems (*ratna*)" and "the ocean," which is a mine of pearls and other gems—into a veritable ocean or mine of poetry himself. Rather than tease the epithets for resonances here or in footnotes to the poem, I let the reader have the satisfaction of doing that on his or her own. A glossary is appended to the translation to assist those unfamiliar with the mythology of Hindu India.

Let me conclude with a Bengali reader's experience of reading Datta's meter. At age nine, Nirad C. Chaudhuri was asked by his father to memorize passages from *Meghanada*. His father claimed that only those who read Datta's blank verse properly could be considered cultured. For decades after the epic came out, Chaudhuri tells us, "bridegrooms were challenged by their sisters-in-law to prove their culture" by reading the *Meghanada*. Of his own acculturation to the new meter, this *amitraksara chanda*—the verse structure that Datta had his friend read Milton in order to fathom—Chaudhuri recounts:

> My father very carefully checked our tendency to stop at the end of the lines—a particularly important precaution because Michael had taken over as the foundation of his blank verse the fourteen-syllable rhyming couplet, and we, finding the metre to be the same, unconsciously read blank verse like couplets and made it sound incredibly grotesque. My father showed us how to read this blank verse—exactly like prose, with attention only to the sense and the punctuation; and he said, if we did that, the rhythm would come out as a matter of course. I did so, and after a little practice with my father, began to recite the rolling verse paragraphs with complete ease.[135]

I invite the reader to recreate Chaudhuri's experience of Datta's poem.

THE SLAYING OF MEGHANADA

CANTO I

Investiture

When in face-to-face combat Vīrabāhu, crown-gem of
warriors, fell and went before his time to Yama's city—
speak, O goddess of ambrosial speech—which best of warriors
did the foe of Rāghava, treasure-trove among that clan
of Rākṣasas, designate commander, then send fresh to
the battle? And by what stratagem did he, the joy of
Ūrmilā, destroy the hope of the Rākṣasas, Indra's
conqueror, that Meghanāda—invincible throughout
the world—and thus free Indra from his terror? I, who am
ignorant, praise your lotus feet and call upon you once
more, white-limbed Bhāratī! Come, chaste woman, favor me, your
servant, as you came and sat once on Vālmīki's tongue (as
though upon a lotus-throne), Mother, when that fowler deep
in the forest with a keen arrow pierced the heron perched
beside his mate. Who in this world comprehends your greatness?
That most mean of men, who robbed, was made immortal, by your
grace, like Umā's husband, Mṛtyuñjaya! O Varadā,
by a boon of yours that thieving Ratnākara came to
be the poet of a mine of poetry! At your touch,
a poison-tree can endue the splendor of a graceful
sandalwood! Alas, Mother, is there like virtue in this
slave? Yet, a mother's love reaches out as strongly to that
dearest of her children who lacks talent, is slow of wit.
Come from on high, compassionate one, appear, enticer
of the universe! Let me, Mother, sing this epic song
filled with virile *rasa*. Grant this thrall the shadow of your
feet. You come also, goddess, you who are the honeybee
Imagination! Glean honey from the flower garden
of the poet's mind and form your honeycomb from which the
folks of Gauḍa might in bliss sip nectar ever after.

Upon his golden throne sat warrior Daśānana—a
mass of brilliance, like the highest peak upon gold-crested
Hemakūṭa mountain. Ministers, counselors, and the
like by the hundreds sat about, bowed humbly. It was a
court unequaled on this earth—made of crystal. In it, gems

shone brightly, as bloom lush lotuses in Lake Mānasa.
White, red, blue, and yellow pillars, row on row, held aloft
an aurous ceiling, as the Indra among snakes[1] spreading
his ten thousand cobra-hoods, obligingly supports the
world. From its valance sparkling diamonds, emeralds, rubies, pearls
dangled, as dangle leafy garlands (intertwined with buds
and blossoms) from a temple. A gem-born luster smiled like
lightning—blinding! Sweet-eyed slave girls waved artful yak-tail whisks;
those moon-faced maids swayed lotus-stem-like arms ecstatically
forth and back. The umbrella bearer held the parasol;
ah, just as Kāma might have stood in Hara's anger's flame,
unburned, so he stood on the floor of that assembly hall,
as bearer of the royal parasol. Before its doors
paced the guard, a redoubtable figure, like god Rudra,
trident clutched, before the Pāṇḍavas' encampment's gateway!
Constant spring breezes delicately wafted scents, gaily
transporting waves of chirping, ah yes! enchanting as the
flute's melodic undulations in the pleasure groves of
Gokula! Compared to such an edifice, O Maya,
Dānava lord, how paltry was that jeweled court built at
Indraprastha with your own hands to please the Pauravas!

In such a court as this there sat the sovereign Rākṣasa,
struck dumb with grief for his son! Tears trickled in endless streams—
dampening his raiment, just as a tree, when its sap-filled
trunk is stricken by sharp arrows, cries silently. In front
of him, palms together, stood the bearer of bad tidings,
ashen gray from dust, his entire body moist with blood. From
the many hundred soldiers who waded into warfare's
sea in the company of Vīrabāhu, only this
one warrior came ashore. That Rākṣasa, spared death's black waves
which had engulfed all the others, was called Makarākṣa—
in strength he matched the Yakṣas' lord. When he learned of his son's
death from this messenger, alas, Naikaṣeya, jewel
among kings, was overcome with gloom that day! Those in the
royal court were saddened by their ruler's grief. His world went
dark, ah me, as does the world at large when the lord of day
is screened off by clouds! But upon regaining consciousness

1. Śeṣa.

moments later, Rāvaṇa, sighing, spoke dejectedly,
"This news of yours, messenger, is like a nightmare! Beggar
Rāghava in face-to-face battle slew the archer who,
by his strength of arms, has harassed even the immortals?
Did Providence, with flower petals, chop down so stately
a *śālmalī* tree?—Ah son, Vīrabāhu, crown-gem of
warriors! for what sin have I lost a treasure such as you?
what fault of mine did you observe, harsh Fate, for which you stole
my wealth? Alas, how am I to bear this anguish? Who else
now will uphold the honor of our clan in this black war!
As in the depths of the forest a woodsman first trims limbs
one by one before the tree is felled, O Providence, so
too does this most forbidding enemy, as you observe,
hack at me relentlessly! I shall be toppled, roots and
all, by his arrows! Were that not to be, would my brother
Kumbhakarṇa, trident-bearer Śambhu's very likeness,
have met his death prematurely because of me? and all
those other soldiers—in defense of this Rākṣasas clan?
Alas, Sūrpaṇakhā, at what ill-fated moment did
you, hapless woman, see that snake, full of *kālakūṭa*
venom, in the fatal Pañcavaṭī Forest? At what
inauspicious time did I (saddened by your plight) transport
to this golden dwelling that flaming beauty, Jānakī?
Ah me, would that I could quit this golden Laṅkā, enter
some dense woods, and thereby cool the burning in my heart through
solitude! Once my gorgeous city seemed a theater
brightly lit by rows of burning lamps and decked with wreaths of
flowers! But one by one those flowers wither now, the lamps
go out; now silent are the *rabāb's* and *vīṇā's* strings,
the flute and *muraja*; why then do I linger any
longer here? For who is there who likes to dwell in darkness?"
So bemoaned Rāvaṇa, Rākṣasa sovereign, dolefully,
like the blind king in Hastinā, alas, when he heard from
Sañjaya's lips how his dearest sons had been slain by blows
from fierce-armed Bhīmasena in the Kurukṣetra war.
Then Sāraṇa, his minister (excellent and learned
confidant) arose and, hands cupped reverently, began to
speak with deference, "O king, renowned all through the world, crest
of the Rākṣasa clan, excuse this thrall of yours! for who

in the world is meet to counsel you? However, reflect
on this, my lordship—when cloud-cleaving pinnacles are crushed
to rubble by a strike of lightning, the mountain as a
whole is never stirred by that oppression. This earthly world
is full of *māyā*, its joys and sorrows are all for naught.
Only the foolish are befuddled by illusion's hoax."

Laṅkā's ruler answered, "What you say is very true, Prime
Minister Sāraṇa! I know indeed this earthly world
is full of *māyā*, its joys and sorrows all for naught. Yet
knowing that, this heart still cries inconsolably. Death has
snatched the flower which had bloomed upon the stalk that is my
heart; now this deflowered heart is sunk in sorrow's sea like
a lotus stalk in water, its blossom-treasure stolen."

And saying thus, the king ordered, with a glance cast toward the
messenger, "Tell me, messenger, how did that champion
Vīrabāhu, bane of the immortals, fall in battle?"

Bowing low before the great king's feet, hands joined together,
that bearer of bad tidings resumed, "Alas, O Laṅkā's
monarch, how shall I recount the peerless tale? how shall I
describe Vīrabāhu's valor? As an elephant in
rut wades through a stand of reeds, so too that elephant of
archers waded through the enemy ranks. Even now my
heart pounds as I recall the way he rampaged! I have heard,
O sovereign of the Rākṣasas, thunder's rumble, lions'
roar, and ocean waves when they crash; I have seen swift lightning
streaks, my lord, run upon the winds. But never have I heard
through all three worlds such a dreadful snap and clatter from the
twanging of a bow! nor ever seen such awesome arrows!

"That legion of grand warriors with Vīrabāhu joined the
battle, like a herd of elephants with their lordly bull.
Dust rose thick as clouds covering the sky—as though those clouds
had come in anger darkening the heavens; a hail of
arrows whirred through the air, flashing like lightning's splendor! Praise
the skill of Vīrabāhu! who can count the foe who fell!

"In this fashion your son, O king, with his troops fought against
the enemy! After some time Rāghava, Indra of
the mortals, joined the fray, a gold diadem on his head,
a tremendous bow in hand, like the bow of Vāsava,
studded with a mix of many jewels." So saying, that

bearer of bad tidings wept in silence, just as weeps a
mourner, reminded of some past heartache! In sympathy,
without a sound, the members there assembled also wept.

Teary-eyed, Rāvaṇa, the love of Mandodarī, spoke
again, "Speak, news bearer, I must hear; how did the son of
Daśaratha slay Daśānana's champion scion?"

"How, O world's sovereign," began once more the bearer of bad
tidings, "how, O wealth of Rākṣasas, can I bear to speak
of that, or you to listen? Rāmacandra pounced upon
your son in battle, as the lion, yellow-eyed, with gaze
afire, gnashing wrathfully awful fangs, leaps upon the
nape of a bull's neck! Then all about swelled the waves of war,
like a raucous ocean dueling with the winds! Sabers
flashed, like tips of flames, from amid ten thousand aligned shields
which resembled smoky billows! Conch shells blared with a roar
like the ocean! What more shall I say, my lord? Through fault from
a former birth, I alone survived! Fie, Providence, for
what sin did you cause such agony for me today? Why
did I not lie upon a bed of arrows on that field
of battle next to Vīrabāhu, the ornament of
golden Laṅkā? But it is not my fault completely. See
this lacerated chest of mine, O gem of kings, caused by
enemy weapons; on my back there are no marks of wounds."

That Rākṣasa was stunned with anguish when he finished what
he had to say. Then Laṅkā's sovereign, as a twinge of pride
and grief shot through his frame, spoke up, "Bravo, messenger! What
brave heart would not yearn to enter battle after hearing
your account? On hearing drumbeats of the double-headed
ḍamaru, does the deadly cobra ever stay at rest
inside his hole? Hail Laṅkā, mother of brave sons! Come—let
us go, my courtiers, and see how Vīrabāhu, crown-
gem of warriors, fell in war; let us gratify our eyes."

That ruler of the Rākṣasas climbed the palace peak, as
the ray-ringed jewel of the day ascends the rising-hill
of gold. On all sides Laṅkā richly shone, crowned with golden
mansions—heart-stealing city! Those edifices made from
gold were encompassed, ring by ring, with flower gardens; there
lay ponds—the homes for lotuses—and silvery fountains,
magnificent trees, and floral sprays—pleasing to the sight,

like the youth of a young maiden; there were temples topped by
diamonds and shops of many hues, adorned with precious stones;
it was as though the world had gathered sundry treasured things
prescribed for *pūjā*, then placed them at your feet, O charming
Laṅkā, you who are the world's desire, residence of bliss.

The Rākṣasa sovereign scanned the highest walls—like staunchest
mountains. Atop, like lions on those mountains, prowled armed guards,
drunk on valor. The abductor of Vaidehī viewed four
lion-gates[2] (closed now) where chariots and charioteers,
horses, elephants, and troops of countless soldiers stood, poised.
That monarch gazed beyond the city and saw there hostile
forces, like grains of sand on some ocean beach, or starry
clusters strewn across the circle of the heavens. Encamped
before the eastern gateway was the warrior Nīla, most
difficult to best in warfare; at the southern gate stood
Aṅgada, a fighter with unseasoned strength as of an
elephant calf or of a poisonous snake who, at the
end of winter, sporting new, vivid skin, sidles to and
fro with hood held high—proudly flicking out its trident tongue!
At the northern gate stood guard the king himself, Sugrīva,
a lion of a hero. And Dāśarathi watched the
western gate—alas, downcast without his Jānakī, like
the lotus-pleasing moon without his moonlight!—backed up by
Lakṣmaṇa; the wind's son, Hanumān; and best of comrades,
Vibhīṣaṇa. The opposition ranks had surrounded
golden Laṅkā, just as a hunting party deep within
the densest jungle, cautiously with teamwork ensnares a
lioness—whose form is charming to the eye, whose force is
furious, like goddess Bhīmā! The king of Rākṣasas
surveyed the nearby battlefield. Jackals, vultures, buzzards,
dogs, and bands of ghouls milled about noisily. Some flying,
some were squatting, others squabbled. Some would beat their wings to
try to scare away their fellow creatures who were just as
greedy. Some, bellowing and squawking, giddy with glee, doused
their flames of hunger; some sucked rivulets of blood! A herd
of elephants had fallen, colossal in bulk; there were
horses swift as winds, now, alas, quite still! Countless broken

2. Major gateways, adorned with the figure of a lion.

chariots, chariot drivers, mahouts, horsemen, lancers,
and troops of soldiers higgledy-piggledy strewn around!
Their armor, shields, sabers, spears, bows, arrows, quivers, cudgels,
battle-axes glinted here, there—gem-studded coronets,
turbans, and accoutrements, all awe-inspiring. Among
instruments sprawled the musicians. Pennon-bearers, staves with
golden flags in hand, had fallen, struck by Yama's staff. As,
alas, the gold-tipped harvest harvested by peasants falls
on the field, so the many Rākṣasas had been felled by
arrows of the Rāghava champion, sun among the
solar clan! Likewise Vīrabāhu—crown-gem of warriors—
fell, crushing hostile heroes, as Ghaṭotkaca, raised in
Hiḍimbā's loving nest, like a Garuḍa, had fallen
at the time Karṇa, wielder of Kālapṛṣṭha, let fly
his missile called Ekāghnī to preserve the Kauravas.
Smarting from excruciating sorrow, Rāvaṇa spoke,
"To recline upon the bed on which you lie today, dear
son, is every champion's fervent longing! For who is
there, when quelling foemen, who fears to die to save the land
of one's birth? He who shies away is a craven coward;
shame be his a hundredfold! But, the heart that is addled
by the wine of affection, my dearest one, turns soft like
a flower blossom. Only Antaryāmī knows how faint
mine is, struck as it is by this lightning bolt. I myself
know not. O Fate, this mortal world is but the playground for
your *līlā*—can it be you are pleased to witness others'
sufferings? Fathers always grieve for sons' misfortunes—O
you who are the father of the world, is this your nature?
Son! my Vīrabāhu! lion among Indras among
warriors! how can I, when bereft of you, hold fast to life?"
So lamented Rāvaṇa, Rākṣasa monarch, who then
turned his gaze to stare out toward the distant sea—the home of
makaras. Out there a line of stones firmly bound one to
another floated on the water, like a static string
of clouds. On either side foam-capped waves, like the hooded best
of snakes, surged in endless, grave hissing. Across that well-built
bridge, broad as a royal causeway, flowed a babbling stream of
beings, like water through a channel during monsoon rains.
In a fit of pique proud Rāvaṇa, bull of heroes, called

to the ocean, "What a pretty garland you wear around
your throat today, O Pracetas! Fie on you, lord of the
waters! Does such apparel become you, O you who are
impassable, invincible? Is this your jewelry,
alas, O jewel-quarry? By what virtue—speak, sir, for
I would hear—by virtue of what deed did Dāśarathi
buy you? You, the adversary of Prabhañjana, yet
fierce as strong winds yourself! Tell me, for what trespass do you
wear this shackle? The juggler fits a chain on a lowly
bear and trots him out for show, but who is capable of
slipping cuffs around the lion's royal paws? This Laṅkā,
golden city, shines refulgent on your chest, O husband
of blue waters, like the Kaustubha gem upon the breast
of Mādhava; why toward her today are you so heartless?
Arise, warrior, with a hero's strength break up this bridge; drown
your shame; cool my searing hurt by scuttling this puissant
enemy of mine beneath unfathomed waters. Do not
tolerate the ugly blemish to remain upon your
forehead, Indra of the waters; I implore you humbly."
Having thus spoken, Rāvaṇa, great king of kings, returned
to his assembly hall and there sat down again on his
golden throne; overwhelmed with sadness, that noble-minded
one remained mute while around him ministers, counselors,
and the like, alas, sat grieving quietly. Suddenly
at that time, there drifted in from all directions soft sounds
of weeping blended with anklets' tinkling, jingling girdles,
and ominous outcries. Escorted by the golden-limbed
women of her retinue, Queen Citrāṅgadā stepped to
the floor of that assembly—hair, alas, disheveled! her
arms, naked, without bangles, like forest-ornamenting
vines when, in snow, they lack gemlike blossoms! Her tear-filled eyes
were as the dewy lotus pads at night! The queen was quite
beside herself, lamenting over Vīrabāhu, as
does a mother bird when some fell snake slips inside her nest
and swallows up her fledglings. A storm of woe blew into
that assembly hall! The womenfolk stood there, appearing
comely as the wives of the divines, their loose and flowing
hair seemed a swirl of clouds, their heaving sighs Pralaya-like
heavy winds, their streams of tears torrential rains, their wailing

moans the thunder's rumble! Laṅkā's sovereign on his gold throne
was startled. Maidens in attendance, tear-soaked, dropped their yak-
tail whisks; the umbrella bearer let slip the parasol
and wept; angry and confused, the guardsman unsheathed his dread
sword; and the ministers, the counselors, and members of
the court, alarmed, broke down crying, causing utter havoc.

Some time passed before Citrāṅgadā, the queen, spoke softly,
gazing as she did toward Rāvaṇa, "Compassionate Fate
gave me a gem; but worthless me, I placed it with you for
safekeeping, O jewel of the clan of Rākṣasas, as
a bird keeps its young in the hollow of a tree. Tell me,
where have you stored it, lord of Laṅkā? Where is my priceless
gem? It is a monarch's *dharma* to safeguard possessions
of the poor. You are the king of kings. Pray tell this lowly
wretch, O monarch, how you kept safe for me that wealth of mine!"

Then hero Daśānana countered, "My love, why in vain
rebuke me! Who ever criticizes one who errs due
to evil forces of the planets, charming one? Alas,
it is Fate's will, my lady, that I must agonize so!
Just look, this golden city, bearer of heroic sons,
is empty now of warriors, as at the height of summer's
heat a garden lacks blossoms, a river wants for water!
Daśaratha's son has left my Laṅkā a shambles as
does a porcupine on entering the bamboo-framed thatched
structure of a pan leaf plantation, trashing it. The sea
wears chains round its leg at his behest! You are consumed by
sorrow for one son, O gentlewoman, but my breast is
sundered both day and night from grieving for a hundred sons!
Alas, dear lady, as strong winds through a forest scatter
cottonlike seeds once pods of the *śimula* split open,
just so these many Rākṣasas, pinnacles upon our
massive clan, have been scattered in this deadly war. Fate stretched
out its arm to level Laṅkā—this I tell you truly."

The Rākṣasa lord fell silent. Moon-faced Citrāṅgadā,
a Gandharva's daughter, wept, head bent with sadness—alas,
bewildered by memories of that foremost of her sons.
Once more, Dāśarathi's adversary resumed speaking,

"Does such lamentation ever suit you, my good woman?
Your best of sons, who slew his homeland's enemies in war,

has gone to heaven. You are the mother of a hero.
Is it right to grieve a son who died engaged in acts of
heroism? My lineage is glorious this day
because of your son's prowess. Why then are you shedding tears,
you whose face is like the moon, streaked by water from your eyes?"
The charming-eyed Citrāṅgadā replied, "He who slays in
war foemen of his native land was certainly conceived
at an auspicious moment. I hold in high esteem the
lucky woman, that mother of such a bloom of warriors.
But consider, husband, where your Laṅkā lies, how distant
from Ayodhyā city! For what cause, from what greed, do tell,
king, did Rāghava come to this land? Yes, golden Laṅkā
tempts the Indra of divines, is unsurpassed throughout all
the world. Surrounding her gleams an ocean like a wall of
silver. We hear his residence is on the Sarayū's
riverside—that little man. Still, does Dāśarathi war
in hopes of capturing your golden throne? Who, a mere dwarf,
would seek to grasp the moon? So, why do you refer to him
as our homeland's enemy, O hero? A snake's head stays
ever bowed; but if one taps upon it, then with hood raised,
that cobra bites the one who tapped his head. Who, please tell me
this, today in Laṅkā set ablaze the doomsday fire? My
husband, by the very fruits of your own deed, alas, have
you doomed the clan of Rākṣasas and are yourself undone!"
That said, Citrāṅgadā, Vīrabāhu's mother, withdrew
sobbing, with her handmaids, to the inner chambers of the
palace. Out of grief and rankled self-esteem that foeman
of Rāghava quit his golden throne, roaring fiercely. "At
long last," declared the sovereign, "my Laṅkā is destitute
of warriors! Whom else shall I send to this black war? Who can
hold aloft the honor of the Rākṣasas? I myself
shall go. Prepare, Indras among warriors, ornaments of
Laṅkā! Let us see how deft he is, this gem of Raghus!
Will the world this day be minus Rāvaṇa or Rāma!"
When that son of Nikaṣā, lion among champions,
had so announced, *dundubhi* drums of war boomed forth from the
floor of the assembly with a thunderous roll. At such
frightful rumblings the Karbūras, intoxicated on
heroism's liquor, equipped themselves, those terrors of

gods, Daityas, and of men. From the elephant barn charged a
herd of tuskers (in might, most difficult to check, like a
stream of rushing water); from the stable pranced a train of
horses, necks arched, spiritedly champing at the bit. Gold-
crested chariots came wheeling out and cast a glow on
the city. Troops of infantry followed, gold turbans wound
round their heads, swords in scintillating scabbards; down their backs
hung leather shields, impregnable in battle; they brandished
cloud-splitting *śāla*-tree-like lances; iron coats of mail
encased their frames. Mahouts appeared like the wielder of the
thunderbolt atop the best of thunderheads; horsemen, like
sons of Aśvinī, gripping fearsome javelins and world-
destroying battle-axes—a luster rose within the
sky, as when a forest fire penetrates some wooded land.
Warrior flag-bearers held on high flags of the Rākṣasa
clan, then unfurled the best of banners, embossed with gems, which
seemed to be the wings of Garuḍa as he flew through the
skies. A martial band produced a deep, resounding clangor
all about; horses in formation neighed impatiently;
elephants were bugling; conch shells blared in earnest; and strummed
bowstrings combined with rattling swords to fill one's ears with sounds!

Golden Laṅkā quaked beneath the weight of champions' feet—
the monarch of the waters roared, wroth! That commotion reached
lovely Vāruṇī, seated on her coral throne under
water in a golden lotus garden where she, with pearls,
was putting up her chignon. Startled, that faithful woman
gazed about her. Speaking to her moon-faced handmaid, in sweet
tones she asked, "For what reason, do tell me, please, confidante,
has Pāśī, monarch of the oceans, suddenly become
so very agitated? Look, our pearl-crowned residence
rocks violently. Perhaps those mischievous winds have blown
in again to do battle with the waves. Fie on the god
Prabhañjana! How could that monarch of the winds forget
so quickly his own pledge, my dear? That day in Indra's court
I begged to have him manacle the winds and throw them all
in prison. With a smile that god pleaded then, 'Grant me leave,
O goddess of the waters, that I might frolic always
with your limpid streams, servants of yours on the surface of
the earth—permit me that, and I shall honor ever your

command.' Then and there, confidante, I consented. So why
now do the gusty breezes come today to torment me?"
    In reply her attendant babbled, "It is pointless to
accuse Prabhañjana, O queen to Indra of the seas.
This is no storm, but rather, monarch Rāvaṇa at his
palace in golden Laṅkā has assumed a tempest's guise
to deflate in battle the warrior pride of Rāghava."
    Vāruṇī spoke once again, "Ah yes, true, my confidante,
Rāvaṇa and Rāma struggle over Vaidehī. The
Rājalakṣmī of the clan of Rākṣasas is my boon
companion. Hurry to her dwelling place; I am eager
to have news of the conflict. Give Kamalā this golden
lotus. Tell her that since she went home, thereby darkening
our ocean dwelling, this flower bloomed where that moon-faced one
had placed her crimson feet while seated on her lotus-throne."
    Attendant Muralā, at Vāruṇī's command, surfaced,
bounding from the waters, as leaps a nimble *sapharī*,
flashing its illusion of shiny, silver-seeming sheen
to the sun. That messengeress reached the lotus-home where
the lotus-lady, love of Keśava, sat upon her
lotus-throne there in Laṅkā city. For just a bit she
paused before the door, to soothe her eyes on the sight in front
of her, charm and grace that would excite the maddener of
Madana.[3] Springtime breezes sauntered there—ever-faithful
followers—murmuring, in hopes of garnering fragrance
from those godly lotus feet. Bouquets shone resplendently
everywhere, just like congeries of gems in Dhanada's
golden vault. Redolent sandalwood and myrrh smoldered in
a hundred golden censers permeating her temple
with their scents. Upon some platters made of gold were arranged
divers gifts and sundry *pūjā* offerings. Golden lamps
in a row were alight, each filled with fragrant oils—softly
glowing, like the glow of fireflies up against the full moon's
radiance! With face averted, moon-faced Indirā sat
glumly—as sat Umā of the moonlike countenance, cheeks
cradled in her palms, when the tenth day of the waxing moon
of Durgā Pūjā dawned, with pangs of separation at

3. Kṛṣṇa.

her home in Gauḍa—so sat bright Kamalā, goddess on
her lotus-throne. Can dolor enter such a blossom-heart?
With measured paces, pretty Muralā stepped into the
temple; and once inside, that messengeress bowed before
the feet of Ramā. Indira—the Rājalakṣmī of
those Rākṣasas—bestowed her blessings, then began to speak,
"What brings you here today, Muralā, please tell me? And where
is my most dear companion, that goddess of the waters?
I think of her constantly. How could I forget all the
kindness faithful Vāruṇī showed to me when I lived with
her? Ramā's hopes are domiciled in Hari's breast—still this
Ramā managed, though bereft of such a one as Hari,
by virtue only of Vāruṇī's salve of love! Tell me,
is she well, that bosom friend of mine, the Indrāṇī of
the seas?" Beautiful Muralā responded, "Vāruṇī
is ensconced safely underneath the waters. Because of
Vaidehī, Rāma wars with Rāvaṇa; she is eager
to have tidings of the battle. This lotus, O chaste one,
it bloomed for joy where you had placed those two reddened feet of
yours; and for that reason, Pāśī's consort sends it to you."
With sad sighs, Kamalā, moonlight of Vaikuṇṭha, answered,
"Alas, friend, the prowess of foolish Rāvaṇa day by
day erodes, like an ocean's shoreline from the pounding surf.
You will be amazed to hear: the hero Kumbhakarṇa,
whose look is ferocious, and Akampana, in warfare
steady as a mountain, fell along with charioteer
Atikāya. Of the many other Rākṣasas, I
am powerless to tell. Vīrabāhu perished—crown-gem
of warriors; those sounds of weeping that you hear within the
inner quarters, Muralā, issue from Citrāṅgadā,
disquieted by grief felt for her son. I am anxious
to depart this city. My heart breaks when I hear day and
night these women sobbing! In each and every household, there
wails, messengeress, a sonless mother and a widow!"
Asked Muralā, "Tell me, O great goddess, which warrior arms
heroically to fight anew today?" Answered the wife
of Mādhava, "I know not who outfits himself this time.
Muralā, come outside and let us see who goes to war."
With that said, Ramā, escorting Muralā, stepped without,

both appearing like Rākṣasa maidens, habited in
silken garments. Their anklets tinkled sweetly, bangles ringed
their wrists, while eye-bedazzling ornamented girdles drew
attention to those slender waists. Before the temple door
both watched wide rows of soldiers marching down the royal way,
like fleet wind-driven waves across an ocean. Along sped
chariots, their fellies clattered as they rolled. Steeds galloped,
in aspect like a dire storm. Elephants alarmed the
earth by the burden of their feet as they lumbered, vaunting
high their trunks as Daṇḍadhara vaunts his deadly scepter.
Instruments of music blared their resonating tones. Gem-
embroidered, rousing banners by the hundreds fluttered. On
either side stood the world-enchanting wives of Laṅkā at
the windows of their golden dwellings, raining down flower
blossoms, calling out their auspicious *ululu* sounds. Said
Muralā, gazing at the moonlike face of Indirā,

"Today I witness on the earth heaven's grandeur, goddess!
It seems to me that Vāsava himself, monarch of the
skies, entered Laṅkā city with an armed force of the gods.
Speak, kind one, kindly tell me, which charioteers are armed
for battle, intoxicated on the wines of valor?"

Said chaste Kamalā of the lotus eyes, "Alas, my friend,
Laṅkā's golden city is without her heroes! They who
were the Indras of great charioteers, terrors of gods,
Daityas, and of men, have been vanquished in this fight so hard
to win! That gem among the Raghus took up the bow at
an auspicious time! See there, that charioteer on the
gold-crowned chariot, that leader among Rākṣasas is
Virūpākṣa, Bhīma's likeness, a warrior who fights armed
with iron arrows, difficult to best in war. And there,
riding on that elephant, look, it is Kālanemi,
bhindipāla clenched in fist, a hero who by his strength
metes out death to foes! Look, that horsemen, Tālajaṅghā, a
tāla palm in stature, with club in hand, he resembles
war-club-wielding Murāri! See, Pramatta, drunk on wines
of warfare, and the Rākṣasa Bhīṣaṇa, whose chest is
hard as stone! What more can I say about the others? There
were hundreds of like soldiers who perished in this struggle,
as when Vaiśvānara penetrates a dense forest, stands

of even the most tall among the trees are reduced to
ashes in the course of that horrific conflagration."
    Asked messengeress Muralā, "Tell me, goddess-queen, why
do I not see Meghanāda, the charioteer who
in battle bested Indra, that lion—yellow-eyed—of
Rākṣasas? Was he slain, chaste one, in that fatal warfare?"
    Replied Ramā of the charming smile, "Perhaps the prince is
strolling leisurely through Pramoda Park and does not yet
know Vīrabāhu fell today in battle. Muralā,
go at once to Vāruṇī. Tell her I shall presently
leave this golden city and return to Vaikuṇṭha. Through
his own fault Laṅkā's ruler comes to ruin. Alas, as
in the monsoon rainy season when a pond of clearest
water is turned turbid by churned mud, just so by sin is
golden Laṅkā sullied! How am I to stay here any
longer? Go, my friend, to where Vāruṇī is seated on
her coral siege in that pearly home of hers. I shall fetch
Indrajit back to Laṅkā's golden city. The fruits of
a former birth will soon come to fruition in this land."
    Bowing to the goddess's feet, then taking leave of her,
Muralā, the winsome messengeress, rose upon the
path of winds, just as a fetching peahen, eyes entranced by
coruscation from the multijeweled brilliancy off
Ākhaṇḍala's bow,[4] flies toward an alluring pleasure grove!
    That pretty lady reached the ocean's shore, then plunged into
those deep blue waters. In the meantime she, the lotus-eyed
love of Keśava, Lakṣmī of the clan of Rākṣasas,
set out to where far away was Meghanāda, gem of
warriors, bane of Vāsava. Through the void sped Indirā.
    Moments later Hṛṣīkeśa's sleek-haired darling reached the
place where ever-winning Indrajit was seated. It seemed
a mansion like Vaijayanta—on verandas rows of
handsome golden pillars topped by diamonds stood, as around
Nandana Gardens stands a file of graceful trees. From the
branches cuckoos cooed; bees hummed as they meandered; flower
buds were blooming; leaves were rustling; vernal breezes blew; and
cascades, gurgling, tumbled. As the goddess stepped up to the

4. The rainbow.

palace made of gold, she saw a host of fearsome-looking
women, bows in hand, turn defiantly toward the brilliant
gates. Down each one's back there swung a braid beside her quiver.
Like lightning streaks were those plaits, interspersed with jewels—gem-
hooded serpents were the arrows in those quivers! Golden
coats of mail covering high breasts seemed like nets of sunbeams
draped upon full-blooming lotuses. The arrows in their
quivers were keenly tipped, yet sharper still the darts from their
almond eyes. They, intoxicated on youth's liquor, paced
like female elephants in heat in spring. Ornamental
girdles sonorously jingled from about their well-formed
hips; around their ankles anklets tinkled. The *muraja*,
vīṇā, flute, and *saptasvarā* sounded; waves of music,
spilled out everywhere, blending with yet other sounds to fill
one's mind with rapture. That best of champions dallied with
these maids of shapely bodies, just as the lord of night sports
with Dakṣa's daughters, or, O Yamunā, daughter of the
sun, as the herdsman danced beneath *kadamba* trees, flute to
lips, sporting with the cowherds' wives upon your splendid banks!

Meghanāda's wet nurse had been a Rākṣasī whose name
was Prabhāṣā. Ramā, wife of Mādhava, took her form,
then appeared, clutching in her hand a cane and wearing white.

Rising from his golden throne, Indrajit, lion among
Indras among warriors, did obeisance to his nursemaid's
feet, then said, "For what reason, Mother, have you come today
to this retreat? Tell me, your humble slave, of Laṅkā's weal."

Kissing him atop his head, that daughter of the ocean
incognita answered, "Alas! Son, what can I say of
golden Laṅkā's predicament! In pitched battle hero
Vīrabāhu, your dear brother, perished! The ruler of
the Rākṣasas, mourning, moved by profound grief over him,
with his troops readies himself today to fight in person."

That great-armed one, aghast, inquired, "What was that you said,
respected lady? Who slew my dearest little brother?
When? I bested the best of Raghus in night combat; I
cut to pieces the opposing army with a rain of
terrorizing arrows. But this news, this strange news, Mother,
wherever did you get it; tell this slave of yours at once."

That pretty Indirā, finest jewel of the ocean,

answered, "My son, alack! it was that wizardly human,
Sītā's husband; though he succumbed to your arrows, yet he
revived. So, be quick, uphold the honor of the clan of
Rākṣasas in this heinous war, crown-gem of Rākṣasas!"

Full of wrath, great warrior Meghanāda tore apart his
garlands, threw away his golden bracelets; lying at his
feet, his earrings shone most elegant, like fetching blossoms
of *aśoka* under an *aśoka* tree! "Fie on me,"
the crown prince chided gravely, "Fie on me! Hostile legions
cincture golden Laṅkā, and here am I midst these charming
women! Does this befit a one like me, Indrajit, son
of Daśānana? Bring my chariot at once. I shall
efface this infamy; I shall slay the enemy throng."

Then that bull among the Indras of the charioteers
dressed in warrior's garb, just like the son of Haimavatī
when he went to conquer Tāraka, the great Asura,
or, like Kirīṭī, disguised as Bṛhannalā, when he
caparisoned himself beneath the *śamī* tree as a
champion, then with Virāṭa's son went to recoup the
cow herd. His chariot was cloud colored; its wheels gave off
lightning flashes; its pennons looked like Indra's bow; and its
steeds were swift of foot. Onto that chariot stepped the crown-
gem of warriors with a hero's pride. At such time pretty
Pramīlā grasped hold her husband's hands (alas, as when a
golden vine hugs tight the king of trees) and weeping, that young
beauty spoke, "Where, companion of my heart, would you consign
your thrall, pray tell me, when you yourself have gone away? How
shall this hapless girl abide apart from you? Alas, my
lord, when deep within the forest, of her own accord a
creeper wraps herself around an elephant's leg and if
unwittingly at play the elephant should lumber off,
still that lordly bull would have proffered her the refuge of
his feet. So why do you, virtues' fund, deny as much to
this slave of yours today?" Meghanāda smiling answered,
"You have bested Indrajit, my chaste one, and secured him
with firm fetters. Who is able to untie those bonds? I
shall return with haste, pure woman, once I have defeated
Rāghava in combat—by virtue of your purity.
Now bid me farewell, my one whose visage is like the moon's."

On the wind's path there arose, with menacing sounds, that best
of chariots, as though Mount Maināka had spread its gold-
hued wings and flown, lighting up the skies! That Indra among
heroes drew back angrily the bowstring and snapped his bow
with verve, just as the Indra among birds screams threateningly
from within the clouds. Both Laṅkā and the ocean quavered!

Sovereign Rāvaṇa was arming, frenzied with heroic
spirits—martial music blared; elephants were trumpeting;
horses whinnied; both troops on foot and charioteers yelled
with fury; silken banners fluttered; and a golden glow
from armor lifted to the skies. At just that moment the
charioteer Meghanāda arrived in full career.

The Karbūras, out of pride, cheered when they saw their best of
champions. That son, bowing to his father's feet, spoke, palms
pressed together, "O monarch of the clan of Rākṣasas,
what is this I hear, Rāghava though dead is yet alive?
I fail to comprehend such *māyā*, Father! But, grant me
your permission; I shall topple, roots and all, that wicked
one today! I shall turn him into ashes with deadly
fiery arrows, and with my wind-weapon, blow him away;
or if you wish, I shall place him, bound, at your regal feet."

Embracing the prince and kissing him atop the head, that
overlord of golden Laṅkā spoke with tenderness, "You,
dear lad, the crown upon our clan of Rākṣasas, are the
hope of hosts of Rākṣasas. My heart wants not to send you
once again into this black war. But alas, Fate has turned
against me. Who ever heard, my son, of stones that float on
water; and who has heard of one, though dead, who lives again?"

He answered with a hero's boldness, that foe of the foe
of Asuras, "What a lowly fellow that human is—
and you, an Indra among kings, fear him? Were you to go
to war while yet this servant lives, then, Father, that disgrace
would be decried through all the world. Meghavāhana would
laugh. God Agni would flare up with anger. Twice I vanquished
Rāghava. Command me once more, Father, so that we might
see by what medicines that warrior will revive this time!"

The king of Rākṣasas replied, "Hero Kumbhakarṇa
was my brother—from trepidation, I, prematurely,
woke him. Alas, look there, this body lies slumped upon the

ocean's shore, like a mountain peak or tree that has been struck
by lightning! Yet if you resolutely wish to fight, dear
son, first propitiate your chosen deity—perform
your ritual sacrifice at Nikumbhilā, my gem of
warriors! For it is you I designate commander. But
mark, the lord of day now descends the setting-hill. In the
morning, dearest child, you will wage war with that Rāghava."

Saying this, the king, sprinkling Ganges water, formally
invested with authority his crown prince. Suddenly
a bard broke into songs of praise, playing passionately
upon the *vīṇā*, "O city of the Rākṣasas, there
are teardrops in your eyes. You, whose hair is loose and flowing,
are distraught by sorrow. Your bejeweled crown and regal
ornaments, alas, O royal beauty, lie fallen on
the ground! Arise, my sweet, cast off this gloom, chaste one. The sun
for Rākṣasas is upon the rising-hill. Your night of
woe is over; your dawn has come at last! Arise, my queen,
and look. His strong left hand holds fast the bow whose strumming would
cause Ākhaṇḍala, home in Vaijayanta, to turn pale!
Gaze upon that quiver. Packed therein are Paśupati-
frightening missiles, like the very Pāśupata! Behold
that Meghanāda, most skilled among the skilled, a lion
among Indras among warriors, whose form is pleasing to
the sweeter sex! Praise be to consort Mandodarī! Hail,
Naikaṣeya, ruler of the Rākṣasas! Hail, Laṅkā
hero-bearer! Dearest Echoes, daughters of the sky, all
listen, then repeat, in full-throated voices: 'Foe-quelling
Indrajit now arms!' Let them quake with terror in their camp—
the Raghu king; Vibhīṣaṇa, disgrace of Rākṣasas;
and all those vile creatures who roamed the woods of Daṇḍaka."

The Rākṣasas' drums and such resounded, and Rākṣasas
exulted. Golden Laṅkā filled with shouts of victory.

Thus ends canto number one,
called "Investiture,"
in the poem
The Slaying of Meghanāda.

CANTO 2

Weapons Acquisition

The sun set, and Twilight appeared—a gem upon her brow.
Night-blooming lotuses now blossomed; in ponds the wan-faced
lotuses of day closed fast their eyes; warbling birds returned
to nests; and cattle, lowing, shambled toward their cow sheds. With
the moon and her radiant stars came Night, smiling. Flirting,
fragrant breezes, blustering about—to all they whispered
sweetly, "What riches did you win kissing which of several
flowers?" The goddess Sleep arrived. And, as tired children
curl up in their mother's lap, just so the many creatures
of land and sea took refuge at that goddess's two feet.
The moon's beloved constellations spread throughout the gods'
abode. Amid the divine assembly sat the sovereign
of gods, on a gold throne—to his left, Puloma's sloe-eyed
goddess daughter. A silver parasol, bright with gems, shone
brilliantly from above that Indra of divinities.
Handling with skill the jewel-studded yak-tail whisks, the fly-
whisk bearers fanned to and fro. Fresh breezes emanated,
gaily wafting honeyed scents from Nandana Gardens. All
around rang out celestial music. Six *rāgas*, with their
thirty-six accompanying *rāgiṇīs*, advanced and started
playing. Urvaśī, Rambhā with the captivating smile,
Citralekhā, and sleek-haired Miśrakeśī danced, charming
with their jingling anklet bells the hearts of a host of gods!
Gandharvas served in golden vessels nectar; others, the
food of the divines. Some bore saffron, musk, and vermilion;
some, the paste of sandalwood; others still, carried garlands
strung with fragrant *mandāra* blossoms. In Vaijayanta,
Vāsava was joyous with his heavenly entourage.
At such a time appeared the Rākṣasas' Rājalakṣmī,
lighting up that godly city with her beauty's brilliance.
Courteously, the spouse of Śacī bowed to Ramā's feet.
Blessing him, then sitting on his golden throne, the one with
lotus eyes, who dwells in Puṇḍarīkākṣa's heart, spoke, "King
of divines, pay heed to why I come today to your court."

Responded Indra, "O daughter of the Indra among
waters, beguiler of the universe, those two red feet
of yours, Mother, are longed for by this universe. He on
whom you mercifully cast your gaze of mercy, mercy-
mistress, his life in this life is indeed fulfilled. By what
merit from a former birth has this slave of yours obtained
that joy? Do explain this to your humble minion, Mother."
Ramā spoke again, "For some time now, treasure of divines,
I have lived in golden Laṅkā. The king of Rākṣasas
worships me. But, alas, finally Fate has turned against him.
Due to his own fault, that sinner puts an end to his own
lineage. Even then, my lord, I am not able to
forsake him. Can one who is a captive flee, Indra of
the gods, if the prison doors remain unopened?
As long as Rāvaṇa lives, I shall be confined within his house.
That son of Rāvaṇa, whose name is Meghanāda, you
know him well, O conqueror of Vṛtra, he is now the
one and only warrior left in Laṅkā. The rest of them
were slain in combat. That champion, a mighty lion,
will attack tomorrow Rāmacandra. Yet once again
Daśānana has appointed him commander. You must
consider well how to protect that Rāghava, so dear
to all the god clan. I tell you—were proud Meghanāda
at Nikumbhilā to complete his sacrifice before
the time he enters combat, the husband of Vaidehī
would find himself in trouble. Mandodarī's son would be
invincible throughout the world, O Indra of divines!
As Vainateya is supreme in strength among the birds,
so that gem of warriors is foremost of the Rākṣasas!"
So saying, Ramā, Keśava's desire, fell silent, ah
me! as the *vīṇā* pauses after entertaining hearts
with melodies! The six *rāgas*, thirty-six *rāgiṇīs*,
and such, on hearing Kamalā's sweet speech, forgot to do
what they do naturally, as in springtime other birds just
sit and listen to the cuckoo's call in a flower grove.
Then spoke that lord of the sky, "From this grave peril, Mother,
who but Viśvanātha can rescue Rāghava? The son
of Rāvaṇa is difficult to best in battle. I

fear him more, much more, than serpents fear the serpent-eater![1]
This very thunderbolt, the one which pulverized the skull
of Vṛtra, the Asura, was repulsed by weapons that
great hero wielded. Hence, worldwide they call him Indrajit.
By a boon from Sarvaśuci, that best of warriors has
become all-conquering. Command your thrall that I might go
with due dispatch to his residence on Mount Kailāsa."
    Spoke the beloved of Upendra, that daughter of the
Indra among waters, "Go, then, lord of the divines, with
haste. Humbly narrate, god, these tidings at the feet of him
who wears the moon, there upon the summit of Kailāsa.
Tell him that chaste Mother Earth cries constantly, unable
to withstand the burden. Tell him that Ananta now is
weary. If the king of Rākṣasas is not uprooted,
the earth will sink to Rasātala! Virūpākṣa is
quite fond of Lakṣmī. Please let him know that she, forsaking
Vaikuṇṭha, has lived for many days in Laṅkā! She thinks
of him constantly in that lonely place, but is it that
he finds some fault with her for which he does not think of her
a whit? What father keeps his daughter from her husband's house—
ask that of learned Jaṭādhara! If you fail to meet
Tryambaka, tell all before the feet of Ambikā."
And saying such, that moon-faced love of Hari said good-bye,
rose, and left. Through the sky the sleek-haired love of Keśava
descended, as gold idols sink in lucid waters, bright,
from beneath the water's surface due to innate brilliance.
    Mātali fetched the chariot. Śacī's husband gazed at
Śacī, speaking very sweetly, "Come along, my goddess,
come with me. When winds are laced with scented nectar, he is
twice as cordial. Mark this, wife, the beauty of a lotus
rests within the nature of its fully blossomed flower."
At her loved one's words, that woman well-endowed with hips smiled
and, taking her husband's hand, stepped onto the chariot.
    That chariot approached with speed heaven's golden doors, which
opened of their own accord with pleasing sounds. Exiting
in haste, that divine conveyance shone splendidly against
the sky. With a start, the world awoke thinking that the sun

1. Garuḍa.

had climbed the rising-hill. *Phiṅgā* birds chirped; other feathered
creatures filled forest groves with morning's song. In their bridal
chambers bashful brides left flower-beds and set to housework.

Near Lake Mānasa beamed brilliantly the lustrous peak of
Mount Kailāsa. Upon its tip sat Bhava's home, like the
peacock-crown on the head of Mādhava. That wondrous blue-
black bodied mountain was arrayed with clumps of golden blooms,
ah me! as though a yellow *dhuti*! Waters gushed from springs—
as if that body were anointed with white sandal paste!

Stepping from his chariot to the footpath, that monarch
of the skies, with his queen of the skies, entered the bliss-filled
abode. There sat Īśvarī, the queen of queens, upon her
golden throne. Vijayā waved a fly-whisk. Jayā held the
royal parasol. Alas, the opulence of Bhava's
residence—how can the poet convey it? Contemplate,
gaze upon it in your mind's eye, all you thoughtful people.

With utmost reverence, great Indra and Indrāṇī bowed
before the feet of Śakti. Ambikā blessed them, then asked—
"Speak the good news, god—both of you, what brings you here today?"

The hurler of the thunderbolts, palms pressed together, spoke,
"What is there in this universe, Mother, of which you are
unaware? Laṅkā's sovereign, hostile to the gods, worried
now by the war, has once again today installed his son
Meghanāda to the post of general. Tomorrow
at dawn that enemy-harassing prince will engage in
battle, after worshiping his chosen deity and
getting from him coveted boons. His prowess, Mother, is
no secret. Rājalakṣmī of the Rākṣasa clan came
to Vaijayanta and so informed this slave of yours, O
Bhagavatī. The love of Hari said chaste Mother Earth
cries out, no longer able to withstand that awful weight;
Śeṣa, upholder of the universe, is weary; and
even she herself, the fickle one, is these days ever
anxious to exit golden Laṅkā city. That goddess
directed me, your servant, to narrate humbly at your
feet these tidings, Annadā. The jewel of the Raghu
clan is a hero favored by the gods. Yet what warrior
in the god clan would dare fight Rāvaṇi upon the field
of battle? That Rākṣasa, Indrajit by name, renowned

throughout the world, renders lusterless in combat, Mother,
the universe-destroying thunderbolt! Consider by
what means, O Kātyāyanī, you can shelter Rāghava.
If you do not bestow him mercy, then, come tomorrow,
overwhelming Rāvaṇi will void this world of Rāma!"

Answered Kātyāyanī, "Naikaṣeya is the finest
among Śiva's worshipers—Triśūlī feels most kindly
toward him. O Indra of divines, can it be that harm to
him could ever come from me! Tāpasendra is absorbed
in meditation now, and thus, O god, is Laṅkā such."

With hands cupped most reverently, Vāsava spoke yet again,
"That sovereign of the Niśācaras, that worst offender
against *dharma* is an adversary of the gods! Think
of this, O daughter of the Indra among mountains. Is
it ever proper, Mother, to extend your mercy to
that wicked one who steals treasures from the poor? Well-mannered
Rāghava forsook his joy and comfort to uphold his
father's solemn vow and in a beggar's garb entered the
deep forest. He had but one priceless gem. Of how he cared
for her, what more can your humble servant say? The vile one
spread illusion's net, then stole that gem! Alas, Mother, when
I reflect on that, my heart fumes in flames of anger! With
his boon from Triśūlī, that Rākṣasa warrior now turns
disdainful of the gods! and greedy for another's wealth,
another's wife—that ever-avaricious, lowly thing!
Yet then, because of what (I fail to understand), do you
grant sympathy to such a fool, compassion-giving one?"

That monarch of the skies fell mute. The queen consort of the
skies, whose speech is like the music of a *vīṇā*, began
to speak in dulcet tones, "Whose heart would not be rent, goddess,
by the sorrows of Vaidehī? She sits day and night in
the Aśoka Grove (like a forest bird now kept encaged)
and in grief that beauty mourns. It is no secret to those
reddened feet of yours, O Mother, what heartaches the moon-faced
one endures without her husband. If you fail to wield the
staff of punishment, O goddess, who will discipline this
dharma-spurning lord of Rākṣasas? Once you overcome
Meghanāda, return Vaidehī to Vaidehī's joy.
Wipe away your servant's blemish, Śaśāṅkadhāriṇī!

For I die of shame, Mother, when I hear from people that
a Rākṣasa downed in war the monarch of the heavens."
Smiling, Umā spoke, "You detest Rāvaṇa, O Jiṣṇu.
And you, Śacī, who surpass them all in loveliness, are
eager for Indrajit's demise. Both of you implore
me to demolish golden Laṅkā. It is not within
my power to effect such a feat. The Rākṣasa host
is by Virūpākṣa given safety. Except for him,
Vāsava, who in the world, tell me please, can fulfill this
wish of yours? Immersed in yogic meditation, O king
of gods, is Vṛṣadhvaja. That Indra among yogis
sits in solitude upon the awesome, cloud-draped mountain
known as Yogāsana. How could one approach him there where
Garuḍa, Indra among birds, is powerless to fly?"
That son of Aditi spoke with humility, "Whose might
except for yours, O Jagadambā, grantor of release,
approaches Bhairava's, the foe of Tripura? Goddess,
lay waste the clan of Rākṣasas and thereby salvage all
three worlds; enhance Dharma's glory; lighten the burden for
Mother Earth; and rescue Rāghava." In such a manner
the adversary of the Daitya clan flattered Satī.
Suddenly that city filled with a rare fragrance; sounds of
bells and conch shells could be heard all around, accompanied
by auspicious jingling, soft and sweet, as when the cuckoos
sing harmoniously in some distant wooded grove. Her
golden throne tottered. In honeyed tones that ideal wife of
Bhaveśa asked her friend Vijayā, "Little moon-face, tell
me, where, why, and who worships me at this untimely time?"[2]
First she chanted *mantras*, then jotted down some figures with
a piece of chalk, computing calculations, and at last
with a smile that confidante reported, "O daughter of
the mountains, the charioteer Dāśarathi worships
you in Laṅkā. I deduce, by my computations, that

2. The annual Durgā Pūjā takes place in Bengal today in the autumn and is known as the "untimely" (*akāla*) Durgā Pūjā. Goddess Durgā, by certain accounts, is to be worshiped in the spring; Rāma, however, needed her help in order to defeat Rāvaṇa and to rescue Sītā, and so worshiped Durgā before he was about to enter Laṅkā. The time happened to be autumn, an untimely time for Durgā's *pūjā*. It is that untimely time that persists as the most auspicious time to worship this goddess.

the Raghu sovereign, hands cupped in supplication, offers
blue lotuses before a water pot on which those two
pretty feet of yours are painted out of bright vermilion.
Confer on him the gift of *abhaya*, O Abhayā.
That finest Raghu, son of Kauśalyā, is your foremost
devotee. Deliver him from danger, O Tāriṇī!"

Satī, queen of queens, arose from her golden throne and once
again addressed Vijayā, "Vijayā, do attend this
godly couple properly. I shall proceed to where sits
Dhūrjaṭi on Mount Yogāsana (that huge mountain peak!)."

And saying this, Durgā, she who moves with elephantine
grace, went inside her golden dwelling. Then the beautiful
Vijayā spoke warmly to Vāsava, Indra of the
gods, together with his heavenly queen, and seated them
upon the golden throne. With utmost satisfaction the
couple partook of the offerings made to them. Jayā,
laughing, hung a string of star-shaped flowers round Śacī's neck;
she placed upon her hair bun an ever-tasteful, ever-
blooming spray of gemlike blossoms. Instrumental music
sounded all about, and a troupe of women sang and danced.
Kailāsa city was entranced, as were all three worlds! When
babies heard the honeyed sounds within their dreams, they smiled, eyes
closed, upon their mother's lap. And sleepless, love-sick maidens
rose aflutter, thinking they had heard their lovers' footfalls
at the door. Cuckoos ceased their songs throughout the forest. And
a band of yogis started, thinking that their chosen god,
from whom they begged a boon, had indeed appeared before them.

When she had slipped into her golden dwelling, that perfect
wife of Bhaveśa reflected, "How can I call upon
Bhaveśa today?" Then, mulling over that a moment,
Satī's thoughts turned to Rati. Umā's wishes instantly
wafted, in the form of ripples of a fragrant breeze, to
where charming Varānanā, enchantress of Manmatha,
dallied with Manmatha in a pleasure garden. Rati's
heart danced like *vīṇā* strings at a finger's touch. Straight away
went that bride of Kāma, hastily, upon the wind's path
to the peak of Mount Kailāsa. Just as, at the end of
nighttime, lotuses lay themselves wide open on a lake,
bowing at the feet of Dawn, harbinger of light's sovereign,

so bowed that love of Madana at the feet of Hara's
darling. Giving Rati her blessings, Ambikā smiled and
said, "That Indra among yogis is immersed in austere
meditation on Mount Yogāsana. Tell me, moon-faced
one, how, by what enticement, can I break his trance?" Bowing
once again, that sleek-haired one replied, "Goddess, you should
assume a most enchanting form. If you so order me,
I shall fetch you divers garments and adorn your sterling
body. As soon as he lays eyes on you, Pinākī will
be enticed, exactly as the sovereign of the seasons
was tempted when he caught sight of the forest, flower-tressed."

So saying, Rati smoothed her hair with aromatic oils,
then plaited it into a captivating braid. Next, that
lovely one assembled sundry ornaments, embossed with
diamonds, pearls, and such. She brought with her paste of sandalwood,
vermilion mixed with saffron, musk, also silken garments
glittering with many jewels. That one with charming eyes
in delight outlined both feet with red lac dye. That daughter
of the Indra among mountains looked the very image
of a world-enchantress. She glowed with twice the splendor of
lustrous gold when rubbed upon a buffing stone. Within a
looking glass the goddess saw that moonlike face of hers, as
the full-bloomed lotus sees its full-blown charm in pellucid
waters. With a smile, the darling of the victor over
Smara spoke, gazing toward the love of Smara, "Summon up
the monarch of your life." At once that love of Madana
called (as the queen among cuckoos calls to Springtime) to her
Madana. Phuladhanu hurried there, as those who live
abroad come eagerly at the strains of their own music.

Said that daughter of the stones, "Come with me, Manmatha. We
shall go to where the sovereign among the yogis sits,
entirely absorbed in yoga. Come at once, my child."

Prostrate at Abhayā's feet, blissful Madana, offspring
of infatuation, answered worriedly, "Why do you,
goddess, give your servant such an order? I am scared
to death, Mother, as I recall that past event! When due
to foolish Dakṣa's blunder, Satī, you abandoned your
corporeal form and, on your own, took birth within the
home of Himādri—it was then that Viśvanātha, out

of grief from loss of you, gave up responsibility
for the universe and commenced to meditate. Later,
Indra, sovereign of the gods, directed me, your servant
to disturb that meditation. At a quite ill-fated
moment I went, Mother, to where god Vāma was immersed
in austere meditation. I seized my flower-bow and
let fly a flower-arrow at that most inopportune
of times. As a lion without warning springs upon the
king of elephants, there filling up the forests with his
terrifying roar, O Bhaveśvarī, just so the sun
whose home is situated in the forehead of your spouse,
sprang forth in anger and consumed this slave of yours. Alas,
Mother, how can I ever, humbly, tell those reddened feet
of yours what burning pain I endured? With forlorn wails I
called to Vāsava, the moon, the winds, and sun; but no one
came. In no time whatsoever I was turned to ashes!
With much trepidation and without enthusiasm,
I think of Bhaveśa—please forgive this slave of yours, O
Kṣemaṅkarī. At your feet I modestly beseech you."
  Śaṅkarī spoke with a smile, consoling Madana, "Come
along with me in best of spirits and be brave at heart,
Anaṅga. By my boon you shall be all-victorious!
The fire who had seized you at that inauspicious moment,
consuming you in his flames, will do today your bidding,
just as the deadly poisons take on the qualities of
medicine, thus saving lives when they are handled wisely."
  Then with hands pressed palm to palm and bowing before Umā's
feet, Kāma said, "What has he to fear in all three worlds, O
Abhayā, to whom you grant *abhaya*? But may I say
this to your lotus feet—how, O daughter of the Indra
among mountains, will you venture out from this abode in
such enchanting garb—do tell this slave of yours. In a flash,
Mother, the world will go insane gazing at your graceful
sweetness—I tell you in all honesty. This well-meant act,
O goddess, will quickly yield contrary ends. When the gods
and Asuras churned the lord of waters and produced the
drink of immortality, the most mischievous sons of
Diti quarreled with the gods for that sweet nectar. Śrī's spouse
arrived upon the scene disguised as Mohinī, a most

exquisitely enchanting woman. When the three worlds saw
Hṛṣīkeśa in disguise, they swooned, struck by one of this
slave's darts! Gods and Daityas both forgot about the nectar
of immortal life. Nāgas bowed ashamed, seeing down her
back her braid; Mount Mandara himself turned motionless at
seeing her high breasts! Remembering all that, O Satī,
a smile comes to my lips. If copper gilded with a film
of gold is dazzling, then consider, goddess, how more awe-
inspiring is the luster of pure gold!" Without delay,
mystifying Ambikā conjured up a golden cloud
and with it veiled her charming figure. It was, alas, as
though a lotus bloom could cloak its moonlike countenance with
sunset's glow! or, as though in heaps of ashes flames could hide,
suppressing their bright grins! or, as though god Śakra, with a
cakra, could mask the wealth of nectar in the lunar orb!

Through a door inlaid with ivory that sweetest smiling
one stepped from her home, like Dawn herself overcast by clouds.
With her was Manmatha, flower-bow in hand, upon his
back a quiver that was packed with keenest flower-arrows—
and she, a lotus, seemed to bloom upon those thorny stalks.

On the very peak of Mount Kailāsa is an awesome
plateau summit called Yogāsana, renowned throughout the
world; it was to there the world-enchanting goddess mounted,
mounted on the king of pachyderms. At once surrounding
caverns closed—crashing, roaring mountain streams fell as silent
as the lord of waters when in peaceful, calm confluence.
The clouds fled far away as does darkness faced with Dawn's
bright laugh. The goddess saw in front of her the ascetic
Kapardī, body smeared with ashes, his eyes shut, drowned in
austere meditation's sea, deadened to the outer world.

To Madana that lady with the most delightful smile
spoke, "What is the point of hesitating, enemy of
Śambara? Shoot your flower-arrows." At the goddess's
command, Mīnadhvaja knelt upon one knee, then twanged his
bowstring, piercing Umā's husband with infatuating
arrows. A thrill shot through Śūlapāṇi. The matted mass
of hair upon his head shook, as, when there is an earthquake,
a stand of trees upon a mountain top will shake, snapping
and cracking. His lordship began to stare! Flames roared from his

forehead, flashing, blazing bright! Seized by fear, Phuladhanu
took refuge in the breast of Bhavānī, as a frightened
lion cub hides when clouds with thunderclaps and lightning streaks
disgorge, as spirited as doomsday fires, dazzling to the
eye. Now, opening his seeing eyes, Dhūrjaṭi arose.
The daughter of the rocks then shed her conjured veil of clouds.

Charmed by a beauty like Mohinī's, that master of all
animals spoke excitedly, "Why do I see you here
alone in this deserted spot, mother of Gaṇendra?
Where is, O Śaṅkarī, your mount, the Indra among beasts?
where are Jayā and Vijayā?" Smiling, Umā of the
most alluring smile replied, "Indra among yogis, you
had forgotten me, your humble servant, and stayed in this
forsaken place so long. That is why I come, my husband,
in hopes of seeing your two feet. Does a wife who loves her
husband go escorted by attendants when she greets him?
At dawn, my lord, does not the *cakravākī* bird proceed
alone to where her heart's mate waits?" Affectionately, god
Īśāna, a trace of joy on his lips, gave Īśānī
a seat upon his deerskin. All about, buds burst open
into bloom; bees, now maddened with a thirst for honey, swarmed;
vernal, southern breezes blew; cuckoos cooed; and a rain of
blown blossoms cleansed by nighttime dew clothed that best of mountain
peaks. In Umā's bosom Kusumeṣu (what more fitting
dwelling place than this for Manasija) sat there strumming
merrily on his flower bow, letting fly a hail of
arrows—by love's scents was Triśūlī made mad! Overcome
by utter shame, Rāhu rushed forth, gobbled up the beaming
moon, while the smiling solar god hid within the ashes!

Then taking on the guise of Mohana, to captivate
his Mohinī, that god spoke, smiling, "I know, my goddess,
all your inner thoughts—why Vāsava has come with Śacī
to our Kailāsa home and for what cause the jewel of
Raghus worshiped you at this untimely time. The son of
Nikaṣā is my greatest devotee, but that foolish
fellow is undone by the fruits of his own deed. My heart
aches just to think about him, Maheśvarī! Alas, my
goddess, what can you give that human being, where will you
find the strength to block what is predestined from another

birth? O Umā, send Kāma to the Indra of the gods.
Direct him to proceed at once, my Maheśī, to the
residence of goddess Māyā. By the grace of Māyā,
hero Lakṣmaṇa will slay the hero Meghanāda."
Mīnadhvaja set off, as the king of birds departs his
nest and flies away, gazing back repeatedly toward his
happy home. Fluffy clouds, golden color, wafting scented
fragrances and raining flower blossoms—lotuses, both
red and white, jasmine, *seṃuti, jāti, pārijāta,*
and so forth, all beloved by gentle breezes—engulfed the
god of gods, that greatest god, there with the greatest goddess.
By the golden door, inlaid with ivory, there awaits
the moon-faced charmer of that Madana, tears in her eyes,
aha! separated from her husband! It was then the
associate of Spring reappeared. Not hesitating,
Manmatha joyously stretched out his arms and drew his spouse
in fond embrace to him, placating her with caring words.
Her teardrops dried, as do the dewdrops on lotus petals
when the sun shows himself upon the sunrise pinnacle.
Regaining her heart's treasure, that richly handsome woman,
her face to his (like the mynah to the parrot during
luscious springtime) spoke very loving words, "You have saved your
servant's life by coming back so soon to her, O joy of
Rati! Whom shall I tell how I worried? I cannot stop
trembling, husband, when I hear the name of godly Vāma
and recall those past events! that overwhelming, spiteful
Śūlapāṇi! Do not venture near him any more, swear
to me, O lord of my existence!" With a honeyed smile
Pañcaśara answered, "In a shady grove, who fears the
solar rays, my beauty? Let us greet the god clan's sovereign."
Manmatha reached where Vāsava was seated on his throne
of gold and, bowing low, relayed the message. Embarking
on his chariot, the charioteer monarch of the
gods sped off to Māyā's dwelling. His spirited steed flew
through the sky, the fly-whisk plume upon its head unswerving;
those chariot wheels rumbled, churning clouds along their path.
In due time, the hero Sahasrākṣa reached the place where
Māyā dwelt. Dismounting from his splendid chariot, that
foremost charioteer among divines stepped within the

temple. Who can ever put in words all of what that god
saw there? There sat the magic queen of Śaktis on a seat
of gold, radiant with added splendor from the sharpest
rays from the sun. With his palms pressed together, Vāsava
bowed most reverently and said, "Give this slave of yours your
benedictions, O great enchantress of the universe."

Upon vouchsafing him those benedictions, the goddess
asked, "Tell me what has brought you here today, Aditi's son?"

Replied the sovereign of the gods, "At Śiva's orders, O
grand Māyā, I have come to your abode. Inform his slave
of yours how, by what strategy, can Saumitri on the
morrow vanquish Daśānana's son? By your grace (so says
Virūpākṣa) the warrior Lakṣmaṇa will overcome
that champion Meghanāda in ferocious combat."

The goddess thought a moment, then replied to Vāsava,
"When Tāraka, the Asura, indomitable, laid
claim to heaven by repulsing you in battle, sovereign
of divines, at such a time that general, the favored
of the Kṛttikās, was conceived within Pārvatī's womb.[3]
To slay the Dānava king, Vṛṣabhadhvaja armed this
warrior personally, forging weapons of tremendous strength.
Observe this shield embossed with gold, and that sword, god, itself
a god of death incarnate, lying sheathed over there. Look,
Sunāsīra, that awesome quiver, inexhaustible,
replete with arrows the likes of venomous serpents, hoods
flared. Gaze, god, upon the bow." Staring at the beauty of
that bow, Śacī's valiant husband smiled and said, "How worthless
is your humble servant's jeweled bow when matched with this. That
best of shields blazes, like the solar orb—dazzling eyes.
That sword shines with furious force, like a flame. Where within
this world, Mother, is another quiver such as that one?"
"Listen, god," resumed the goddess Māyā, "Ṣaḍānana
vanquished Tāraka by the power from those weapons. And
by the force of those same weapons, hero, Meghanāda
soon will die—I speak the truth. Yet not a warrior within
all three worlds, neither god nor human, can in a fair fight
slay Rāvaṇi. Send this weaponry to Rāma's younger

3. By some accounts Kārttikeya was conceived in Pārvatī's womb; by other accounts not.

brother. I myself tomorrow shall proceed to Laṅkā
and there protect Lakṣmaṇa, god, in his battle with the
Rākṣasas. Go now to the land of the divines, treasure
of the godly host. When Dawn, the friend of flowers, opens
up the golden portals of the east tomorrow with her
lotus hand, that lion among Indras among warriors
will free you from your fear of Indrajit, constant dread of
yours—Laṅkā's lotus-sun will sink behind the setting-hill."
In ecstasy, the Indra of the gods praised that goddess,
gathered up the weapons, and then headed home to heaven.
The champion Vāsava took his seat upon the golden
throne within the gods' assembly hall and called on champion
Citraratha, "Bear these weapons carefully and go, great
hero, straight to golden Laṇkā. Saumitri the lion
will slay in combat Meghanāda come tomorrow by
the grace of Māyā. How that will happen, goddess Māyā
will inform him. You tell Rāghava, O sovereign of the
Gandharvas, that the denizens of heaven wish him well, that Hara's
love, Pārvatī herself, was pleased with him today. Bestow
upon him *abhaya*, high-minded one. If Rāvaṇi
is killed in battle, Rāvaṇa is sure to perish too.
And that jewel of the Raghu clan, Vaidehī's bliss, will
again regain his chaste Vaidehī. Mount my chariot,
O best of charioteers, and be on your way. Lest the
Rākṣasas catch sight of you in Laṅkā and engage you
in hostilities, I am ordering the clouds to veil
the sky; I am summoning Prabhañjana and shall have
him loose the winds a while. Then lightning will come out to dance;
and I shall fill the world with swelling, rumbling thunderclaps."
Bowing humbly to the feet of the Indra among gods,
the charioteer Citraratha gathered cautiously
that weaponry and then proceeded to the mortal world.
The lord of gods called upon Prabhañjana and said, "Quick,
raise a cataclysmic storm in Laṅkā city, sovereign
of the winds; set free imprisoned gales at once; bring on the
clouds; and quarrel somewhat raucously with the hostile lord
of waters!" That god exuberant, just like a lion
springing when his chains are broken, went to where the winds were
being held within the dark recesses of a mountain

cavern. From afar Pavana heard the loud and mindless
howling; he watched the mountain lurch from forces far inside
as though unable by its strength alone to hold in check
those mighty winds. By touch, the god pushed aside the stony
portal. With screams that menace, winds sped forth, as do waters
when embankments suddenly give way! Earth quaked; the ocean
roared! Rows of waves shaped like massive mountains tumbled, crashing
loudly, driven mad in combat with the winds! Clouds clamored
noisily as they scudded here, there. Lightning laughed, followed
by the crackling roar of thunder. The lord of stars, his stars
in tow, fled; all the while clouds surged over Laṅkā, belching
flames. Throughout the forest, timber snapped, toppling with a thud,
while violent storms whipped through the skies, streaming rain as if
to drown creation in Pralaya's deluge, dumping hail.

The Rākṣasas in panic dashed inside their homes. Amid
that camp, where stood the valiant Indra among Rāghavas,
came unannounced the charioteer Citraratha, like
the ray-ringed sun, a royal robe cloaked his figure! Round his
waist there shone an ornamental girdle with a mass of
brilliance like constellations of the zodiac—from it
hung the best of swords, brightly coruscating! How shall the
poet pen the golden glow from his godly quiver, bow,
shield, armor, lance, and coronet of sunbeams? That godly
shine bedazzled, and soon a scent from heaven filled the land.

Most respectfully that best of Raghus bowed before the
godly messenger, then asked, "Heavenly inhabitant,
what land but heaven, ah me, is adorned by such grandeur,
such grace? Why are you here today, forsaking Nandana
Gardens—please tell your servant that. I have no throne of gold,
O god. What shall I offer as a seat? Yet if you, lord,
feel some compassion toward your slave, accept this water for
the washing of your feet, and take these presents, and kindly
sit upon this seat of *kuśa* grass. Rāghava, alas,
is but a beggar!" And blessing him, that charioteer
took a seat on the *kuśa* grass, then spoke in sweetest tones,

"My name is Citraratha—hear me out, Dāśarathi.
I am a faithful devotee and serve the Indra of
the gods, come rain or shine. The Gandharvas are under my
command. I journeyed to this city in accordance with

Indra's orders. That monarch of the gods and the god clan
wish you well. Gaze at these weapons, gem of men. The king of
gods sends them to your younger sibling. Great goddess Māyā
will come at dawn to explain by what course of action the
champion Lakṣmaṇa will slay the champion Meghanāda,
on the morrow. You are beloved by the gods, O jewel
of the Raghu clan. Abhayā herself is pleased with you!"

Replied the son of Raghu, "At these auspicious tidings,
O best of Gandharvas, I am afloat in a sea of
bliss! Yet I am but an ignorant mortal—alas, how
shall I ever show you my appreciation? Tell me!"

That messenger said with a smile, "Listen, gem of Raghus,
gratitude for gods, protection of the poor, suppression
of one's senses, treading ever on the path of *dharma*,
serving constantly the goddess Truth, even offerings
of sandalwood and flower blossoms, foods, and garments made
of silk and such the gods will scorn if he who offers them
is himself untrue. This basic fact I tell you truly."

Rāmacandra bowed. Charioteer Citraratha gave
his blessings, then departed for the city of the gods
in his godly chariot. The raucous tempest calmed; the
ocean settled down. Golden Laṅkā smiled again as she
gazed upon the moon with starry entourage. Entering
the gentle waters, moonlight once more bathed her silvery
form while out of curiosity the lotus blossoms
grinned. Anew, cadaver-eating jackals ran out on the
battleground along with droves of vultures, ghouls, and buzzards.
The Rākṣasas, drunk from all the liquor of heroics,
came out-of-doors once more, brandishing their awesome bludgeons.

Thus ends canto number two,
called "Weapons Acquisition,"
in the poem
The Slaying of Meghanāda.

CANTO 3

Reuniting

In Pramoda Park wept Pramīlā, that youthful daughter
of a Dānava, pained because apart from her dear spouse.
The moon-faced one, eyes filled with tears, paced constantly about
the flower garden, just like the maid of Vraja, ah me,
when she, in Vraja's flower groves, failed to find her Kṛṣṇa,
yellow-clad, under a *kadamba* tree, flute at his lips.
That lovesick woman, time and again, would step inside her
home, then reemerge, like a pigeon, inconsolable
in her empty pigeon house. Anon, she would climb to the
roof of her dwelling and gaze toward distant Laṅkā, dabbing
with the loose end of her sari her ceaseless tears. Mute were
the flute, *vīṇā*, *muraja* drum, finger cymbals, and the
strains of song. The faces of her retinue turned somber
at the sorrow of their pretty mistress. And who is there
who has not seen the sullen faces of the flowers when
their forest mistress burns in separation from her Spring?
To Pramoda Park came goddess Night. All atremble, chaste
Pramīlā in trilling tones began to speak, though sniffling,
as she flung her arms around the neck of an attendant
named Vāsantī, redolent with scents of spring, "Vāsantī,
look, dark Night has come as though a deadly snake to bite me.
Where, oh where, companion, is the conqueror of foes, my
Indrajit, sovereign of the Rākṣasa clan, at this time
of peril? 'I shall be back soon,' that hero said, and went
away. I fail to comprehend the reason for this long
delay. If you should know, my confidante, do tell me, please."
Replied the attending Vāsantī, like Spring's companion
cooing in the spring, "How am I to say just why the lord
of your life is late today? But, dispel your worries, you
whose husband lives. Your champion will return once he routs that
Rāghava. What do you have to fear, O friend? Who in a
battle can better him whose body is impervious
to the arrows of both Asuras and gods? Come, let us
saunter through the garden. We shall gather fragrant blossoms
and string the finest garland. We shall smile as we lay that

garland round your lover's neck, as when, with glee, the people
tie the victory pennant to the winning chariot's crest."
At that, those two walked through the grove where moonbeams
played on ponds
thus causing lotuses to smile. Bumblebees buzzed, cuckoos
cooed, blossoms blossomed, and a line of fireflies shone from the
forehead of a row of trees (like a jeweled part in her
sylvan hair). Southern breezes blew, causing leaves to murmur.
Both filled the loose ends of their saris with blossoms. Who can
say how many flower petals were pearled with dewdrops from
Pramīlā's eyes? A little ways away that woman spied
a sad sunflower, face turned pale, aha, pining for her
sun, and went and stood beside her saying sweetly, "I too
suffer that same agony, darling of the sun, which you
endure on this darkest night. The world now seems most gloomy
to these hapless eyes of mine. My heart, it burns in flames of
lovesick separation. That sun's radiance, which I must
witness to survive, he is hidden past the setting-hill.
Yet day after day shall I gain again the monarch of
my life (as you, chaste one, will gain yours by the grace of Dawn)?"
Having gathered up a bunch of flowers from that garden,
chaste Pramīlā heaved a sigh, dejected, then addressed her
confidante, "There now, I have plucked this heap of blossoms, friend,
and shall string a graceful garland; but where ever shall I
find those two feet which I wish to worship with this floral
offering? I cannot think who might impede my king of
beasts. Come, dear one, let us now all go to Laṅkā city."
Confidante Vāsantī answered, "How will you enter on
this day Laṅkā? The troops of Rāghava, like an ocean
impossible to cross, surround her. There thousands upon
thousands of the Rākṣasas' foes tromp about with weapons
in their grasp, like Daṇḍadhara, punishing staff in hand."
Pretty Pramīlā, Dānava maid, became incensed. "What
was that you said, Vāsantī? When once the stream departs her
mountain cave, heading for the sea, who is capable of
standing in her way? I, the daughter of a Dānava,
a bride within the clan of Rākṣasas—Rāvaṇa is
my father-in-law, and Meghanāda is my spouse—am
I to fear, my friend, that beggar Rāghava? We go this

day to Laṅkā proper by the strength of our own arms. Let
us see by what stratagem the gem of men prevents us!"

Thus said, that faithful wife, with a gait which matched the king of
elephants, went inside her home of gold, seized by anger.

As when the great foe-harassing charioteer Pārtha
following that sacrificial stallion wandered to their
queendom, those warrior-women dressed for battle eagerly,
enraged by blasts from the conch shell Devadatta, just so
all the four directions resounded with the boom of drums
as those women strode out frenzied by the wine of valor,
unsheathing swords, twanging bowstrings, and brandishing their shields,
while the brilliance from their golden armor glistened, lighting
up the city! In stables, horses whinnied as they, with
ears erect, listened to the chink of anklets, the clatter
of belled waistbands, just as deadly cobras dance and sway when
they hear the rapid drumbeat of the double-headed drum
called *ḍamaru*. From stalls, elephants responded with ear-
piercing trumpeting, as the monarch among clouds trumpets
from afar in deep, sonorous blasts. Gaily, Echo woke
in caverns and on mountain tops in forests—filling of
a sudden the environs with her reverberations.

A most wrathful, most hot-tempered woman by the name of
Nṛmuṇḍamālinī saddled up a hundred horses
in a mix of trappings and then led them gleefully from their
stable to a nearby platform where a hundred warrior-
women mounted them, swords rattling within scabbards against
their steeds' flanks. The crests upon their coronets bobbed high and
low; down their backs ornamented braids swung fetchingly in
concert with their quivers. Handheld lances seemed like spiky
stalks emanating from lotus blossoms. Those horses neighed,
overcome with ecstasy, just as Virūpākṣa shouts
ecstatic while he holds upon his chest that Dānava-
destroyer's pair of lotus-feet! Martial music sounded;
immortals in the heavens gave a start, as did Nāgas
in Pātāla, and likewise men within the world of man.

Spirited Pramīlā dressed, overcoming with anger
her shyness and fear. The glow from the diadem atop
her chignon shone, ah alas, like Indra's bow upon the
crest of clouds. Her eyebrows drawn with black kohl were like the eye-

pleasing crescent moon upon Bhairavī's forehead. That bright-
eyed one covered her high breasts with armor and strapped a gold,
jewel-studded cummerbund artfully round her waist. Down
her back beside her quiver hung a shield, dazzling to the eyes
like the orb of the sun. Along her thigh (ah, round like
a banana tree, light of the forest!) flashed a well-honed
saber in its golden casing. Her hand grasped a long lance,
and many bangles sparkled on her arms. That Dānava
was fitted out like Haimavatī when, wild from wines of
valor, she crushed Mahiṣāsura in pitched battle or
when she vanquished Śumbha and Niśumbha. Like Ḍākinīs
and Yoginīs the band of mounted maids ringed the chaste wife.
That pretty one rode Vaḍabā—flame atop the mare's fire!
As clouds call out commandingly from the skies, just so this
callipygous woman called out to her retinue in
rich, full tones, "Hear me out, Dānava maids, foe-conquering
Indrajit is now a virtual captive inside Laṅkā.
I am at an utter loss to comprehend why my life's
lord tarries there so long, neglecting me, his thrall. I will
go there, to his side; we will breach the monstrous enemy
lines and march into the city, overcoming the armed
forces of the Raghus' best—on this I give to you my
word, warrior-women. If we fail, then I shall perish in
the struggle—whatever has been written on my forehead!
We were born among the Dānava clan, my Dānava
maids. It is the fate of Dānavas to kill in combat,
or to drown within the river of our enemies' blood!
We have honey on our lips, deadly poison-glances in
our eyes! Are these tender, lotus-stalk-like arms devoid of
power? Come, one and all, let us see the manliness of
Rāghava. We shall have a look at that handsome form which
drove my auntie, Sūrpaṇakhā, mad with passion when she
saw him in the Pañcavaṭī Forest; we shall gaze on
warrior Lakṣmaṇa; and we shall bind up with a *nāga-
pāśa* that cinder smudge upon the clan of Rākṣasas—
Vibhīṣaṇa! We shall trample under foot the hostile
camp, as cow elephants do a clump of reeds. My ladies,
you must be like lightning and fall upon our enemy!"
Those female Dānavas let loose a menacing sound, just

like a herd of female elephants—gone mad in springtime.
As the progress of a forest fire is most difficult
to check when accompanied by its friend, the wind, just so that
chaste one headed toward her spouse, unchecked. Golden Laṅkā shook;
the ocean roared; thick clouds of dust flew up on every side—
yet when have clouds of smoke ever had the force to screen out
flames at night? With the brilliance of just such flames, the woman
Pramīlā proceeded with her band of warrior-women.
Shortly, that moon-faced one reached the western gate. At once a
hundred conch shells blared, a hundred awesome bows were strummed by
those women, threateningly. Laṅkā quaked with terror. Mahouts
shuddered on their elephants, charioteers upon their
chariots, the best of horsemen on their mounts, the monarch
on his throne, and clan wives in their inner quarters. In their
nests birds shivered, lions in mountain lairs, wild elephants
in jungles. Aquatic creatures dove to deeper waters.
Hanumān, fearsome-looking son of Pavana, sallied
forth aggressively, growling out his words, "Who are you who
on this night come out to die? Hanumān stands vigilant
at this gateway—Hanumān whose very name when heard will
cause the lord of Rākṣasas to tremble on his throne! The
jewel of the Raghu clan himself stands guard, together
with his ally Vibhīṣaṇa, lionlike Saumitri,
and a hundred other warriors, so very difficult
to best in combat. Is this some joke that you dissemblers
have assumed the guise of women? I know Niśācaras
are accomplished sorcerers. But I shall shatter with strength
of arms the power of your *māyā*—I shall smash the foe
when and where I find him with my fright-instilling bludgeon."
The attending Nṛmuṇḍamālinī (that wrathful, hot-
tempered woman) twanged her bow inflamed, shouting threateningly,
"Barbarian, bring here at once that lord of Sītā! Who
wants you, you wretched little beast! We, by choice, have not struck
the likes of you with our weapons. Does the lioness pick
a quarrel with a jackal? We spared your life, now scamper
off, jungle-dweller! Simpleton, what is there to gain by
killing you? Be off with you, call the lord of Sītā here,
and your master Lakṣmaṇa, and call that blemish on the
clan of Rākṣasas, that Vibhīṣaṇa! Foe-conquering

Indrajit, whose wife is pretty Pramīlā—his woman
now will enter Laṅkā, by force of arms, to worship at
her husband's feet! What man of arms, you fool, can block her way?"

With force like that of mighty winds, Hanumān, an Indra
among heroes and son of Pavana, rushed forward, but
then that champion saw with trepidation there among those
warrior-women Pramīlā, the Dānava, in attire
most colorful. A brilliance, lightninglike, played upon her
diadem. Her fine coat of mail glistened from her stunning
figure, shining like a mesh of sunbeams interlaced and
tinged with gems. Hanumān stood wonderstruck as he thought to
himself, "When I leapt the ocean none can leap and landed
here in Laṇkā, I espied fearsome Bhīmā, ferocious,
a falchion and a human skull in hand, and wearing round
her neck a string of severed heads. I saw Rāvaṇa's sweet-
hearts, Mandodarī and those other Dānava daughters
all. I watched the wives and young girls of the Rākṣasas (like
slivers of the moon) return alone in dark of night, each
to her own abode. I saw that lotus of the Raghu
clan in the Aśoka Grove (alas, distressed by sorrow).
But never have I seen throughout the world such beauty and
such sweetness as she has! Praise the warrior Meghanāda,
that such a brilliant streak of lightning should be forever
bound by bonds of love to the body of a cloud like him!"

And thinking to himself these words, the son of Añjanā
spoke in deep tones (as storms Prabhañjana), "O pretty one,
my lordship, sun among the solar clan, bound the captive
sea with fetters made of stone, then ventured to this city
accompanied by some thousand warriors. The Rākṣasas' king
is his foe. Your ladyship, tell me, for what reason do
you come here at this odd hour? Speak, and have no fear in
your heart. I am Hanumān, servant of the Raghus. That
wealth of Raghus is an ocean of compassion. What quarrel
do you have with him, bright-eyes? What favor do you beg? Tell
me promptly—you have come on what account? Speak. I shall make
your wishes known, your highness, at the feet of Rāghava."

The chaste one answered—aha, that message sounded to the
ears of Hanumān like the strains played on a *vīṇā* thick
with honey! "That best of Raghus is my husband's foe. Be

that as it may, I personally have no quarrel with him.
My husband, lion of Indras among warriors, is world-
victor by the might of his own arms. What need have I to
battle with his adversary? We are all mere women,
maids among this clan. But consider this, warrior, lightning's
splendor, which delights the eye, kills men on contact.
Here, champion, take with you my messengeress. The lovely
woman will relate to Rāma what I seek. Go with haste."

Messengeress Nṛmuṇḍamālinī, who resembles
her who wears the necklace strung with human heads, stepped forward
fearlessly into the enemy's ranks, just as a ship
under sail frolics in the waves without concern, even
though afloat upon the waters of a shoreless ocean.
Hanumān went on ahead to lead the way. The warrior
throng seemed startled by that woman, just as a householder
is alarmed when in the dead of night he espies a fire
in his home. That irascible woman smiled to herself.
All those warriors stared aghast. They milled about uneasy,
banding together here and there. Anklets chimed from her feet,
as did the ornamental waistband round her midriff. An
awesome lance in hand, she with hips well endowed strode forward
dominating everyone with piercing dartlike glances.
The apex of her diadem made of peacock feathers
danced smartly there atop her head. A gemmed necklace flashed from
the cleavage between her shapely breasts. Down her back dangled
one jewel-studded braid, waving like Kāma's flag in spring.
With a young cow elephant's saunter, that voluptuous
one proceeded, casting light in all directions, just as
moonlight, the confidante of lotuses, shines upon a
clear lake, or as the rays of Dawn on mountain pinnacles.

Inside his tent sat the gemstone of the Raghus. Before
him stood Lakṣmaṇa, lion among champions, his hands cupped
reverently together. Off to one side was their ally
Vibhīṣaṇa, and the other warriors, most ferocious
in their mien and as spirited as the Rudra clan. The
cache of those god-given weapons shone resplendent from a
wooden altar, colored crimson by red sandalwood and
covered with a flower offering. Incense smoldered in
its censers while rows and rows of oil lamps burned on all four

sides. Everyone gazed in awe at the godly weaponry.
Some praised the sword; some marveled at that best of shields, with gold
overlaid, like clouds graced by the sun at sunset; others
spoke of the quiver; still others, of the armor, a mass
of brilliance. High-minded Rāghava himself held up that
best of bows, saying, "By the might of these two arms I, at
Vaidehī's bridegroom-choosing ceremony, broke the bow
named Pināka. I better not string this one! How is it,
brother Lakṣmaṇa? Would you like to bend it?" Suddenly
the ranks cried out, and "Victory to Rāma!" rolled through the
skies in a raucous din, like the crashing roar of ocean
waves. The Rākṣasa charioteer, in panic, glanced at
Dāśarathi, then that lion spoke, "Look, Indra among
Raghus, beyond the camp. Does Dawn approach in dead of night?"

Wonderstruck, all gazed out past the tents. "That woman seems like
Bhairavī," said the gem of men. "Is she Dānava or
goddess, friend, please look. Laṅkā is a place of *māyā*; she
is full of wizardry; and your elder brother can assume
any shape at will. Look carefully, for that sorcerer
is not unknown to you. It was a stroke of luck, O best
of Rākṣasas, when I got you on my side. Who but you,
friend, speak, could save these weakened forces in such peril? You
are Rāma's lasting savior in this land of Rākṣasas!"

Just then the messengeress, escorted by Hanumān,
reached the tent. Politely bowing, hands cupped reverently, that
woman spoke (as if the *rāgiṇīs*, all thirty-six, had
blended into song!), "I bow respectfully before your
feet, Rāghava, and to all the other venerable ones—
my name is Nṛmuṇḍamālinī. I am the servant
of the Daitya woman, pretty Pramīlā, pleasure of
Indrajit, lion of Indras of warriors." Offering
his blessings, warrior Dāśarathi asked, "Why have you made
your way here, messengeress? Tell me in detail by what
deed, auspicious one, I might please your mistress? Say at once."

The one who looked like Bhīmā answered, "You are the best of
warriors, Raghu lord. Please come fight with her. If not, then let
her pass, for that beauty will enter golden Laṅkā to
do obeisance to her lord, her husband. You slew many
Rākṣasas by might of your own arms. A Rākṣasa's wife

now begs battle; battle her, O Indra among warriors.
We are a hundred women strong—whomever you prefer
will fight you by herself. Take up bow and arrow, if you
choose, best of men, sword and shield, or mace—and always we are
anxious for barehanded combat! Your choice, my lord, but please
be quick about it. For your sake that chaste one holds in check
her troops, as the huntress, a Kirāta, holds her cheetah
when that lethal one goes wild on spotting a herd of deer."

Saying thus, that good woman bowed her head, as a blossom
fully blown (dewdrop studded) offers salutation by
the lowering of its head before the gentle breezes.
Answered the Raghu sovereign, "Listen, my sleek-haired one, I
never quarrel without cause. The Rākṣasas' sovereign is
my foe. You are all young girls and wives within the clan. For
what offense should I act bellicose toward you? Merrily,
with fearless hearts, enter Laṅkā. Rāma, my good lady,
was born of Raghu kings, kings of warriors; your mistress, bright-
eyed messengeress, is a warrior's wife, her attendants,
warrior-women. Tell her, gentlewoman, I profusely
praise her wife's devotion, her strength and valor—I beg from
her to be excused without a battle. Hail Indrajit!
Hail pretty Pramīlā! It is known throughout the world, O
messengeress, that Rāghava is but a beggar now;
by twist of Fate he became impoverished, a mere forest
dweller. What gift (one which would befit you), comely one, could
I give today? I give my blessings. May you be happy!"

Thus said, his lordship turned to Hanumān, "Hero, let them
pass. Oblige this host of women by most cordial conduct."

With obeisance to Sītā's husband, the messengeress
took her leave. Smiling, friend Vibhīṣaṇa spoke, "See there, O
Raghu sovereign, see the prowess of Pramīlā out there!
Note, my lord, that matchless marvel. I know not who could wage
a winning war with such a host of women, truly bold
Bhīmā-like Cāmuṇḍā—foe of the Raktabīja clan!"
Added Rāghava, "My heart was gripped by fear when I saw
the figure of that messengeress, best of Rākṣasas.
Then and there I put aside all thought of fight. Only a
fool, my friend, would antagonize a tigress such as that.
Come, companion, let us have a look at your nephew's wife."

Just as when a forest fire far away penetrates a
wooded stand, filling full of flames all ten directions, that
Indra of Rāghavas saw in smokeless skies before him
a glowing mass which tinged with gold the gathered clouds. Alarmed,
he listened to the clatter of their bows, the trotting hooves
of horses, the threatening shouts, the jangle of their swords sheathed
in scabbards. Their instruments of music rang out, blending
with other sounds, as if waves of warbling birds were carried
by a thunderstorm. Banners fluttered—glimmering from gems
embossed. Horses pranced, then cantered smoothly; their belled trappings
jingled. On either side stood tall a column of soldiers
like two mountain ranges—between them marched that female corps,
just as lumber through a mountain pass cow elephants who
fill the land with trumpeting and cause the earth to tremble.

Ahead, the wrathful, hot-tempered Nṛmuṇḍamālinī,
mounted on her kohl-black steed, held a golden banner staff
in hand. Behind her, the musicians stood just like a troupe
of heaven-sent Vidyādharīs, ah, peerless upon the
face of the earth; *vīṇā*, flute, *mṛdaṅga* drums, small cymbals,
and the like, blended in sweet tripping notes. Behind them, in
among lance-wielding warrior-women was Pramīlā, like
a crescent moon among a constellation! in prowess,
just like Bhīmā! All about her there danced lightning's splendor,
born of gems. And through the welkin brandishing his flower-
bow, Rati's husband wantonly accompanied her, striking
her repeatedly with unfailing blossom-darts. Like the
buffalo-destroying Durgā on her lion's back; like
Śacī, Indra's consort, on Airavata; like Ramā,
wife of Upendra upon the Indra among birds—like
them all, that purest heroine appeared resplendent
astride her Vaḍabā, who was herself the queen of mares
caparisoned in jewels! Slowly, deliberately, as though
oblivious to the hostile throng, that troop of women
marched. Some strummed their bowstrings; others shouted, brandishing their
swords; some vaunted lances; others laughed; while still others roared
like lionesses, deep in the forest, or Bhairavī,
driven mad by love and valor's strong intoxication!

Glancing toward that best of Rākṣasas, Rāghava spoke, "How
amazing, Naikaṣeya! I have never seen, never

even heard of such a one in all of the three worlds! Have
I awakened to a dream? Tell me honestly, greatest
jewel of friends. I cannot fathom this. It unnerves me here
to witness such a strange illusion, friend, so do not you
deceive me too. From charioteer Citraratha's mouth I
heard the news that goddess Māyā would descend to help her
slave. Is it she who perpetrated such a hoax, disguised
as faithful consort, and is it she who now proceeds to
Laṅkā? Tell me, wise one, who is doing the beguiling?"

Answered Vibhīṣaṇa, "I tell you truly, this is no
nocturnal dream, Vaidehī's husband. There is a Daitya
by the name of Kālanemi, renowned throughout the world,
a foe of the divines; this pretty Pramīlā is his
daughter. The woman, my lord, was born from part of goddess
Mahāśakti and so is just as powerful as the
'Great Śakti.' Who can match that Dānava in prowess? The
captivating woman, O Indra among Rāghavas,
keeps under foot the Indra among Rākṣasas, that
lion, yellow-eyed, who defeated on the battlefield
lightning-hurling Sahasrākṣa—as Digambarī keeps
under foot Digambara. To save the world, Providence
wrought these bonds that bind the hero Meghanāda, deadly
elephant upon a rampage. Just as streams of water
damp a dreaded forest fire, the enemy of woodlands,
so does this chaste wife damp with loving conversation that
doomsday fire constantly. The deadly hooded viper,[1] its
strike now overpowered, remains submerged under fragrant
waters of the Yamunā. Hence, those who dwell amid this
universe live in happiness—gods in heaven, Nāgas
in their lowly Pātāla, men within the world of man."

The Raghu sovereign spoke, "It is true what you say, best of
friends; charioteer Meghanāda is the greatest of
the charioteers. I have not seen skill like his in all
of the three worlds! and I have fought with Bhṛgurāma, a
mountain of a warrior, immovable in battle. It
was, indeed, an auspicious moment, friend, when your nephew
seized the bow and arrow. What shall I do now, tell me, gem

1. Kāliya; see Yamunā in Glossary.

of Rākṣasas? When the mighty lioness joins her mate
within the forest, who can protect my herd of deer? See
there, the ocean filled with *halāhala* poison surges
all about us with an awful roar. As Nīlakaṇṭha
(conqueror of Nistāriṇī's heart) saved the world, just so,
my friend, by your power save those under your protection.
Consider well, O champion, your elder brother is as
fatal as a snake, his poison fangs, that greatest hero,
Indrajit. If I could somehow break those fangs, my fondest
hopes would be fulfilled; if not, I declare to you, I bound
the sea and ventured onto golden Laṅkā all for naught."

Bowing low before his brother's feet, champion Saumitri
spoke, "Why should we any longer fear the Rākṣasa, O
Raghu sovereign? He who has the favor of the lord of
gods, what need he fear in all three worlds, my lordship? For sure,
Rāvaṇi will fall, defeated by my hand tomorrow.
When and where does that which is not *dharma* triumph? The king
of the Rākṣasas practices non-*dharma*; on the field
of battle, Meghanāda will be stripped of strength due to
those iniquities. For the father's faults, the son shall die.
Tomorrow he who is the sun to lotus Laṅkā will
descend the setting-hill; so said Citraratha, divine
charioteer. So, my lord, for what reason do you fret?"

Replied Vibhīṣaṇa, "What you say is true enough, O
elephant of warriors. Where there is *dharma*, there follows
victory. By his own transgressions, alas, is the sovereign
of the Rākṣasas now ruined. Meghanāda, foeman
of the monarch of the skies, will die by your arrows. But
you must be careful. This Dānava, Pramīlā, displays
great prowess; and Nṛmuṇḍamālinī—like the goddess,
she who wears a garland made of human heads—is fond of
battle. One who lives beside a forest in which roams the
deadly lioness should be always vigilant. Who knows
when, where, and on whom that Bhīmā will pounce next. If from Night
he obtains protection, we shall kill him in the morning."

Then the gem of Raghus addressed friend Vibhīṣaṇa, "If
you would, O best of Rākṣasas, take Lakṣmaṇa along
with you from gate to gate and look in on the soldiers. See
who stands guard tonight and where. All were greatly wearied by

the battle waged with Vīrabāhu. Check around—what is
Aṅgada about; where is Nīla, the great hero; our
ally, Sugrīva, where is he? At this western gate, I
myself shall keep the watch, bow in hand." "By your command," the
champion answered, then set off with the joy of Ūrmilā.
The two of them shone splendidly like Tāraka's slayer
accompanied by the sovereign of the gods, or like the moon,
that fount of nectar, in the presence of the lord of light.

Faithful Pramīlā reached the golden gates of Laṅkā. Horns
blared; war drums rumbled with their ear-splitting pounding. Gigantic
Rākṣasas thundered like Pralaya's thunderclouds, or like
a herd of elephants. Rākṣasa Virūpākṣa flew
into a rage, a *prakṣveḍana* weapon in his hand;
likewise Tālajaṅghā, who held a palm-tree club; and just
so did Pramatta, whose appearance terrified! Horses
whinnied; elephants began their trumpeting; chariot
wheels squawked and squealed; ferocious pikemen brandished pikes; iron-
shafted *nārācas* were launched, blocking out the lord of Night.
The heavens, on fire, filled with tumult, as when, earth quaking,
grumbling thunderously, a volcano spews forth streams of fire
out into the dead of night! In panic, Laṅkā shuddered.

Hot-tempered Nṛmuṇḍamālinī hollered loudly, "Whom
would you slay with your weapons, timid ones, in this darkness?
We are not the foes of Rākṣasas but rather are their
faithful wives! Open up your eyes! See for yourselves!" At once,
gatekeepers seized the bolt and tugged, as it creaked and groaned. With
sounds like that of thunder, those gates now parted. Joyous, the
pretty one entered golden Laṅkā to cries of "Victory!"

As when moths spot a flame, then cluster round in glee, so too
came the townsfolk on the run from all directions. The wives
among them produced auspicious calls of *ululu* and
showered them with flowers while, inspired, bards extolled them
to the strains of music. Those dashing women marched ahead,
as do waves of fire through a densely wooded forest. The
Vidyādharī-like musicians played on their *vīṇā*, flute,
muraja drums, and tiny cymbals. Horses neighed as they
pranced high. Swords jangled in their sheaths. Babies woke up startled
in their mother's lap. Many maiden Rākṣasas opened
peepholes, peered through, then, delighted, praised the prowess of that

Pramīlā. Shortly she, consumed by love, reached her husband's
home—like a serpent, jewel lost, on finding it again!

Foe-defeating Indrajit spoke in a lighthearted vein,
"After besting Raktabīja, you now return, I guess,
to Kailāsa and your home, my moon-faced one? If you so
order, I shall fall before your feet, for I am your most
constant servant, O Cāmuṇḍā!" Smiling, his wife said, "By
the grace of your two feet, my lord, this slave has overcome
the world; I cannot, however, overcome Manmatha.
Contemptuous of the arrow's fire, yet ever do I
dread the fires (most inexplicable) of separation
from you. It causes me to come to whom my heart desires
always! as the playful river flows to the sea at last."

So saying, that chaste one stepped into the house, divesting
her person of her martial raiment. She then put on a
white silk sari with gem-embroidered border and fastened
tight across her comely breasts a bodice. On her hips shone
an ornamental girdle; a diamond necklace and a
string of pearls swung to and fro upon her bosom. The part
in her hair was lined with a twinkling starry headdress from
which a single jewel dangled on her forehead, while the
hue of gems sparkled from her tresses, and earrings from her
ears. That stunning beauty had donned these many ornaments.
The crown-gem of Rākṣasas, Meghanāda, floated on
the sea of bliss as the couple took their seat upon a
throne of gold. A troupe of singers serenaded, dancing
girls performed—as do Vidyādharas and Vidyādharīs
in their heavenly abode. Forgetting their own sorrows,
birds sang from inside cages. Fountains gurgled, gushed upward,
as does the ocean at a moonbeam's touch. Spring breezes blew
honeyed tones, as when the king of seasons sports with woodlands
lovingly throughout sweet springtime in some secluded spot.

Accompanied by Vibhīṣaṇa, lionesque Saumitri
at this point proceeded to the northern gate; high-minded
Sugrīva stood guard himself, vigilant with his troop of
warriors, immovable in war—like peaks of the Vindhya
mountain range. At the eastern gate was Nīla, an awesome
figure; goddess Sleep importuned him there in vain. Before
the southern gate prowled prince Aṅgada, as does a hungry

lion hunting food, or as does Nandī, with spear in hand,
before Kailāsa's peak. Smokeless bonfires in the hundreds
burned round about encircling Laṅkā, like the moon in a
clear sky amid encircling stars. At each of the four gates
a company of warriors stood watch—as when, by the grace
of rain clouds, cultivated crops grow day by day and on
a platform raised beside the field a peasant stands alert,
scaring off the herds of deer, huge water buffalo, and
other sorts of herbivorous beasts. These troops of warriors,
the bane of Rākṣasas, were on duty all round Laṅkā.

Quite satisfied, the two of them retraced their steps to the
tent where, composed and calm, waited warrior Dāśarathi.

With a smile, Umā, in Kailāsa, addressed Vijayā
saying, "Gaze down, my moon-faced one, toward Laṅkā. In warrior's
garb shapely Pramīlā now enters through the city gates,
escorted by her ranks of women. The luster from her
golden breastplate reaches to the skies. They stand dumbfounded,
look, that gem of mankind, Rāghava, Saumitri, their friend
Vibhīṣaṇa, and all those other warriors. Who in the
world of men possesses such exquisite beauty? I once
dressed in such attire, during the Satya *yuga*, in
order to destroy the Dānavas. There, listen to that
ominous sound! Drawing back the bowstring, that lady snaps
it angrily and shouts. All about, the monstrous army
trembles. See, the diadem upon her hair bun dances.
That woman with the fairest skin now crests, now troughs as her
mount canters on—ah, goodness me—like a golden lotus
upon the undulating ripples of Lake Mānasa!"

Her confidante, Vijayā, answered, "True enough, what you
say, Haimavatī—who indeed in the world of mankind
has such beauty? I know Pramīlā, heroic daughter
of the Dānavas, is your thrall. But consider this, O
Bhavānī—how will you keep your promise? Indrajit, in
power, is himself world-victor; now Pramīlā has joined
with him—flame, the wind's companion, has joined the wind itself!
Tell me now, Kātyāyanī, how will you rescue Rāma?
And how will champion Lakṣmaṇa destroy the Rākṣasa?"

Śaṅkarī thought a moment, then replied, "My beautiful
Pramīlā was born a part of me, Vijayā. I shall,

come morning, withdraw from her my power. As the gem, which
dazzles from the touch of brilliant sunlight, turns lackluster
at the close of day, in like fashion I shall enervate
that woman on the morrow. No doubt, in combat champion
Lakṣmaṇa will vanquish Meghanāda! Pramīlā and
husband will come here. Rāvaṇi will serve our Śiva; and
we shall welcome Pramīlā, making her my companion."

That said, Satī went inside her house. On silent footsteps
goddess Sleep approached Kailāsa, whose inhabitants gained
respite on their beds of blooms. The crescent moon on Bhava's
forehead brightened, spreading through the house a silvery cast.

Thus ends canto number three,
called "Reuniting,"
in the poem
The Slaying of Meghanāda.

CANTO 4

Ashoka Grove

I bow before you, guru among poets, before your
lotus feet, Vālmīki. O crown-gem upon the head of
Bhārata, I, your slave, humbly follow after you just
as the wretched poor follow as camp followers of an
Indra among kings when that king goes on a pilgrimage
to a sacred spot. Meditating day and night on foot-
prints you have left, how many pilgrims before me have gained
entrance to fame's temple, by subduing world-subduing
Śamana—to become immortal. Śrī Bhartṛhari;
scholar Bhavabhūti, called Śrīkaṇṭha; a man of marked
mellifluence, Kālidāsa—known throughout Bhārata
as the favorite son of Bhāratī; most captivating
Murāri, epitome of his namesake's melodic
flute; and poet Kṛttivāsa, a repository of
achievements, ornament of this Bengal.—O forefather,
how am I to sport with regal geese upon the lake of
poetic *rasa* if you do not guide me? I shall string
anew a garland after plucking blossoms tenderly
from your literary garden. I strive to beautify
our language with divers decorations, but where shall I
(impoverished me!) obtain that gem cache, Ratnākara, if
you do not help? Show compassion, lord, to this needy one.
Golden Laṅkā, swimming in a sea of bliss, was ringed with
golden lamps, like an Indra-among-monarch's queen in her
necklace made of precious stones. From building after building
music could be heard; troupes of dancing girls performed, singers
sang sweet strains; loving women dallied lovingly with their
men, honeyed high-pitched giggles bubbling from their lips. Some were
occupied with love play; others sipped on spirits made of
sugarcane. On doorways garlands strung with fruits and flowers
hung. From the fronts of houses banners fluttered; lamps burned in
windows; and streams of people flowed through the thoroughfares in
uproarious waves of sheer delight, as during some grand
festival when the city's residents go wild. Heaps of
blossoms rained down from all sides—the town grew redolent with

sweet aroma. Laṅkā that night was awake at midnight;
Sleep went door to door, but none bid her step inside his home
or even begged the boon of rest. "Tomorrow Indrajit,
Indra among warriors, will slay Rāma. He will put down
Lakṣmaṇa. He, with a lion's roar, will drive that pack of
jackal foes to the ocean's shore. He will bind and drag back
here that Vibhīṣaṇa—will chase away that Rāhu from
the moon, and thus the eyes of earth will be refreshed when once
again they gaze upon this wealth of nectar moonbeams." Hope,
a sorceress, sang her song down streets and lanes, by temples,
parks, from doorways, and in homes that night in the stronghold of
those Rākṣasas—and why should not they float on joyful seas?

In the Aśoka Grove, alone, aggrieved, the beloved
of the Rāghava wept silently in her darkened hut.
Unruly guardian matrons had abandoned that chaste
one and were pacing some ways off, all intoxicated
by the thrill of gaieties—just as the tigress leaves a
dying doe and, bold at heart, further prowls the forest. The
woman's face was pale, aha, like sunstone crystal in
the dark recesses of a mine (where rays of sunshine fail
to reach) or like Ramā, *bimba*-lipped, beneath the waters.
Pavana sighed like a mourner at a distance, heaving
with emotions. In sorrow, leaves quaked and rustled. Birds perched
mutely on branches. Blossoms fell in piles round about tree
trunks as though the trees, consumed by burning heartaches, were of
themselves tearing off their finery. Afar a river—
the loud lapping of her ripples like snuffling cries—headed
for the ocean as if to tell the lord of waters of
this tale of woe. Moonbeams could not so much as penetrate
that thick forest. In foul waters does the lotus ever
bloom? Yet still that grove was splendid from her matchless beauty.

The woman sat alone, like radiant Prabhā in a
somber hovel. At such a time pretty Saramā came
crying and sat at the chaste one's feet—pretty Saramā,
the Rākṣasas' Rājalakṣmī, dressed as one of their wives.

For some time that bright-eyed one dabbed at her tears, then in a
soothing voice spoke, "Those uncouth matrons left you here alone,
my lady, and returned to the city where all enjoy
the celebrating on this night. Learning that, I came to

worship at your feet. I brought along a container of
vermilion. If you permit, I shall place a dot upon
your pretty forehead. You are a married woman; this garb
of yours hardly suits you. Alas, he is a wicked one,
that lord of Laṅkā! Who could ever tear the petals off
of such a lotus blossom—I fail to comprehend how
he could strip the jewelry from your exquisite person!"
    Opening her canister, the wifely Rākṣasa with
tender care put a spot of powder in the part within
that woman's hair; another spot of color brightly shone
upon her forehead, ah yes, as from Twilight's forehead shines a
gem-star.[1] That dot affixed, Saramā took dust from that one's
feet. "Forgive me, Lakṣmī. I have touched the body craved by
gods, but your slave remains a lifelong servant at your feet."
    And with that, the youthful woman sat down once again at
those feet. Ah goodness me, it was as if a golden lamp
radiated brightly in the ten directions from the
foot of a *tulasī* tree. In a soft voice Maithilī spoke,
    "You reproach Daśānana all for naught, O moon-faced one.
I myself shed my ornaments, casting them away when
that sinful one seized me in our forest hermitage. I
scattered them along the path, as markers. It was that bridge
which brought my clever Raghu lord to this golden Laṅkā.
Gems, pearls, precious stones, what is there in this world which I would
not renounce, my dearest, to regain my treasured husband?"
    Said Saramā, "My lady, this servant of yours heard of
your *svayamvara* from your own ambrosial lips and why
that jewel of the Raghus went into the forest. Please
tell me, chaste one, how that Indra among Rākṣasas snatched
you away? I beg you—slake your humble servant's thirst with
showers of ambrosia. Your unmannerly guardswomen
are now far away. Take this time to tell that tale to me,
for I would hear. By what ruse did that thief trick Rāma and
the worthy Lakṣmaṇa? And by what *māyā* did he slip
into the Raghu's house and purloin such a gem as you?"
    Just as the sacred stream pours out in mellow tones from the

1. Bengali wives put vermilion powder in the part in their hair, a sign that they are married; the spot of color on the forehead is cosmetic adornment.

mouth of Gomukhī, in like manner spoke Jānakī, that
honey-tongued chaste wife, to Saramā with affection, "You
are Sītā's ardent well-wisher, friend. So, if you would like
to hear of past events, then I shall tell you. Listen well.

"We were living, bright-eyes, on the Godāvarī's bank, like
a pair of pigeons who had built their nest atop some tree,
quite tall, and lived contentedly. Round us lay a dense wood,
named Pañcavaṭī, one that seemed much like the garden of
the gods on earth. High-minded Lakṣmaṇa looked after me
at every moment. And I ask you: what does one lack who
has the storehouse of the Daṇḍaka at his disposal?
Warrior Saumitri would always find me fruits and roots. At
times my lord would track wild game; but, dear friend, that heroic
Indra among Rāghavas—he is known throughout the world
as an ocean of compassion—abstained from taking life.

"I forgot all about my former happiness. I, the
daughter of a king, a wife within the Raghu clan—but
in that forest, friend Saramā, I found even greater
joy. In all the four directions round our cottage flowers
full with color bloomed daily—how can I describe it? Spring
roamed the Pañcavaṭī Forest constantly. The king of
cuckoos used to wake us in the morning, cooing sweetly.
Tell me, moon-faced one, what queen opens up her eyes to such
a flattering panegyric? The ecstatic peahen
with her peacock used to dance before my door. Is there a
pair of dancers in this world, good woman, equal to that
twosome? Guests would regularly visit us, bull and cow
elephant calves, fawns, feathered friends, some with golden plumage,
some white, some black, some variegated, like Vāsava's
bow upon the crest of the best of clouds. All were gentle
creatures. I ministered to each and every one with the
tenderest of care; I would nurture them with utmost love,
as a river—itself brimming with water through favor
of the clouds—nurtures the thirsty in a desert. A pond
served as my mirror. I used to pluck blue lotuses (price-
less gems) and wear them in my hair; I would adorn myself
with an array of flowers. My lord would smile, addressing
me teasingly as Vanadevī. Alas, true friend, shall
I gain again the lord of my life? Will these hapless eyes

within this worthless life span once more light upon those feet—
lotuses in hope's lake, objects of my heart's desire? O
harsh Fate, for what transgression do you judge your thrall at fault?"
    Saying that, her ladyship succumbed and wept in silence.
Chaste Saramā cried too, drenched in the water of her tears.
    Moments later, Saramā, the Rākṣasa wife, wiping
dry her tears, addressed chaste Sītā's feet, "If it pains you to
recall the past, my lady, then enough! What is the good
of living it again? I see your tears and want to die!"
    Replied the honey-spoken one (as honey-throated as
kādambā waterfowl), "If, alas, this luckless woman
(dear, you lucky one) should not cry, then who in the world should?
Listen, I shall recount for you what happened. For just as
during the monsoon rains, sweet confidante, a swollen stream,
tormented by floodwaters, overflows her banks and spills
her waters left and right, so too does the agitated
heart spill its tale of woe to others.[2] That is why I speak—
please hear me out. Whom else has Sītā in this hostile land?
    "We were happy on the Godāvarī's riverbank in
that Pañcavaṭī Forest. Alas, companion, how shall
I describe the charm of those deep woods? I would in my dreams
always hear the sylvan *vīṇā* in Vanadevī's hands;
or I would sometimes sit upon a lake shore and watch the
amorous play of heavenly maidens, clothed in sunbeams,
as they sported among lotus clusters. Wives, pure at heart,
of some sage's family would at times, smiling graciously,
come to this servant's cottage, as beams of moonlight come to
a darkened home. I would now and then spread out a deerskin
(oh my, speckled in a hundred shades!) beneath some tree and
sit, speaking to the shade as if she were my bosom friend;
or from time to time I skipped and played with a doe in the
forest and sang again the notes I heard the cuckoo sing.
I gave the young vine to the tree in marriage, chaste one. And
when the couple budded, I kissed the tender sprouts, calling
all of them with pleasure my granddaughters; when the bee buzzed,
respectfully I would hail him as my grandson-in-law.
Sometimes I strolled contentedly with my lord along the

2. Rivers are feminine in Bangla.

river's edge; we would gaze into tremulous waters at
what seemed to be a new sky, new stars, a novel splendor
to the lord of Night. Sometimes we would climb a hillock, dear
friend, and I would sit there at my husband's feet, like a vine
at the foot of a mighty mango tree. With the greatest
sympathy my lord would gratify me with a rain of
nectar-words—ah me, whom shall I tell? how shall I tell of
that? In Kailāsa, so I have heard, Kailāsa's denizen,
Vyomakeśa, sits upon a golden throne with Gaurī;
there in front of Umā, Pañcamukha with eloquence
expounds on topics from the Āgamas, the Purāṇas,
the Vedas, and the Pañcatantra. In like fashion, my
good-looking one, I too used to hear such talks. Even now,
in this deserted forest, I seem to hear that honeyed
discourse. Could such music to this servant's ears be silenced,
O cruel Fate?" In sadness, that wide-eyed woman fell mute. Then
pretty Saramā spoke, "When I listen to your tale, wife
of Rāghava, contempt for courtly pleasures wells up in
me! Willingly would I forsake the comforts of the realm
to go into like exile in the forest. Yet still, it
frightens me to think such thoughts. When the sun's rays penetrate
the dreary woods, my lady, those beams of light themselves make
bright the surrounding forest; when Night comes to a land, all
faces pale at her arrival! So, why should not all be
glad, sweet one, wherever you set foot—you who are bliss to
this world, enchantress of the universe. Tell me, madam,
by what ploy did the sovereign of the Rākṣasas abduct
you? This slave of yours has heard the *vīṇā*'s strains, the call of
the best of cuckoos in among new leaves during springtime's
succulent months, but never in this world have I heard such
honey-coated speech as yours. Look there is the sky, that moon,
whose radiance pales before your beauty, that god, fount of
nectar, smiles as he imbibes your words of nectar, lady.
The cuckoo and all other birds are hushed so as to hear
your tale—I tell you. Speak, faithful wife, fulfill all longings."

The darling of the Rāghava continued, "In this way,
friend, I spent many happy days in the Pañcavaṭī
Forest. Your sister-in-law, that naughty Sūrpaṇakhā,
showed up and ultimately brought disaster. I die of

shame, friend Saramā, recalling what she did! Fie on her!
a blemish upon womankind! That tigress sought to serve
devotedly the best of Raghus after shunting me
aside! Livid with rage, Saumitri the lion drove her
off. Then other Rākṣasas came running, and a battle
royal rang throughout the woods. Frightened, I withdrew inside
our cottage. Whom can I tell, companion, how much I wept
due to the bowstrings' twanging? I shut my eyes, cupped my hands
in prayerful supplication, and called upon the god clan
to save Rāghava. Both anguished cries and leonine roars
rose into the skies. In a faint, I fell upon the ground.

"I know not how long, my fondest, I remained in such a
state; with his touch that greatest Raghu revived your servant.
In a soft voice (indeed, as the gentle breezes sound in
flower gardens during springtime) my husband spoke, 'Arise,
queen of my heart, treasure of this Raghu son, joy of the
Raghu palace! Does such a bed befit you, my gold-limbed
one!' O Saramā, my bosom friend, shall I ever hear
again those sweet tones?" Then, without any warning that chaste
one swooned and collapsed; but Saramā was there to catch her.

Just as deep within the forest the feathered one, twitching
in excruciating pain, falls upon the ground once the
Niṣāda has taken aim at the lilting bird song on
that tree branch and let fly his arrow, just so plummeted
that pure wife of a sudden to the lap of Saramā.

After a while the bright-eyed woman regained consciousness.
Saramā, weeping, spoke, "Forgive my blunder, Maithilī.
I have made you miserable today for no good reason,
alas, senseless me." In a gentle tone of voice that sleek-
haired love of Rāghava replied, "What blunder, friend? Listen
well; I shall resume my tale of days gone by. You have heard
from Sūrpaṇakhā what deception Mārīca had wrought
(as mirages on the desert lead astray!). Alas, my
dear, at an ill-fated moment I, intoxicated
by my greed, begged for that stag. Grabbing bow and arrow, my
Raghu sovereign headed out, leaving me with Lakṣmaṇa,
my brother-in-law, for my protection. That *māyā*-deer
darted off like lightning lighting up the forest. Behind,
fast as the foe of elephants, my husband gave it chase—

unlucky me, I lost the reason for my happiness!
"Then suddenly, kind one, I heard a cry for help far in
the distance, 'Where are you, brother Lakṣmaṇa, at this
time of peril? I am dying!' Saumitri the lion gave
a start. I too started, grasped his hand, and pleaded, 'Warrior,
go with the speed of wind into that woods; see who summons
you! My heart cries out at hearing such a plea! Go quickly—
perhaps it is our Raghu lord who calls, charioteer!'
"Responded Saumitri, 'My lady, how shall I carry
out your order? How can you stay here by yourself, alone,
in these desolate woods? Who knows how many Rākṣasas
with magic powers are afoot in the vicinity?
Of what are you afraid? Who in all three worlds can bring harm
to the ornament of the Raghu clan, who in strength is
Bhṛgurāma's mentor?' Then again I heard that cry for
help, 'I am dying! At this time of peril, where are you,
brother Lakṣmaṇa? Where are you, my Jānakī?' I could
contain myself no longer, dearest one! Letting go the
hand of Lakṣmaṇa I uttered, at that fateful moment,
'My mother-in-law, Sumitrā, a most kind woman—who
says she bore you in her womb, cruel thing? Providence made your
heart of stone! Now I know some mean-souled tigress deep within
the jungle bore and reared you, meanest one! Coward, you
insult to the warrior clan! I shall go, I shall see who
summoned me pathetically from that forest there!' Full of
rage, his eyes now red, that gem of warriors grabbed his bow; in
a wink, he strapped the quiver to his back, stared at me, and
said, 'I honor you as if you were my mother, daughter
of Janaka, as though my very mother. That is why
I tolerate this scolding quite unwarranted. I am
going. Stay inside; be ever on your guard. Who knows what
might take place today. It will not be my fault; I leave you
on your orders.' With that, the champion headed for the woods.
"How much more, my dear companion, shall I tell you of what
passed through my mind as I sat in that deserted spot? The
morning wore on; with joyful sounds, birds, deer, and such, many
fawns, strict vegetarians, elephant calves, both bull and
cow, arrived. To my surprise, I saw a yogi, lustrous
like Vaiśvānara, with ashes covering his body,

an ascetic's *kamaṇḍalu* water pot in hand and
a pile of matted hair upon his head. Ah, confidante,
if only I had known that, in disguise, in amongst the
flowers lurked that vile thing, a deadly viper, a deadly
poison in among pure waters—had I known, would I have
ever fallen prostrate on the ground, head bowed before him?
"Said the one of sorcery, 'Give alms, O Raghu woman
(you who in these woods are Annadā!), to your famished guest.'
"The loose end of the sari, with which one covers up one's
head, I drew out and down, then across my face, dear friend, and,
with palms pressed tight, I uttered, 'Do please have a seat upon
that deerskin mat beneath the tree and rest a while, my lord.
The Indra among Rāghavas will soon return, with his
brother, Saumitri.' That scoundrel said (I failed to see through
his feigned rage), 'I told you, I, your visitor, am hungry.
Give me alms. If you will not, then say so, and I shall go
look elsewhere. Do you, Jānakī, withhold from a guest this
day your hospitality? Do you, Raghu wife, wish to
pour this inky smirch upon the Raghu clan? Tell me, is
it pride that makes you heedless of a Brahmin's curse? Give me
alms, else I shall curse you and be gone. Venal Rākṣasas
are presently the enemies of Sītā's husband—due
to a curse of mine.' So I overcame my shyness and,
alas, dear companion, apprehensive went out bearing
alms—not realizing I had put my foot into his
snare. Then and there your brother-in-law, with a grin, grabbed me.
"Once, my moon-faced one, I was walking through the forest with
the Rāghava; a doe was grazing by a distant bush.
Suddenly I heard an awful clamor; seized with fright I
looked and saw a lightning-bolt-like tiger strike that deer! 'Save
her, husband,' I said, falling at his feet. With a flaming
arrow that best of warriors turned that tiger in a flash
to ashes. With tender care I hugged that forest beauty
then set her free, my friend. The sovereign of the Rākṣasas,
like that very tiger, seized me in his clutches! But no
one happened by to free this hapless doe, my lovely,
at that moment of disaster. I filled the forest with
my woeful cries. And, I heard sounds of wailing; perhaps
Vanadevī, a mother pained by her servant's plight, was

weeping. However, all that crying was in vain. Iron
will melt by fire's power; does a stream of water soften
it? Then will, my dear, the hardened heart yield to drops of tears?
"Off came the mass of matted hair; away, the ascetic's
water pot. In regal charioteer's attire that fool
hoisted me onto his golden chariot. He spoke much,
that perverse fellow, roaring angrily at times, at times
sweet talking; Saramā, I die of shame recalling that!
"That charioteer drove his chariot. And just as cries
the frog, held in the jaws of some lethal snake, so too I
cried, pretty woman, and to no avail. Those golden wheels
creaked and rattled, inundating with their noise the forest,
alas, drowning out this luckless woman's screams for help. When
trees, frightened by the power of Prabhañjana, thrash and
crash about, who can hear the pigeon coo? Finding myself
in difficulty, I forthwith, friend, stripped off my bracelets,
bangles, necklace, my tiara, choker, earrings, anklets,
and ornamental girdle. I scattered them along the
way. That is why no ornaments adorn my wretched frame,
Rākṣasa wife. You rebuke Daśānana all for naught."
The moon-faced one fell silent. Then Saramā spoke, "Your slave
is thirsty still, Maithilī; please give another draught of
nectar to her. Such a gift makes ears today seem useful!"
In sweetest tones that one whose face is like the moon resumed,
"If you indeed are bent on knowing, then listen well, my
woman, for who but you will hear Vaidehī's woeful tale?
"Just as the Niṣāda, once he has caught a bird within
his snare, returns home joyously, Laṅkā's sovereign in like
fashion drove his chariot; and alas, dear one, just as
that bird cries as it flutters anxiously, attempting to
break free from fetters, likewise I too cried, my pretty one!
" 'O sky, I have heard you carry sounds (I prayed silently),
shout out this slave's plight there where are that Raghu crown-gem and
my husband's brother, Lakṣmaṇa, that world-conqueror! O
Samīra, you who carry scents; I, at your courier-
feet, respectfully implore you: go quickly to where roams
my lord! O cloud, you who bellow fearsomely, call to my
husband with your thunderous rumblings! O bumblebee, honey
maker, leave your blooms and buzz the news of Sītā round the

grove where that warrior, Indra among Rāghavas, is now;
sing Sītā's song of woe in your *pā*-note tune, O cuckoo,
companion of Springtime! His lordship will listen to you
if you sing!' In this manner I lamented, but none heard.

"The golden chariot moved on, nimbly dodging the sky-
splitting mountain peaks, forests, rivers, streams, and sundry lands.
You have seen with your own eyes, Saramā, the speed of that
Puṣpaka; what is the point of saying more about it?

"A short while later I heard in front of us a lion's
terrifying roar. Our team of horses, frightened, bolted;
the golden chariot lurched unsteady. With my eyes wide
open I saw perched upon a mountain's back a warrior,
the spitting image of Bhairava, like some black cloud when
Pralaya happens! 'I know you,' boomed that best of warriors.
'You thief, you are Laṅkā's Rāvaṇa. What married woman
have you filched today, horrid one? Whose house did you darken,
snuffing out its lamp of love? You make a habit of this
sort of thing, I know well. By slaying you with keen arrows,
I shall wipe away today the stain on all who would bear
arms! Come forward, witless one! Fie on you, Rākṣasa king!
Is there a reprobate as shameless in this whole wide world?'

"And with that said, my friend, the Indra among champions roared.
I myself fainted on the spot, there in the chariot.

"When I regained consciousness I found that I was lying
on the ground. Through the skies, the Rākṣasa charioteer
in his chariot warred with that other warrior, shouting
menacingly. Can a woman's tongue, my lovely lady,
recount such conflict? Afraid, I shut my eyes. And sobbing,
I importuned the god clan to come to the aid of that
warrior to overcome the Rākṣasa, my enemy,
then rescue me, this slave, from present danger. I resolved
to plunge into the forest, to flee to distant lands. But
alas, dear, I, stumbling, fell, as if felled by a violent
earthquake. I then prayed to Mother Earth, 'In this forsaken
land, O Mother, open up your bosom, purest woman,
and take in this unfortunate one! How can you bear your
saddened daughter's torment? Come quickly! That foulest one will
soon be back, alas, my mother, as a thief goes back in
dead of night to where he buried secretly his stash of

jewels—another's riches! Come rescue me, O Mother!'
"A booming battle raged throughout the skies, my pretty one.
The earth shook; the environs filled with noise. Again I lost
consciousness. Listen, gentlewoman, listen closely, friend,
to this unprecedented tale. In a dream I saw my
mother, my chaste Mother Earth. That lady of compassion
came to me, her thrall, and drawing me to her side, uttered
these sweet words, 'It is according to Fate's wish, my child, that
the king of Rākṣasas should kidnap you, dear one; because
of you, that lowlife with his line will be expunged. I can
not bear this burden, and so it was that I conceived you
in my womb, dear one, to lay waste Laṅkā. At the fateful
moment when foul Rāvaṇa had touched your person, I knew
Fate had finally turned toward me; and I gave my blessings to
you. You, Maithilī, eased your mother's suffering. Now I
shall open up the doors on what will come to pass; do look.'
"Companion, I saw before me a cloud-piercing mountain;
there, as though all drowning in a sea of sorrow, were five
warriors. At such a time my Raghu sovereign arrived with
Lakṣmaṇa. On witnessing my lord's drawn face, confidante,
I grew worried—what more can I say of how I wept? Those
five warriors bowed before the Rāghava king and his younger
brother. Together, they then went into a charming city.
"The Raghu warrior, having slain the local raja in
pitched battle, placed the finest of those five upon the throne.
Messengers ran off in all the four directions; warriors,
thousands and thousands, lion-like, came scampering, raising
a horrible din. The earth trembled, my friend, beneath the
weight of those warriors' feet. Afraid, I closed my eyes. But my
mother, smiling, said, 'Of what are you, Jānakī, afraid?
King Sugrīva, best of allies, marshals troops to free
you. The champion your husband slew was known as Vāli, a
king renowned throughout the world. That city is Kiṣkindhyā.
Look there, a company of heroes, all comparable to
Indra, arms.' I looked and saw arrayed those Indras among
warriors, streaming like a flow of water during monsoon
rains, roaring threateningly. The dense forest split asunder
with a horrendous thud; streams dried up; forest creatures dashed
away, panic stricken; the whole world, friend, filled with rumblings.

"The army reached the ocean's shore. There I saw, Saramā,
my dear, stones afloat on water; many hundred warriors
grabbed hold of mountains, wrenched them free with a mighty heave, and
flung them in the water. Artisans at work in concert
built a wondrous bridge. By my lord's command, the monarch of
the waters, that very Pāśī, placed fetters round his own
legs. With that ocean, incapable of being spanned, now
spanned, the soldiers swaggered on across. And this golden land
reeled beneath the pressure of those hostile feet. 'Victory,
Raghu sovereign, victory!' all cheered. I wept for joy, my
confidante. Inside his golden dwelling place I saw the
sovereign of the Rākṣasas on his throne of gold. Within
the assembly hall there stood one warrior, wise like Dharma
incarnate, who said, 'Worship the best of Raghus; return
Vaidehī lest you and yours should perish.' But the foe of
Rāghava, drunk upon the liquor of this worldly life,
kicked and swore at him. His feelings hurt, that elephant of
warriors defected to my life's lord's side." Said Saramā,
"My ladyship, how can I ever tell you how saddened
by your sorrow was the sovereign Rākṣasa's heroic
younger brother. We both cried far more than I can tell you,
chaste one, when we thought of you." "I know," replied beautiful
Maithilī, "I know that Vibhīṣaṇa is my greatest
benefactor. Likewise, you, friend Saramā. That luckless
Sītā lives today is due solely to your kindness, kind
one. But listen, I continue with my marvelous dream.

"Then the Rākṣasa throng prepared for war; the Rākṣasa
musicians played; and a great cacophony rose into
the skies. I shivered, friend, to see that band of warriors, as
spirited as Hutāśana, mighty as a lion.
How shall I speak of all the battle that ensued? There flowed
a river of blood. I saw a pile of corpses, mountain
high, hideous, grisly. There came the headless Kabandha—
ghosts, ghouls, and Dānavas—vultures, buzzards, and all manner
of carrion-eating birds; packs of jackals and countless
dogs gathered there. Laṅkā filled with fear-instilling noises.

"I saw the Karbūra lord once more in his assembly
hall, but now his face seemed haggard, tears washed his eyes, for he
was grieving. His pride had been humbled in pitched battle by

the prowess of the Rāghava, my dearest! Sadly the
Rākṣasa king spoke, 'Aha, Fate, is this what you had in
mind? Go, all of you, and carefully awake my brother
Kumbhakarṇa, the very double of trident-holding
Śambhu. Who can save the clan of Rākṣasas if he can
not?' That group of Rākṣasas sped off; music issued in
shrill blasts; and the womenfolk let out calls of *ululu*.
Cutting a huge figure, that Rākṣasa charioteer
strode in among the troops. But my lord, with keenest arrows
(who, dear, in the world shows such dexterity?), split his head
in two! That domineering champion died, as he awoke,
before his time! I got a tingling feeling, bosom friend,
when I heard them holler out, 'Hail! Victory to Rāma!'
Rāvaṇa wept. And golden Laṅkā wailed aloud with grief.

"I became, my friend, uneasy when I heard the weeping
all around. I said to my mother, as I hugged her feet,
'My heart bursts, Mother, from the sorrows of the Rākṣasa
clan. This servant of yours ever is distressed to see the
distress of another; forgive me, Mother.' Mother Earth
responded smiling, 'Dearest Raghu wife, what you have seen
is absolutely true. Your husband will rout Laṅkā and
punish Rāvaṇa. Open up your eyes and look once more.'

"I saw, dear Saramā, a gathering of heavenly
maidens, various jewelry upon their limbs, wearing
garlands made of *mandāra* blooms and attired in silken
garments. They gathered round me, smiling. One said, 'Arise, chaste
one, vile Rāvaṇa was finally killed in war.' Another
said, 'Arise at once, treasure of that Raghu son, bathe in
scented waters, woman, and dress in sundry finery.
Goddess Śacī, consort of the Indra of the gods, will
bestow this very day Sītā to the spouse of Sītā.'

"I spoke, friend Saramā, hands humbly palm to palm, 'What use,
O heavenly maids, are these clothes and jewelry to this
thrall? With your permission, I shall go like this to my lord;
let the gem of men see poor Sītā in her beggar's rags!'

"The godly maidens answered, 'Listen, dearest Maithilī.
Gems crystallize deep in dirty mines, but the giver cleans
one off before presenting it into the monarch's hand.'

"Now weeping, now smiling, friend, I hurriedly got dressed. I

glimpsed my husband not far removed, alas, dearest, looking
like the ray-ringed sun god on the golden rising-hill. Half
crazed, I ran, my sweet-faced one, and fell at his feet. Just then
I awoke. Suddenly, O bosom friend, a room turns black
when the lamp goes out; that same thing happened to me—my world
went dark all around. O Fate, why did I not die then and
there? In hopes of what does this wretched life remain within
my body?" The moon-faced one fell silent, as a *vīṇā*,
silenced when its strings snap. Saramā (Rājalakṣmī of
the clan of Rākṣasas, but dressed as one among their wives)
spoke sobbingly, "You shall have your husband back, daughter of
Janaka. I tell you, this dream of yours is true. Stones do
float on water; hero Kumbhakarṇa, terror of gods,
Daityas, and of men, has indeed been felled in combat; and
now Vibhīṣaṇa serves the winning Raghu lord with his
thousands upon thousands of brave warriors. Paulastya sure
will die, thus receiving his just punishment; that wicked
one will take with him his entire line. Now tell me, what
next happened. My eagerness to hear the story knows no
limit." Once again the chaste one spoke in sweetest tones, "I
opened up my eyes, my moon-faced friend, and saw before me
Rāvaṇa; on the ground, alas, lay that lion among
warriors, like the highest mountain peak, now crushed by lightning.

"The enemy of Rāghava then spoke, 'Open wide your
lotus eyes; see, my dear, the prowess of a Rāvaṇa,
you whose face is like the moon. The world-renowned Jaṭāyu
dies today by the very strength of these, my arms. It was
his own fault that he, the stupid son of Garuḍa, should
perish. Who told that rustic fool to pick a fight with me?'

" 'I died in warfare, Rāvaṇa, defending *dharma*,' said
that champion in a weakened voice. 'I fell in face-to-face
combat and shall go to the gods' abode. But what is there
for you anon? Consider! Greedy one, you, a jackal,
lusted for a lioness. So, who can save you now, O
Rākṣasa? O lord of Laṅkā, you have placed yourself in
jeopardy by stealing this fine jewel of a woman.'

"With that, the warrior ceased to speak. Laṅkā's sovereign hoisted
me again onto the chariot. Hands cupped reverently,
I cried out, friend, to that best of warriors, 'My name is Sītā,

Janaka's daughter, a servile wife among the Raghus,
sir! If you, my lordship, meet the Rāghava, tell him this
sinful one abducted me, finding me alone at home!'
"With a percussive clamor, the chariot lifted off
into the sky. Next I heard a horrible racket; straight
ahead I saw the ocean full of billowing blue waves.
Fathomless, shoreless waters mounted surging crests of white-
caps, in constant motion. I wished to leap into that sea,
my friend, and drown; but that heinous one prevented me from
doing so. In my heart I called out to the sovereign of
the waters and the creatures in the sea, but none heard or
paid attention to this woman in distress. The golden
chariot rushed through the firmament with desire's speed.
"There ahead Laṅkā shone before us radiantly. This
golden city, friend, is a pleasing beauty mark upon
the ocean's forehead. But even were a prison made of
gold, my dear, would its glow seem beautiful to a prisoner's
eyes? Just because the cage is golden, is a bird therein
incarcerated, dearest, content in that confinement?
Constantly unhappy is the bird who frolics in the
forest when you place it in that cage. I was born at a
star-crossed moment, pretty Saramā. Tell me, friend, who
has ever heard a tale like this? I am both the daughter
of a king and wife in a line of kings, yet still I am
confined to prison!" That beautiful one broke down and wept,
her arms about Saramā's neck; and Saramā wept too.
Moments later bright-eyed Saramā wiped away the tears,
then said, "My lady, who can contravene Fate's decree? What
Mother Earth has said is true. It is Fate's wish, and that is
why Laṅkā's sovereign kidnapped you, bringing you to this land.
That wicked one, inclusive of his whole clan, will perish.
What other warriors are there in this warrior-spawning land?
Where, chaste woman, are all the soldiers who can conquer the
three worlds? Look there, on the seashore, that pack of scavengers
gorge themselves gleefully on a pile of corpses. Listen
well, widowed women sob in house after house. Your night of
sorrow soon will end. I told you, your dream will come true. A
troupe of Vidyādharīs will shortly garland you with blooms
of *mandāra* and adorn that shapely form of yours. You

will greet the Rāghava, just as charming Mother Earth greets
sweetly succulent Spring. Do not forget, pure wife, this slave
of yours. However long I live I shall keep your image
in the temple of my heart and worship it joyfully,
just as daily, when Night arrives, the pond in ecstasy
offers worship to that wealth of moonlight. You have suffered
much in this land, sleek-haired one. But this thrall of yours is not
to blame." Said Maithilī with music in her voice, "My boon
companion, Saramā, what greater sympathizer in
this world have I than you? To me, you are a river in
the desert, Rākṣasa wife! You took the form of cooling
shade to soothe sun-scorched me! You are the very essence of
compassion in this place of no compassion! You are a
lotus in these muddy waters! You are the jewel that
is imbedded in the forehead of this snakelike golden
Laṅkā! What more can I say? Sītā is a pauper, while
you, dear, are a priceless gem! When the impoverished find
such a gem, do they ever treat it lightly, lovely one?"
Bowing low to Sītā's feet, Saramā responded, "Bid
this slave of yours farewell, kind one. My heart wants not to leave,
lotus of the Raghu clan. But the sovereign of my heart
serves Rāghava. If Laṅkā's lord were to learn I addressed
your two feet, he would be furious and I in danger."
Maithilāi spoke, "Companion, go home quickly; I hear foot-
steps in the distance; perhaps the matrons are returning."
Like a doe once frightened, fleet-footed Saramā was off;
her ladyship remained behind in that deserted grove,
like a solitary flower blossom in the forest.

Thus ends canto number four,
called "Aśoka Grove,"
in the poem
The Slaying of Meghanāda.

CANTO 5

Preparations

Star-studded Night smiled from her heavenly abode, but, at
Vaijayanta, Mahendra fretted. Arising from his
flower-bed, the celestial regions' lord sat mute on his
gemmed throne—other gods lay fast asleep in golden temples.
Feigning wounded pride, the queen of the skies spoke coyly, "By
what fault, O monarch of divines, has your thrall offended
you? Else why do you withhold the touch of your feet from our
bedchamber? See there, Menakā's heavy eyelids droop shut
for a moment, then again she opens wide, startled; and
look at Urvaśī, practically unmoving now. Charming
Citralekhā seems as if a painted doll. It is in
dread of you, husband, that respite-giving goddess Sleep keeps
her distance; for whom else does she have to fear? In dead of
night, tell me, please, who is still awake, anywhere? Is there
some Daitya army camped at heaven's gates, set to attack?"
Replied the foe of Asuras, "I am worried, goddess.
How will champion Lakṣmaṇa slay the Rākṣasa? Chaste one,
invincible is Rāvaṇi, Indra among warriors."
"You have, my husband, garnered weapons," responded ever
youthful Paulomī, "with which the champion Tārakāri
slew Tāraka. It is your good luck that Virūpākṣa
sides with you. Pārvatī herself decreed, upon request
of me, her humble servant, that what you wish would come to
pass tomorrow. Māyā, queen among the goddesses, will
herself arrange the slaying—so, why worry, dearest spouse?"
Replied the foe of Daityas, "What you say is very true,
queen of the Indra among gods; those weapons I, indeed,
have sent to Laṅkā. But by what stratagem will Māyā
maintain Lakṣmaṇa in his war with Rākṣasas, my wide-
eyed one—that I cannot imagine. I am well aware
Sumitrā's son is a great hero; but when, my goddess,
is the elephant an even match against the king of
beasts? I have heard the roll of thunder, my fine-featured one,
the loud crackling of the clouds; I have seen the lightning flash,
those streaks of fire ever scintillate upon my transport.

But my heart quakes, goddess, when Meghanāda roars enraged,
when that archer sets to bow a fiery arrow cluster
and howls his hideous howl; even Airāvata quails
when faced with that one's ghastly bludgeon!" Heaving a sigh of
dejection, the lord of the divines fell silent; herself
sighing sadly (a true wife's heart laments her husband's grief
always), heaven's queen took her seat beside the Indra of
the gods. Urvaśī, Menakā, Rambhā, and the charming
Citralekhā stood around them, just as on a pond at
night beams of nectar from the moon surround in silence closed
lotus blooms, or as a row of lamps surrounds Ambikā's
altar during the autumn Durgā Pūjā when Bengal,
beside herself with joy, welcomes home her ever longed-for
little mother! Without a sound the couple sat there. At
that very moment there arrived the goddess Māyā. A
refulgence born of gems increased twofold in that godly
dwelling, just as golden splendor from *mandāra* blossoms
in the paradisiacal garden, Nandana by
name, is accentuated from sunbeams' intertwining.

With much deference that god and goddess bowed before her
lotus feet. Māyā blessed them both, then took her seat upon
her throne of gold. Hands cupped in supplication, the wealth of
the divines inquired, "Your wish, Mother? Inform this slave."

Replied the one possessed of *māyā*, "I am setting off
for Laṅkā, Āditeya; there I shall satisfy your
wish and crush the crown-gem of the clan of Rākṣasas this
day by stealth. Notice, Night slips away. Purandara, soon
that world-delighting Dawn will make her smiling presence known
upon the summit of the rising-hill; lotus-Laṅkā's
sun will then descend the setting-hill. I shall escort, O
enemy of Asuras, Lakṣmaṇa to the temple
of the sacrifice called Nikumbhilā. And I shall snare
the Rākṣasa in a net of *māyā*. Himself devoid
of weapons, that hero weakened by a blow from godly
weaponry and helpless (like a lion in a snare) will
perish—who can contravene Fate's edict? Rāvaṇi shall
die for sure in battle; but once the ruling Rākṣasa
is informed, how will you rescue Rāmānuja, Rāma,
and wise Vibhīṣaṇa, the Raghu's ally? Overwrought

with grieving for his son, that champion will then join the fray,
O Indra of the gods, fierce-armed like Kṛtānta himself.
Who can best him? Consider what I say, lord of the gods."
Answered Śacī's husband, the slayer of Namuci, "If
Meghanāda were to fall, felled by Saumitri's arrows,
O grand Māyā, I, with an army of the gods, would join
the war against the Rākṣasas tomorrow and rescue
Lakṣmaṇa. By your grace, O goddess, I have no fear of
Rāvaṇa! You first strike a blow, Mother, spreading out your
net of *māyā*. Strike down the pride of the Karbūra clan,
that Rāvaṇi, in war a fearsome fighter. Rāghava-
candra is the favored of the god clan; the immortals
would do battle for him, Mother, as though their very lives
depended on it. I personally tomorrow shall go
to earth, shall burn those Karbūras with swift shafts of lightning."
"That is indeed your proper task, thunderbolt-wielding son
of Aditi," said Māyā, "I am heartened by your words,
best of gods. Now by your leave, I shall be off to Laṅkā."
With that, the queen of Śaktis blessed them both and left. Sleep then
drew near and humbly bowed before the Indra of the gods.
Grasping Indrāṇī's lotus hand lightheartedly, the great
Indra went inside their sleeping chamber—blissful haven.
Citralekhā, Urvaśī, Menakā, and Rambhā—all
departed quickly for their own quarters. There they shed their
bracelets, waistbands, jingling girdles, anklet bells, and other
ornaments; they doffed their bodices, then lay upon their
flower beds, those celestial beauties, figures just like sun-
beams. Breezes—melodious, mellifluous—wafted, now
through ringlets, now atop high breasts, now across their moonlike
faces—amorous, they sported, as do tipsy honey-
bees when they come upon full-blown blossoms in the forest.
Grand goddess Māyā reached heaven's golden gates; on their own
those gold doors opened sweetly. That captivating woman,
once outside, calling goddess Dream to mind, spoke liltingly,
"Go to Laṅkā, to where champion Saumitri is encamped.
Dressed as Sumitrā, take your seat at the head of his bed
and tell him this, voluptuous one, 'Get up, my child, for
Night has gone. At Laṅkā's northern gate among a stand of
trees there shines a lake; on its bank rests a golden Caṇḍī

temple. Bathe in that lake, then pluck a bunch of flowers and
offer worship most devotedly to that mother who
quells Dānavas. By her grace, celebrated one, will you
with ease destroy the frenzied Rākṣasa. Alone, my pet,
proceed into those woods.' Goddess Dream, without adieu, go
to Laṅkā. See there, Night retreats. There can be no delay."
    Off went Dream, the goddess. Blue skies intensified while stars
appeared as if to flake away and fall to earth. Quickly
she descended into Rāmānuja's tent; disguised as
Sumitrā, that sorceress sat by his head and whispered
tenderly, "Get up, my child, for Night has gone. At Laṅkā's
northern gate among a stand of trees there shines a lake; on
its bank rests a golden Caṇḍī temple. Bathe in that lake,
then pluck a bunch of flower blossoms and offer worship
reverently to the mother who quells Dānavas. By her
grace, O celebrated one, will you with ease destroy
the frenzied Rākṣasa. Go alone, my pet, into those woods."
    Startled, that hero rose and gazed round about. Alas, an
unchecked gush of tears made moist his chest. "O Mother," cried out
plaintively that Indra among warriors, "why are you so
callous toward this slave of yours? Show yourself again that I
might worship those two feet of yours; to take the dust from them
would gratify my heart's fond dream, Mother fondest! When I
call to mind how much you wept as I bid farewell, my heart
breaks! In this worthless life of mine, Mother, shall I ever
see your pair of feet again?" Wiping dry the rivulets
of tears, that elephant of warriors strode with the gait of
pachyderms to where his lord, monarch of the Raghus, stood.
    Said the younger-born, bowing to his elder brother's feet,
"I just saw a wondrous dream, sovereign of the Raghu clan.
Near the head of my bed sat my mother, Sumitrā, who
said most tenderly, 'Get up, my child, for Night has gone. At
Laṅkā's northern gate among a stand of trees there shines a
lake; on its bank rests a golden Caṇḍī temple. Bathe in
the lake, then pluck a bunch of flowers and offer worship
most devotedly to the mother who quells Dānavas.
By her grace, celebrated one, will you with ease destroy
the frenzied Rākṣasa. Alone, my pet, proceed into
those woods.' Having said that, Mother disappeared. I cried out

but got no answer. What is your command, gem of Raghus?"
Vaidehī's joy asked Vibhīṣaṇa, "What do you say, O
best among confederates? You are known throughout the world
as Rāghava's rescuer in this land of Rākṣasas."
Replied the finest of the Rākṣasas, "There is in the
woods, my lordship, a Caṇḍī temple on the lake shore. The
ruler of the Rākṣasas worships Satī in that grove.
No one else ever goes there, intimidated by that
frightful place. I have heard that Śambhu—fearsome trident in
his hand—stalks about the entrance. He who worships Mother
there is victorious throughout the world. What more can I
say? If you have the nerve, Saumitri, to penetrate those
woods, then, O charioteer, all your wishes will come true."
"O most excellent of Rākṣasas, this servant follows
Rāghava's command," responded hero Lakṣmaṇa, "if
ordered, I shall go forth with ease into that forest. Who
is there to thwart me?" In honeyed tones the monarch of the
Rāghavas declared, "You have suffered much on my account,
dear one. When I dwell on that, my heart wants not to impose
upon you further. But what am I to do? How could I
go against a godly order, Brother? Proceed with care—
and with the force of *dharma*, great hero! Let favor from
the god clan protect you, as if armor made of iron!"
Bowing to Rāghava's feet and hailing Vibhīṣaṇa,
Saumitri, sword in hand, set off fearless, moving in haste
toward the northern gateway. There confederate Sugrīva
stood alert, the very image of a Vītihotra
in among his troops. On hearing footsteps, the champion barked
gruffly, "Who are you? For what purpose are you here on this
dark night? Speak at once, if you wish to live! Otherwise, I
shall crush your head with stones!" Retorted Rāmānuja good-
naturedly, "Destruction to the clan of Rākṣasas, O
gem of warriors! I serve Rāghava." Advancing smartly,
Sugrīva saluted Lakṣmaṇa his comrade, Indra
among warriors. Mollifying with kind words Kiṣkindhyā's
king, the joy of Ūrmilā continued further northward.
A while later, that one of mighty limbs reached the entrance
to the grove, and much to his surprise saw not far ahead
a gigantic figure. From its forehead shone a crescent

moon, just like the gemstone on a monstrous serpent's forehead.
Atop its head sat a pile of matted hair onto which
there poured the frothy waters of the Jāhnavī, like some
silvery streak of moonlight on an autumn night across
the surface of a heap of clouds. Its body had been smeared
with ashes; in its right hand, a trident massive like a
śāla tree. Saumitri recognized the lord of Bhūtas.
Unsheathing his shining sword, that lion among warriors
roared, "Charioteer Daśaratha, son of Raghu's son,
Aja, world-renowned—it is his son—this slave—who bows
before your feet, Candracūḍa! Let me pass, for I shall
march into the woods and worship Caṇḍī; if unwilling,
then battle me, your minion! The overlord of Laṅkā
is engaged in deeds opposed to *dharma*; should you choose to
wage war on his side, Virūpākṣa, then let us fight—I
brook no delays! With Dharma as my witness, I challenge
you—if Dharma be for justice, I shall win for certain!"

As the king of mountains, hearing crackling thunder, answers
back with echoing rumbles, in like style Vṛṣadhvaja
bellowed gravely, "I do commend your bravery, Lakṣmaṇa,
crown-gem of champions. How can I fight you? The propitious
goddess is pleased with you, lucky one." Kapardī, keeper
of the gate, stepped aside; Saumitri strode into the woods.

At a ferocious lion's roar that warrior stiffened. The
dense forest reverberated on all sides with sounds of
crashing. Out leapt a lion whose yellow eyes shone blood-red;
he flicked his tail and gnashed his teeth together. With a cry
of "Hail to Rāma," that charioteer bared his sword. The
māyā-lion turned and fled, as does darkness in the face
of Hutāśana's might. Calmly, resolutely, that wise
one advanced bravely. Of a sudden clouds, booming, belching,
masked the moon. Winds whipped up, howling. Streaks of lightning lit the
skies, while the land, following those momentary gifts of
brilliance, seemed twice as dark. Thunderbolts clapped violently as
they struck the earth repeatedly. Prabhañjana, by strength
of arms, toppled trees. A forest fire gained access to those
woods. Golden Laṅkā shook, and a ways away the ocean
roared as though some thousand conch shells, blaring on a field of
battle, blended with the clatter of the strumming bowstrings.

Like a stolid mountain, the hero stood his ground in that
hellish confrontation. Then, as suddenly as it all
began, the conflagration was extinguished; the raucous
storm subsided; the husband of the stars showed himself once
more; and stars shone beautifully throughout the sky. Mother Earth,
coifed in her flower-tresses, gaily smiled. Sweetly scented
fragrances cavorted while the gentle breezes murmured.

Wonderstruck, the high-minded one with determination
strode on. Suddenly the woods swelled with the tinkling of bells.
A flute, a *vīṇā*, a *mṛdaṅga* drum, small cymbals, and
a *saptasvarā* sounded; surging with that music were
other tones born of women's voices, pleasing to the mind.

That hero saw before him, in a grove filled with flowers,
a troupe of damsels, like some starry constellation that
had fallen to this earth. A few of them were bathing in
the lake, crystal clear, looking ever so like moonbeams at
midnight. Fine silken bodices adorned the bank while their
figures, in those limpid waters—ah, golden lotuses
upon Lake Mānasa. Some gathered blossoms for bouquets;
others dressed their locks of hair, those chains of love. Still others
held in hand *vīṇās* crafted out of ivory, pearls inlaid—
strings of gold glistened from atop those repositories
of music's *rasa*. A number of the giddy maids were
dancing; in the cleavage, twixt two plump breasts, necklaces of
jewels swung from side to side, ankle bells jingled round their
feet, and ornamental girdles jangled on those buttocks.
Men perish from the fatal bite of deadly cobras—but,
when they feast their eyes on those gem-studded serpents swaying
to and fro, down the backs of maidens, men's hearts, from passion's
venom, merely are inflamed. They flee in terror when they
spot the hooded snake, Kṛtānta's messenger—yet, alas,
when these other cobras bob and weave, how can men help but
want to wrap them round their head and neck, as does Umā's spouse,
the serpent-wearing trident-wielder. On tree limbs cuckoos,
those companions of Springtime, were aroused and singing; not
far off, water fountains splashed and played. Wantonly, breezes
coursed, looting aromatic treasures from the flower houses.

Without the slightest trace of reticence, that troupe of maids
crowded round the foe-conqueror, singing, "Welcome, O crown-

jewel of the Raghus! We are not Niśācarīs but
rather denizens of heaven. We dwell, O champion, in
a golden temple within the paradisiacal
park called Nandana; there we gaily sip elixir of
eternal life. Unending springtime ever flowers in
youth's garden; our paired lotus-blossom breasts are constantly
in full bloom; the nectar never dries upon our pondlike
lips; we are immortal maidens, your lordship. All of us
extend to you our most cordial of welcomes. Come, sir, with
us—we shall give to you, O gem of virtues, the pleasures
men, age after age, performed severe austerities to
obtain. Disease, sorrow, and the like—all those worms which eat
away life's flower in this mortal world—not one of them
infests the land where we reside in eternal bliss." Palms
pressed together Saumitri spoke, "O covey of divine
lovelies, please forgive this slave of yours. My elder brother,
a charioteer renowned throughout the world, is Rāma-
candra; Maithilī is his spouse; the lord of Rākṣasas
found her alone in the forest and abducted her. Once
I have overcome that Rākṣasa in mortal combat,
I shall free chaste Jānakī. Grant me a boon, maids divine,
that this pledge of mine might come to pass. I was born into
the world of man; I respect you all as though you were my
mother." With that the strong-armed one raised his head and saw the
woods deserted. The women gone as in a dream, or as
evanescent bubbles found in water. Who comprehends
Māyā's *māyā* in this mundane world of *māyā*? Again,
calmly and somewhat circumspect, the hero pushed on, awed.

Thereupon that best of champions spied a lake not far off.
On its bank stood the Caṇḍī temple, a hundred golden
gem-encrusted steps led down to the water. That hero
saw a lighted lamp in the temple; by the altar's base
lay a heap of flowers; a bronze gong, a conch shell, and a
bell were sounding; there was water in a pot; and smoke rose
from a censer, blending with the redolence of floral
scents, permeating the surroundings with sweet aromas.
That Indra among champions climbed down to the water and
there bathed; with utmost care he plucked a bluish lotus; at
that, the ten directions filled with luxurious perfume.

Saumitri, a lion of Indras among warriors, went
inside the temple and offered worship properly to
her who rides a lion.[1] "O Varadā," Rāmānuja
called out, prostrating himself, "bestow upon this slave a
boon. Let me slay the Rākṣasa champion, Mother, this I
beg of you. O Antaryāminī, can the human tongue
articulate all you know about man's inmost thoughts? Pure
woman, sate each unspoken longing of this heart." Afar,
clouds boomed; Laṅkā trembled under sudden bolts of lightning.
The woods, the temple, and the lake itself rocked shore to shore,
shaking violently—as though caught in a major earthquake.

Before him hero Lakṣmaṇa saw the great Māyā on
her golden throne. The sheer intensity of her brilliance
dazzled his eyes momentarily with coruscation
as of lightning. Blinded, that hero saw about him a
darkened temple. Then Satī smiled. With that, the darkness at
once disappeared, and the high-minded one gained supernal
vision! as waves of honeyed voices wafted through the skies.

The grand Māyā spoke, "Most pleased with you today, son of chaste
Sumitrā, are all the gods and goddesses. Vāsava
has sent you weapons of the gods. On Śiva's orders I
myself have come to expedite this task of yours. Take up
your godly weapons, warrior, and then with Vibhīṣaṇa
traverse the city proper to where Rāvaṇi worships
Vaiśvānara in the temple of the Nikumbhilā
sacrifice. Pounce precipitately on that Rākṣasa,
as a tiger strikes, and destroy him. By my boon you two
will enter sight unseen; I shall sheathe you in a veil of
māyā, like a sword inside its scabbard. Now go with a
stout heart, you of renown." That gem of champions bowed low to
the feet of Māyā, then proceeded in great haste to where
the best of Rāghavas awaited. Awake now, birds were
cooing in flower groves, like musicians at festivals,
who fill the land with propitious strains. Trees shed blossoms on
that best of champion's head; breezes blew in mellow murmurs.

"Your mother, Sumitrā, conceived you in her womb at a
most auspicious moment, Lakṣmaṇa!" came a message born

1. Durgā.

of the firmament. "Songs that praise your deeds will fill three worlds
this day, I proclaim! You, Saumitri, shall do that of which
the gods have been incapable! You shall be immortal,
like that clan of gods!" Sarasvatī spoke no further, but
the birds cooed more melodiously in their pleasure grove.

That cooing went inside the happy home, that gold temple
where the Indra of warriors, hero Indrajit, reposed
upon his flower bed. To music from the forest grove
awoke that elephant of warriors. That Indra among
charioteers held Pramīlā's lotus hand in his, and
in a honeyed tone of voice, ah, goodness me, as when a
bee hums mysteries of love into a lotus blossom's
ear, he spoke (kissing her closed eyes affectionately). "The
birds, cooing, call you, my beauty, my golden Dawn. Open,
dearest one, your lotus eyes. Arise, my eternal bliss.
My wife, this heart of mine is like the sunstone, and you, a
picture of the sun—I, lackluster when you close your eyes.
You are the ultimate fruit upon the tree of fortune
in my world. The pupils of your eyes, priceless gems. Arise
and see, moon-faced one, how blossoms in that lovely arbor
bloomed with your stolen charms." Startled, that woman rose in a
hurry—as do those cow herdsmen's wives at the flute's lush sounds!

Demurely, she covered her figure out of modesty.
Again, the prince spoke with affection, "Finally dark Night
recedes. Were that not so, would you have bloomed, my lotus; would
these two eyes of mine have been consoled? Come, darling, let us
offer our obeisance before my mother's feet, then I
shall take my leave. Later I shall proffer worship to god
Vaiśvānara and gratify, by a hail of arrows
like terrifying lightning, Rāma's wish for war with war."

They dressed, that daughter-in-law and son of Rāvaṇa—both
unequaled in this world: Pramīlā, the finest among
females, and hero Meghanāda, the finest of the
males! The pair emerged from their bedchamber—like the morning
star accompanied by the newly risen sun. Ashamed, pale-
countenanced fireflies faded away (no longer sipping
the elixir-dew off flower petals). Bees darted back
and forth, in hopes of nectar; upon a tree limb sang a

cuckoo his honeyed, fifth-note song.[2] Rākṣasas' melodic
instruments resounded; guardsmen bowed; cries of "Victory
to Meghanāda" rose into the skies! Joyously the
couple took their seat inside their jeweled palanquin, which
conveyance bearers bore to Queen Mandodarī's golden
quarters. It was an edifice from which emanated
splendor—embossed with emeralds, diamonds, ivory—unmatched in
all the world. Whatever was eye-pleasing that Providence
created shone in or round about those quarters. Before
the door paced sentry maids, *praharaṇas* in their hands like
Death's very scepter. Some were on horseback, some on foot. All
about sparked rows of stellar lamps. Vernal breezes wafted,
bearing fragrances from groves of myriad flowers. Soft
sounds of the *vīṇā* billowed forth, like some enchanting dream.

Into such a golden dwelling went the conqueror of foes
with gorgeous Pramīlā whose face seemed like the moon. A
certain Rākṣasī by the name of Trijaṭā came on
the run. Said the lion among warriors, "Listen, my good
Trijaṭā, upon completion of the Nikumbhilā
sacrifice, I, according to my father's order, shall
fight Rāma, shall destroy the enemies of Rākṣasas;
and so, I wish to worship now my mother's feet. Go, with
this message. Say, 'Your son and daughter-in-law are waiting
at the doorway, O queen of Laṅkā.' " Prostrating herself
humbly, Trijaṭā (the horrid Rākṣasī) said to that
champion, "Prince, Queen Mandodarī presently is in the
Śiva temple. For your well-being she worships Umā's
spouse, forgoing food and sleep. Who in this world, champion, has
a son like you? And who has such a mother?" So saying,
that messengeress fast departed, showing lightning's speed.

A troupe of female eulogists, to accompaniment from
instruments, sang out, "O Kṛttikā, O Haimavatī,
come see your Śaktidhara, your Kārttikeya, waiting
at your door with bright-eyed Senā. Come gaze with joy upon
your daughter-in-law, who even puts Rohiṇā to shame,
and your son, whose good looks force the moon to admit he is

2. See *pā* in Glossary.

but stained. You lucky woman, you! Hero Indrajit, world-
conquering champion—pretty Pramīlā, chaste world-charmer!"

The queen of Laṅkā exited the Śiva temple, where-
upon the couple bowed before her feet. Ecstatic, the
queen drew them both close to her, kissed the tops of their heads, then
wept. Goodness me, a mother's heart—in this world it is in
you that love is stored, just as flowers are the storehouse of
aromas, and oysters, pearls' containers, those gem-filled mines.

An autumn moon of a son, a daughter-in-law who is
autumnal moonlight, and the queen of the Rākṣasa clan
herself the very essence of star-crowned Night—streams of dew-
tears fell upon her leaf-cheeks, making them more beautiful.

Said the Indra among warriors, "Your ladyship, bless this
thrall of yours. Once the Nikumbhilā sacrifice has been
properly completed, I shall go to battle on this
very day and vanquish Rāghava. That scoundrel slew my
baby brother, Vīrabāhu. I want to see by what
power he can stop me. Give me, Mother, your foot-dust. With
your blessings I today shall free Laṅkā from this danger
with volleys of keen arrows. I shall shackle, then haul back
that traitor, Uncle Vibhīṣaṇa! shall plunge Sugrīva
and Aṅgada beneath the sea's unfathomed waters!" The
queen replied, wiping tears with the gemmed end of her sari—

"How can I bid farewell to you, my child? To the dark sky
of my heart, you are the full moon. That heroic spouse of
Sītā is in battle dauntless; the champion Lakṣmaṇa
is overpowering; Vibhīṣaṇa, compassionless,
acts like a deadly serpent. Intoxicated on the
wine of greed, an idiot can kill with ease his own, just
as a tiger racked by hunger kills and eats his cubs. I
tell you, it was at an inauspicious time, child, that my
husband's mother, Nikaṣā, conceived vile Vibhīṣaṇa
in her womb. That venal one has wrecked our golden Laṅkā."

Smiling, the charioteer answered to his mother, "Why,
Mother, do you fear that Rāghava and Lakṣmaṇa, those
enemies of Rākṣasas? Twice on father's order I
overcame them both in hard-fought combat, with volleys of
flaming arrows. By the grace of your two feet this humble
servant has always proved victorious in warfare with

gods, Daityas, and with men. Uncle Vibhīṣaṇa knows, your
ladyship, the prowess of your son; so do the god clan's
charioteers, lightning-flinging Sahasrākṣa foremost
of their lot; likewise does the Indra among Nāgas in
Pātāla; and so the Indra among mortals on this
earth. Why, tell me Mother, do you fear for me today? That
Rāma is beneath contempt! Why should you, pray tell, fear him?"

The queen, with warm affection, kissed his head and said, "He is
a man with a wizard's powers, my child, this husband of
Vaidehī, or else he is assisted by the whole god
clan. When you bound them both with *nāgapāśas*, who was it
who then loosed those bonds? Who saved them, in a fight at night,
when you shackled Rāghava and all his forces? All this I
fail to comprehend. I have heard tell that when Maithilī's
lord so orders, stones float on water, fires die, and rains pour
down! A man of wizardry, this Rāma! How, my dearest
child, can I bid you leave to vie with him again? Alas,
Fate, why oh why did star-crossed Sūrpaṇakhā not wither
in her mother's womb!" So saying, the queen wept silently.

Said the elephant of warriors, "By dwelling on events
gone by, you lament now, Mother, for no good reason. Our
enemies are at the city's gates. How could I relax
until I crush them in pitched battle? When Hutāśana
attacks a house, who is there who stays asleep inside? The
Rākṣasa clan, famed, feared in all three worlds by gods, Daityas,
and men alike, should I—your ladyship, O Mother—should
I, Indrajit, the son of Rāvaṇa, let Rāghava
inflict infamy upon our clan? My grandfather, your
father, Maya, an Indra among Danu's scions—what
would he say if he learned of this? What of all my uncles,
your charioteer brothers? The entire universe
would laugh! Command your humble thrall. I shall go do battle,
Mother, shall destroy that Rāghava! Just listen: birds are
cooing in the garden. The sun's foe yields. I must worship
my deity of choice and then, with a contingent of
Rākṣasas most difficult to overcome, I shall join
the fight. Return now, madam, to your residence. Soon I,
victorious in combat, shall be back and with fervor
worship at your pair of lotus feet! Father's permission

I have gained—now please give me yours. Who can contend with your
servant, ladyship, once you have yielded him your blessings?"
Then wiping tears away with the jeweled free end of her
sari, the queen of Laṅkā answered, "If you have to go,
my dear—may Virūpākṣa, guardian of Rākṣasas,
guard you in this deadly conflict. This I beg at his two
feet. What more can I say? You desert me in this room now
void of my affections' fancy." The queen cried as she spoke,
but glanced toward Pramīlā. "Stay with me, little mother; I
soothe my wretched heart gazing at your moonlike face. Mother
Earth in the moon's dark fortnight is cheered by beams of starlight."
That one of strong limbs bowed before his mother's feet, then took
his leave. Weeping, the royal consort with her son's wife went
again to her quarters. Shunning his palanquin, the prince
walked the path leading to the woods—with determination
that best of charioteers strode on down the flowered path-
way to the entrance of the temple of the sacrifice.
Suddenly, from behind, there came the sound of ankle bells.
Ever recognizable, ah yes, to a lover's ears
are the sounds his woman's footsteps make. That Indra among
warriors smiled, embracing rapturously in the confines
of his arms that lotus-face, that Pramīlā. "Alas, my
lord," said the pretty one, "I had planned on going with you
to the temple and outfitting you in your warrior's garb.
But what was I to do? Mother-in-law would have me take
refuge in her home. Yet I, however, could not stay there,
without gazing once again upon your feet. I have heard
that even just a sliver of the moon shines bright from the
brilliance of the sun; so is it with this slave of yours, O
sun among the Rākṣasa clan! Without you, I swear, the
world is gloom, my lord!" Then onto her pearl-studded breast, her
eyes rained pearls of even greater radiance. Compared to
those, what worthless things are dewdrops upon lotus petals?
Responded the finest of warriors, "I shall soon return,
after overcoming Rāghava in battle, O my
Laṅkā-beautifier. Go back, my darling, to our queen
of Laṅkā. Rohiṇī, chaste wife of mine, rises prior
to the moon! Did Fate create, faithful wife, those lotus eyes
to cry? Why, my pet, have storm clouds gathered in those vaults of

light? Give your consent, beauteous one—just look, Night, tipsy
on the liquor of delusion, has fled quickly, thinking
you to be Dawn—grant me permission, most chaste woman, that
I might carry on, to the temple of the sacrifice."

As when the champion Kusumeṣu, on Indra's orders,
left his Rati and set off that fateful moment to break
Śiva's meditation; just so, alas, set off then this
Kandarpa-like hero Indrajit, leaving his pure wife
Pramīlā, the epitome of Rati. At a most
ill-fated time Madana embarked upon his journey;
at an equally ill-fated moment set off hero
Meghanāda—the hope of the Rākṣasa clan, in all
the world invincible! Ah, the march of destiny, who
has the power to impede its progress? As Rati once
lamented, so too, presently, did youthful Pramīlā.

All this time the Rākṣasa wife had been brushing back her
tears. She stared in the direction of her husband some ways
off and spoke in a mellifluous voice, "I know why you
roam dense forests, O king of elephants. Once you have seen
that gait of his, how could you, shameless, show your face again,
vain one? Who would say your waist is slender, lion, once his
eyes have seen the beast with yellow eyes amid our clan of
Rākṣasa? That is also why you remain forever
exiled to the forest. You may slay the elephant, but
this lion of a warrior with his awesome bludgeon has
subdued in battle Vāsava, eternal enemy
of the clan of Daityas and sovereign of the clan of gods."

With this, that chaste wife, her hands together in a sign of
supplication, gazing toward the sky, still weeping, prayed, "This
Pramīlā, your humble slave, O daughter of the Indra
among mountains, beseeches you. Cast your glance of mercy,
maid of mercy, upon Laṅkā. Protect him, the greatest
of the Rākṣasas, in this struggle. Clothe that champion in
impregnable armor. I, a vine, supported always
by you, Satī, this vine's life depends upon that kingly
tree. Please see to it, Mother, that no battle-ax befalls
him. What more can your servant say? You are Antaryāmī.
But for you, O Jagadambā, who is there to save him?"

As breezes waft a wealth of fragrance into the quarters

of the king, just so the voice-bearing firmament bore those
prayers of Pramīlā to the residence on Kailāsa.
Indra trembled fearfully. Observing this, the sovereign
of the winds, with a zephyr's speed, floated them away. That
chaste wife, wiping her teary eyes, turned back—as cowherd wives,
about to lose their lover, bid good-bye to Mādhava
on the Yamunā's shores, and empty-hearted return to
empty houses, so, weeping still, that woman went back home.

Thus ends canto number five,
called "Preparations,"
in the poem
The Slaying of Meghanāda

CANTO 6

The Slaying

Hero Saumitri the lion left that woods, returning
to the camp where the lordly Raghu king was waiting. That
noble-natured one moved swiftly, as when a huntsman spies
the king of beasts in the forest, then runs for his weapons—
to choose with haste his deadliest club for mortal combat.

Moments later, that most celebrated one reached the spot
where the Raghu charioteer stood. Bowing before that
pair of feet, then showing deference to Vibhīṣaṇa,
their best of friends, the high-minded one spoke, "This faithful thrall
of yours has found success today, my lord, by your blessings.
With your two feet in mind, I proceeded to the forest
and there did *pūjā* to Cāmuṇḍā, my lordship, in her
golden temple. To confuse your servant, a myriad
of chaste maids spread their net of *māyā*—how shall I, who am
so ignorant, recount all of that before your feet? I
came upon Candracūḍa, guardian of the gates, but
he let me pass without a struggle due to the power
of your virtues, my lord—just as the greatest serpent slips
away, powerless against the virtues of a potent
antidote!—and thereupon this slave of yours entered that
forest. Next a lion threatened, snarling, but I turned him
back; a most raucous storm blew in with terrifying howls;
forest fires, ever so like doomsday's conflagration, raged
throughout the land, burning trees in all directions; but, in
a moment's time, that companion of the wind[1] went out of
its own accord, and the wind god vanished. It was then I
saw in front of me a gathering of heavenly maids,
sporting in the sylvan grove; with hands cupped reverently, I
honored them, begged a boon, my lord, then bid farewell to them
all. Not far off, a temple shone resplendently within
the woods, brightening up that fair land. I descended to the
lake, bathed my body, and with a blue lotus offering
I worshiped Mother fervently. Māyā appeared before

1. Agni.

me, granting me a boon. Said that lady of compassion,
'Most pleased with you today, son of chaste Sumitrā, are all
the gods and goddesses. Vāsava has sent you weapons
of the gods. On Śiva's orders I myself have come to
expedite this task of yours. Take up your godly weapons,
warrior, and then with Vibhīṣaṇa traverse the city
proper to where Rāvaṇi worships Vaiśvānara in
the temple of the Nikumbhilā sacrifice. There pounce
precipitately on that Rākṣasa, as a tiger
strikes, and destroy him. By my boon you two will enter sight
unseen; I shall sheathe you in a veil of *māyā*, like a
sword inside its scabbard. Now go with a stout heart, you of
renown.' Tell me, what is your wish, O jewel among men?
Night departs, and we must not delay. Shall I slay that son
of Rāvaṇa, my lordship, please command this slave of yours!"

The Raghu lord replied, "Alas, how—when living beings,
panic-stricken, run panting for their lives with wind's speed on
seeing in the distance that messenger of Death, by whose
venom gods and men alike are reduced to ashes—how
can I send you into such a serpent's hole, you who are
more than life to me? Sītā's rescue is not to be. For
naught, Ocean, did I shackle you, slay countless Rākṣasas
in war, and bring that Indra among kings with retinue
and army to this golden Laṅkā. Alas, for no good
cause at all did bloody torrents, the likes of rain, drench this
earth. Kingdom, wealth, father, mother, kin and comrade—by quirk
of luck I lost them all. All I had left in my darkened
room was the lamp, Maithilī; now misfortune (ah Fate, by
what fault am I deemed guilty at your feet?) has extinguished
even that. Who is there left in my line, Brother, whose face
I can gaze upon and by so doing sustain this life
of mine? Shall I live on in this mortal world? Come, let us
once again return, Lakṣmaṇa, to our forest refuge.
At an inauspicious time, befuddled by the lure of
Hope, we came, Brother, to this city of the Rākṣasas."

Saumitri the lion answered with a warrior's brashness,
"What makes you, Raghu lord, so fearful? In all three worlds whom
should that hero fear who has in his possession godly
powers? Sahasrākṣa, the gods' sovereign, takes your side, so

too does Virūpākṣa, that denizen of Kailāsa,
and the maiden of the mountain, his ever faithful wife.
Look there, toward Laṅkā—the anger of the gods, like blackened
clouds, hovers over golden hues on all four sides. Smiles of
the gods, my lord, illuminate this camp of yours, just see!
Direct this slave of yours, and I shall take up my godly
weapons and march into the Rākṣasa's abode; I shall
for sure destroy the Rākṣasa, by favor of those feet
of yours. You are sage, my lord. Why do you fail to heed the
orders of the gods? You always tread *dharma*'s path; why then,
Aryan, do you today engage in this un-*dharmic*
act? Who has kicked the consecrated water pot, and where?"[2]

With honeyed words, the ally, hero Vibhīṣaṇa, spoke,
"What he says is true, O charioteer, Indra among
Rāghavas. Rāvaṇi, bane of Vāsava and throughout
the world invincible, is in prowess like the over-
powering messenger of Death. But today it makes no
sense for us to dread him. In a dream, O jewel of the
Raghus, I saw the Rājalakṣmī of the Rākṣasas.
Sitting by my head, my lord, and making bright the camp with
her purest rays, that faithful wife addressed this lowly one,
'Alas, Vibhīṣaṇa, your brother is now drunk with pride.
Would I, who abhor defilement, willingly reside in
such a sinful household? Does the lotus ever bloom in
muddy waters? When does one see stars in a cloudy sky?
Due to former deeds of yours, however, the immortals
are favorably disposed toward you. You will inherit the
umbrella and the scepter and the vacant kingly throne.
By Fate's decree, I today install you, famed one, as lord
of all the Rākṣasas. This coming day Sumitrā's son,
the lion, will slay your nephew Meghanāda. You will
act as his accomplice. Carry out the gods' command with
care, my future king of Karbūras.' I awoke and sensed
the entire camp was permeated by a scent from

2. To touch anything with one's feet is disrespectful and inauspicious, causing ill consequences. Someone, somewhere must have committed the very inauspicious act of kicking a consecrated pot, one in which the divinity resides. How else, implies Lakṣmaṇa, can one account for his brother's strange behavior?

heaven, and I heard somewhat removed heavenly music,
playing softly in the sky. At the gateway to the camp
I, astounded, saw that charming woman who charms him who
inflames Madana.[3] A chignon that resembled massive
clouds hid from view the nape of her neck; in her hair glistened
strings of jewels—ah me! compared to that, lightning's luster
streaking through roiling thunderheads is of small consequence!
Then suddenly Jagadambā vanished. For a time I
stood there staring, thirsty-eyed, but my want was not fulfilled;
Mother did not show herself again. Listen well to all
I have to say, charioteer Dāśarathi. Just give
the order; I shall go where Rāvaṇi does *pūjā* to
god Vaiśvānara in the sacrificial temple. O
keeper of men, keep strictly to the gods' command. I tell
you, your cherished goal will for sure be reached, best Rāghava."

Sītā's husband answered, eyes filled with tears, "When I recall
those days gone by, best of Rākṣasas, my troubled heart cries
out. How can I cast this jewel of a brother into
unplumbed waters? Alas, O friend, when mother Kaikeyī,
heartless—it was my bad luck—followed Mantharā's selfish
scheme and I, therefore, forsook the comforts of the kingdom
to preserve the good name of our father, that fond brother,
moved by love for brother, quit the courtly life of his own
free will. Mother Sumitrā wept. From an upper level
in the women's quarters his wife Ūrmilā wailed. And all
the other city residents—how can I tell you how
much they all pleaded? But he would pay no heed at all to
their entreaties. Instead, following behind me (like my
very shadow), my brother entered eagerly the woods,
freely giving up for good his youthful adolescence.
Said mother Sumitrā, 'You steal away my heart's desire,
Rāghava. Who knows by what magic's power you have tricked
my baby. Now I must entrust my treasure to your care.
Guard prudently this precious gem of mine, I beg of you.'

"Sītā's rescue, best of friends, is not to be. Let us turn
back to our forest sanctuary. Difficult to beat

3. Lakṣmī, wife (charmer) of Viṣṇu/Kṛṣṇa, who in turn charmed Madana.

in combat is that Indra among charioteers, that
Rāvaṇi, bane of gods, Daityas, and of men. Sugrīva,
Indra of the mighty ones; prince Aṅgada, most learned
when it comes to warfare; Hanumān, son of the wind and
strong beyond all measure, like Prabhañjana, his father;
Dhūmrākṣa, a ball of fire upon the battlefield, most
cometlike; there is Nala and there Nīla; Keśarī—
a lion of a champion from the vantage of his foes;
and all the other soldiers, godlike in appearance and
as heroic as the gods; you, O great charioteer—
when you with help from all these are unable to defeat
that Rākṣasa, how then, pray tell, can Lakṣmaṇa engage
him all by himself? Alas, Hope is a sorceress, I
tell you, friend, for she is why we leapt across the waters
that cannot be crossed and came to the Rākṣasas' domain."

Then of a sudden, in the regions of the firmament,
Sarasvatī, born of the skies, spoke in dulcet tones, "Tell
me, is it proper for you, husband of Vaidehī, to
doubt the word of gods, you who are the favorite of the
god clan? Why, O hero, do you spurn the gods' advice? Cast
a glance into the void." Amazed, the Raghu king saw there
a peacock fighting with a snake. The peacock's screeching cries
commingled with the hissing of the cobra, filling ten
directions with a frightful dissonance. Wings spanned the sky,
looking like a mass of clouds; amid it all flashed *halā-*
hala poison, intense as any fiery holocaust.
Both fought fiercely. From fear, the earth began to tremble; the
ocean waters constantly were swelling, churning. The next
moment that best of peacocks plummeted to earth, quite dead;
the reptile hissed loudly—victorious in their struggle.[4]

Said Rāvaṇānuja, "You saw with your own eyes that strange
sight; it is not devoid of portent, mark my words, husband
of Vaidehī; mull it over! It is no shadow play; the
gods have shown you through this *māyā* what will happen—today
leonine Saumitri will void Laṅkā of her hero!"

The jewel of the Raghu clan then entered once again

4. Birds, Garuḍa in particular and peacocks also, are the enemy of snakes and normally best them.

his tent and armed his beloved younger brother with those
godly weapons. Ah, that handsome warrior cut a gallant
figure, looking much like Skanda, the foe of Tāraka.
Upon his chest that high-minded one wore a coat of star-
studded armor; from his belt there flashed a brilliant saber,
embossed with precious stones. Down his back a shield glinted, like
the solar orb itself; beside it swung a quiver made
of ivory, gold-inlaid, and packed with arrows. In his left
hand that archer held firm the godly bow; on his head there
shone a coronet radiating all around (as though
fashioned from rays of the sun); from that crown bobbed constantly
a tuft of hair, just as a lion's mane bobs loosely on
the lion's back. Rāghavānuja dressed all excited,
shining brightly—just like the ray-ringed sun god at high noon.

Hastily that hero left the camp—high spirited, like
a stallion at the sound of horns when the waves of warfare
crest and crash! Out went that best of warriors; out with him went
Vibhīṣaṇa attired in warrior's garb, fearsome when in
battle! Gods showered them with flowers; auspicious music
rang across the skies; Apsarās danced throughout the void; earth,
heaven, and the netherworld filled with shouts of "Victory!"

Gazing toward the skies, hands cupped in supplication, that best
of Raghus prayed, "Beggar Rāghava begs for refuge at
your lotus feet today, Ambikā. Do not forsake, O
goddess, this humble slave of yours. How hard I have striven,
Mother, to maintain *dharma*—all this is not unknown to
those reddened feet of yours. Now, please, let this worthless being
savor *dharma*'s fruits, O Mṛtyuñjaya's darling. Satī,
protect my brother—more dear to me than life, this youth, this
Lakṣmaṇa—in his battle with the Rākṣasa. Quell that
most turbulent Dānava. Save the gods, Nistāriṇī!
Preserve your humble subjects, O slayer of the demon
buffalo; trample under foot the frenzied Rākṣasa!"

In such a manner the enemy of Rākṣasas praised
Satī. Just as breezes waft a wealth of fragrance into
royal quarters, so too the air, which carries sound, bore the
prayer of Rāghava to the residence at Kailāsa.
Indra of the heavens smiled in heaven, and Pavana

of his own accord moved it swiftly through the carrier
of sound. On hearing that sweet prayer, Mother—daughter of the
mountain—overjoyed, said, "Be it so," and gave her blessings.
Dawn, she who is dispeller of both gloom and sorrow, flashed
a smile on the rising-hill, as Hope, indeed, does upon
a sad heart. Birds cooed in wooded groves, bumblebees darted
here and there. Night softly sauntered off, taking with her stars;
splendidly a single star yet shone upon Dawn's forehead
but shone with all the brilliance of a hundred stars. Flower
blossoms now bloomed in her tresses—a novel star array.
Turning to that best of Rākṣasas, Rāghava then said—
"Be cautious, friend. The beggar Rāma has entrusted to
you, best of charioteers, Rāma's priceless gem. No need
of further words—my life and death this day are in your hands."
Hero Vibhīṣaṇa reassured the great archer, "You
are favored by the gods, O jewel of the Raghu clan;
whom do you have to fear, my lordship? Champion Saumitri
will, of course, best in combat the champion Meghanāda."
Bowing to those feet of the Indra of the Rāghavas,
Saumitri started off with his comrade Vibhīṣaṇa.
Layers of thick clouds enveloped both of them, just as fog
in the winter season encircles mountain peaks at the
break of day. Invisible, the two advanced toward Laṅkā.
The goddess Māyā stepped into that golden temple where
Kamalā—Rājalakṣmī of the clan of Rākṣasas,
dressed in wifely Rākṣasa attire—was seated on her
lotus throne. Smiling, that Ramā, Keśava's beloved,
queried, "What brings you on this day, O great goddess, to this
city? Voluptuous one, please tell me of your wishes."
Answered Māyā, the queen of Śaktis, with a gentle smile,
"Today hold in check your power, daughter of the ocean;
godlike charioteer Saumitri will penetrate this
golden city, and by Śiva's orders that champion will
vanquish haughty Meghanāda in the temple of the
Nikumbhilā sacrifice. Your radiant power is
like the fires of annihilation, O radiating
woman, and hence, what enemy is there capable of
entering this city? Show sympathy to Rāghava,

O goddess, I beseech you. Grant him a boon, O wife of
Mādhava; spare Rāma, a follower of *dharma*'s path."
    With a forlorn sigh, Indirā replied, "Who can fail to
heed your word, you who are adored throughout the universe?
But my heart cries out as I contemplate all this. Alas,
that best of Rākṣasas and his consort Mandodarī
do my *pūjā* lovingly—what more can I say? True, it
is through his own fault that the wealth of Rākṣasas is lost.
I shall therefore hold in check my power, goddess, for how
can I impede the course of destiny? Tell Saumitri
he may enter, without fear, the city. Appeased, I grant
him this boon: may Sumitrā's hero son in the coming
battle best the foe-defeating son of Mandodarī."
    To the western gate walked Keśava's desire—most fetching,
she, like a full-blown bloom at dawn cleansed by dewdrops. With that
pretty one went Māyā. Succulent banana saplings
withered; auspicious water pots shattered on their own; the
waters of this world went dry. For, that sustaining power
blended then and there with the red lac dye which lined her feet,
as at Night's departure the gossamer of nectar moon-
beams blends into the net of solar rays. Laṅkā's beauty
faded, ah! as when the jewel on the forehead of the
cobra's mate is lost. Afar, clouds of a sudden rumbled
loudly; the sky wept rain; the lord of waters tossed and turned;
Mother Earth quaked violently, lamenting, "Oh, my city
of the Rākṣasas, this plight of yours—you who used to be,
O golden lady, the very ornament of this world!"
    The two of them climbed the city ramparts and viewed not far
away godlike Saumitri, like sun-god Tviṣāmpati,
veiled in fog, or like the lord of fire, that Vibhāvasu,
cloaked in billowing smoke. Alongside was charioteer
Vibhīṣaṇa—the wind with wind's companion—difficult
to overcome in combat. Who could save today, alas,
the hope of Rākṣasas, that Rāvaṇi? As the tiger,
maneuvering for position, moves under cover of
the brush when he spots a fine stag off in some dense woods—or
as the crocodile, the likes of Yama's discus weapon
incarnate, with swiftness glides undetected out toward that
distant bather he caught sight of in the middle of the

river—so too did champion Lakṣmaṇa with companion
Vibhīṣaṇa proceed with speed to slay the Rākṣasa.[5]

With a sigh of resignation and bidding her good-byes
to Māyā, pretty Indirā returned to her own home.
Mādhava's beloved wept. Mother Earth in joy soaked up
those teardrops—as oysters suck in tenderly, O cloud maids,
water from your eyes and form priceless pearls whose excellence
is born when chaste Svātī shines in the circle of the sky.

By the strength of Māyā's power, that pair of warriors marched
into the city. At Saumitri's touch the portals flew
wide open with a thunderous clatter, but whose ears did
that racket reach? Alas! all Rākṣasa charioteers
were made deaf by Māyā's trickery; none saw those foemen,
like Kṛtānta's messengers, overpowering, serpents
slithering slyly into a bed of blooming flowers.

Quite surprised, Rāmānuja gazed all around and saw a
force of four divisions at the gateway—mahouts on their
elephants, horsemen on their steeds, great charioteers in
chariots, and on the ground foot soldiers, messengers of
Śamana—fearsome, like Bhīma, unbeatable in war.
A glow like creation's final fire filled the firmament.

Nervously the heroes gazed upon the all-consuming
blazing Virūpākṣa, a stellar Rākṣasa, who held
a *prakṣveḍana* weapon and rode astride a golden
chariot. There stood the champion Tālajaṅghā, as tall
as a *tāla* palm—like a Gadādhara, enemy
of Mura. And there was Kālanemi upon the back
of an elephant, a warrior with the power to deal
death to foes. Fond of the fight and deft as well, Pramatta
stayed besotted always on the liquor of heroics.
Cikṣura, a Rākṣasa who seemed an equal to the
sovereign of the Yakṣas—and there were other mighty
heroes, terrors all to gods, Daityas, and mankind. Calmly,
with utmost care, the two proceeded. Saumitri, silent,

5. Besides the obvious connotations of the tiger and the crocodile as dangerous and their homologation here with Lakṣmaṇa and Vibhīṣaṇa, there is the Bangla saying *"jale kumir ḍāṅāy bāgh"* (a crocodile in the water and a tiger on the shore), meaning something comparable to "between a rock and a hard place," or, as Datta himself might explain it, "between Scylla and Charybdis."

observed on either side of them hundreds and hundreds of golden temples, shops and gardens, ponds and fountains; stabled horses, elephants within stalls; countless chariots the hue of fire; arsenals; and charming theaters adorned with precious stones, ah yes! just as in the city of the gods! Who is able to describe Laṅkā's many riches—the envy of the gods! coveted by Daityas! Who can count the jewels in the ocean or stars throughout the sky!

Within the city those champions gaped in rapt attention at the Rākṣasa king's palace. Golden colonnades and diamond columns glistened; the pinnacles protruding from that edifice reached the sky, resplendent like the peaks of Mount Hemakūṭa. Ivory embossed with the charm of gold enhanced the windows and the doors, a delight to the eye, looking splendidly like shafts of sun at daybreak on a mound of snow. That much celebrated Saumitri stared in stupefaction, then spoke to friend Vibhīṣaṇa, Indra of champions, "Among monarchs, your elder brother is to be praised, best of Rākṣasas, a sea of glory in this world. Ah, who owns such riches on the surface of this earth!"

With a dejected sigh hero Vibhīṣaṇa spoke, "You are right, gemstone of champions. Who, alas, does indeed own such riches on the surface of this earth? But nothing is forever in this mundane life. One goes, another comes—that is the way of the world, just like waves upon the sea. Come quickly, O best of charioteers, and carry out this day the slaying of Meghanāda; gain for yourself immortality, my lord, by drinking fame's elixir."

The two moved posthaste, unseen, by the grace of Māyā. Hero Lakṣmaṇa watched wives of Rākṣasas—who even put to shame doe-eyed lovelies—on the bank of a pond, gold water jugs perched on their hips, sweet smiles upon their honeyed lips. Lotus flowers bloomed in lakes that morn. Here and there a charioteer of imposing stature would emerge. Foot soldiers, decked out in iron armor, left their flowered beds. Someone blew a conch shell brazenly, putting all at once an end to sleep. Syces saddled up their mounts. Elephants trumpeted loudly, trunks flaunting *mudgaras*, on their backs resplendent silk trappings, fringed with pearl pendants. Chariot

drivers loaded diverse weaponry and golden banners
carefully onto their chariots. Enchanting morning
music could be heard within the many temples, ah me,
just like that played in homes throughout Bengal during *dola*
when all the gods appear on earth to worship Ramā's mate!
Flower-maids sauntered to and fro, gathering flower blooms,
filling all the paths with floral scents and brightening with
color their surroundings, just like Dawn, friend of the flowers.
Elsewhere others scurried here, now there, bearing loads of milk
and yogurt. Gradually the hustle and bustle and the
noise intensified as townsfolk woke throughout that city.

Someone said, "Come, let us mount the wall. If we fail to get
there early, we shall not secure a spot where from to view
the spectacular fight. I wish to soothe my eyes upon
our prince in martial garb and all those other excellent
warriors." Another answered boastfully, "What is the point,
I ask you, of ascending the city walls? Our prince will
best both Rāma and his younger brother Lakṣmaṇa in
an instant, for who in the world can stand his ground against
those arrows? Our enemy subduer will burn his way
through the opposition forces just as fire rages through
dry grasses. He will strike his uncle Vibhīṣaṇa a
frightful blow, then manacle that cur. Surely the victor
will come to the assembly hall to receive his royal
favors, so let us head for that assembly hall ourselves."

What more shall the poet say of all that hero saw and
heard? Smiling inwardly, the famous one, divinely brave
like a god himself and bearing godly weapons, moved on,
followed by charioteer Vibhīṣaṇa. Close ahead
there shone the temple of the Nikumbhilā sacrifice.

Upon a cushion made of *kuśa* grass sat Indrajit
worshiping his chosen deity in private, clad in
silken clothes with a shawl made of the same, on his forehead
a mark of paste made from sandalwood, around his neck, a
garland. Incense smoldered in a censer; all about burned
lanterns fueled with purified ghee. There were heaps of flower
blossoms and a *koṣā-koṣī* dish and spoon, fashioned from
rhinoceros horn and filled with you, O Jāhnavī, your
water, you destroyer of defilement! To one side lay

a golden bell and sundry offerings on a golden
platter. The door was closed. All alone, the Indra among
charioteers sat in a trance as though Candracūḍa—
Indra among yogis—O Mount Kailāsa, on your crest!

As a tiger, driven by hunger, enters like Yama's
messenger a cow shed, so fierce-limbed Lakṣmaṇa entered
that god's house by Māyā's power. His sword clattered in its
scabbard; shield and quiver clanged together violently; the
temple trembled underneath the weight of that warrior's feet.

Startled, Rāvaṇi opened wide his eyes. The hero saw
in front of him a godlike charioteer—brilliantly
coruscating like the ray-ringed solar god at midday!

Prostrating himself in obeisance, the champion, with hands
cupped in supplication, said, "O Vibhāvasu, at a
most auspicious time your humble slave worshiped you today;
and thus, my lord, you sanctified this Laṅkā with the touch
of your two feet. But, for what reason, tell me, brilliant one,
have you come disguised as the mortal Lakṣmaṇa, foe of
Rākṣasas, to grace your devotee? What is this *līlā*
of yours, shining one?" Again that hero bowed to the ground.

Dreadful Dāśarathi, with a warrior's daring, answered,
"I am not god Vibhāvasu. Observe well, Rāvaṇi.
Lakṣmaṇa is my name, born to the Raghu clan. I have
come here, lion of all warriors, to vanquish you in war;
do battle with me instantly!" As a wayfarer stands
transfixed with terror if suddenly he sees upon his
path the king cobra, hood raised, just so that hero stared in
Lakṣmaṇa's direction. A fearless heart today had just
turned fearful! a lump of iron melted from high heat, ah
yes! The sun, by Rāhu, had been swallowed, darkening that
mass of brilliance of a sudden! Summer's heat dried up the
lord of waters! By stealth, Kali entered Nala's body!

Astonished, the champion spoke, "If truly you are Rāma's
younger brother, then tell me, charioteer, by what guile
did you penetrate today the city of the king of
Rākṣasas? There are hundreds and hundreds of Rākṣasas—
in power the terror of the Yakṣa sovereign—who, with
fearsome weaponry in hand, guard the city gates. The high
walls of this city are like mountains; upon those ramparts

pace ten thousand soldiers, like deadly discus weapons. By
what strength of *māyā*, hero, did you fool them all? Who is
the charioteer throughout this universe, born of gods
or of men, who single-handedly could defend himself
against that throng of Rākṣasas in battle? Why then do
you mislead me, your humble servant, with this illusion;
tell this slave that, Sarvabhuk! What grand jest is this of yours,
O jester? Saumitri is no formless god; how could he
penetrate this temple? Look there, the door is still now closed.
Your lordship, grant this devotee of yours a boon that I
may free Laṅkā of her fears by slaying Rāghava this
day, that I may drive away the ruler of Kiṣkindhyā,
and that I might offer shackled at the feet of our great
king the traitor Vibhīṣaṇa. Hear that, everywhere horn
blowers sound their war horns. Were I to tarry, those troops of
Rākṣasas would become dispirited; bid me farewell."

Responded godlike leonine Saumitri, "I am your
god of death, unruly Rāvaṇi! That serpent slithers
through the grass to bite him whose time has come! You are ever
drunk with pride; made hero by the power of the gods, you,
fool, constantly disdain those gods! You are undone at last,
rank one. By order of the gods, I challenge you to fight!"

So saying, the hero boldly bared his sword. Dazzling the
eye with the brilliance of the fire that ends the world, that most
excellent of sabers glinted, as do lightning-flash-filled
thunderbolts in the hands of Śakra. Then said the son of
Rāvaṇa, "If truly you are Rāmānuja, the fierce-
armed Lakṣmaṇa, then I shall certainly oblige your wish
for war with war; is ever Indrajit dissuaded from
the battlefield? But first accept my hospitality,
champion supreme, and abide within this edifice—you
may be the enemy of Rākṣasas, yet now you are
my guest. I shall dress myself in warrior's garb, for it is
not the practice, among the brotherhood of warriors, to
strike an unarmed foe. This code of conduct, best of warriors,
is not unknown to you, Kṣatriya—need I say more?"

In a voice like that of thunder, Saumitri spoke, "Once he
has caught a tiger in his snare, does the hunter ever
set him free? I shall slay you here and now, you imbecile,

in like fashion. You were born among the Rākṣasas, O
evildoer; why with you should I heed the *dharma* of
Kṣatriyas? I slay a foe by whatever means I can."

Said the conqueror of Vāsava (like Abhimanyu,
seeing all the seven champions, that champion, out of rage,
became the very essence of some molten iron), "You
are a blemish on the brotherhood of Kṣatriyas, fie
on you a hundredfold, Lakṣmaṇa. You are without shame.
Were the Kṣatriya fraternity to hear your name, in
disgust those charioteers would place hands over ears. You
stole into this temple in the manner of a thief; like
a thief, you I shall punish. Were a snake to steal into
the nest of Garuḍa, would he again return to his
own hole, you reprobate? Who has brought you here, foul fellow?"

In the twinkling of an eye the strong-limbed one picked up the
koṣā dish and hurled it with a dreadful roar at the head
of Lakṣmaṇa. To the ground the hero crashed, felled by that
horrific missile, as the king of trees falls crashing from
the force of the lord of winds. His godly weapons clattered,
and the temple shook as though caught in a violent earthquake.
There flowed a rivulet of blood. Quickly Indrajit seized
the godly sword—but was incapable of lifting it.
He grabbed the bow, drew it toward him, but the bow stayed steadfast
in Saumitri's grasp. Furious, he then clasped the shield, but
his strength proved powerless to carry out that task. As, in
vain, an elephant tugs at mountain peaks, his trunk wrapped round,
so tugged that Indra among champions at the quiver. Who
in the world comprehends Māyā's *māyā*! That proud one stared
at the door, defiant, in a rush of temper. Startled,
that best of warriors saw before him—a tremendous pike
in hand and looking like some Dhūmaketu—his uncle
Vibhīṣaṇa, a one most formidable in warfare.

"At last," the foe-conqueror said sadly, "I realize
how this Lakṣmaṇa gained entry to the city of the
Rākṣasas. Alas, O Uncle, was such conduct proper
on your part, you whose mother is chaste Nikaṣā, you who
are blood brother to the greatest of the Rākṣasas? and
to Kumbhakarṇa, the very image of the trident-
wielding Śambhu? and whose nephew has bested Vāsava?

You show the way to your own home, uncle, to a thief? You
seat a lowly Caṇḍāla in the residence of kings?
But I do not rebuke you, for you are one who is to
be revered, one comparable to my own father. Please step
aside from the doorway. I shall go to the armory,
then shall send Rāmānuja to the place of Śamana.
Today I shall expunge in war Laṅkā's ignominy."

Replied Vibhīṣaṇa, "Your efforts will prove futile, my
knowing lad. It is Rāghava I serve; how could I do
him harm, whom I am asked to guard?" Rāvaṇi responded
deferentially, "O brother of my father, your words
make me wish to die. You, the slave of Rāghava? How do
you bring such language to your lips, O uncle, please tell that
to this thrall of yours. Fate has set the crescent moon upon
the brow of Sthāṇu—does that moon ever plummet to earth
to wallow in the dust? O Rākṣasa charioteer,
how could you forget who you are? into what exalted
clan you were born? Who is that lowly Rāma after all?
The regal geese sport upon a crystal lake among the
lotuses—my lordship, do they ever go paddle into
muddy waters, home of algae scum? The lion, Indra
of the beasts, when does he ever, O you lion among
warriors, address the jackal as a friend? He is but a
dumb dog, and you, most wise; nothing is beyond the ken of
those feet of yours. He is just a little-minded mortal,
O champion, this Lakṣmaṇa; if that were not the case, would
he have called an unarmed soldier to do battle? Now tell
me, grand charioteer, is this the *dharma* seemly to
grand charioteers? There is no child in Laṅkā who would
not laugh at such a claim. Out of my way. I shall be back
soon enough. We shall see today by what godly force this
foul Saumitri fends me off in combat. In battles with
gods, Daityas, and with men, you have seen through your own eyes, O
best of Rākṣasas, the prowess of your humble servant.
Shall we see if your slave shies from such a puny human
being? That braggart, insolent, entered here, this temple
of the Nikumbhilā sacrifice—command your thrall and
I shall make the worthless mortal pay. Into the city
of your birth, uncle, that forest dweller has set foot. O

Providence, do depraved Daityas stroll in paradise's
Nandana Gardens? Is the blooming lotus an abode
for worms? Tell me, uncle, how am I to tolerate an
affront like this—I, who am your brother's son? And you, too,
O jewel among Rākṣasas, how do you abide it?"

As when a snake is made to bow its upraised head by the
power of a mighty *mantra,* just so, shame-faced and glum,
that charioteer, Rāvaṇa's younger brother, answered,
glancing at the son of Rāvaṇa. "I am not to blame,
my child. You rebuke me all for naught. By the error of
his deeds, alas, has our king brought ruin on this golden
Laṅkā, and destroyed himself. The god clan religiously
abstains from sin, but Laṅkā city overflows with it.
And Laṅkā sinks within these blackened waters, just as earth
will do, come Pralaya. That is why, for protection, I
have sought the refuge of the feet of Rāghava. Who is
there who wants to drown for the wayward ways of someone else?"

The bane of Vāsava grew livid. Gravely, as when the
Indra among clouds rumbles angrily in the sky at
midnight, that Indra among warriors spoke, "You who follow
dharma's path, younger brother of the king of Rākṣasas,
are renowned throughout the world—according to what *dharma,*
pray do tell this humble servant, please, let me hear, did you
abandon all of these—your kin, your caste, your brothers? It
says in the learned books that even if outsiders are
with virtue and your people virtueless, still then your own,
devoid of virtue, are to be preferred—outsiders are
forever only that. Where, O best of Rākṣasas, did
you learn this lesson? But I, in vain, do reprimand you.
In such company, O brother of my father, why would
you not but learn barbarity? He who travels with the
lowest of the low becomes himself a lowly creature."

At this point, through the care of Māyā, Saumitri regained
consciousness and, with a roar, that hero twanged his bowstring.
Taking aim, that champion pierced foe-besting Indrajit with
the keenest of his arrows, just as the enemy of
Tāraka, the great archer, pierced Tāraka with a hail
of arrows. Alas, there flowed a rivulet of blood (just
as a stream of water courses down the body of a

mountain in the monsoon season), moistening his clothes and
muddying the ground. That charioteer, beside himself
with pain, snatched up the conch shell, bell, the plate of offerings,
whatever was within the temple, and enraged hurled them
one by one—as charioteer Abhimanyu, unarmed
against the strength of arms of seven charioteers, threw
first the crests of chariots, their wheels, then broken swords, torn
leather shields, pierced armor, whatever he could lay his hands
upon. But illusive Māyā, stretching out her arms, caused
all those things to fall wide of the mark, just as a mother
brushes back mosquitoes swarming round her sleeping son with
a wave of her lotuslike hand. Enraged, Rāvaṇi ran
at Lakṣmaṇa, letting out a wild roar, like a lion
challenging the beaters there before him.[6] But because of
Māyā's *māyā,* in all the four directions that hero
saw horrific Daṇḍadhara mounted on his monstrous
water buffalo; saw Śūlapāṇi with the trident
in his grip; saw Caturbhuja with the conch, the discus,
and the mace in his four hands; and saw, with trepidation,
the multitude of the god clan's charioteers in their
vehicles from heaven. Dejected, the hero sighed and
stood there enervated, ah me, like the moon when swallowed
up by Rāhu or like the lion caught within a snare.
    Rāmānuja let drop the bow, then bared his wondrous sword;
the eye was dazzled by light from its broad blade. Alas, the
blinded conqueror of foes, hero Indrajit, struck by
that falchion fell upon the ground drenched with blood. Mother Earth
quaked violently; boisterously the ocean swelled. And at once
the whole universe filled with a stupendous noise. In the
heavens, on the earth, and throughout Pātāla, both mortal
and immortal beings, in sheer terror, anticipated
some disaster. There, as the sovereign of the Karbūras
sat in his courtly hall upon his golden throne, his crown
of gold of a sudden slipped from his head and tumbled down,
as the pinnacle on a chariot when severed by
an opposing charioteer teeters, then falls beneath

6. Hunters are served by beaters, whose function is to circle round behind the prey and drive it toward the hunters for the kill.

the car. Seized with misgivings, the champion, king of Laṅkā,
remembered Śaṅkara. Pramīlā's right eye slightly twitched.[7]
Absentmindedly, alas, that chaste wife, unawares, wiped
the vermilion from her pretty forehead.[8] For no reason,
Mandodarī, queen consort of the Rākṣasas, swooned. And,
asleep in their mothers' laps, babies cried mournful wails, just
as Vraja's children cried the time their precious Śyāma made
the land of Vraja dark, setting off for Madhupura.

Felled in unfair combat, that foeman of the Asuras'
foes, that hope of the Rākṣasa clan, addressed the champion
Lakṣmaṇa with harsh words, "Disgrace to the community
of warriors, you, Sumitrā's son! Shame on you a hundred
times! I, the son of Rāvaṇa, fear not Śamana. But
what will be an eternal sorrow in my heart, base one,
is that by a blow from your weapon I shall die today.
I—who in pitched battle subdued Indra, the subduer
of the clan of Daityas—am to die now by your hand? For
what false step has Providence meted out such punishment
upon this humble servant—shall I ever understand?
What else can I say to you? When the lord of Rākṣasas
gets word of this, who will save you, O meanest of all men?
Even though you plunge into the sea's unfathomed waters,
our sovereign's wrath will navigate to that domain—burning
like Vāḍaba. That rage of his, like a forest fire, will
incinerate you in the woods, if you flee into the
forest, you beastly thing. Even Night, you fool, will not be
capable of hiding you. Dānava, divine, or man—
who is fit to rescue you, Saumitri, when Rāvaṇa
is angered? Who in the world will wipe away your blemish,
blemished one?" Saying this, that noble-minded one recalled
with sadness in those final moments the lotus feet of
both his mother and his father. Anxious, he grew calm as
he thought of Pramīlā, his eternal bliss. Tears blended

7. The twitching of the right eye of a woman is ominous; for a man, it is the left eye twitching that is an inauspicious sign.

8. The vermilion atop the forehead, running into the central part of a woman's hair, is a mark of marriage for Bengali Hindu women. If such a woman's husband dies, she breaks her conch-shell bangles, another sign of a married woman, and wipes the vermilion from her head.

with his blood as both flowed freely, alas, dampening the
earth. The sun to lotus Laṅkā had reached his setting-hill.
Like dying embers or gentle rays of Tviṣāmpati,
just so the mighty one lay on the surface of the earth.

His eyes awash with tears, Rāvaṇa's younger brother spoke,
"You who always rest on finest silken bedding, fierce-armed
one, from what aversion do you lie now on the ground? What
would the king of Rākṣasas now say, were he to see you
lying on such bedding? and Mandodarī, chief queen of
the Rākṣasas? and pretty Pramīlā whose countenance
is like that of the moon of autumn? and all of Diti's
daughters, who in beauty shame the godly maidens? and chaste
Nikaṣā, your aged grandmama? What will they all say,
the clan of Rākṣasas, and you, the crown-gem of that clan?
Get up, dear lad. It is I, your uncle, calling you—I,
Vibhīṣaṇa! Why do you not pay heed, you who are more
dear than life to me? Arise, dear boy, I shall open wide
the door immediately, as you requested. Proceed now
to the armory, efface today in battle Laṅkā's
stain. O pride of Karbūras, does the ray-ringed solar god,
delight to eyes of all the world, ever go beyond the
setting-hill at noon? Then why today do you, dressed as you
are, famed one, lie upon the ground? The horns blow, listen there,
they call to you; the king of elephants is trumpeting;
horses whinny shrilly; armed is the Rākṣasas army,
an Ugracaṇḍā when it comes to war. The enemy
is at the city gates, get up, foe-conqueror. Preserve
the prestige of this clan of ours in the coming battle."

In such a manner hero Vibhīṣaṇa wailed with grief.
Saddened by his comrade's sadness, leonine Saumitri
spoke, "Restrain your sorrow, crown-gem of Rākṣasas. What is
the purpose of such fruitless lamentation? It was Fate's
decree that I slay this soldier; you are not to blame. Come,
let us now return to camp where Cintāmaṇi worries,
separated from his humble servant. Listen well, O
champion, auspicious music emanates from the homes of
heavenly beings." The best of charioteers then heard
celestial melodies, most enchanting, like in a dream.

The two left hurriedly, just as a hunter, when he slays
the young of a tigress in her absence, flees for his life
with wind's speed, panting breathlessly, lest that ferocious beast
should suddenly attack, wild with grief at finding her cubs
lifeless! or, as champion Aśvatthāmā, son of Droṇa,
having killed five sleeping boys inside the Pāṇḍava camp
in dead of night, departed going with the quickness of
a heart's desire, giddy from the thrill and fear, to where lay
Kuru monarch Duryodhana, his thigh broken in the
Kurukṣetra war! They both traveled unseen, by Māyā's
grace, to where the champion, the joy of Maithilī, was camped.
    Bowing to those lotus feet, Saumitri the lion spoke
with utmost deference the following, hands together,
"By the grace of your two feet, jewel of the Raghu clan,
this humble slave proved superior to the Rākṣasa
in combat. Meghanāda—that hero, that conqueror
of Śakra—is no more." Then planting a kiss atop his
younger brother's head and hugging him affectionately,
his lordship spoke, eyes wet with tears, "I have gained again this
day by your strength of arms my Sītā, O Indra of great
physical prowess. You, of all the heroes, are to be
most lauded. Praise be to mother Sumitrā. Praise to your
father Daśaratha, the progenitor of you and
most valued of the Raghu clan. Fortunate am I, your
elder brother; lucky is your place of birth, Ayodhyā.
This fame of yours will be proclaimed throughout the world for all
time to come. But remember, offer *pūjā* to the strength-
bestowing gods, my fondest one. Man is forever weak
when dependent on his own strength only; and if success
is realized, it is by the good graces of the gods."
    Addressing Vibhīṣaṇa, ally supreme, the husband
of Vaidehī intoned warmly, "At a most auspicious
moment, O companion, I came upon you in this land
of Rākṣasas. You, in the guise of a Rākṣasa, are
good fortune for the Rāghavas. You today have placed
the clan of Rāghavas in your debt by your merit, gem
of merit. As the king of planets is the monarch of
the day, so too, I say to you, the king of friends is you.
Come everyone, worship her who is beneficent, that

Śaṅkarī." And from the sky the gods in great delight rained down blossoms. Jubilant, the army bellowed, "Hail, spouse of Sītā!" In terror, golden Laṅkā woke to peals of glee.

Thus ends canto number six,
called "The Slaying,"
in the poem
The Slaying of Meghanāda.

CANTO 7

Felling with the Shakti Weapon

It was then Āditya showed himself upon the rising-
hill, looking just like Padmayoni, asleep on lotus
petals, as he, most pleased, opened his lotus eyes and gazed
at Mother Earth. Overjoyed, blossom-tressed Mother Earth smiled,
a string of pearls about her throat. As propitious music
waxes in a temple at the time of celebration,
so swelled waves of sweet notes throughout forest groves. Lotuses
shone in splendor upon pellucid waters while on land
the golden sunflower coveted as much attention.

As the blossoms bathed their bodies in Night's dew, so too chaste
Pramīlā with shapely breasts bathed in scented waters, then
plaited her hair. A strand of pearls beautified that glossy
head, like a shaft of moonlight across a cloud in autumn.
That woman whose arms were delicate as lotus stalks picked
up gem-studded bracelets to adorn her lotus-stalk-like
limbs—but it was as if the harsh bonds of those bangles brought
anguish to her arms! and alas, her golden necklace seemed
to pain that supple throat of hers. Surprised, the faithful wife
summoned confidante Vāsantī, the one who is most sweet
with scents of springtime, "Why, my dearest, do I find myself
incapable of wearing jewelry? What causes all the
wailing I hear far off in Laṅkā? My right eye twitches
constantly; my heart cries out. I know not, fond friend, alas—
I know not into what dark peril I shall plunge today.
My heart's lord attends the sacrificial temple; go to
him, Vāsantī. That jewel of a warrior must not join
in combat on this inauspicious day. Tell my life's lord
that this slave of his implores him, embracing his two feet!"

She whose speech is, like a *vīṇā*, full of melody fell
silent. Confidante Vāsantī answered, "Listen well, O
you of fetching countenance, the wailing grows louder all
the time. I cannot tell you why the residents weep. Come,
let us go immediately to the god's shrine where her
highness, Mandodarī, worships Āśutoṣa. Giddy
on the spirits of battle, the horses and elephants,

charioteers and chariots, promenade the highway
of the king. How could I reach that sacrificial temple,
my married mistress, where your husband, who always wins in
warfare, outfits himself in martial garb?" So the two of
them proceeded to the Candracūḍa temple, where the
queen of Rākṣasas was imploring Candracūḍa to
protect her son—but all in vain! Anxiously they hastened.

Girīśa, at home on Mount Kailāsa, grew sullen. That
Dhūrjaṭi, dejected, sighed repeatedly, then glancing
at his Haimavatī spoke, "Goddess, your wish is won; that
monarch among charioteers, Indrajit, succumbed in
deadly battle. Hero Saumitri, adhering to the
scheme of Māyā, slew him while in the temple. The treasure
of the clan of Rākṣasas is my finest devotee,
moon-faced one. I am ever saddened by his sorrows. You
see this trident in my hand, Satī, the grief one feels for
sons strikes deeper than do blows from this. Ever present, ah,
alas, is the agony—even all-destroying time
proves powerless to numb the pain. Has Rāvaṇa, Satī,
yet heard his sterling son has died in battle? He will at
once succumb unless I, with my gift of *rudra tejas*,
save that Rākṣasa. I pleased Vāsava at your behest,
faithful wife; permit me now to favor Daśānana."

Kātyāyanī replied, "Do as you wish, enemy of
Tripura. Vāsava's desire will be fulfilled; that for
which he begged before your feet now comes to pass. My lord, the
warrior Dāśarathi is a devotee of this slave
of yours. Let that fact be kept in mind, O Viśvanātha.
To those lotus feet of yours what more shall your servant say?"

With a smile Śūlī called to mind brave Vīrabhadra. When
that warrior, most formidable of stature, had fallen
prostrate at his feet, Hara spoke, "Dear lad, Indrajit this
day has lost his life in combat. Saumitri slipped into
the sacrificial temple and slew him, by the grace of
Umā. The messengers are scared to give this message to
the lord of Rākṣasas. Moreover, messengers among
the Rākṣasas do not know by what deception warrior
Saumitri bested that unbeatable Rākṣasa in
war. But for the gods, charioteer, who in this world is

capable of comprehending godly *māyā*? Quick, go
to golden Laṅkā, O you whose arms are strong, dressed as a
messenger for the Rākṣasas. By my command, give aid—
confer my *rudra tejas*—to the son of Nikaṣā."

Through the sky went the warrior Vīrabhadra, fearsome in
appearance. Aerial beings all round bowed timidly.
The sun was voided of its brilliance by the brightness of
his charm, just as the nectar-ray-ringed moon lacks rays of light
in the presence of the splendor of the sun. The frightful
shadow of a trident fell upon the surface of the
earth. With resounding roars the lord of waters paid homage
to Bhairava's minion. That warrior reached the city of
the Rākṣasas; and golden Laṅkā shook with tremors from
the force of his landing, just as branches quaver when the
Indra among birds, Garuḍa, alights upon a tree.

That warrior went inside the sacrificial temple and
saw the Indra among warriors on the ground, alas, like
a blooming *kiṃśuka* tree felled amid the woods from the
power of Prabhañjana. Moist-eyed, he gazed upon the
prince. Immortals' hearts are pained to witness mortal sorrow.

Before the golden throne—where sat warrior Daśānana,
crown-gem of Rākṣasas—Vīrabhadra showed himself in
messenger's attire, now covered with ashes and lacking
brilliance like a sun concealed. Bowing slightly, that warrior
blessed the Rākṣasa and teary eyed stood before him, palms
together. Surprised, the monarch queried, "For what reason,
messenger, does your tongue hesitate to carry out its
appointed task? Rāma, the human being—you are not
a servant of that Rāghava! Then why, O bearer of
the news, is your face so ashen hued? The sun to lotus
Laṅkā, vanquisher of gods and Daityas, prepares today
for battle—can you bear me tidings that are ominous?
If Rāghava died in battle from his lethal, thunder-
bolt-like bludgeon, then convey that news. I shall reward you."
With deliberation, that one spoke, incognito, "My
lord, alas, how can I, worthless me, relate before your
feet misfortune's tidings? At the outset, Karbūra king,
grant this slave of yours *abhaya*." Anxiously the hero
answered, "What need have you to fear, messenger? Tell me at

once—weal and woe happen in this world by Fate's decree. I
bestow on you *abhaya*, now promptly give me the news!"

The hero, Virūpākṣa's emissary costumed as
a message bearer, spoke, "O best of Rākṣasas, warrior
Meghanāda, pride of Karbūras, died today in war!"

As when deep within the woods a Niṣāda wounds the king
of animals with a mortal arrow and that lion,
roaring wildly, slumps to the ground, so too slumped that monarch
to the floor of his assembly hall. Counselors of his,
wailing loudly, weeping, gathered all around that champion.
Some fetched pitchers full of cooling water; others fanned him.

With the *rudra tejas*, Vīrabhadra soon brought to his
senses that most excellent of Rākṣasas. The hero,
reacting as does gunpowder to fire's touch, commanded
the messenger, "Speak, messenger, who slew ever-winning
Indrajit today in battle? Tell me without delay!"

Replied the one in disguise, "By deception Saumitri
the lion entered the temple of the Nikumbhilā
sacrifice, Indra among kings, and in an unfair fight
that wicked one slew the Indra among warriors. Alas,
I saw him there within the temple, that warrior, just like
a blooming *kiṃśuka* tree felled amid the woods from the
power of Prabhañjana. You, the finest warrior, the
lord of Rākṣasas—assuage your grief today with acts of
valor. Let the women of the clan of Rākṣasas soak
the earth with teardrops. But you in warfare slaughter with your
awesome bludgeon that deceitful foe, the slayer of your
son, and appease, great archer, the denizens of this land!"

Then suddenly that godly messenger disappeared, and
the assembly hall filled with a perfume divine. The lord
of Rākṣasas caught a glimpse of a pile of matted hair
and the shadow of a monstrous trident. Bowing, his hands
cupped in supplication, that Śaiva spoke, "Have you at last,
your lordship, remembered me, your hapless servant? Stupid
me, alas, how shall I ever understand your *māyā*,
illusory one? But first, I shall carry out your orders,
knower of all. Thereafter shall I humbly narrate to those
lotus feet of yours everything this heart of mine contains?"

Angered—powerful today by the great *rudra tejas*—

that fine Rākṣasa exhorted, "Each archer in this golden
Laṅkā, muster hastily a four-division army!
On the field of battle shall we forget our suffering—
if indeed a person can forget insufferable pain!"

The rumbling of drums of war surged across the floor of that
assembly while horn blowers sounded resonating blasts
upon their best of bull's horns, as though it were the very
moment of Pralaya! At that frightful din the Bhūtas
on Mount Kailāsa's crest quickly armed, as did Rākṣasas
everywhere; Laṅkā reeled underneath the weight of warriors'
feet. Flame-hued chariots of war exited smartly, gold
pennants waving; elephants, all smoky gray, brandished in
their trunks huge cudgels; and out pranced snorting steeds. Cāmara,
bane of the immortals, roaring, joined the four divisions
of the army; with the charioteers drove Udagra,
a terror in combat; among the ranks of elephants
rode Vāskala, like cloud-borne Vajrī, fierce thunderbolt in
hand among his clouds; shouting menacingly, the hero
Asilomā, commander of the cavalry, appeared;
and Biḍālākṣa, a fearsome Rākṣasa, wroth in war,
marched with the infantry. Then came the standard-bearers, flags
flying, as though a rash of comets of a sudden streaked
through the sky. And Rākṣasa music rang out all around.

As the Dānava-quelling Caṇḍī, born from the power
of the gods, laughed jauntily while she, Satī, armed herself
with godly weaponry, so in Laṅkā armed the corps of
fearsome Rākṣasas—in war a wrathful Ugracaṇḍā.
Her arms possessed the strength of the king of elephants; Her
feet moved with equine speed; the crown upon Her head was made
of golden chariots; bejeweled banners formed the loose
end of Her sari; *bheri* kettledrums, *turi* horns, the
dundubhi and *dāmāmā* and other drums produced Her
lion's roar! Weapons—*śela, śakti, jāṭi, tomara,*
bhomara, śūla, muṣala, mudgara, paṭṭiśa,
nārāca, and *kaunta*—shone brightly as Her teeth! The fire
of Her eyes was born of armor's brilliance! Mother Earth quaked
constantly; with fear the ocean tossed and rolled; the mountains
were atremble—from that roar of Bhīmā—for once again
it seemed that Caṇḍī had been born and thundered angrily!

Back at camp that champion, the sun among the solar clan,
startled, addressed his boon friend Vibhīṣaṇa saying, "See
there, companion, how Laṅkā lurches time and time again
as if in the throes of a violent quake. Billows of
smoke arise and, like thick clouds, blot out the lord of daylight.
A frightful luster glows throughout the sky, as though born of
flames of the world's final fires. Listen there, hear those crashing
waves, as if the sea churns in the distance to dissolve the
universe within Pralaya!" That Rākṣasa, crown-gem
of friends, spoke, his cheeks gone wan with fright, "What can I say, my
lord? The land trembles under foot of Rākṣasa warriors,
not from any earthquake. That light you see throughout the sky
springs not from doomsday fires, O husband of Vaidehī. The
ten directions are aglow from the combined brilliance of
their weapons, luster born of golden armor. That uproar,
hero, which now deafens ears is not the rumble of the
sea; it is the ranks of Rākṣasas roaring, maddened by
the heady wines of valor. Distraught by sadness for his
Indra among sons, Laṅkā's lord dons the charioteer's
attire. Tell me, how are you to rescue Lakṣmaṇa and
all the many other warriors, warrior, from dire peril?"

His lordship answered sweetly, "Go quickly, O best of friends,
and summon here at once my commanding officers. This
humble thrall is ever given shelter by the gods. Those
supernal beings will be the rescue of their servant."

Then taking up a horn, that best of Rākṣasas let out
a chilling blast. Kiṣkindhyā's lord came forward, striding with
the saunter of a king of elephants; then came warrior
Aṅgada, wise in ways of warfare; Nala and Nīla,
divinelike in appearance; Hanumān, fiercely strong, like
Prabhañjana; the hero Jāmbuvāna; the warrior
Śarabha, bull of warriors; Gavākṣa and Raktākṣa,
dreaded by the Rākṣasas; and all the other generals.

Hailing that contingent of great warriors in accordance
with the proper courtesies, hero Rāghava spoke out,
"Overwhelmed by sorrow for his son, the Rākṣasa king
today armed hurriedly together with his Rākṣasa
legions; Laṅkā trembles constantly beneath the weight of
warriors' feet. You all are world conquerors in war; prepare

with haste; defend Rāghava today in this hour of
his direst need. By quirk of luck I became a friendless
forest exile. You all are Rāma's refuge, strength, and force
in battle. But one charioteer is yet alive in
Laṅkā—slay him today, my warriors. By your aid I placed
shackles on the sea; in pitched battle I downed the champion
Kumbhakarṇa, the counterpart of that trident-clutching
Śambhu; Saumitri slew ferocious Meghanāda, the
bane of gods, Daityas, and of men. Save my clan, my honor,
and my life, supporters of the Raghus, and rescue her,
the Raghu wife, incarcerated by the wiles of that
Rākṣasa. You have bought this Rāma with the coin of your
affection; by vouchsafing generosity, now bind
firm with a noose of gratitude today the entire
Raghu line, O you who dwell within the southern regions."

The Raghu lord, teary eyed, fell silent. With a sound like
that made by the clouds, Sugrīva thundered, "Either I shall
die or I shall cause that Rāvaṇa to die; this I vow,
O finest of the champions, at your feet! I now enjoy
the comforts of a kingdom, my lordship, by virtue of
your favor—you are my source of wealth and honor; by a
noose of gratitude is your humble subject ever bound
to your lotus feet! What more can I say, O champion? There
is not a warrior in our ranks who fears Kṛtānta when
asked to carry out a task for you! Let the Rākṣasas
arm; we shall fight unafraid!" The officers all roared with
rage; that massive army bellowed, "Victory to Rāma!"

Affronted by those horrid cries, the ranks of Rākṣasas
thundered in heroic frenzy, like Dānava-quelling
Durgā in answer to the howls from Dānavas. Golden
Laṅkā filled to overflowing with raucous shrieks and shouts.

Those noises reached the place where Kamalā, Rājalakṣmī
of the clan of Rākṣasas, sat upon her lotus throne.
That chaste wife gave a start. Her lotus eyes saw Rākṣasas
arming everywhere, blind with fury; Rākṣasa banners
fluttered in the air, a sign portending ill for any
living creature. The Rākṣasas' musical instruments
blared forth loudly. And Indirā—whose face is like the
autumn moon—beat a path through the void to Vaijayanta.

Musicians, both various and sundry, performed in that heavenly place; Apsarā maidens danced; Kinnaras sang melodiously. Among the gods and goddesses sat the monarch of the gods upon his golden throne. To his left was Śacī of the charming smile. Inexhaustible vernal breezes wafted by, exhaling sweetly; and all about, Gandharvas rained down heaps of *mandāra* blossoms.

There within that godly convocation stepped the love of Keśava. Bowing to her, Indra spoke, "Give me, please, the dust from on your feet, O Mother; for by your grace this slave of yours is freed of fear—wicked Rāvaṇi lost his life today in battle. Now I can pursue the pleasures of this heaven unencumbered. Compassionate one, what does he lack on whom you cast your sympathetic glance?" With a smile pretty Indirā, gem par excellence of the jewel-laden sea, replied, "Foe of Daityas, your enemy may have fallen to the ground; but with his throng of Rākṣasas, the king of Laṅkā, that distraught monarch, makes ready to avenge the slaying of his son. Thousands of Rākṣasas gird up with him. It was to announce this news, my lord, that I traveled here. High-minded Saumitri accomplished your task for you. Now save him, Āditeya. Great is he who risks his life to rescue a helpmate when in danger. What more, Śakra, can I tell you? The prowess of the clan of Rākṣasas is not unknown to you. Do ponder, O spouse of Śacī, by what means you might help rescue Rāghava."

Replied the sovereign of the gods, "See there, in the north of heaven, O Jagadambā, there in the province of the sky, a fine array of immortals. If that great archer, monarch of the Rākṣasa clan, ventures out desiring battle, I shall war with him upon the battlefield, kind one. I fear not Rāvaṇa, Mother, stripped of Rāvaṇi."

Much impressed, Ramā surveyed the troops of Vāsava in heaven's northern sector. As far as her divine eyes saw, that pretty gazed on chariots and elephants, on steeds and horsemen, on mahouts, charioteers, and infantry, victorious in combat, all victors over Yama. There were Gandharvas, Kinnaras, and the gods, as full of fire as the final fire of this *yuga*. There was general

Skanda, foe of Tāraka, aboard his peacock-bannered
chariot; and there was charioteer Citraratha
on his multicolored vehicle. The sky glowed like a
woods engulfed by flames; in silhouette against all that loomed
rows of elephants majestically, like smoky billows.
Flame-shaped spearheads, glittered, blinding, bedazzling eyes. Flags flared
stylishly, as though static streaks of lightning; shields glinted,
outgleaming the solar orb; and armor sparkled brightly.
    The love of Mādhava inquired, "Speak, Āditeya,
treasure of the gods, where are Prabhañjana and all the
other guardians of the compass points? Why is it that the
ranks in heaven seem so vacant in their absence?" Śacī's
hero husband answered, "I ordered the direction-guards
to guard today their respective regions, Jagadambā.
In this battle of the gods and Rākṣasas (both clans near
invincible), who can say what will happen? Mother Earth
perhaps this day shall drown, as at the time of Pralaya;
this vast creation might be plunged into the nether realm."
    Keśava's sleek-haired darling blessed that monarch of the gods.
Then she, the Mother, returned most hurriedly to Laṅkā
transported on gold-hued clouds. There Kamalā went within
her own shrine, sadly sitting on her lotus throne—all ten
directions were illumined by her beauty's rays, but her
face was drawn, ah, due to sorrows of the Rākṣasa clan.
    Drunk on the heady wines of warfare, the sovereign of the
Rākṣasas donned his martial gear—his legions of Indras
among charioteers circled him with an effulgence
as bright as the golden peak of Mount Hemakūṭa. Not
far off, martial music played; Rākṣasa banners fluttered
in the breeze; and countless Rākṣasas shouted threateningly.
At that instant Queen Mandodarī rushed into the court,
alas, like a flustered pigeon who finds her nest devoid
of fledglings. Scurrying behind her came her retinue
of confidantes. The queen collapsed before those royal feet.
    With tenderness the Rākṣasa king helped his chaste wife to
her feet, then spoke sadly, "Fate has at present turned against
us both, Indrāṇī of the Rākṣasa clan. That we yet
live is only to avenge his death. Return now to your
empty quarters—I am headed for the battlefield. Why

do you detain me? An eternity, my lady, we
shall have during which to grieve. We shall renounce the worthless
pleasures of the realm, purest wife, and dwell in solitude—
the two of us—and reminisce on him day after day.
Go back. Why would you douse this flame of wrath with the water
of your tears, O Queen Mandodarī? The stately *śāla*
tree that enhanced the woods was felled today; the highest peak
upon that best of mountains' crest was crushed; the moon, jewel
of the skies, has been forever swallowed up by Rāhu."

Tugging, coaxing, her companions escorted her to the
women's quarters. Consumed with rage, the Rākṣasa lord stepped
outside and, turned to the Rākṣasas, ranted with fury—
"He, by whose might this Rākṣasa force proved dominant in
war with gods, Daityas, and with men—he, the volley of whose
arrows harassed Indra, of the gods, in the company
of his godly charioteers, and the Nāgas in the
depths of Pātāla, and men within the world of man—he
is dead this day, that monarch among warriors, slain in
unfair combat, warriors! Saumitri in a sneak-thief's guise
stole into the temple and in that out-of-the-way place
slew my son while he sat unarmed! Just as one away from
home dies sad at heart, distant from his native land, in like
manner died today the ornament of golden Laṅkā,
within this very golden Laṅkā, without seeing there
in front of him as death approached those objects of his love—
father, mother, brother, and devoted wife! For a long
time now I have protected all of you as though you were
my sons—ask the world over, what family rivals that of
the Rākṣasas in fame? However, all for naught have I
vanquished gods and men, and planted in this mundane world the
tree of glorious achievements. Cruelest Fate this day has
at last turned utterly against me, and that is why the
irrigation trough around that tree of mine dried up in
this unseasonable summer's heat. Still then, I do not
weep or wail. Of what use is crying? Shall I get him back
again? Alas, do streams of tears ever melt Kṛtānta's
stony heart? Now I shall join the fray and best that stupid
Saumitri, transgressor against *dharma,* who in warfare
stoops to deception. Should my efforts prove futile today,

I shall not return—I shall not set foot again within
this city as long as I shall live! Such is my promise,
Rākṣasa charioteers. You in battle are the bane
of gods, Daityas, and of men; you are world-victors. As you
march onto the battlefield, recall him. Meghanāda
died in battle. When one has heard such news, who within this
clan of Karbūras would wish to go on living? Hero
Meghanāda was the pride of our own Karbūra clan."

With remorseful sighs, the great archer ceased his speech. Out of
rage, and of grief, those Rākṣasas let loose a baleful howl,
dampening the ground, ah me, with a downpour from their eyes.

On hearing that horrendous hooting cry, the army of
the Raghus, boisterous, thundered back. And the Indra of the
heavens shouted from on high. Vaidehī's husband became
incensed, as did Saumitri the lion, and Sugrīva,
Aṅgada, Hanumān, and the other valued generals,
all Yamas to the Rākṣasas—Nala, Nīla, and high-
minded Śarabha—that huge army bellowed out their shouts
of "Victory to Rāma!" Roiling clouds rumbled as they
veiled the skies. The universe was dazzled by lightning streaks
as thunder clapped. Those jets of light flashed grins that looked much like
Cāmuṇḍā's many smiles when that goddess, giggling, giddy
on warfare's liquor, crushed the frenzied Dānava forces.
The jewel of the day, the dark's destroyer, sank within
those clouds of gloom. Winds, with the breath of Vaiśvānara, blew
everywhere. Forest fires raged through woodlands. Flood waters
roared as they, without warning, swallowed villages and cities.
Earth tremors toppled trees and buildings. Living creatures cried
out loud, and then gave up the ghost, just as at Pralaya!

In sheer terror, panic-stricken Mother Earth fled sobbing
to Vaikuṇṭha. There, upon his throne of gold in all his
gracefulness, sat Mādhava. That faithful wife bowed before
the god and prayed, "Time after time, O spouse of Ramā, sea
of kindness, you assumed so many incarnations and
thereby saved me, your most humble subject. During the flood
you, as Tortoise, placed this slave of yours upon your tortoise
shell. I found myself between the tips of your tusks (which looked
like smudge marks on the body of the moon) that time when you,
friend of the needy, descended in the body of the

Boar. You eased this servant's suffering by taking on the
guise of Human-Lion and dismembering the Daitya
Hiraṇyakaśipu. As the dwarf Vāmana, you dwarfed
Bali's pride. I lived, my lord, by your grace. What more can I
say? This thrall finds sanctuary at your feet. And so, I
fall before those lotus feet in this time of grave danger."
Smiling, and in the sweetest of tones, the foe of Mura
asked, "For what cause are you upset today, tell me, Mother
Earth, mother of the world? Who troubles you this time, dear child?"
Answered Mother Earth, weeping, "What is there you do not know,
omniscient one? Look, my lord, toward Laṅkā. The Rākṣasa
king is drunk on war. So too is that hero, Indra of
the Rāghavas. Likewise is that charioteer, the Indra
of the heavens! Three rut elephants, they give trouble to
your servant. That godlike sovereign among charioteers,
Lakṣmaṇa the lion, slew fierce Meghanāda today
in battle. Beside himself with bitter grief, the treasure
of the Rākṣasas vowed to kill in combat Lakṣmaṇa.
Indra, with bravado fit a warrior, vowed to defend
him. Alas, any moment now the deadly battle will
begin in golden Laṅkā, O Pītāmbara, sparked off
by tempers of the gods, the men, and Rākṣasas. How shall
I endure this ghastly torment, O lord, please tell me that."
With a smile, the lord of Ramā glanced toward Laṅkā. He saw
Rākṣasa forces setting out in countless numbers, blind
with fury, arrayed in four divisions. In the lead marched
"Prowess," sending tremors through the earth; on behind came "Din,"
deafening the ear; "Dust" followed, forming heavy clouds that
blocked one's vision. Golden Laṅkā reeled most violently. The
spouse of Śrī observed the Raghu army on the outskirts
of the city, as Prabhañjana, the waves' eternal
enemy, shows himself from afar to them who ride the
ocean's surface. Puṇḍarīkākṣa watched the god clan on
the run toward Laṅkā, just as Garuḍa, king of birds, on
espying at a distance his staple diet—hooded
cobra—swoops screaming. The universe filled with grave rumblings.
Abandoning their meditations, yogis fled; frightened
mothers held their babies in their arms and cried; animals
dashed off in all directions terrified. Cintāmaṇi

(he who is the swan upon the "mind-lake" of Yogīndra)
pondered for a moment then replied to Mother Earth, "Chaste
wife, I see your situation is most awkward. By the
gift of *rudra tejas*, Virūpākṣa made that monarch
of the clan of Rākṣasas powerful today. I find
no other resolution. You simply have to go to
him, Mother Earth!" Weeping, she answered to those lotus feet,
"Alas, my lord, that powerful destroyer, Triśūlī,
is constantly engaged in pure destruction. That foe of
Tripura displays an inexhaustible supply of
tamas. O Sauri, the deadly snake only wants to spew
his caustic venom, and thus burn the living! But you, an
ocean of compassion, supporter of the universe,
if you bear not the burden of this universe, then tell
me, who else will? Save your servant, O lord of Śrī, this is
my entreaty most humbly put before your reddened feet!"
Replied the deity, with a smile, "Return to where you
were, Mother Earth. I shall carry out this task for you by
holding godly might in check. Devendra will be power-
less to rescue Lakṣmaṇa; Umā's grieving lord will not
be able to avenge the sorrow of the Rākṣasas."
Much relieved, Mother Earth repaired to earth. Then his lordship
said to Garuḍa, "Fly through the firmament, winged one, and
pilfer the power of the gods during this day's fight, just
as the sun, enemy of darkness, purloins quantities
of water, or just as you, my Vainateya, filched the
amṛta. By my orders, go make the gods impotent."
Spreading his gigantic wings, that monarch of the birds flew
the skies. His monstrous shadow fell upon the earth below,
darkening the countless forests, mountains, streams, and rivers.
Just as flames leap out through doors and through windows when a fire
flares up in a house, just so from all four city gates leapt
Rākṣasas, howling wrathfully. The Raghu army roared
in all directions; and the forces of the gods then made
their entry to the fray. First came that best of elephants,
Airāvata, driven mad by the thrill of battle. On
his back rode lightning-tossing Sahasrākṣa, lustrous as
Mount Meru's pinnacle caught within the rays of sun, or
like the sun himself at noon. Then came the charioteer

general Skanda, the foe of Tāraka, riding in his
peacock-bannered chariot. And warrior Citraratha
in his vehicle of many hues. And Kinnaras and
Gandharvas and Yakṣas on their several different mounts and
chariots. In terror, Laṅkā listened to music from
the heavens. That land shook, startled by the godly noises.

The gem of men prostrated flat upon the ground in front
of Indra, then spoke, "I am a servant to the servants
of the gods, O sovereign of the god clan! How many deeds
of merit I must have done in former births—what can I
say? For that is surely why today I gained the refuge
of your feet in these most trying times, O Vajrapani.
Is that the reason that the denizens of heaven on
this day have sanctified this soil with the touch of their feet?"

Replied the monarch of the skies, addressing Rāghava,
"You are favored by the god clan, gem among the Raghus.
Climb aboard this godly chariot, charioteer, and,
by strength of arms, destroy the Rākṣasa who transgresses
against *dharma*. By his own wicked acts is that treasure
of the Rākṣasas now lost. Who can save him? Just as we
procured elixir through the churning of the waters, so
too shall we gods today churn this Laṅkā. We shall thrash those
Niśācaras and deliver unto you, champion, that
faithful and most pure Maithilī. How much longer must that
Ramā sit beneath the waters, with the world in darkness?"

Raucous fighting raged between the gods and humans and the
Rākṣasas. Ten thousand conch shells, like the sea itself, blared
all around. Heroic archers twanged their bowstrings until
the ear no longer heard. Arrows shot across the skies, and,
with the might of lightning bolts, they pierced leather armor, shields,
and bodies, causing blood to flow in torrents. Rākṣasa
and human charioteers, both were leveled. Elephants
fell in heaps, as do leaves in a garden stripped by forces
of Prabhañjana. Chargers, whinnying, collapsed. And the
battlefield filled with an excruciating dissonance!

Cāmara, scourge of the divines, attacked the godly ranks
with the full force of all four divisions. Charioteer
Citraratha, that champion on a chariot, brilliant
as the sun, sped to the fray, like a lion when he spies

his mortal enemy, the elephant. With ferocious
shouts, Udagra, monarch among charioteers, beckoned
to Sugrīva. Chariot wheels ground round and round, making
noises like a hundred streams cascading. With his troop of
elephants, Vāskala—as unstoppable himself as
a bull elephant—spotted Aṅgada some ways away;
that young prince grew enraged, as do little lion cubs when
they see a herd of deer. Asilomā, livid, keen sword
in his hand, surrounded with his horses Śarabha, bull
among those warriors. Biḍālākṣa (as destructive as
Virūpākṣa) began to war wildly with Hanumān.
Into combat on his godly car rode charioteer
Rāghava, aha, like a second monarch of the skies,
that wielder of the thunderbolt. He whose banner shows a
peacock, Skanda, enemy of Tāraka, gazed upon,
to his surprise, the handsome champion Lakṣmaṇa, likeness
of himself in the mortal world. Dust clouds rose round about;
golden Laṅkā tottered; the ocean roared. That hero, spouse
of Śacī, drew up his array of troops, magnificent.
    Out came the Rākṣasas' king astride his Puṣpaka. Its
wheels screamed loudly, spitting sparks. The team of horses neighed with
spirit. A luster, born of gemstones, blinding to the eye,
ran ahead, just like Dawn when Āditya in his one-wheeled
chariot ascends the rising-hill. And the Rākṣasas
shouted uncontrollably when they caught sight of their lord.
    Addressing his best of chariot drivers, that finest
charioteer spoke, "The humans do not fight alone this
day, O driver, have a look. Like fire amid the smoke, just
so a regiment of the enemies of Asuras
shines splendidly amid the Raghu ranks. Indra comes to
Laṅkā now that he has heard of Indrajit's demise in
battle." And remembering his son, the king, that treasure-
trove of Rākṣasas, roaring angrily spoke in grave tones,
"Steer this chariot, O driver, to where thunder-clutching
Vāsava stands now!" That chariot traveled with desire's
speed. The Raghu army turned and fled, as forest dwellers
flee, short of breath, when they eye a raging bull elephant!
Or, as birds and beasts flee terrified when fearsome thunder
clouds, filled with flashing lightning, whip across the skies, belching

loudly! Twanging his bowstring, that lion among Indras
among warriors pierced then and there the drawn battle lines with
his sharpest arrows, as easily and simply as flood
waters, with a strong surge, cave in levees made of sand! Or,
as a tiger in the nighttime crashes through a pasture's
fences! But Śikhidhvaja drove his chariot ahead,
and with resolve drawing back his bowstring, that great hero,
foe of Tāraka, blocked the other charioteer's path.
With hands together, cupped in supplication, and bowing
to that champion, Laṅkā's monarch solemnly spoke, "This thrall,
my lord, worships day and night Śaṅkarī and Śaṅkara!
Why then do I find you here today, unashamedly
among the enemy throng? For what reason, Kumāra,
do you render such assistance to Rāma, that hateful
human? You are an Indra among charioteers. In
an unfair fight, Lakṣmaṇa killed my son. Now I must kill
that loathsome, that deceitful fighter. Do not block my way!"
    The son of Pārvatī spoke, "I must defend Lakṣmaṇa
today, O sovereign of the Rākṣasas, by order of
the sovereign of the gods. Through strength of arms, O strong-armed one,
defeat me, or you shall not realize this goal of yours."
    Angered and, moreover, powerful this day, due to the
great *rudra tejas*, the riches of the Rākṣasa clan,
like Agni incarnate, shouted threateningly and hurled his
weapons, wounding Śaktidhara in the fray with a hail
of arrows. Abhayā, turning to Vijayā, said, "Look
there, dear companion, over there toward Laṅkā, the monarch
of the Rākṣasas mercilessly pierced Kumāra with
sharp arrows. Look there in the sky, the Indra among birds
is pilfering the power of the gods. Go, my dear, with
lightning's speed and halt Kumāra. O follower of mine,
my heart breaks when I see those bloody rivulets on my
baby's supple body. Sadānanda shows compassion
to his devotees, even more than to his son. That is
why Rāvaṇa is now most difficult to overcome
in battle, dearest girl." That female messenger darted
as sunbeams down the blue sky's path. Addressing Kumāra,
that moon-faced one whispered in his ear, "Please sheathe your weapons,
Śaktidhara, on orders of Śakti herself. The king

of Laṅkā is at present possessed of *rudra tejas*!"
Smiling, god Skanda, Tāraka's adversary, turned his
chariot about. With a triumphant roar the lord of
Rākṣasa laid low countless soldiers, then sped off to where
Vajrapāṇi sat astride the back of Airāvata.

Gandharvas, by the hundreds, and mortal men circled round
that Indra among Rākṣasas; but with threatening shouts, the
champion dismissed all of them in the twinkling of an eye,
as a conflagration turns a stand of trees to ashes.
That throng of warriors fled, giving up disgracefully. Just
then the foeman of the Daitya clan came forward, irate,
like Karṇa seeing Pārtha in the Kurukṣetra war.

That Rākṣasa, yelling, threatening, hurled a huge lance aimed
at Airāvata. But, in mid-flight the monarch of the
skies shattered it abruptly with a rain of arrows. The
sovereign of the Karbūras shouted brashly to the lord
of the divines, "Heroic spouse of Śacī, Rāvaṇi,
in mortal fear of whom you shiver constantly in your
Vaijayanta, is dead, killed through perfidy today in
warfare, according to your plan! I suppose that is why
you have come to Laṅkā city, shameless one! You cannot
be slain, immortal. But if you could, I would have quelled you
in an instant, as quells Śamana! Still you cannot save
Lakṣmaṇa, I give my word on that, god!" And clenching in
his fist an awesome war club, that best of charioteers
leapt to the ground—Mother Earth reeled beneath the weight of his
two feet, and his sword in its scabbard clattered on his hip.

With a holler, Kuliśī, the thunder-flinger, enraged,
seized a thunderbolt. At that very moment Garuḍa
stole away his strength; the lightning-hurling god was rendered
powerless to move a single shaft of lightning. The king
of Rākṣasas then bashed the skull of the monarch among
elephants with his fearsome war club, as Prabhañjana,
uprooting in a storm sky-piercing trees, bashes mountain
peaks. Stopped dead there in his tracks by the colossal blow, that
pachyderm fell to his knees. Grinning, the Rākṣasa once
more stepped up onto his chariot. Chariot driver
Mātali commandeered a wondrous chariot, but the
foe of Diti's sons forewent the chase in a fit of pique.

Then bow in hand, roaring like a lion, Dāśarathi
wheeled into the battle on a car come from the heavens.
    The Rākṣasa sovereign spoke, "I do not seek you today,
husband of Vaidehī. Live a little longer on this
earth in safety. Where is your younger brother, that heinous
fighter who resorts to treachery? It is he whom I
shall kill. You return to camp, best of Rāghavas." The great
archer then let out a ghastly roar as that champion caught
sight of Rāmānuja at a distance. Like a lion
among cattle, that Indra among champions was mauling
Rākṣasas—now from his chariot, now on the ground.
    The Puṣpaka sped along, grinding, growling. Its wheels, like
discs of fire, rained sparks everywhere. The royal banner on
that chariot's crest shone splendidly, like Dhūmaketu
incarnate! As the monarch among falcons, when it spots
a pigeon off some ways, spreads its wings and dashes through the
skies, so too dashed that Rākṣasa, on observing upon
the battlefield his son's slayer, that champion Saumitri.
Both gods and men ran here, there, everywhere, hollering, to
protect their lord of champions. And troops of Rākṣasas came
on the run, once they caught sight of their lordly Rākṣasa.
    The son of Añjanā, having bested in a battle
the Rākṣasa warrior Biḍālākṣa, now appeared—that
Hanumān, mighty like Prabhañjana, howled fearsomely!
    Just as heaps of cotton fly in ten directions, blown by
the forces of the god of winds, just so ran Rākṣasas
helter-skelter, on catching sight of that warrior, Yama's
likeness. Angered, Laṅkā's sovereign, with his sharpest arrows
harassed that champion. Hanumān grew agitated, like
a mountain seized by tremors. That Indra among warriors
called to mind his father's feet at this time of jeopardy,
and, from pure joy, the wind bestowed his own powers on his
son—as likewise the sun endues the moon, that beloved
of lotuses, with a gift of his own rays. But the fine
charioteer Naikaṣeya, mighty, by virtue of
great *rudra tejas*, warded off that son of Pavana—
Hanumān beat a retreat, fleeing from the battlefield.
    Then along came Kiṣkindhyā's sovereign, having put to flight
warmonger Udagra. Smiling, the lord of Laṅkā spoke,

"Have you not forgone the pleasures of your kingship at a
rather awkward moment, barbarian, to come to this
golden city? Was not your brother's wife, that Tārā, your
guiding star?[1] Why would you abandon her and come away,
here among the brotherhood of charioteers, hey you,
Kiṣkindhyā's lord? I let you go. Now run along to your
homeland. Why would you want to make of her a widow once
again, you fool? What other 'husband's brothers' does she have?"[2]
With a ferocious roar, hero Sugrīva answered back,
"Who is there in this world, Rākṣasa king, who acts opposed
to *dharma* as much as you do? Lusting for another's
wife, immoral one, you plunged your entire line into
utter ruin. You, Rākṣasa, are a disgrace to the
Rākṣasa clan. You shall die by my hand today! I will
rescue my friend's wife, after putting you to death right now!"

With that, the hero let loose a shout and hurled a mountain
peak. That mountain crest darkened skies as it sailed along; but
with arrows finely honed that skilled charioteer, king of
Rākṣasas, reduced the pinnacle to rubble. The crown-
jewel among Rākṣasas then strummed his bow again, and,
with a hideous howl, that champion pierced Sugrīva with
his keenest arrow. That high-minded one, in pain from the
devastating wound, fled away. In utter panic, the
Raghu forces scattered to the four directions (with a
gushing, rushing noise, as when waters break embankments). The
gods, not in possession of their powers now, fled with the
humans, as with smoke fly burning embers when blown briskly
by the god of winds. Right in front of him that Rākṣasa
saw godlike Lakṣmaṇa. Hero Rāvaṇa, frenzied when
in combat from the wine of valor, yelled in a threatening
voice—champion Saumitri, at heart fearless, shouted back with
a sound like that made by an elephant in rut. That skilled
archer, maddened, twanged his bow named Devadatta. "At last,
Lakṣmaṇa," said Rāvaṇa with rage, "we meet on this field

1. Tārā, a proper name, also means "star, astral body."

2. The kinship term of reference for a woman's "husband's younger brothers" is "debara/deor"; the "debara" is considered to be the one to support the elder brother's wife, in the elder brother's absence.

of war, lowly human! Where is god Vajrapāṇi now?
and the peacock-bannered Śaktidhara? and the sovereign
of the Raghu clan, your brother? and king Sugrīva? Who
is there to save you now, wretched lout? At this moment of
impending death, think on both your mother, Sumitrā, and
Ūrmilā, your spouse! For I am now about to feed your
flesh to beastly carnivores. The earth will soak up rivers
of your blood! It was an ill-fated moment when you crossed
the sea, foul one, and, dressed every bit the common sneak thief,
slipped into Rākṣasa quarters, stealing there that jewel
of a Rākṣasa—priceless throughout the entire world."
    Roaring wildly, the sovereign set an arrow, resembling
fire's flame, to his bowstring. With snarls of a vicious lion,
growling, leonine Saumitri answered back, "I was born
a Kṣatriya, sovereign of the Rākṣasas, so I have
no fear of Yama. Why do you try to frighten me? You
are distraught today, grieving for your son, as much as you
are capable, charioteer. But soon I shall end your
melancholy and send you where your best of sons resides."
    There ensued a monstrous battle. Gods and men looked on in
sheer amazement at both of them as over and over
again Saumitri, with aggressive shouts, parried volleys
of sharp missiles. The Rākṣasa king, astounded, spoke, "I
commend you on your warrior's skills, lionlike Saumitri!
Good charioteer, you show more might than Śaktidhara,
but there is no escaping from my clutches on this day!"
    Then remembering his best of sons, that champion flung,
with extreme malice, his missile by the name of Śakti!
That monstrous leveler of enemies, like a streak of
lightning, brightened up the skies and gave out with a clap of
thunder. In horror, gods and men shivered. Lakṣmaṇa, like
a star, plummeted to earth felled by that deadly blow. His
godly weapons clanked and rattled, dulled, coated with bloody
streams. That noble one lay there, like a mountain wrapped in snakes.
    Just as deep within a woods the hunter, having shot the
best of deer with his unfailing arrows, runs rapidly
toward him, so did that hero, king of the Rākṣasas, leap
from his chariot and run to seize the lifeless body.
All around there swelled a hue and cry. With gasps of sorrow

both god and human charioteers gathered round champion
Saumitri. In their home on Kailāsa, Śaṅkarī, at
the feet of Śaṅkara, said, "Lakṣmaṇa has fallen, my
lord, in warfare with the sovereign of the Rākṣasas. There
lies Sumitrā's child, sprawled out in the dust. You have pleased the
Rākṣasas, you who are devoted to your devotees.
You humbled Vāsava's warrior pride. But, my lord, I beg
of you, Virūpākṣa, preserve the corpse of Lakṣmaṇa."
    Smiling, Śūlī said to champion Vīrabhadra, "Restrain
the lord of Laṅkā, warrior." And with the swiftness of a
heart's desire, Vīrabhadra went, then spoke gravely in the
ear of Rāvaṇa, "Go back, Rākṣasa king, to golden
Laṅkā. What need have you in this battle with a slain foe?"
    The dreamlike godly messenger then disappeared. Roaring,
that lion of a champion ascended once again his
chariot. Rākṣasa martial music issued forth, and
with resounding voices Rākṣasas yelled. The Rākṣasa
legion marched into the city—as ferocious goddess
Cāmuṇḍā, victorious in battle, having vanquished
Raktabīja, returned shouting, dancing wildly, a smile
upon her bloody lips, her body drenched in streams of gore!
As the gods en masse sang Satī's praises, so the bards with
joy extolled in victory songs the Rākṣasas' army!
    Meanwhile, bested in war, the sovereign of the gods, in a
fit of rage, strode through the godly ranks on back to heaven.

Thus ends canto number seven,
    called "Felling with the Śakti Weapon,"
    in the poem
The Slaying of Meghanāda.

CANTO 8

City of the Spirits

As an Indra among monarchs, his royal tasks complete,
removes his crown, gently sets it down, and then disappears
into his chamber, so too the lord of day had doffed his
crown jewel, the darkness-dispelling sun, on that summit
of the setting-hill. Night accompanied by her stars arrived
as did that soothing fount of nectar, Night's beloved moon.
Many a hundred bonfires blazed around the battlefield.
There, where charioteer Saumitri lay upon the ground,
Vaidehī's husband fell speechless. His tears flowed uncontrolled,
mingling with his brother's blood, and wet the earth like a spring
that trickles down a mountainside, dissolving ocher dust,
then seeps out on the ground below. The Raghu troops seemed stunned
by grief—Vibhīṣaṇa, wild in war, and Kumuda, and
Aṅgada, Hanumān, heroes Nala and Nīla, and
Śarabha, Sumālī, Subāhu, a lion among
warriors, and Sugrīva—all condoled their lordship's sorrow.
Once their lord regained consciousness, he, grief-stricken, chided—
"When I renounced the kingdom and went to live in exile
in the forest, Lakṣmaṇa, as night set in, O expert
archer, bow in hand, you, at the door of our hut would stand
alert to guard me. Yet here today in the Rākṣasas'
enclave—this day, this very city of the Rākṣasas!—
I, among foes, here founder in these perilous waters.
Still then, O great-armed one, you forsake me, seeking respite
upon the ground? Who will rescue me today, please tell me?
Stand up, brave one! Since when do you not heed your brother's words?
But if by some ill luck of mine—I who am unlucky
always—if you have indeed abandoned me, then tell me
honestly, you who are to me much more than life, for I
must hear. What misdeed is hapless Jānakī at fault for,
in your opinion? Day and night she weeps as she, confined
by Rākṣasa, thinks of Lakṣmaṇa, her husband's brother.
How did you forget—Brother, how could you ever forget
this day the one who like a mother always cared for you
so warmly? O pinnacle of Raghu's clan, she, a clan

wife, shall she remain incarcerated by Paulastya?
Is it right that you should rest before you first destroy in
combat such a wicked thief—you who are invincible
in battle, bold as omnivorous fire? Arise, my fierce-
armed one, victory pennant of the Raghu clan! Minus
you I am helpless, a charioteer whose chariot
is missing wheels. With you supine on this bed, O hero,
Hanumān is powerless, a bow without its bowstring.
Aṅgada wails pitifully; friend Sugrīva, noble-
minded, is heartsick; good charioteer Vibhīṣaṇa,
Karbūra supreme, he too mourns; a host of heroes grieves.
Get up, console these eyes, my brother, by the gaze of yours.
"If, however, you have tired of this awful war, then,
O archer, let us go back to our forest home. Sītā's
rescue, fondest one, is not to be—that luckless woman.
It is not for us to vanquish Rākṣasas. But if you
do not accompany me, how shall I, Lakṣmaṇa, show
my face upon the Sarayū's far shore where Sumitrā,
your mother who so loves her son, laments? What shall I say
when she asks me, 'Where, O Rāmabhadra, is the object
of my love, your little brother?' How shall I answer to
your wife, Ūrmilā, and to the people of the city?
Stand up, dear child. Why do you turn a deaf ear today toward
this plea your brother makes, for love of whom you quit the realm
with its amenities and took to the forest? Out of
sympathy, you always used to cry whenever you would
see these eyes of mine moist with tears. Tenderly you dabbed those
teary rivulets. Now I am drenched with water from my
eyes, yet you, who are to me much more than life, will you not
so much as glance my way? Lakṣmaṇa, does such behavior
ever suit you, Brother (you who are renowned throughout the
world as one devoted to his brother!), you who are my
everlasting joy? All my life I held firm to *dharma*
and worshiped the gods—and is it this the gods have given
in return? O Night, compassion-filled, you who nightly make
the flowers, withered by the summer's heat, succulent with
drops of dew, revive this blossom. You who are a fount of
nectar, god of nectar rays, pour down your life-bestowing
juices, save Lakṣmaṇa—save beggar Rāghava, kind one."

The foe of Rākṣasas, forlorn, wailed upon the field of
battle, cradling his dearest younger brother. All about,
the warrior throng howled with sadness, just as howls a stand of
stately trees at midnight when winds blow deep in the forest.
At her home upon Kailāsa, the mountain's daughter[1] was
empathizing with the saddened Raghu lad. From the lap
of Dhūrjaṭi to his lotus feet the droplets of her
tears trickled, like dew upon the hundred-petaled lotus
at dawn. Her lordship queried, "For what reason, my pretty,
are you distressed today, tell me?" "What is there which you do
not already know, my god?" replied the goddess Gaurī,
"Out of grief for Lakṣmaṇa, Rāmacandra mourns wildly
in golden Laṅkā. Listen! My heart is stirred by Rāma's
sorrow. Who in the world, O lord of the universe, will
ever worship this slave of yours again? You embarrassed
me greatly today, lord. You have plunged my reputation
into waters of disrepute. This servant of yours falls
at your feet, at fault for disturbing your meditation,
O Indra of austerities—just for that, I guess, you
punish me so? Ill-fated was the moment Indra came
to me! Ill-fated, when Maithilī's spouse did my *pūjā*!"
The great goddess sobbed silently, her feelings hurt. Smiling,
Śambhu answered, "Why so glum, daughter of the Indra of
mountains, over this mere trifling matter? Send that warrior,
Indra among Rāghavas, to Kṛtānta's city with
Māyā; by my favor, charioteer Dāśarathi,
in corporeal form, shall gain access to spirit world.
His father, King Daśaratha, will inform him by what
means the brother might regain his life. Stay your gloom, my
moon-faced one. Present to Māyā, prettiest, my trident.
There in Yama's land of darkness it will shine a fiery
pillar and illuminate that realm. The spirits there will
honor it, as loyal subjects do the regal scepter."
At her Mount Kailāsa home, Durgā called to mind Māyā.
At once that sorceress appeared and, with hands together,
bowed before Ambikā. In soft tones Pārvatī spoke, "Go
to Laṅkā, beguiler of the universe. Maithilī's

1. Pārvatī.

mate laments, beside himself from grief for Saumitri. Speak
to him with sweet words and guide him to the land of spirits.
His father, Daśaratha, will advise him by what means
high-minded Saumitri might gain again his life, along
with all the soldiers slain in this destructive war. Hold this
trident of Triśūlī's in your lotus hand, chaste lady.
This best of weapons, like a pillar made of fire, will glow,
illuminating Yama's land of darkness." With a bow
to Umā, Māyā set off. The shadows in the Milky
Way drifted far away, as though outshone by the brilliance
of her beauty. Those myriad stars smiled—like gems inlaid
on a ray of sun. In her wake she left across the face
of the sky a trace of light as that beauty, like a ship
in ocean waters, headed for Laṅkā. Soon that goddess
landed where the sullen jewel of Raghu's clan stood among
his army. Golden Laṅkā filled with heavenly fragrance.

At Rāghava's ear, Mother whispered, "Wipe away your streams
of tears, charioteer Dāśarathi, your beloved
brother shall revive. Bathe in the sea's sacred waters, then
come with me at once to Yama's quarters. Noble one, you
will enter bodily the land of spirits by virtue
of Śiva's favor. Your father Daśaratha will make
known how well-marked Lakṣmaṇa will again live. O fierce-armed
one, come now. I shall excavate a tunnel. Fearlessly,
fine charioteer, proceed through it. I shall go ahead
of you to show the way. Tell everyone, Sugrīva and
all commanders, that they should stand guard over Lakṣmaṇa."

Astounded, Rāghavendra alerted all his generals
to take heed. Then that noble one set out for the seashore—
to that place of holy pilgrimage. Once he had bathed his
body in these sacred currents, the most fortunate one
propitiated all the gods, his ancestors and such,
giving offerings of drinking water, then with dispatch
proceeded to the entrance of his tent, alone. Now the
jewel of men saw his quarters bright by godly power.
Hands cupped in supplication, that charioteer performed
worship with flowers meant especially for the goddess.
Adorning his imposing figure in fine warrior garb,
that lord of warriors bravely ventured into the tunnel—

for what does he with whom the gods find favor have to fear?
On went that best of Rāghavas, as goes a traveler
down a path through a darkened forest when at night the beams
the nectar-rayed moon, smiling, casts penetrate the woodland.
And on ahead proceeded goddess Māyā in silence.
In a while that best of Raghus, startled, heard waves crashing,
as though a thousand oceans swelled, bellowing angrily.
He gazed with trepidation not far away upon a
monstrous city, ever cloaked in night. The Vaitaraṇī,
like a moat, flowed by resounding thunderously! In fits and
spurts waves bubbled hotly, just as milk in heated vessels
surges upward, bursting into puffs of vapor, panicked
by the fire's power. The gem of day does not show itself
in splendor in that sky, nor does the moon, nor stars. Thick clouds,
packing wind and spewing forth great balls of fire, roam throughout
deserted pathways, howling wildly, like Pinākī at
Pralaya when, inflamed, he sets his arrows to his bow!
Taken aback, the Raghu lord gazed upon a wondrous
bridge that spanned the river—sometimes fiery, sometimes wrapped in
dense smoke, beautiful sometimes, as though it were built of gold.
Beings by the millions were ever running toward that bridge—
some wailing, agonized, while others acted jubilant.
Vaidehī's husband asked, "Tell me, kind woman, why does the
bridge repeatedly assume a different guise? And why do
countless beings (like moths who spot a flame) dash to that span?"
The goddess Māyā answered, "It is a bridge of many
natures and can at will change its form, O Sītā's husband.
To sinners it is veiled in smoke from its fiery power;
when virtuous beings come along, it turns most pleasant
and beautiful, like a golden path to heaven. Over
there, those countless souls you see, gem of men, left their bodies
in the mortal world; all are on their journey to the land
of spirits to enjoy, or suffer, as it were, the fruits
of deeds on earth. They who followed *dharma*'s ways cross the bridge
to the northern, western, and eastern gates. Sinners, in great
misery, forever swim the river. Yama's henchmen
harass them upon the sandy shore, while in the water,
their sin-filled hearts burn as if in scalding oil. Come along
with me. You soon shall see what men's eyes have not seen before."

With deliberate steps the best of Raghus walked behind;
ahead, like a golden lamp, the sorceress illumined
that horrific land. Beside the bridge, Rāma, seized with fear,
spied a monstrous figure, a messenger of Yama, with
punishing rod in hand. Thundering, that emissary
of Kṛtānta interrogated, "Who are you? By what
power, O brash one, did you come into this land, alive
and with your body whole? Speak at once, or I shall crush you
here and now by a blow from this staff!" Goddess Māyā smiled,
and to that messenger Mother vaunted Śiva's trident.

Head bowed, that henchman spoke to the chaste lady, "Can it be
within my power, faithful one, to halt your progress? See,
the bridge turns gold with joy, as does the sky when greeting Dawn."

They both crossed the Vaitaraṇī River. On ahead that
Raghu sovereign saw a city's iron gates—wheel-shaped rings
of flames spun constantly, spewing sparks everywhere. On
the face of that imposing gate, the jewel of men saw
written there in fiery letters, "By this path sinners go
to suffer constant sorrow in the realm of sorrows—you
who enter, give up all hope as you step inside this land!"

Before the gates that charioteer caught sight of Fever,
gaunt and frail. Now his skinny body quaked with cold, now burned
in horrid heat, like the waters' sovereign, from the forces
of Vaḍabā's fire. Bile and phlegm and gas—they all attacked
him, causing loss of consciousness. Beside this malady
sat Gluttony, gross of belly, regurgitating half-
digested food, foul thing, scooping up more tasty morsels
with both hands, wolfing them down. Near him Inebriation
grinned, his eyelids heavy from a drunken stupor—sometimes
dancing, sometimes singing, sometimes quarreling, crying sometimes,
but always the senseless fool, always a destroyer of
one's senses. Next to him was nasty Prurience, body
putrid as a corpse, yet that sinner lusted after sex—
his heart ever sizzled in the flames of carnal craving.
There beside him sat Consumption spitting blood and hacking,
coughing night and day. Asthma wheezed and gasped, in gripping pain.
Cholera, his eyes lackluster, waves of blood from mouth and
anus spewed like streams of purest water—in the form of
thirst, this foe attacks repeatedly. There stood that frightful

messenger of Yama, spasmodic Tetanus by name,
who grips one's weakened body cruelly, like a tiger, who,
when preying on some forest creature, stalks now, then pounces
on its quarry, clawing it exuberantly. Nearby,
beside that sickness, sat Insanity—violent at
times, inflamed like fire when offered an oblation of ghee,
at other times completely catatonic—now decked out
in odd apparel, then again, stark naked, like Kālī,
Hara's darling, on the field of battle—sometimes frenzied,
singing songs and clapping gaily—sometimes sobbing—sometimes
with a broad grin on her twisted lips—at still other times
slitting her own throat with a sharp knife, swallowing poison,
drowning in a well, hanging by the neck—sometimes, for shame!
strutting coyly, lewdly, a most lascivious woman
seducing lustful men—and without discriminating
between feces, food, and urine, she, alas, would sometimes
mix them all together and eat heartily—at times she
is bound in chains, other times she seems composed, just like a
river without current, in the absence of any breeze!
Who can describe all the other maladies that were there?

Rāghava eyed a charioteer in battle on a
fire-colored chariot (his clothes drenched in blood, a sharp-edged
sword in his hand). At the chariot's prow stood Wrath, attired
in driver's garb. A necklace made of human heads around
his throat, a pile of corpses heaped before him. He noticed
Murder, fearsome falchion in hand. His arms upraised, alas,
always in the act of slaying. And from a tree limb, rope
around his neck, swung Suicide noiselessly, tongue lolling,
fright-filled eyes wide open. Speaking sweetly to the Indra
among Rāghavas, goddess Māyā said, "All these ghastly
messengers of Śamana you see in sundry guises,
Raghu hero, they roam the surface of the earth without
rest, just as a hunter through dense forests stalks his deer. Step
into Kṛtānta's city, spouse of Sītā. Today I
shall show you under what conditions souls reside within
this land of souls. Here we have the southern gate; eighty-four
hell-pits lie within this sector. Now come along at once."

The courageous spouse of Sītā stepped into Kṛtānta's
city, ah me, just like Springtime, king of seasons, into

a charred forest, or like elixir into a lifeless
body. Darkness filled the city, while all around arose
wails of agony; both the land and waters shook nonstop
from quakes; a massive line of roiling clouds in angry fits
spit deadly fire; fetid winds wafted, as though a thousand
corpses were then being cremated at a burning ground.

After a while, that best of Raghus saw in front of him
a huge lake—deadly fire rolled like water in crashing waves.
In it swam a million beings, twisting, writhing, screaming
with agony! "Alas, heartless Fortune, did you create
us in these many forms for this? Ah, intolerable!
Why did we not succumb to searing gastric juices in
our mothers' womb? Where are you, gem of day? And you, O lord
of Night, moon with the nectar-rays? Will our eyes again be
soothed by gazing on you two again, O gods? Where are our
sons, our wives, our relatives? Where, ah, are those possessions
for which we labored constantly by many schemes—for which
we did our shady deeds, while indifferent to *dharma*?"

In this manner, the sinful souls lamented time and time
again wallowing within that lake. From the void came the
answer, booming savagely, a message born of that void,
"Why, O hapless ones, do you cavil in vain at your fate?
Here you suffer all the consequences of your actions.
For what reason did you hoodwink *dharma* with such evil
conduct? The rule of Fate is known as fair throughout the world."

When the heavenly message ceased, Yama's monstrous henchmen
bashed in heads with staves. Worms gnawed away. Diamond-taloned flesh-
consuming raptors swooped down upon those wispy figures,
ripping out intestines, screeching hideously. And the
lands around were ringing with the screams of tortured sinners.

Sadly, Māyā spoke to Rāghava, "This fiery lake is
known as Raurava, listen, gem of Raghus. Base-minded
ones who steal another's riches remain here forever.
If those who judge are partial to injustice, they too end
up in this lake, as do all other beings guilty of
such flagrant sins. Here the fires never are extinguished, the
worms never cease gnawing. I tell you, this is no common
conflagration which consumes these spirits in this loathsome
hell, best of Raghus. Fate's rage, assuming fire's form, burns here

perpetually. Come along, charioteer, I shall
show you Kumbhīpāka, the hell in which Yama's henchmen
fry sinners in hot oil. Listen, O hero, not far off
that is their sound of crying. By my *māyā* power I
have blocked your nostrils, otherwise you could not stand it here,
O charioteer, best of Raghus. But let us go to
where in dark pits those who have committed suicide moan
pitiably, ever captive." With hands cupped together,
that sovereign among men spoke, "Please forgive this slave of yours,
Kṣemaṅkarī. I shall perish here and now from others'
sorrows, if I see more suffering like this. Mother, who
would willingly be born into this world knowing these might
be the consequences? Man is helpless—can he, Mother,
ward off the sorcery of sin?" Answered Māyā, "There is
not a venom in this world, O great archer, for which there
is no antidote. But if one shuns that medicine, then
who can save him? The noble one who fights sin through his deeds
is always looked upon with sympathy by gods—Dharma
shields that one in armor quite impregnable. Were you to
witness all these pits of punishment, O charioteer—
but enough of that, let us now proceed along this path."

On a ways, the spouse of Sītā stepped into a forest—
silent, boundless, tall; no birds called; no breezes blew within
that frightful woods; flowers—they which beautify a forest—
would not bloom. Here, there sunlight trickled through dense foliage,
but it was without strength, like the smile an invalid makes.

Beings by the thousands congregated suddenly round
that Raghu lord, eager, just like flies around a vat of
honey. Someone queried in a most pathetic voice, "Who
are you, O embodied one? Speak, by what virtue have you
ventured to this land? Are you god or mortal man, tell us
now. Speak, gratify us all, O fount of virtue, with your
nectar-laden rain of speech. Since that day Yama's henchmen
wrenched away our wretched lives, we have been without sounds made
of human tongue. Our eyes are content now that they have seen
your form, fine-limbed hero. Please satisfy these ears with speech."

The foe of Rākṣasas replied, "This slave of yours was born
among the Raghu clan, O spirits. The charioteer
Daśaratha is my father. His chief queen Kauśalyā,

is my mother. They call this servant of yours by the name
of Rāma. Alas, I dwell through ill luck in the forest.
By Triśūlī's orders, I am to meet my father. That
is why, my friends, I came today to Kṛtānta's city."

Retorted one among the spirits, "I know you, Indra
among champions. By your arrows I lost my body in
the Pañcavaṭī Forest." With a start, the gem of men
gazed at Rākṣasa Mārīca—now incorporeal.

Rāmacandra asked, "For what sin have you come here to this
hellish forest, Rākṣasa, tell me that?" "The cause of this
harsh punishment, alas, is mean Paulastya, Raghu king!"
answered he, devoid of form. "It was to do his bidding
that I deceived you, and consequently am condemned to
this hell." Then along with Dūṣaṇa came Khara (Khara,
or the sharp one, sharp as the keenest sword in battle, when
he was alive), who, angered when they saw the Raghu lord,
pride wounded, both slipped away, just as a viper, lacking
poison fangs, humbled, hides when it spots a mongoose. All of
a sudden the forest filled with a colossal roar. Those
ghosts dashed off. Dry leaves were flung about, as when a cyclone
blows. Māyā told the monarch among champions, "Hear me, gem
of Raghus, these spirits live in diverse pits. At times they
come and wander through this forest of lament, lamenting
silently. See there, Yama's messengers mercilessly
drive them all away, each to his proper place." The one who
is the sun to Vaidehī's lotus heart saw herds of ghosts
with Yama's minions' horrifying shadows in pursuit.
Those ghosts ran swiftly panting, just as a deer herd fleet of foot
bounds off breathless, pursued by a hungry lion. Eyes moist,
Rāmacandra, sea of kindness, went sadly with Māyā.

A moment later that finest warrior shuddered as he
heard agonized screaming. He saw off in the distance some
thousand women, pallid, like the moon in daytime skies. One
of them tore at her long hair saying, "I always used to
bind you prettily, to bind the hearts of randy menfolk,
unheedful of my deeds and *dharma*, driven mad by youth's
intoxicating wine." Another scratched her breasts with her
own fingernails and said, "Alas, I spent my days for naught
adorning you in pearls and diamonds. And, in the end, what

came of that!" Yet another woman, from remorse, gouged out
her eyes (as cruel vultures do the eyes of carrion)
saying, "I used to outline you with kohl, wicked organs,
then smile and fling my arrows with your sidelong glances. In
mirrors I would gaze upon your brightness and feel contempt
for doe eyes. Is this, finally, the spoils of vanity?"

That throng of women departed, whimpering. Behind them
marched a matron of Kṛtānta, gruesome serpents hissing
through her tresses; her nails resembled sabers; her lips were
smeared with blood; her two banana-breasts hung down below her
navel, ever swinging to and fro; and flames leapt from her
two nostrils, then blended, augmenting the fire of her eyes.

Addressing Rāghava, Māyā spoke, "All such women as
you see before you, gem of Raghus, were much enamored
of clothes and fineries while on the surface of the earth.
These wanton women, driven by libido, would always
dress like the forest floor in springtime so as to lure the
hearts of desirous men to play at love. Now where is that
fetching beauty, prize of youth, alas?" Impulsively, an
echo echoed, "Now where is that fetching beauty, prize of
youth, alas!" Weeping, those women left, each for her own hell.

Again Māyā spoke, "Gaze once more before you, O foe of
Rākṣasas." That gem of men then saw another group of
women, infatuating with their beauty, their chignons
laced with fragrant blossoms, the might of Kāma's fire in their
doelike eyes, the sweetest of ambrosial juices upon
their lips! Their necks, replete with jewels, were like the conch shell
of the king of gods; a filmy bodice made from gold threads
clothed the pulchritude that was their breasts with a mere pretext
of clothing, to show them off the more, intensifying
sensual cravings in hearts of lustful men. Their midriffs
were quite svelte. From within blue silk (most sheer) their rounded thighs,
in contempt, it seemed, for any covering at all, showed
teasingly their banana-tree-shaped splendor, as did those
Apsarās' exquisite naked bodies while cavorting
in the waters of Lake Mānasa. Ankle-bells rang from
their feet, an ornamental girdle round their hips. *Vīṇā*,
rabāb strings, and tiny cymbals, each merrily in its
own style, blended sweetly with *mṛdaṅga* drums' gay beat. Those

shapely women undulated on those waves of music.
From elsewhere there appeared a gathering of handsome men,
laughing softly, good-looking like the warrior-god, hero
Kārttikeya, the favorite of the Kṛttikās, or,
O Rati, like your own Manmatha, for whom your heart craves.
On noticing that group of men, the womenfolk, in a
tizzy from lust's juices, flung their arrows of flirtatious
sidelong looks—bangles jingled musically round their wrists.
On their hot breath rose the pollen from the flowers in their
garlands and, like dust, soon blurred good judgment's sun. The men had
lost the battle, but is there strength in men to win such wars?
Just as the bird and his mate lose themselves in games of love
while frolicking, these suave sophisticates caught hold of those
coquettes, sauntered to the woods—for what purpose, eye told eye!
Suddenly the forest filled with shrieks! Astounded, Rāma
saw those men and women wrestling with each other, rolling
on the ground, biting, scratching, pummeling with clenched fists and
kicking. They tore their hair, gouged eyes, clawed at nose and mouth with
adamantine fingernails. Earth was soaked by streams of blood.
Both the parties struggled fiercely, just as Bhīma, dressed in
women's clothing, fought with Kīcaka in Virāṭa. There
came all of Yama's henchmen, quickly driving the two sides
apart, beating them with iron *lāṭhis*. In gentle tones,
pretty Māyā spoke to Rāghava, joy of Raghu's clan,
"Listen, my child, these men in life were slaves to Kāma; those
seductive women served Kāma as his handmaids. They both
indulged their carnal appetites unbridled, ah alas,
drowning *dharma* in the waters of non-*dharma*, shedding
shame—now punishment is meted out in Yama's city.
Just as a mirage deceives the thirsty person on a
desert and just as the golden grace of *mākāla* fruit
defrauds the famished, such is the case with copulation.
The cravings of both partners are never satisfied in
full. What more need I say, my child, look for yourself. Such pain,
O lucky one, many sinners suffer in the mortal
world, before they come to hell. This is Fate's decree: He who
spends his youth immorally becomes debilitated
later on in life. Undampable are the flames of sex,
which will consume one's heart; unquenchable is the rage of

Fate that, like lust's fire, burns one's body, mighty-armed one, I
tell you. In the end, this is the lot of just such sinners."
Bowing low before the feet of Māyā, the gem of men
said, "All these strange things I have witnessed in this land, by your
grace, O Mother, who could possibly describe them all? But
where is the kingly sage? I shall beg at his feet for young
Lakṣmaṇa. Lead me to his dwelling place—this is my wish."
Smiling, Māyā replied, "This city is huge, Rāghava,
I have shown you but a tiny portion. Were we two to
wander, champion, endlessly for twelve years through Kṛtānta's
realm, even then we would not see all the sections. Beyond
the eastern gate reside, with husbands, faithful wives who were
devoted to their mates; that portion of this city is
unparalleled in heaven or on earth; magnificent
mansions stand in pleasant floral groves; most delightful ponds
always brim with lovely lotuses; spring breezes humming
sweetly flow forever; many of the finest cuckoos
sing constantly their special *pā* note. Spontaneously
vīṇās sound, as do *muraja* drums, small cymbals, flutes, and
seven honeyed tones from *saptasvarās*. Yogurt, milk, and
ghee gush from springs continuously, all about; mangoes,
the ambrosial fruit, ripen in the orchards; Annadā
herself serves sumptuous foods. Delicious fare of every
sort (what one chews, sucks, licks, or drinks) one has for the asking,
as in heaven from the ever fruitful wish-fulfilling
vine, great archer. We do not have business there. Go, hero,
through the northern gate and amble for a while in that fine
place. Soon you shall see your father's feet, jewel among men."
Heading north, the two of them proceeded hurriedly. The
spouse of Sītā saw some hundred mountains bald and scorched, ah,
as though from flames of godly fury! Some held heaps of snow
on the summits of their highest peaks; others of them roared
repeatedly, disgorging fire, melting boulders in their
fiery streams, blanketing the sky with ashes, filling the
surrounding countryside with rumblings. His lordship saw a
hundred endless deserts; hot winds blew ceaselessly, driving
on ahead dunes of sand, like waves. That warrior observed a
vast expanse of water, sealike, its far shore unseen. In
one spot raged a storm, whipping up whitecaps tall as mountains.

In another, still waters stood, growing stagnant. Monstrous
frogs cavorted there, croaking gravely, and a tangle of
gigantic snakes, bodies endless like that of Śeṣa! In
yet another place *halāhala* poison simmered, just
as in the ocean at the time of churning it. Sinners
piteously roamed this land, whining. Snakes struck, scorpions
stung, and there were insects with huge pincers. Flames beneath the
earth's surface, bitter cold in the air! Alas, who ever
finds a moment's rest before this northern gate! With quickened
pace, that finest charioteer moved along with Māyā.

When the shore draws near, once the helmsman with great effort has
traversed a lonely stretch of water, and the wind, bosom
friend of fragrance borne from flower gardens, rushes out to
greet him, and his ears are soothed to hear the cuckoo's call, mixed
with human voices, after many days away—then that
boatman is afloat upon a sea of ecstasy. With
like feelings did the best of Raghus hear some music not
far off. That noble one, dumbfounded, saw golden mansions
all around, lush gardens filled with golden blossoms, deep ponds,
repositories for the fresh blue lotuses. In a
pleasant voice Māyā said, "It is through this gate, O warrior,
all great charioteers who fall in face-to-face battle
go to savor everlasting happiness. Limitless,
O noble one, is the sense of joy in this locale. Come
along by this garden path, my firm-armed one, for I shall
show to you the celebrated, by whose fame the city
of Sañjīvanī is scented, like a fragrance through a
garden. In the land of virtue, Fortune's smile shines like the
moon, sun, and stars, brilliantly, day after day." Intrigued, that
warrior walked on briskly. Ahead went Māyā, trident in
hand. In due course, that hero noticed a field before him—
like a battleground. In one place, spears stood stately like some
śāla forest. Elsewhere an array of horses whinnied,
fitted in their martial trappings. Yet elsewhere trumpeted
an Indra among elephants. Shield-wielding soldiers gamed,
gripping sword and shield. Someplace else some wrestlers grappled on
the turf. Banners fluttered, as if exhilarated by
the battle. In yet another region on his flowered
seat, a golden *vīṇā* in his hand, enchanting to his

audience, sat the poet singing songs in praise of the Kṣatriya clan. Inspired by that music, warriors cheered. Heaps of *pārijāta* blooms were rained down, I do not know by whom, filling the environs with sweet scents. Apsarās cavorted, and Kinnaras vocalized, as in heaven.

Māyā spoke to Rāghava, "All charioteers slain in face-to-face combat in the Satya *yuga* you see on this field today, crest-jewel of Kṣatriyas. Look there, Niśumbha, body gold-hued like Mount Hemakūṭa; the glow from his diadem ascends the skies, a valorous charioteer—Caṇḍī, born of gods' joined powers, vanquished in pitched battle that monarch among champions. Look, Śumbha, stately as the trident-holder Śambhu. And over there, mighty Mahiṣāsura, breaker of horses. And there, the champion and fine warrior Tripura, Tripurāri's foe. And Vṛtra and other Daityas, renowned throughout the world. See there Sunda and Upasunda, once more floating calmly on the waters of fraternal love." The noble Rāghava inquired, "Tell me, kind one, why do I not see Kumbhakarṇa, Atikāya, Narāntaka (he who means the death to mortal men in warfare), as well as Indrajit, and all other Rākṣasa charioteers?"

Replied the sorceress, "Before one's funeral is performed, one does not gain access to this city, O husband of Vaidehī. On the city's fringes such beings wander unless and until their obsequies are carried out by friends—I relate to you what Fate decrees. Take note, O best of charioteers, a fine warrior heads our way. I shall stand beside you, O jewel among men, invisible. Enjoy a pleasant talk." So saying, Mother disappeared.

Startled, the best of Raghus gazed upon that sterling lord of warriors. Lightning danced atop his diadem. From that prodigious figure, his raiment shone quite dazzling to the eye. Lance in hand, he strode the stride of a bull elephant.

Coming closer, that lord of champions, addressing Rāma, questioned, "For what purpose do you travel here today in your physical form, crown-jewel of the Raghu clan? It was in unfair combat that you slew me, to gratify Sugrīva. But put aside your fears. We know no malice

in Kṛtānta's city, for here everyone has subdued
his passions. The stream of human life, which flows so murky
on the surface of the earth, courses limpid through this land.
I am Vāli." Much chagrined, the gem of men recognized
that monarch of Kiṣkindhyā, an Indra among warriors.
Vāli added, smiling, "Come along with me, O warrior
Dāśarathi. See that garden not far off, my lord, full
of golden flowers; charioteer Jaṭāyu strolls through
that arbor all the time, in your father's company. That
hero will be overjoyed to see you. The noble one
gave his life, acting in accord with *dharma*, in order
that he rescue a chaste woman then in danger. For that
reason is his honor boundless. Now come along quickly."

The foe of Rākṣasas queried, "Tell me kindly, O good
charioteer, are all equally content within this
realm?" "In the deep recesses of a mine," Vāli answered,
"a thousand precious stones are formed, O Rāghava. All are
not of equal radiance, mind you; but is there any,
tell me, jewel among Raghus, totally devoid of
luster?" In this way the two of them conversed at leisure.

Through that pleasant grove where babbled constantly a stream of
nectar waters, the gem of men saw Jaṭāyu, son of
Garuḍa, a godlike charioteer, ensconced upon
a platform fashioned out of ivory and inlaid with
a profusion of gems! Notes from the *vīṇā* were heard all
about. A glow the tint of lotus petals made those woods
radiant, as does sunshine filtered through temporary
awnings at the house wherein there is a celebration.
Fragrant vernal breezes wafted there. Affectionately
that warrior spoke to Rāghava, "My eyes are soothed today
to see you, jewel of the human family, offspring of
my friend! Praise be to you! Auspicious one, your mother had
conceived you at a most auspicious moment! Praise be to
my erstwhile companion, Daśaratha, he who gave you
life! You are favored by the god clan; hence you can come in
your own body to this city. Speak, my precious, let me
hear the news of battle. Has the wicked Rāvaṇa been
felled in combat?" Bowing out of deference, his lordship

spoke most sweetly, "By grace of those two feet of yours, revered
elder, I slew countless Rākṣasas in heated warfare.
Rāvaṇa, sovereign of the Rākṣasas, is now the sole
surviving warrior in that city of the Rākṣasas.
It was by that one's arrows that noble Lakṣmaṇa, my
younger brother, lost his life. Your slave has come today on
Śiva's orders to this land most hard to reach. Please tell this
servant where his father, friend of yours, may be found, warrior."
    Hero Jaṭāyu spoke, "That kingly sage resides among
the other royal sages, through the western gate. It is
not prohibited for me to venture to that land. I
shall escort you. Come along, O enemy subduer."
    That noble one observed fascinating places of all
sorts, golden mansions, many godlike charioteers. On
banks of lakes, in flower gardens, beings gamboled in great
delight, just as in the springtime honeybees buzz about
in pleasant wooded groves, or as at night fireflies light up
the ten directions. The two proceeded with quickened pace,
as thousands of those beings crowded around Rāghava.
    Hero Jaṭāyu announced, "This grand charioteer was
born among the Raghus. In somatic form, by Śiva's
orders, he comes to this city of the spirits to gaze
upon his father's feet. Bless him, then be off, all of you,
each to his own station, creatures." All wished him well, then left.
The two proceeded blissfully. In one direction a
golden-bodied mountain peak held its crown of trees up to
the skies, like the crown of matted hair upon Kapardī,
mendicant with matted hair. Little streams skipped and gurgled.
Diamonds, other gems, and pearls were visible in crystal
waters. Here and there in valleys, green tracts of earth were decked
with flower blossoms. Lakes had formed, embossed with lotuses.
Constantly the finest cuckoos cooed throughout the woodlands.
    The son of Vinatā's son, addressing Rāghava, spoke,
"Look, jewel among Raghus, the western gate, all of gold,
the houses in this wondrous land are made with diamonds. Look
there, beneath that golden tree above whose stately head is
spread a canopy of emerald leaves sits Dilīpa, gem
of men, upon a throne of gold, beside his faithful wife

Sudakṣiṇā. Worship with devotion the founder of
your lineage. In this land dwell countless royal rishis—
Ikṣvāku, Māndhātā, Nahuṣa, all world-recognized.
Step forward, honor your forefather, O mighty-armed one!"
    Advancing, that monarch of charioteers fell prostrate
at the couple's feet. Conferring his blessing, Dilīpa
asked, "Who are you? Tell me how you came in bodily form
to this land of spirits, godlike charioteer? When I
gaze upon your moonlike face, my heart is buoyed up, on a
sea of bliss." Sudakṣiṇā then spoke in honeyed tones, "O
fortunate one, tell us at once, who are you? Just as when
in foreign lands the sight of one's own countryman pleases,
just so are my eyes delighted, seeing you. What righteous
woman in her womb conceived you at a most auspicious
time, high-minded lad? If indeed you are born of gods, O
godly one, why bow before us two? If not a god, then,
like a god among mankind, which clan do you glorify?"
    Dāśarathi, hands cupped in supplication, answered, "Your
son, named Raghu, kingly sage, renowned the whole world over,
that world-conqueror, by his own might, gained conquest over
the entire world. To him was born a son, named Aja—
protector of the earth; Indumatī married Aja;
from her womb was born high-minded Daśaratha; his chief
queen is Kauśalyā; your thrall was born of her. The sons of
mother Sumitrā, lion Lakṣmaṇa and Śatrughna,
are vanquishers of foes in battle. Mother Kaikeyī,
your lordship, bore my brother Bharata in her belly."
    The regal sage responded, "So you are Rāmacandra,
coronet of the Ikṣvāku clan. I bestow upon
you blessings. May your fame be constantly proclaimed across
the world, for as long as moon and sun rise in the sky, famed
one. My lineage shines upon the surface of the earth
due to all your virtues, O paragon of virtue. That
gold mountain you see there, at its base and famous in this
region stands a banyan tree, its name Imperishable,
atop the Vaitaraṇī River's bank. Beneath that tree
your father worships faithfully king Dharma on behalf
of you. O mighty-armed, ornament of the Raghu clan,

go to him. Warrior Daśaratha grieves for your sorrows."

The gem of men, excited, bowed before those lotus feet, bade good-bye to warrior Jaṭāyu, and set out on his own (accompanied by Māyā in the void) to where that scintillating golden mountain stood, then saw that best of warriors underneath the tree Imperishable—on the Vaitaraṇī's riverbank, whose waters run like nectar through this land—its golden branches, emerald leaves, its fruit, alas, who can describe the luster of that fruit? that king of trees, prayed to by the gods, and grantor of salvation.

From afar the kingly sage caught sight of his fine son, stretched out his arms (chest wet with tears) and said, "Have you, who are to me much more than life, come at last to this land most hard to reach, by favor of the gods, to please this pair of eyes? Have I recovered you today, my long lost treasure? Aha, how shall I tell you, Rāmabhadra, how I suffered in your absence? Just as iron melts in fire's power, so did I, in sorrow over you, and left my mortal body prematurely. I shut my eyes, alas, my heavy heart on fire. Harsh Fate, my child, for misdeeds of mine has written pain and struggle, ah me, on your forehead, you who always tread the path of *dharma*! That is why all this happened. That is why, alas, Kaikeyī, like a female elephant in heat, trampled under foot the creeper of my hopes, that which made the garden of my life so beautiful." Warrior Daśaratha wailed while Dāśarathi wept in silence.

That best of Raghus spoke, "O Father, now your servant bobs upon a shoreless sea. Who can save him in these dire straits? If what transpires on the earth is known within this city, then it is surely not unknown to those fair feet of yours the reasons why your slave has ventured to this region. Well before his time, alas, my dearest younger brother died today in cruelest battle! If I cannot have him back, I shall not return to where the gem of day and moon and stars shine gloriously! Order me and I shall die right before you, Father! I cannot live in separation from him!" cried the gem of men at his father's feet. Moved by his child's sorrow, Daśaratha said, "I do know for what

reason you have traveled to this city, son. Earnestly
I worship sovereign Dharma, gladly making offerings
of water with my cupped hands, all for your well-being. You
shall have your Lakṣmaṇa, you who bear auspicious markings.
Life is yet confined within his body, like a captive
held inside a crumbling prison. On the peak of fair Mount
Gandhamādana grows the greatest curative, my dear,
Viśalyakaraṇī, a golden creeper. Fetch it and
revive your younger brother. King Yama himself freely
told of such a remedy today. Devoted servant,
Hanumān, son of the swift, he who moves with speed, send him.
In an instant he, that awesome hero, the equal of
Prabhañjana, will bring the medicine. In due time you
will vanquish Rāvaṇa in a fierce battle. By your darts
that wicked one will perish, and with him his entire
lineage. My daughter-in-law, Lakṣmī of the Raghu
clan, that little mother, will return and once again will
brighten up the Raghu household—yet it is not your luck,
dear child, to savor happiness. For just as myrrh, alas,
enduring suffering, smolders in its censer as it
scents with sweet aroma the surroundings, so too famed one,
will the homeland of the Bhāratas be filled with your sweet
fame. It is due to sins of mine that Fate has punished you—
I perished for my own sins, in separation from you.

    "Only half the night has now elapsed on earth. Return at
once by godly might to Laṅkā, hero. Dispatch forthwith
warrior Hanumān. Fetch the cure while yet it is still dark."

    Daśaratha blessed the champion Dāśarathi. In hopes
of taking dust from his father's feet, the son had offered
lotus hands to those lotuslike extremities—but in
vain, for he failed to touch those feet! In a reassuring
voice, Aja's son, born of Raghu, said to Daśaratha's
child, "This is not my former body that you see here, you
who are much more than life to me. It is but a shadow.
How can you, corporeal one, touch this shadow? Like an
image in a mirror, or in water, is my body.
Now without delay, my dearest one, return to Laṅkā."

    Bowing, speechless, toward those feet, that noble one departed,

accompanied by Māyā. Shortly that hero reached the
spot where good warrior Lakṣmaṇa lay still upon the ground.
That throng of warriors stood about, sleepless in their sorrow.

Thus ends canto number eight,
called "City of the Spirits,"
in the poem
The Slaying of Meghanāda

CANTO 9

Funeral Rites

Night turned to morning. Encircling Laṅkā there arose a
monstrous roar, proclaiming boldly victory for Rāma.

He left his golden throne and, morose, sat upon the ground,
alas, that Rāvaṇa, ruler of the Rākṣasas. Then
it was he heard terrifying sounds, the likes of crashing
ocean waves. Surprised, that finest charioteer inquired,
glancing toward Sāraṇa, "Speak plainly, O wise and best of
counselors, for what reason does the hostile throng shout, they
who through the night were miserable with sorrow? Quickly tell
me. Has that unfair fighter, stupid Saumitri, once again
revived? Who knows why the clan of gods, benign, would do such
a thing. That Rāma, who chained the ever-moving currents,
by whose force of *māyā* stones float on the water's surface,
who survives though slain in combat twice—is there anything
within this world of which he is incapable? Tell me,
I must hear, O best of ministers, what has happened now?"

Hands cupped in deference, that best of ministers replied
with regret. "Who comprehends gods' *māyā* in this world of
māyā, Indra among kings? Gandhamādana, sovereign
among mountains and a god by nature, came himself last
night bearing a panacea and resuscitated
Lakṣmaṇa, O king. That is why their legions shout for joy.
As at winter's end a snake possesses twice the vigor,
likewise champion Saumitri shows a renewed spirit—now
intoxicated by the wine of valor. And so too,
with Sugrīva, the southerners are enlivened, like a
herd of elephants, my lord—one hears—with its lordly bull."

Disheartened, that finest charioteer, Laṅkā's sovereign,
sighing spoke, "Who can reverse the will of Fate? When vanquished,
even immortals die, but that foe whom I had slain in
face-to-face combat, did he revive again through divine
might? O Sāraṇa, by my bad luck, even Kṛānta
has forgotten his prime duty. If once the lion sinks
his teeth into the deer, does he ever let him flee? But
what is the point of useless grieving? I knew then all was

lost—when that sun, pride of Rākṣasas, set in darkness, when
my brother Kumbhakarṇa, the utter likeness of the
trident-bearing Śambhu, died in war, as has now our prince,
victor over Vāsava, a second Śaktidhara
in this world.[1] For what purpose do I cling to my own life?
Shall I yet again regain them both upon this earth? Go,
my Sāraṇa, to the skilled charioteer Rāghava.
Tell that champion: 'Rāvaṇa, the wealth of Rākṣasas, O
great-armed one, begs this of you—stay with your army in this
land for seven days, forgoing all hostilities, O
charioteer. My sovereign wishes to perform his son's
cremation rites properly. Observe the warriors' code of
ethics, Raghu monarch. A warrior always proffers due
respect to brave opposing warriors. By your strength of arms,
O hero, golden Laṅkā, bearer of brave warriors, is
now warriorless. You are to be praised among the warrior
brotherhood. You grasped the bow at an auspicious moment,
gem of men. Kind Fate has shown you favor; and, by divine
authority, the king of Rākṣasas now finds himself
in jeopardy. Good warrior, grant today a foeman's wish.'
Hasten now, best of ministers, to the camp of Rāma."

With praises to the Indra of the Rākṣasas, that most
excellent of counselors, his entourage in tow, set
forth. Without a word, the warders opened wide the gateway
loudly. In measured steps that minister of Rākṣasas
moved out somberly toward the ever roaring ocean's shore.

Inside his tent sat his lordship, jewel of the Raghu
clan, submerged within a sea of bliss. In front of him stood
Saumitri, monarch among charioteers, like a tree
now free of snow with new sap flowing, or like the moon in
full phase in a joyous sky, or like a lotus, at night's
end, full blown. And on his right, the Rākṣasa ally, that
hero Vibhīṣaṇa, with all the generals—those most
difficult to overcome in war—as though the Indra
of the gods were flanked by warriors from among the god clan.

Promptly, a courier relayed this news in brief:

1. The earlier death of his brother Kumbhakarṇa presaged the death of his son Meghanāda ("victor over Vāsava") and Rāvaṇa's own inevitable demise as well.

"A minister from the clan of Rākṣasas, Sāraṇa,
my lord, renowned throughout the world, is at the entrance to
our camp, accompanied by his retinue—what is your
order, gem of men, please tell this thrall of yours." The best of
Raghus declared, "Bring at once, courier, with courtesy
that most excellent of counselors to this place. For who
does not know that in combat messengers must not be slain?"
Sāraṇa then stepped inside the tent and spoke (praising those
two royal feet), "Rāvaṇa, the wealth of Rākṣasas, O
great-armed one, begs this of you, 'Stay with your army in this
land for seven days, forgoing all hostilities, O
charioteer. My sovereign wishes to perform his son's
cremation rites properly. Observe the warriors' code of
ethics, Raghu monarch. A warrior always proffers due
respect to brave opposing warriors. By your strength of arms,
O hero, golden Laṅkā, bearer of brave warriors, is
now warriorless. You are to be praised among the warrior
brotherhood. You seized the bow at an auspicious moment,
gem of men. Kind Fate has shown you favor; and by divine
authority the king of Rākṣasas now finds himself
in jeopardy. Good warrior, grant today a foeman's wish.' "
The Raghu lord replied, "The greatest of my enemies,
O Sāraṇa, is your master. Nonetheless, by his grief,
I tell you truly, I am most aggrieved. Whose heart would not
be consumed at seeing Rāhu devour the sun? The kingly
banyan tree who, in forests, burns beneath the sun's fierce rays,
he too at such a death is ashen faced. In times of woe
one's own and an outsider are alike to me, O best
of ministers. Return to golden Laṅkā. I and my
forces shall not take up arms for seven days. Tell the lord
of Rākṣasas, O learned one, persons firm in acting
in accord with *dharma* do not ever strike another
follower of *dharma*." The hero, speaking thus, fell mute.
Head bowed, the minister of Rākṣasas replied, "You are
the finest of the clan of men, jewel of the Raghus;
in learning, intelligence, and might of arms you have no
equal in the world. This action of yours is quite fitting,
hear me out, magnanimous one. Do good men ever do

improper deeds? Just as hero Naikaṣeya is the
ruler of the Rākṣasas, so you, O Rāghava, are
sovereign among men. At some star-crossed moment—excuse my
emotions, charioteer, I beg before your feet!—but,
at some star-crossed moment, the two of you encounter one
another as though bitter foes. Who can alter edicts
made by Fate? That same Fate, O great-armed one, who created
Pavana as hostile to the sea, who made the Indra
among beasts the foe of Indras among elephants, the
Indra of the birds antagonistic to the serpents.
It is through deceit wrought by His *māyā* that Rāghava
is the enemy of Rāvaṇa—whom else can we blame?"

On securing such a favor, he sped home in great haste
to where the lord of Rākṣasas sat quiet, his vestments
moist from outpourings of tears, ah me, grief stricken. Meanwhile,
the sovereign among men gave his chiefs the order. Gaily
each cast off his battle garb and, in his own tent, rested.

Where sat Vaidehī in the Aśoka Grove—as, alas,
sat chaste Kamalā beneath unfathomed seas, apart from
her husband—to there came Saramā, Rājalakṣmī of
the Rākṣasa clan, clad in wifely Rākṣasa attire.
With praises to those lotus feet, that gentlewoman sat
before her. Maithilī, speaking in honeyed tones, queried,
"Please tell me, moon-faced one, why have this city's residents
wept and wailed these past two days? I listened fearfully to
war cries from the battlefield all yesterday; forests shook—
as though from earthquakes—underneath those warriors' distant foot-
falls; in the sky I noticed arrows, leaping like fire's flame
tips; at the close of day, the Rākṣasa forces backtracked
to their city to triumphal shouts while musicians played
a stirring air. Who won? Who lost? I implore you, tell me,
please, Saramā. My agitated heart, alas, dearest,
feels no solace. Here I know not whom to query. I get
no answer when I ask the sentry women. And, O friend,
hideous Trijaṭā, that red-eyed one, sharp sword in hand,
looking ever so like Cāmuṇḍā, came to cut me up
last night, blind with rage. But these sentry matrons held her back;
and that is why, my sleek-haired one, this hapless thing yet lives.

My heart still skips a beat when I call to mind that fell one."
Chaste Saramā replied with sweetest speech, "It is your good
fortune, lucky one, that Indrajit has lost his life in
combat. Hence Laṅkā mourns so, day and night. Finally, my
lady, that heroic king of Karbūras is weakened.
Mandodarī whimpers; the women of the Rākṣasa
clan are overwhelmed with grief; joyless are the Rākṣasa
charioteers. On the strength of your virtue, lotus-eyed,
your brother-in-law, skilled charioteer Lakṣmaṇa, did
in combat that of which the gods were unable—he slew
him who had bested Vāsava—invincible worldwide."
She of the pleasing tongue responded, "You are to my ears
Suvacanī incarnate, always, in this city, my
dearest, O Rākṣasa wife. Praise Saumitri, a lion
of Indras among warriors. At a very auspicious
moment did my mother-in-law, Sumitrā, conceive, O
friend, a son like him within her womb. Now at last, perhaps
Fortune, in its mercy, has thrown open wide my prison
doors. Rāvaṇa, most nefarious of charioteers,
now stands alone in Laṅkā. Let us see what happens—let
us see what further grief is written on my forehead.[2] But
listen well. Gradually the wailing sounds intensify,
friend." Said Saramā-Suvacanī, "The Indra among
Karbūras, by treaty with the Indra of the Raghu
clan, is taking to the ocean's shore for funeral rites
his son, chaste one. For seven days and nights, in this land of
Rākṣasas none shall bear arms in hostility—this pledge
the gem of men made at Rāvaṇa's request—an ocean
of compassion is that Indra among Rāghavas, your
highness. Pretty Pramīlā, the Daitya woman—her heart
splits in two, O faithful wife, when she contemplates all this—
pretty Pramīlā, who to the funeral pyre will give
her body, she, a chaste wife seeking for her husband—O
you who are devoted ever to your husband—she will
enter the godly city of divines today. Did not
chaste Rati die along with her life's lord when Kandarpa,

2. Shortly after birth, Fate comes and writes one's future upon one's forehead.

my gentle woman, burned to death in Hara's anger's fire?"
That Rākṣasa wife, already wet from the water of
her tears, sobbed, overflowing with anguish. Then she who is,
as Sītā, compassion incarnate on the surface of
the earth, she who by another's sorrows is herself made
sad, spoke—eyes suffused with liquid as she told her friend, "I
was born at an ill-omened time, Saramā Rākṣasī.
The lamp of joy, companion, I extinguish always in
whatever house I enter, I who am the essence of
inauspiciousness. Fortune has inscribed this wretched luck.
My husband, finest among men, just see, is banished to
the forest. And a forest exile, O dear girl who bears
auspicious markings, is my husband's brother, high-minded
Lakṣmaṇa. Confidante, over sorrow for his son my
father-in-law gave up his life. Ayodhyā city is
now dark, my dear. The kingly throne sits vacant. Jaṭāyu
succumbed by strength of fearsome arms from monstrous forces while
defending to the death the honor of this humble slave.
Now over there—that Vāsavajit, because of me, the
luckless one, he too is dead and all of those Rākṣasa
charioteers—who can even count their number? Now will
die that youthful female Dānava, incomparable in
beauty in this world. At the start of spring, ah me, such a
bloom is made to wither!" "Your fault," responded Saramā,
wiping back her tears, "whatever are you saying, pretty
one? Who was it stripped away and bore you, golden creeper,
here, first having tricked the king among the mango trees? Who
plucked the lotus of the Raghu's fancy and brought her to
this land of Rākṣasas? By the fruits of his own deed is
Laṅkā's ruler ruined. What more can this humble servant
say?" Most doleful, Saramā wept. At the sorrow of the
clan of Rākṣasas, Rāghava's beloved wailed in that
Aśoka Grove, saddened from the sadness felt by others.
The western gates swung open with the noise of thunder. Out
came thousands of Rākṣasas, hands clenching golden staves from
which fluttered silken banners. In file they walked on either
side of the royal way. Silent were those standard bearers.
Ahead of all there went the kettledrums upon the backs

of elephants, drums which filled the land with solemn booming;
on foot came soldiers, row by row; then horse columns and the
elephants; charioteers in their chariots, driven
at a measured pace; and the instruments of music made
their mournful sounds. As far as one could see, that joyless throng
of Rākṣasas proceeded toward the sea. Their glittering
gold armor overwhelmed the eye. Their golden banner-staves
shone with sunbeams' brilliance. On their heads were diadems;
on belts hung scabbards; hands held spears; from eyes, alas, ran tears.

Out came the warrior-women (Pramīlā's maidservants), in
valor just like Bhīmā, beautiful as Vidyādharīs,
clothed in battle dress—Nṛmuṇḍamālinīs mounted upon
black horses—sullen faces, ah yes, like Night without her
moon. Teary streams flowed unchecked, dampening their uniforms,
dampening their mounts, dampening the earth herself. Some sobbed
openly; other women cried in silence; some gazed toward
the Raghu army angrily, eyes filled with fire, as a
tigress (once ensnared) stares at the nearby hunting party.
Aha, where is that laughter, light of lightning? Where are those
darting sidelong glances which are capable of piercing
all in passion's combat? Amid the women sentries pranced
Vaḍabā, unsaddled, empty of her beauty, as a
stalk without its bloom. Female servants all about waved their
fly-whisks to and fro; there walked with them a train of ladies
weeping all along the way; a tumult rose into the
sky. Pramīlā's heroic garb shone resplendent, loosely
draped upon the back of Vaḍabā—sword, armor, quiver,
bow, and diadem, aha, studded with such priceless gems.
A jeweled waistband, her coat of mail interlaced with gold—
both of them now lackluster; for the waistband, yes, recalled
her thin waistline, while the coat of mail remembered her high
pair of lovely breasts, like peaks of mountains. Slave girls scattered
cowry shells, parched rice, gold coins, and the like; songstresses sang
woefully; Rākṣasīs beat their comely bosoms, weeping.

Out came chariots moving slowly, among them was that
best of chariots, rich hued, lightning's sparkle on its wheels,
flags, the colors found in Indra's bow, on its pinnacles—
but this day it was devoid of splendor, like the empty
splendor of an idol's frame without its lifelike painted

image, at the end of an immersion ceremony.[3]
The Rākṣasa charioteers let out an awful wail,
beside themselves, pounding chests at times with tremendous blows.
Inside the chariot blazed the fearsome bow, quiver, shield,
falchion, conch, discus, mace, and other weapons; a superb
coat of armor; a crown like concentrated sunshine; and
all the rest of the heroic accouterments. Singers
sang their songs of pathos, bemoaning the Rākṣasas' plight.
Some strew gold coins, as trees cast off their flowers when they writhe
in violent storms. Water bearers sprinkled scented water,
keeping down dusty billows which had ceased to tolerate
the footsteps' burden. Toward the seashore moved that chariot.

Upon the cushion of a gold palanquin, bloom-strewn, sat
pretty Pramīlā beside the body—as Rati in
the mortal world accompanies disembodied Kāma.
A vermilion dot upon her forehead, round her neck a
garland, bangles ringed her lotus-stalk-like limbs; ornaments
of many sorts adorned this wifely Rākṣasa. Females
wielding fly-whisks wept and waved their fine fans up and down, while
others, crying, flung flowers hither and yon. With sadness
now uncontrolled, these Rākṣasa womenfolk wailed aloud.
Where, alas, was that light which ever glowed upon her moon-
like face? Where, ah me, that charming smile which always shone so
beautifully upon those nectared lips, as the maker-
of-the-day's rays on those *bimba*-like red lips of yours, O
lotus? Vowed to silence, that moon-faced one turned heart and head
toward husband, as though her lord were present now. When the king
of trees withers, so too wastes away the vine, that lovely
bride who chooses for herself her bridegroom. A prodigious
throng of charioteers filed out on either side, in hand
bared swords off which flashed sunbeams, as luster from their golden
armor stunned the eyes. And all about, those learned in the
Vedas recited scripture aloud; the *hotṛ* priest, while
carrying the sacred fire, recited the great *mantra*;

3. *Visarjana*, also called *bhāsān*, is the ceremony following Durgā Pūjā, for instance, when the image of the deity is immersed in the Ganges. The image consists of straw on a stick frame, all of which is covered with clay. When dry, the clay is painted. Once immersed, the clay washes away, leaving the stick and straw frame.

sundry ornaments and articles of clothing, sandal
paste, musk, saffron, flowers, and vermilion were transported
by the Rākṣasa wives on golden platters; gold jars held
sacred Ganges water. Everywhere were lamps of gold that
glowed. Huge *ḍhāka* drums reverberated, smaller *ḍhola*
drums resounded, and *kāṛās*, tumbler-shaped percussions, barked,
small cuplike cymbals clanged, *mṛdaṅga* drums and hollowed gourds
were played; dish-round gongs and conch shells blared, while those among the
Rākṣasīs not widowed, moist with tears, called out *ululu*—
ah, an auspicious sound on that most inauspicious day.

Out stepped the king of Rākṣasas, Rāvaṇa, dressed in white,
white shawl and garland of *dhuturā* round his neck, as though
about the throat of Dhūrjaṭi himself. On all four sides
but at a distance stood his ministers, heads bowed. Silent
was that sovereign of the Karbūras, eyes full of tears, and
silent his counselors and those best of Rākṣasas who
wielded some authority. Bringing up the rear, weeping,
were residents who lived within that Rākṣasa city—
the children, women, and old men. That city, empty now,
grew dark as Gokula without Śyāma. Slowly, toward the
sea they moved, awash in tears. Sounds of mourning filled the land.

His lordship spoke to Aṅgada in mellow tones, "Go with
a thousand charioteers, O prince and hero, and in
friendly fashion accompany the Rākṣasa legion
to the ocean's shore. Go cautiously, good warrior. My heart
is agitated by the misery felt by Rākṣasas.
At such times of crisis, I do not distinguish others
from my own, O prince. Since, on seeing champion Lakṣmaṇa,
the ruler of the Karbūras, remembering what has
taken place, might anger, you, prince, go instead. Crown-jewel
among kings, your father bested Rākṣasas in combat;
kindly, courteous one, perform this act to honor him."

With ten hundred charioteers went the gracious warrior
Aṅgada, heading seaward. And in the sky the god clan
gathered—the sovereign of the divines on Airāvata,
along with his fine-figured woman, the ever youthful
Śacī, and peacock-bannered Skanda with his peacock flag,
a general and the enemy of Tāraka. In

a multicolored chariot arrived charioteer
Citraratha; upon a deer there came the monarch of
the winds; Kṛtānta rode his monstrous water buffalo;[4]
in his own Puṣpaka he drove—the Yakṣa, sovereign of
Alakā; Night's husband came, that peaceful fount of nectar
who pales before the power of the sun; the smiling twins,
Aśvinī's sons, were there, and many other gods. Godly
dancing girls appeared, and the Gandharvas and Apsarās,
Kinnaras and Kinnarīs. Artfully the instruments
of heaven sounded through the skies. Gods and sages came from
curiosity, as did other residents on high.

They reached the seashore whereat Rākṣasas quickly built a
proper pyre. Bearers brought sweet scented sandalwood and ghee
in quantities. With sacred Mandākinī water, those
Rākṣasas washed carefully the corpse, then dressed it in fine
silken garments, and placed it on the pyre. Solemnly, their
purohit recited *mantras*. Having bathed her body
in that sacred place of pilgrimage, the ocean, the most
chaste of faithful wives, that pretty Pramīlā, divested
herself of ornaments and jewels, bestowing them on
all those present. With obeisance to her revered elders,
that one of honeyed speech addressed the group of Daitya maids
saying sweetly, "O companions, after all this time my
life today comes to an end in this arena of the
living. Return, all of you, to our Daitya homeland. Speak
politely at my father's feet, Vāsantī, all the news.
And to my mother." Alas, the tears began to stream. That
chaste wife kept silent—the Dānava women sobbed out loud.

Then a moment later, holding back her grief, that pretty
one spoke up, "Tell my mother, that which Fortune wrote upon
the forehead of this humble servant finally today
has come to pass. To whose hands my parents gave this humble
slave, it is with him, my dear, I go this day—within our
world what refuge is there for a wife without her husband?
What more shall I say, my friend? Do not forget her, dearest
ones—this is Pramīlā's most earnest plea to all of you."

4. Each Hindu deity has his or her specific vehicle or *vāhana*. Pavana, the wind god, rides a deer; the god of death, Kṛtānta, has a water buffalo as his mount.

That purest wife then mounted the pyre (as though onto a
floral throne) and sat with peace of mind at her husband's feet,
a garland of full-blown blossoms wrapped around her chignon.
The Rākṣasa musicians played, and aloud those versed in
texts recited from the Vedas. The women Rākṣasa
gave out auspicious calls of *ululu* which, when joined with
ululations, rose into the skies. Flowers showered all
around. The Rākṣasa maidens, as was proper, proffered
sundry ornaments and articles of clothing, sandal
paste, musk, saffron, vermilion and so forth. The Rākṣasas
carefully arranged on all four sides sharp arrows smeared with
ghee, arrows used for killing beasts, just as is done the ninth
day during Durgā Pūjā in households of the Śākta
devotees, O Śakti, before your altar's pedestal.

The monarch of the Rākṣasas stepped forward, then spoke with
anguish, "It was my hope, Meghanāda, that I would close
these eyes of mine for the final time with you before me—
transferring to you, son, the responsibility for
this kingdom, I would set out on my greatest journey. But
Fate—how shall I ever comprehend His *līlā*? That joy
eluded me. It was my hope to soothe my eyes, dear lad,
by seeing you upon the Rākṣasas' regal throne, on
your left my daughter-in-law, the Lakṣmī of this clan of
Rākṣasas, as consort. Futile were those hopes. For due to
fruits of a previous birth I observe you both today
upon the throne of Time.[5] That sun, the pride of Karbūras,
is forever swallowed up by Rāhu. Did I serve with
care Śiva just to gain but these ends? How shall I ever
turn back now—ah, who can tell me how I might return to
Laṅkā and our empty home? By what feigned consolation
shall I console your mother—who can tell me that? 'Where are
my son and daughter-in-law?'—Queen Mandodarī, when she
asks me, 'For what pleasures did you leave them at the seashore,
sovereign of the Rākṣasas?'—what shall I say to make her
understand? Alas, what can I say? Son. Preeminent
of warriors. Victorious in battle always. Little

5. The word is *kāla*, which glosses as both "time" and "death."

mother, Lakṣmī of the Rākṣasas. For what transgression
did Fate write this cruel pain upon the monarch's forehead?"

At his Kailāsa home, Śūlī was beside himself. His
matted hair tilted to one side upon his head; with a
vicious roar his serpents hissed; from his forehead flames leapt forth;
the Tripathagā poured down her frightful crashing waves, like
swiftly flowing streams through mountain caverns. Mount Kailāsa
shook violently. In panic the universe quaked. Fearful,
faithful Abhayā, hands cupped humbly, addressed Maheśa,

"For what reason are you angry, lord? Tell me, your servant,
please. He died in war, that Rākṣasa, by Fate's decree. Do
not blame the Raghu warrior. If you wrongly harm him, lord,
first burn me to ashes." And at that, Mother hugged his feet.

With feeling, raising Satī, Dhūrjaṭi replied, "My heart
breaks, Nagendra's daughter, from the Rākṣasas' woe. You know
how I love the champion Naikaṣeya. But, for your sake,
Kṣemaṅkarī, I forgive that Rāma and his brother."

To Agni, god of fire, Triśūlī commanded sadly,
"Sanctify them by your touch, you who are most pure, and bring
at once to this auspicious home that Rākṣasa and wife."

In the form of lightning streaks, Agni ran to earth. Then at
once the pyre burst ablaze. All, startled, looked upon that
fiery chariot. There on a seat of gold within the
chariot sat the warrior, vanquisher of Vāsava,
in celestial form. On his left, pretty Pramīlā whose
splendor of unending youth shone from her graceful figure
and on whose honeyed lips, a smile of everlasting joy.

With great speed that best of chariots climbed its skyward path
as the god clan in concert rained down flowers, and the
universe filled with blissful sounds. The Rākṣasas put out
those brilliant flames in streams of pure milk. With utmost care they
gathered up the ashes and immersed them in the ocean.
Having washed that cremation site using water from the
Jāhnavī, Rākṣasa craftsmen by the thousands built with
golden bricks a temple on the spot where stood the pyre—
that temple's lofty spire, cleaving clouds, rose to the sky.

After bathing in waters of the sea, those Rākṣasas
now headed back toward Laṅkā, wet still with water of their

grief—it was as if they had immersed the image of the
goddess on the lunar tenth day of the Durgā Pūjā.
Then Laṅkā wept in sorrow seven days and seven nights.

Thus ends canto number nine,
called "Funeral Rites,"
in the poem
The Slaying of Meghanāda

NOTES TO INTRODUCTION

1. For most of his life, he used "Dutt" as the Anglicized spelling of his surname. In 1866 while in Europe, he writes his main benefactor back in Calcutta, the renowned Isvar Chandra Vidyasagar, "I am 'published' Barrister as Michael Madhusudan Datta, Esquire. You might drop the vulgar form 'Dutt' "; Ksetra Gupta, ed., *Madhusudana racanavali* (The collected works of Madhusudan) (Kolkata: Sahitya Samsad, 1974; rpt. 1980), 618. I accede to his wishes expressed in that letter and refer to him as Datta.

2. South Asian names and the spellings of names in the Roman alphabet have changed over time. In the case of place names, I shall from here on use the English spellings current during Datta's lifetime and call Kolkata Calcutta and Chennai Madras.

3. Sisir Kumar Das, *Sahibs and Munshis: An Account of the College of Fort William* (New Delhi: Orion Publications, 1978), 150.

4. Gauri Viswanathan, *Masks of Conquest: Literary Study and British Rule in India* (New York: Columbia University Press, 1989).

5. Sushil Kumar De, *Bengali Literature in the Nineteenth Century, 1757–1857* (Kolkata: Firma K. L. Mukhopadhyay, 1962), 480.

6. Ibid., 481.

7. Ibid., 486ff.

8. Ibid., 488.

9. A somewhat comparable institution, Haileybury College, had been opened in England in 1805 and continued to serve as a training ground for young civilians headed for Company service in India. The philosophy driving that educational institution would appear to have been far more Anglicist than Orientalist from the very outset, interested in fully preparing the new recruits before they could become corrupted by actual India; Sumanta Banerjee, *The Parlour and the Streets: Elite and Popular Culture in Nineteenth Century Calcutta* (Kolkata: Seagull Books, 1989), 34–35.

10. David Kopf, *British Orientalism and the Bengal Renaissance: The Dynamics of Indian Modernization, 1773–1835* (Berkeley and Los Angeles: University of California Press, 1969), 241–42.

11. Ibid.

12. Gupta, *Madhusudana racanavali*, 638.

13. Ibid., 639.

14. De, *Bengali Literature*, 491.

15. Suresh Chandra Maitra, *Maikela Madhusudana Datta: jivana o sahitya* (Michael Madhusudan Datta: life and literature) (Kolkata: Puthipatra, 1975), 33.

16. Concerning his age and the year when he entered Hindoo College, the earliest biography of Datta gives thirteen and 1837; Yogindranath Basu, *Maikela Madhusudana Dattera jivana-carita* (A biography of Michael Madhusudan Datta) (5th ed.; Kolkata: Chakravarti, Chatterjee, 1925), 25 and 48. The editor of Datta's collected works cites Brajendranath Bandyopadhyay's opinion that the year was 1833, noting that the college magazine (March 7, 1834) mentions Datta reading aloud at the college's awards ceremony; Gupta, *Madhusudana racanavali*, xi. More recent biographers, first Maitra and then

Ghulam Murshid, opt for the date given in the earliest biography. Maitra cites overwhelming evidence of a second, older Madhusudan Datta at Hindoo College in the early 1830s; *Maikela Madhusudana Datta,* 32–33. Murshid agrees with Maitra; *Ashara chalane bhuli: Maikela-jivani* (Fooled by hope's deception: a Michael biography) (2d ed.; Kolkata: Ananda Publishers, 1997), 28.

17. Thomas Babington Macaulay, "Minute on Education," in *Sources of Indian Tradition*, edited by Wm. Theodore de Bary (New York: Columbia University Press, 1958), 2: 44–45.

18. Ram Mohun Roy, "Letter on Education," in *Sources of Indian Tradition*, 2: 40–43.

19. Macaulay, "Minute on Education," in *Sources of Indian Tradition*, 2: 47.

20. Ibid., 2: 49.

21. Amalendu Bose, *Michael Madhusudan Dutt* (New Delhi: Sahitya Akademi, 1981), 9.

22. Maitra, *Maikela Madhusudana Datta*, 28.

23. Murshid, *Ashara chalane bhuli*, 19–20.

24. Gupta, *Madhusudana racanavali*, 622.

25. Ibid., 622–23.

26. Ibid., 438.

27. Ibid., 454.

28. Nagendranath Som, *Madhu-smriti* (Remembrances of Madhu) (3d ed.; Kolkata: Vidyodaya Library, 1989), 8; Murshid, *Ashara chalane bhuli*, 39.

29. Gupta, *Madhusudana racanavali*, 41.

30. Ibid., 556.

31. Ibid., 602.

32. Ibid., 438.

33. Ibid., 519–20.

34. Ibid., 520.

35. Ibid., 524.

36. Ibid., 525–26; letter dated and timed, "Kidderpore, 27 Nov., [1842] Midnight."

37. Quoted in Basu, *Maikela Madhusudana*, 124.

38. Ibid., appendix, 4.

39. Murshid, *Ashara chalane bhuli*, 65.

40. Gupta, *Madhusudana racanavali*, 467.

41. Murshid, *Ashara chalane bhuli*, 71.

42. Gupta, *Madhusudana racanavali*, 528–29.

43. Ibid., 528.

44. Murshid, *Ashara chalane bhuli*, 84.

45. Ibid., 66; photocopy of the relevant page from the college registry appears on page 88.

46. Ibid., 107.

47. I want to thank Rachel Fell McDermott for questioning today's generally held but erroneous belief that Madhusudan became Michael Madhusudan upon converting to Christianity. It was due to her prodding that I came to see the obvious, which has been in plain view all along.

48. Amalendu Bose sees a direct connection between the decline in his income and the decline in the importance of Persian, which Raj Narain spoke, as a useful language in the courts; *Michael Madhusudan Dutt*, 26. Persian, however, had begun its decline a decade earlier and probably had no bearing on his financial situation. Other biographers suggest that Raj Narain had, for reasons unknown, been disqualified by judges from pleading appeal cases; Murshid, *Ashara chalane bhuli*, 86.

49. Murshid, *Ashara chalane bhuli*, 87–88.

50. Gupta, *Madhusudana racanavali*, 530.

51. Ibid.

52. Murshid, *Ashara chalane bhuli*, 94. Other biographies have him leaving Calcutta earlier in December and arriving the day before Christmas.

53. Ibid., 100, 102.

54. Ibid., 103 n. 29.

55. Gupta, *Madhusudana racanavali*, 530–31.

56. In *Kim*, Kipling immediately declares his hero to be "English," but how English is he? In Kipling's words, Kim was "white—a poor white of the very poorest. The half-caste woman who looked after him (she smoked opium, and pretended to keep a second-hand furniture shop by the square where the cheap cabs wait) told the missionaries that she was Kim's mother's sister; but his mother had been nurse-maid in a Colonel's family and had married Kimball O'Hara, a young colour-sergeant of the Mavericks, an Irish regiment. He afterwards took a post on the Sind, Punjab, and Delhi Railway, and his Regiment went home without him. The wife died of cholera in Ferozepore, and O'Hara fell to drink and loafing up and down the line with the keen-eyed three-year-old baby." Rudyard Kipling, *Kim* (New York: New American Library, 1984), 19. That Kim's mother served as a "nurse-maid in a Colonel's family" does not, quite obviously, preclude her from being "half-caste," just like the woman who is said to have looked after Kim. I thank Amanda Hamilton, who studies the Anglo-Indian community in nineteenth-century India, for calling my attention to Kim's wonderfully ambiguous pedigree.

57. Murshid, *Ashara chalane bhuli*, 102–3.

58. Gupta, *Madhusudana racanavali*, 531.

59. From "Visions of the Past," cited ibid., 478.

60. And, looked at differently, "The Captive Ladie" is also "Orientalist," Rosinka Chaudhuri tells us in her study of nineteenth-century poetry by Indians, primarily English-language poetry; *Gentlemen Poets in Colonial Bengal: Emergent Nationalism and the Orientalist Project* (Kolkata: Seagull Books, 2002), 108. "Orientalist poetry" by Indians is that which "used form and style borrowed from English poetry and themes taken from Orientalist translations of Indian classics [by such Englishmen as Sir William Jones and H. H. Wilson] or the ancient and medieval history of India [compiled by the likes of James Tod among others]"; ibid., 152. But "Orientalism," a term today with many valences, need not be inferred as negative here, for Orientalist poetry of this kind, writes Chaudhuri, contributed to the engendering of a nationalism of sorts, a nationalism that "signified a pride in, and an awareness of, an indigenous culture and tradition"; ibid., 132.

61. From "The Captive Ladie," cited in Gupta, *Madhusudana racanavali*, 507.

62. Ibid., 531.

63. Ibid., 538.

64. Ibid., 534.

65. Ibid., 535.

66. Ibid.

67. Ibid., 536–37.

68. Quoted in Basu, *Maikela Madhusudana*, 159–60; Bethune's letter dated July 20, 1849.

69. Ibid., 160–61.

70. Nilmani Mukherjee, *A Bengali Zamindar: Jaykrishna Mukherjee of Uttarpara and His Times, 1808–1888* (Kolkata: Firma K. L. Mukhopadhyay, 1975), 169–70. The society formally started in 1851; planning had begun the previous year.

71. Viswanathan, *Masks of Conquest*, 142–65.

72. Gupta, *Madhusudana racanavali*, 630–31.

73. Ibid., 539.

74. Basu, *Maikela Madhusudana*, appendix, 20.

75. Murshid, *Ashara chalane bhuli*, 346.

76. Basu, *Maikela Madhusudana*, appendix, 13.

77. Gupta, *Madhusudana racanavali*, liv; Isvar Chandra Singh's letter dated May 8, 1859.

78. *Ekei ki Bale Sabhayata?* (Is this called civilization?), in Gupta, *Madhusudana racanavali*, 241–54.

79. Goutam Chattopadhyay, ed., *Awakening in Bengal in Early Nineteenth Century (Selected Documents)* (Kolkata: Progressive Publishers, 1965), 1: lxi–lxvii. As noted earlier, there were two Madhusudan Dattas at this time, both associated with Hindoo College. This may be the senior one, not our poet.

80. Only two plays were performed at this important and innovative theater, one for which Datta produced a translation and one his original composition. The premature death of the younger of the Paikpara rajas kept the doors of this theater closed for good; Asutosh Bhattacarya, *Bamla natyasahityera itihasa: prathama khanda, dvitiya bhaga, madhyayuga (1873–1900)* (History of Bangla dramatic literature: Volume one, part two, middle period [1873–1900]) (3d ed.; Kolkata: A. Mukherji, 1968), 426.

81. Gupta, *Madhusudana racanavali*, 575; letter written to the actor Keshav Gangopadhyay, after finishing his drama *Krishnakumari* in September of 1860. The play was not performed until February of 1867, the very month Datta returned from Europe.

82. The classic studies of *Ramayanas* in Bangla remain Dinesh Chandra Sen's *The Bengali Ramayanas* (Kolkata: University of Calcutta, 1920) and more recently Asit Kumar Banerjee, ed., *The Ramayana in Eastern India* (Kolkata: Prajna, 1983). For a brief discussion of some of the variations among Rama narratives, see Edward C. Dimock, Jr., Edwin Gerow, C. M. Naim, A. K. Ramanujan, Gordon Roadarmel, and J.A.B. van Buitenen, *The Literatures of India: An Introduction* (Chicago: University of Chicago Press, 1974), pp. 72–80. For a more in-depth examination of aspects of the *Ramayanas* in several different linguistic traditions, see Paula Richman, ed., *Many Ramayanas: The Diversity of a Narrative Tradition in South Asia* (Berkeley and Los Angeles: University of California Press, 1991).

83. Gupta, *Madhusudana racanavali*, 558.

84. Ibid., 562.

85. Rabindranath Tagore, "Meghanadavadha kavya," in *Rabindra-racanavali, acalita samgraha* (The collected works of Rabindranath Tagore: Out-of-print material) (Kolkata: Visvabharati, 1962; first published in *Bharati*, August, 1882), 2: 80.

86. Ashis Nandy, *The Intimate Enemy: Loss and Recovery of Self under Colonialism* (Delhi: Oxford University Press, 1983), 19.

87. Harekrishna Mukhopadhyay, ed., *Krittivasi Ramayana* (Kolkata: Sahitya Samsad, 1957), 351–52.

88. Gupta, *Madhusudana racanavali*, 557.

89. This hierarchy of vulnerability is implicit from the very beginning of the war: Ravana will be the last to die. In Krittivasa it is made explicit as follows: "But for Virabahu and Indrajit, there are no warriors; once they have perished, Ravana shall be destroyed"; and "If Virabahu does not die, Ravana will not perish"; Mukhopadhyay, *Krittivasi Ramayana*, 330 and 335.

90. Gupta, *Madhusudana racanavali*, 557.

91. *Marksavadi*, no. 5 (September[?] 1949): 132.

92. Gupta, *Madhusudana racanavali*, 547.

93. Ibid., 551.

94. Ibid., 556.

95. Ibid., 551–52.

96. Ibid., 554.

97. Ibid., 558.

98. Ramananda Chattopadhyay, ed., *Kasidasi Mahabharata* (3d ed.; Kolkata: Pravasi Press, 1962), 300.

99. See Norvin Hein, *The Miracle Plays of Mathura* (New Haven: Yale University Press, 1972); Richard Schechner, *Performative Circumstances: From the Avant Garde to Ramlila* (Kolkata: Seagull Books, 1983); Anuradha Kapur, *Actors, Pilgrims, Kings, and Gods: The Ramlila at Ramnagar* (Kolkata: Seagull Books, 1990); and Philip Lutgendorf, *The Life of a Text: Performing the Ramcaritmanas of Tulsidas* (Berkeley and Los Angeles: University of California Press, 1991).

100. Basu, *Maikela Madhusudana*, appendix, 15.

101. Sen, *Bengali Ramayanas*, 251.

102. Bishvanath Bandyopadhyay has written a persuasive article demonstrating the correspondences between Sulocana of the Jagadrami *Ramayana* and Datta's Pramila; "*Pramilara utsa*" (The Origins of Pramila), *Desh*, 22 Phalgun, 1388/March 6, 1982, 9–10. Bandyopadhyay concedes that there is little if anything of the warrior woman in Sulocana. But that aside, the two female characters and their actions are too alike for the similarities to have been coincidental. Dinesh Chandra Sen had earlier suggested that Datta must have read the Jagadrami *Ramayana; Bengali Ramayanas*, 251. In a letter to the editor, following publication of Bandyopadhyay's article, a reader wondered in print whether we can trust the Jagadrami *Ramayana* as a credible, legitimate text; Sushanta Sarkar, "*Pramilara utsa*," *Desh*, 20 Caitra 1388/April 3, 1982. I have no answer for him. Furthermore, he asks, why have literary historians been so disinterested in this text? Again, no answer from me.

103. Gupta, *Madhusudana racanavali,* 546.

104. Ibid., 564.

105. Raj Narain Basu, *Se kal ar e kal* (Then and now) (1879; reprint, Kolkata: Bangiya Sahitya Parishad, 1956), 95.

106. Pramathanath Bishi, *Bamla sahityer naranari* (Men and women in Bangla literature) (Kolkata: Maitri, 1966), 25.

107. William Radice, "Xenophilia and Xenophobia: Michael Madhusudan Datta's *Meghnad-badh kabya,*" in Rupert Snell and I.M.P. Raeside, eds., *Classics of Modern South Asian Literature* (Wiesbaden: Harrassowitz, 1998), 147.

108. Ibid., 150.

109. Ibid., 152.

110. Ibid., 163.

111. Gupta, *Madhusudana racanavali,* 557.

112. Ibid., 558.

113. Ibid., 561.

114. Ibid., 564.

115. Ibid., 567.

116. Ibid., xxxiii.

117. *Bangadarshan,* 2: 5 (August, 1873): 232.

118. *Bangadarshan,* 8: 6 (September, 1881): 262.

119. Ibid., 263.

120. Ibid., 264.

121. Rabindranath Tagore, "Meghanadavadha kavya," in *Rabindra-racanavali, acalita samgraha,* 2: 78.

122. Ibid., 79.

123. Ibid., 81 (misprinted as 79).

124. Rabindranath Tagore, *Jivanasmrti* (Reminiscences); cited in *Rabindra-racanavali, acalita samgraha,* 2: 718.

125. Harold Bloom, *The Anxiety of Influence: A Theory of Poetry* (New York: Oxford University Press, 1973).

126. I wish to thank Abdul Mannan Syed, the current executive director of the Nazrul Institute, Dhaka, Bangladesh, who called my attention to the fact that Nazrul renamed his wife. Such a practice was not unprecedented. Rabindranath Tagore's wife's name had been changed, from Bhabatarini to Mrinalini, by the Tagores on the occasion of her marriage into the family.

127. Karunamaya Goswami, *Kazi Nazrul Islam: A Biography* (Dhaka: Nazrul Institute, 1996), 15.

128. Subodh Chandra Sengupta, ed., *Samsada Bangali caritabhidhana* (Samsad's biographical dictionary of Bengalis) (Kolkata: Sahitya Samsad, 1976).

129. Pramatha Chaudhuri, "Sabuja patrera mukhapatra" (*Sabuj Patra*'s manifesto), in *Nana-katha* (Miscellany) (Kolkata: By the author, [1919]), 109–10.

130. Introductory notes by Abinash Chandra Gangopadhyay speak of this production of *Meghanadavadha kavya* as the first production mounted at the newly renamed National Theatre; see Debipada Bhattacharya, ed., *Girisa racanavali* (The collected works of Girish Chandra Ghosh) (Calcutta: Sahitya Samsad, 1964), 147.

131. Ibid., 29, 31.

132. Edward Thompson, *Rabindaranath Tagore: Poet and Dramatist* (2d ed.; London: Oxford University Press, 1948), 16.

133. Gupta, *Madhusudana racanavali,* 548–49.

134. Mukhopadhyay, *Krittivasi Ramayana,* 335.

135. Nirad C. Chaudhuri, *The Autobiography of an Unknown Indian* (Berkeley and Los Angeles: University of California Press, 1968), 186.

abhaya, the negative of the word "fear" (*bhaya*); by extension, "assurance that no harm will be done."

Abhayā, "she who assures that no harm will be done"; epithet of Durgā.

Abhimanyu, "fearless and wrathful"; name of the warrior son of the Pāṇḍava Arjuna and Kṛṣṇa's sister Subhadrā. A major figure in the great Bhārata war, Abhimanyu knew how to penetrate the best of (i.e., the virtually impenetrable) military formations but did not know how to exit from the hostile forces so arrayed. (Two explanations account for this great warrior's vulnerability. While still in his mother's womb, Abhimanyu had heard his father discussing military strategy with the other Pāṇḍavas, and thus learned from him how to breach formidable enemy alignments; Abhimanyu failed, however, to gain knowledge of the means by which to exit from those opposing ranks, for his mother fell asleep before Arjuna had finished speaking to his brothers. According to another tale, the moon was cursed, for failing to pay due deference to the sage Garga, to be incarnated in the world of humans as Abhimanyu; although a sage's curse once uttered cannot be retracted, Garga out of pity lessened its severity by declaring that Abhimanyu, at the end of his sixteenth year, could be slain in battle and would then return to heaven.) Abhimanyu is slain at the completion of his sixteenth year by seven opposing Kaurava warriors. In Kāśīrāmadāsa's *Mahābhārata,* the fight of the seven against the one is referred to as an unfair battle (*anyāya śamara*), exactly the way weaponless Meghanāda characterizes his fight to the death with a heavily armed Lakṣmaṇa supported by Meghanāda's own uncle in the sixth canto of *The Slaying of Meghanāda.* In the *Mahābhārata,* Abhimanyu fights valiantly but futilely, ripping off parts of chariots and hurling them at his attackers, again similar to what Meghanāda, in *The Slaying of Meghanāda,* does in the temple with the various paraphernalia required for *pūjā* as he attempts in vain to save his life.

Āditeya, "son of Aditi"; epithet of Indra; matronymic from Aditi, mother of the gods.

Aditi, mother of the gods; the antithesis of Diti, progenitress of the Daityas (also known as Asuras, Dānavas, Karbūra, Rākṣasas, that is, the antigods by whatever name).

Āditya, the sun god, who daily ascends the "rising-hill" in the east, rides across the sky in his one-wheeled chariot, and descends the "setting-hill" in the evening.

Āgama, a class of Hindu texts, often including esoteric lore and framed as a conversation between Śiva and his wife Pārvatī, with the former instructing the latter.

Agni, fire or the god of fire; Meghanāda's chosen deity. Fire and wind support each other, hence the epithet of "wind's companion" for Agni.

Airāvata, "produced from the ocean"; name of Indra's elephant mount, one of the many objects produced from the primordial ocean when churned by the Suras (gods) and the Asuras (antigods).

Aja, a patriarch within Rāma's lineage; grandfather of Rāma; see Dilīpa.

Akampana, "nontrembling"; name of a Rākṣasa warrior.

Ākhaṇḍala, "breaker"; epithet of Indra; "Indra's bow/Ākhaṇḍala's bow" is the rainbow.

Alakā, city ruled by Kubera, the god of riches, located in the Himālaya mountains.

Ambikā, "mother"; epithet of Durgā.

amṛta, the negative of the word "dead" (*mṛta*); by extension, "ambrosia, an immortality-producing elixir, the nectar of the gods." One of the many products that came out of the primordial ocean when churned by the Suras (gods) and the Asuras (antigods), the *amṛta* was initially appropriated by the Asuras. In order to obtain it from the Asuras, Viṣṇu assumed the guise of Mohinī, an enchantingly beautiful woman, and thereby distracted the Asuras. Viṣṇu's mount Garuḍa, also known as Vainateya, stole away the *amṛta* from the preoccupied Asuras, depriving them of that powerful elixir.

Anaṅga, "he who is without a body"; epithet of the god of love, Kāma, who at the behest of the other gods aroused Śiva sexually, breaking the great sage's yogic meditative trance. Angry, Śiva with fire from his third eye incinerated Kāma, who thereafter was devoid of bodily form, though he continued to exist incorporeally.

Ananta, "the one without end"; epithet of Śeṣa and of Vāsuki, both Nāga monarchs and mythological cobras; Vāsuki (Ananta) supports the entire world on his many heads; see Śeṣa.

Aṅgada, nephew of Sugrīva and crown prince of the southern kingdom of Kiṣkindhyā, allied with Rāma against the Rākṣasas.

Añjanā, mother of Hanumān.

Annadā, "she who is a giver of food"; epithet of Durgā.

Antaryāmī, "he who resides within"; the god who knows one's inner thoughts.

Antaryāminī, "she who resides within"; the goddess who knows one's inner thoughts.

Apsarā, a class of celestial demigoddesses or nymphs, known for their exceptional beauty and their dancing ability.

Asilomā, "he whose body hairs are swords"; name of a Rākṣasa warrior.

aśoka, a variety of flowering tree.

Aśoka, "nonsorrow"; name of the grove on the island kingdom of Laṅkā wherein Sītā is held captive.

Asura, a class of enemies of the gods; the negative of Sura (god); often considered synonymous with Daitya, Dānava, Karbūra, and Rākṣasa.

Āśutoṣa, "he who is satisfied readily"; epithet of Śiva.

Aśvatthāmā, son of Droṇa, ally of the Kauravas against the Pāṇḍavas in the war narrated in the *Mahābhārata*. After the one hundred sons of Dhṛtarāṣṭra had been slain or lay dying, Aśvatthāmā, whose father fought and died on the side of Dhṛtarāṣṭra's sons, vowed to avenge the Kauravas' defeat by slaying the Pāṇḍavas. He with two accomplices set out for the Pāṇḍavas' camp. As night set in, they rested, but Aśvatthāmā noted that an owl stayed alert at night to catch its prey while other birds slept, which led him to propose a night attack. When the three conspirators reached the encampment, they found its entryway guarded by Śiva, who refused to give them passage. Aśvatthāmā then emptied his quiver on Śiva, but the god proceeded to swallow those arrows without being wounded. Unsuccessful through brute force, Aśvatthāmā performed a *pūjā* to Śiva and ultimately threatened to offer himself up as a human sacrifice unless the god grant him a boon, thereby allowing his vow of vengeance be fulfilled. He also requested and received Śiva's falchion with which to do his dirty work. Śiva assented to these requests and stepped away from the gate. Aśvatthāmā then entered, slew Dhṛṣṭadyumna and Śikhaṇḍī, both brothers of Draupadī (common wife of the five Pāṇḍavas), and decapitated the five Pāṇḍavas' five sleeping sons, thinking them to be the senior Pāṇḍava warriors. Aśvatthāmā presented the five severed heads to the dying Duryodhana, eldest of the one hundred Kauravas, who realized that his cousins, the Pāṇḍavas, yet lived but that their offspring were now dead. With that knowledge, Duryodhana succumbed.

Aśvinī, mother of the Aśvins, twin divine warriors. By one account, Saṃjñā, wife of the sun, finding the heat of her husband intolerable, assumed the appearance of a horse (*aśva*) and went wandering off in the land of Uttarakuru. Sūrya, the sun, came to know of her whereabouts, went there, and impregnated his Aśvinī ("she who has the appearance of a horse"). Aśvinī, also known as Vaḍabā (see Vaḍabā), gave birth to twin sons, charioteers both, who were known not only for their handsome appearance but also for their skill as medical practitioners to the gods. Aśvinī, by another account, is considered one of the twenty-seven (later increased to twenty-eight) stars (*nakṣatras*: constellations or lunar "houses" through which the moon passes), all twenty-seven of which are beautiful wives of Candra, the moon.

Atikāya, "whose body is huge"; name of a Rākṣasa warrior.

Ayodhyā, the kingdom and capital city of Daśaratha, to be inherited by Rāma, located in northern India, on the Sarayū River.

Bali, a Daitya humbled by Viṣṇu in his fifth of ten *avatāras* or incarnations. Bali prided himself on his dominion over the three worlds: heaven, earth, and the nether region called Pātāla. Viṣṇu, appearing before him in the form of Vāmana or "the dwarf," asked Bali for as much territory as he, Vāmana, could traverse in three strides. Haughty Bali acceded to the request of this dwarfish being, whereupon Vāmana increased in size and strode through heaven and earth in two paces, but left the humbled Bali sovereignty over the lower regions.

Bhagavatī, name of Durgā that emphasizes her role as supreme goddess; feminine of Bhagavān (supreme lord).

Bhairava, name of Śiva that emphasizes his violent, terrible, formidable aspect.

Bhairavī, name of Durgā that emphasizes her aspect as the spouse of the formidable Śiva; also an epithet of the goddess as Kālī.

Bharata, (1) one of the three half brothers of Rāma, the other two being Lakṣmaṇa and Śatrughna. When, due to a boon granted his mother, Bharata was to assume the throne of the deceased Daśaratha, he demurred and placed Rāma's sandals on the throne instead; see Kaikeyī. Also, (2) progenitor of the Bhāratas, the lineage engaged in the internecine war recounted in the *Mahābhārata;* see Bhārata (2).

Bhārata, (1) name for India and for the "continent" (*varṣa*) that is premodern India (canto 4); also, (2) descendants of Bharata (canto 8).

Bhāratī, name of Sarasvatī, goddess of speech, the arts, and learning; her complexion is white.

Bhartṛhari, name of a famed Sanskrit poet, author of *Bhaṭṭikāvya* (Bhaṭṭi's verse narrative), a work illustrating grammar and poetic conceits while at the same time narrating the tale of Rāma; Bhaṭṭi is considered the Prakrit form of Bhartṛ.

Bhava, "essence, existence"; epithet of Śiva.

Bhavabhūti, name of a famed Sanskrit poet, author of the drama *Uttararāmacarita* (The later history of Rāma).

Bhavānī, name of Durgā.

Bhaveśa, "lord of existence"; epithet of Śiva.

Bhaveśvarī, "goddess of existence"; epithet of Durgā.

bheri, a kettledrum.

Bhīma, "ferocious (masculine)"; (1) epithet of Śiva that emphasizes his more violent aspect; also, (2) a shortened form of Bhīmasena, second eldest of the five Pāṇḍava brothers.

Bhīmā, "ferocious (feminine)"; epithet of Durgā in her more violent aspect.

Bhīmasena, second eldest of the five Pāṇḍava brothers; see Bhīma (2).

bhindipāla, a weapon whose nature is uncertain—either a short javelin thrown by hand or shot through a tube, or a stone fastened to a cord, a sling.

Bhīṣaṇa, "monstrous, terrible"; name of a Rākṣasa warrior.

bhomara, a spear whose shaft is twisted like an auger.

Bhṛgurāma, another name for Paraśurāma or "Rāma with the ax," who is the sixth of the ten *avatāras* of Viṣṇu and an extremely formidable fighter. A Brāhman by caste, Bhṛgurāma/Paraśurāma is said to have slain with his ax all of the Kṣatriyas (the warrior caste). The word *bhṛgu* itself suggests strength, having as it does as one of its literal meanings, "sheer cliff or mountain plateau."

Bhūta, "ghost, spirit"; Śiva is the lord of the Bhūtas.

Biḍālākṣa, "cat-eyes"; name of a Rākṣasa warrior.

bimba, a red fruit.

Bṛhannalā, "big reed"; pseudonym of Arjuna. After the eldest Pāṇḍava had lost (been cheated) at dice, the five brothers and their common wife, Draupadī, went into forest exile for twelve years, according to the terms of the wager. The thirteenth year they were to dwell incognito. If identified, they would have to live another twelve years exiled. The thirteenth year was spent in the domain of Virāṭa, king of the Matsyas. Arjuna chose to disguise himself as a eunuch and dress in women's clothes, hiding with conch shell bangles the calluses on both arms (he was ambidextrous) produced by the bowstring. He took the name Bṛhannalā and passed himself off as a song and dance instructor for the girls of the palace. As the thirteenth year ended, the Kauravas, in league with another king and not knowing the Pāṇḍavas' whereabouts, invaded the Matsya kingdom where they rustled King Virāṭa's cattle. The king and all the Pāṇḍavas save Arjuna were out fighting the invaders when news of the stolen cows reached prince Uttara, who was still in the palace. Virāṭa's son accepted the eunuch as his chariot driver, then set off to engage the enemy. But, intimidated by the mighty Kauravas, Uttara could not bring himself to fight. The two retreated to a particular *śamī* tree in which the Pāṇḍavas had stashed their weapons and regalia when donning disguises for the thirteenth year. Arjuna changed back into his martial attire. Now fully accoutered, Arjuna, this time with Uttara as his chariot driver, retrieved the cow herd then routed Karṇa, Duryodhana, and the supporting Kaurava forces.

cakra, a discus weapon; a chariot wheel.

cakravākī, a particular bird, female; as a poetic conceit, the couples, *cakravāka* and *cak-*

ravākī, are said to be separated at day's end and to mourn for each other the whole night long.

Cāmara, "yak-tail fly-whisk"; name of a Rākṣasa warrior.

Cāmuṇḍā, epithet of Durgā in her more frightful aspect. The name is derived from Caṇḍa and Muṇḍa, two gigantic demons whom Durgā slew.

Caṇḍāla, one of the lowest castes in the Hindu hierarchy, metonymic for the lowest of the low in society, an untouchable.

Caṇḍī, name for the goddess Durgā in her more ferocious aspect; the incarnation of the goddess desired by the gods—and created from their combined powers—for the purpose of defeating the buffalo Asura (see Mahiṣāsura), the iconic reenactment of the slaying of which is central to the annual Durgā Pūjā festival in Bengal; she who vanquished the Asura Raktabīja and the Asura brothers Śumbha and Niśumbha.

Candracūḍa, "he who wears the moon as a crown"; epithet of Śiva.

Caturbhuja, "he who has four arms"; epithet of Viṣṇu.

Cikṣura (also spelled Cikkura), "loud, like the crack of lightning"; name of a Rākṣasa warrior.

Cintāmaṇi, "gem of thought; mythic wishing gem"; epithet of Viṣṇu (canto 7). Since Rāma is, from one perspective, an *avatāra* of Viṣṇu, the epithet can also apply to Rāma (canto 6). Moreover, since *cintā* means not only "thought" but also "worry" in Bangla, the suggestive meaning of the epithet could be "gem of worries," an apt rendering in both occurrences in *The Slaying of Meghanāda.*

Citralekhā, name of one of the members of the class of celestial demigoddesses called Apsarās, known for their exceptional beauty and their dancing ability.

Citrāṅgadā, one of Rāvaṇa's queens, mother of Vīrabāhu, and daughter of Citrasena, a heavenly Gandharva. (Cf. the Kṛttivāsī *Rāmāyaṇa,* "Laṅkā Kāṇḍa.") Though unrelated to this character, there is in the *Mahābhārata* a Citrāṅgadā, who resides in Manipura and has a son by Arjuna.

Citraratha, "he whose chariot is bright or of many colors"; name of the leader of the class of celestial demigods called Gandharvas, known for their musical skills but also for their expertise in warfare.

Daitya, a class of enemies of the gods; matronymic from Diti; often considered synonymous with Asura, Dānava, Karbūra, and Rākṣasa.

Ḍākinī, a class of female goblinlike demigoddesses who attend upon Śiva and Durgā.

Dakṣa, (1) father of the twenty-seven stars (*nakṣatra*: a constellation or lunar "house" through which the moon passes), all twenty-seven of which are considered beautiful wives of Candra, the moon (canto 1). Also, (2) father of the goddess in her first anthropomorphized incarnation when she is known as Satī. He plans to perform a grand sacrifice but, intentionally and foolishly, excludes his son-in-law, Śiva, from the guest list. Satī, the epitome of the faithful wife, sides with her husband and is mortified to death, literally, by her father's rudeness toward Śiva. Hearing of his wife's demise, an enraged Śiva trashes Dakṣa's sacrifice, killing the host sacrificer, his father-in-law. Beside himself with grief, he stays constantly near his wife's lifeless body. Concerned that Śiva will be preoccupied with mourning, unmindful of his responsibilities as supreme lord of the universe as long as his wife's corpse is present, the other gods send Cakrapāṇi (Viṣṇu, with discus in hand) to dismember Satī with his discus into fifty-one parts, to be scattered across the South Asian subcontinent. Where those parts landed became the fifty-one *mahāpīṭhas* or sacred places of pilgrimage for worshipers of the goddess. Śiva, still despondent, goes off into the mountains to meditate. Once again the gods fear that a meditating Śiva will leave the universe devoid of a supreme lord. They prevail upon the goddess to incarnate again, this time as Pārvatī, daughter of the Himālayas, also known as Himādri. Kāma is thereupon enlisted to break Śiva's trance so that he might become attracted to Pārvatī and thus resume an active role in governing the world (canto 2).

dāmāmā, a large war drum.

ḍamaru, a small, hourglass-shaped drum with heads on either end; played by Śiva and by present-day snake charmers.

Dānava, a class of enemies of the gods; matronymic from Danu; often considered synonymous with Asura, Daitya, Karbūra, and Rākṣasa.

Daṇḍadhara, "staff-holder"; epithet of Yama, who wields the staff (*daṇḍa*) of punishment (*daṇḍa* also means "punishment").

Daṇḍaka, a forest in southern India in which are not only the smaller Pañcavaṭī Forest (where Sītā, Rāma, and Lakṣmaṇa were residing when Sītā was abducted by Rāvaṇa) but also Kiṣkindhyā, kingdom of Sugrīva and "the southerners."

Danu, mother of the Dānavas.

Daśānana, "he who has ten heads"; epithet of Rāvaṇa, who has ten heads and twenty arms.

Daśaratha, "he who has ten chariots"; father of Rāma, Bharata, Lakṣmaṇa, and Śatrughna. Kauśalyā (mother of Rāma), Kaikeyī (mother of Bharata), and Sumitrā (mother of Lakṣmaṇa and Śatrughna) are the three wives of Daśaratha.

Dāśarathi, epithet of Rāma, primarily; can be used for his three half-brothers (refers to Lakṣmaṇa, canto 6); patronymic from Daśaratha.

Devadatta, "given by the gods"; (1) name of Arjuna's (Pārtha's) conch-shell battle horn; also, (2) name of the bow given to Lakṣmaṇa by the gods.

Devendra, "Indra (lord, foremost) of the gods"; epithet of Indra.

ḍhāka, a large barrel-shaped drum.

Dhanada, "giver of wealth"; epithet of Kubera, god of riches. He is also lord of the class of demigods known as Yakṣas; and he is a half brother (same father, different mother) of Rāvaṇa, though Kubera himself is aligned with the gods, not with the Rākṣasas.

dharma, translated variously as Duty, the Law, and Religion; it is that which one ought to do, that to which one should be steadfast.

Dharma, a god who embodies, so to speak, moral duty, just law, and the best of what is meant by religion. Dharma, in Bangla Hinduism, is a somewhat minor folk deity; Dharma is also a name by which Yama, the god of death, is known. Datta's Dharma, however, is a more generalized, all-encompassing, moral deity.

ḍhola, a drum held horizontally and played on both ends with two hands.

Dhūmaketu, "comet, falling star"; literally, "banner of vapor or smoke"; a comet augurs ill, bringing with it disaster; a name for fire and the sun.

Dhūmrākṣa, "he whose eyes are smoke"; name of a Rākṣasa warrior.

Dhūrjaṭi, name of Śiva.

dhuti, the dhoti or lower cloth worn by men.

dhuturā, a particular plant, its fruit and its flowers, associated with Śiva. Śiva indulges in a narcotic made from *dhuturā*.

Digambara, "he who is clad only by the sky"; name of Śiva, naked and lying supine with Kālī standing or dancing upon his chest.

Digambarī, "she who is clad only by the sky"; name of goddess Kālī, when naked and standing or dancing upon the chest of her spouse Śiva.

Dilīpa, a patriarch within Rāma's lineage. (Dilīpa begat Raghu, who begat Aja, who begat Daśaratha, who begat Dāśarathi, the patronymic name for both Rāma and his half brothers.)

Diti, mother of the Daityas; the antithesis of Aditi, progenitress of the gods.

dola, "swing"; the name of the swing festival when child Kṛṣṇa is swung. It is one of the most joyous and festive times in the Hindu calendar, a time when people throw red powder—or dissolve the powder in water and sprinkle it—upon one another, imitating the sportive play between Kṛṣṇa and the Gopīs or cowherd women in Vṛndāvana. This same festival also goes by the name of Holi.

Droṇa, an expert in weaponry; he taught his skills to the Kauravas, fought on their side, and died in the great Bhārata war.

dundubhi, a large war drum.

Durgā, the goddess, consort of Śiva. Her annual, autumnal *pūjā* is the major Hindu festival in Bengal. (1) On the sixth day of the waxing moon during the appropriate autumn month, Durgā (in this context called Gaurī, Haimavatī, Pārvatī, Umā, among myriad other names) arrives home in Bengal, having come from her husband's in the Himālayas. From then on through the ninth day of the waxing moon, she is visiting her parents, and her *pūjā* is joyously performed all over Bengal. On the tenth day of the waxing moon, called Vijayā or Vijayā Daśamī, "the victorious tenth," she must leave her father's home and return to the proper place for a married woman, beside her husband, in this case, Śiva, who resides on Mount Kailāsa. On that day the Durgā icons are immersed in the Ganges, and the vital force of the goddess leaves the clay and straw image, traveling upstream to her husband's abode where she stays until the next year, when again she will pay a visit to her parents and her childhood home, much to everyone's delight. (2) Durgā in her iconography for the Durgā Pūjā does not appear as the young Bengali married daughter arriving home for the annual visit but instead as the supreme ten-armed goddess, slayer of the buffalo demon (see Mahiṣāsura). In that powerful aspect, she has for her *vāhana* or conveyance the lion, hence the epithet "she who rides a lion" (canto 5). Note that Vijayā, besides being the "victorious" tenth day of the waxing moon, is the name of one of Durgā's two heavenly attendants, Jayā being the other. Furthermore, in the Durgā Pūjā iconography, Durgā, along with her husband Śiva, has four children, Lakṣmī, Sarasvatī, Kārttikeya, and Ganeśa (see Gaṇendra).

Duryodhana, eldest of the one hundred Kauravas, all of whom are slain in the great Bhārata war.

Dūṣaṇa, "defiling, violating"; name of a Rākṣasa general who, along with a Rākṣasa named Khara, is slain by Rāma and Lakṣmaṇa in the Pañcavaṭī Forest well before the battle on Laṅkā. Both Dūṣaṇa and Khara were sent against Rāma and Lakṣmaṇa by Sūrpaṇakhā to avenge her humiliation at the hands of Lakṣmaṇa; see Sūrpaṇakhā.

Ekāghnī, "single-slayer"; epithet of the Śakti missile obtained from Indra by which Karṇa, allied with the Kauravas, slew Ghaṭotkaca, who was fighting for the Pāṇḍavas; the powerful missile could be used by Karṇa to slay but a single enemy; see Ghaṭotkaca and Karṇa.

Fate, a translation throughout *The Slaying of Meghanāda* of the word Vidhi; see Vidhi.

Gadādhara, "he who holds a club"; epithet of Viṣṇu.

Gandhamādana, the mountain on the Indian mainland (as opposed to Laṅkā) whereon grows the restorative herb Viśalyakaraṇī, by which Lakṣmaṇa is revived.

Gandharva, a class of celestial demigods who are the heavenly musicians and also knowledgeable about warfare.

Gaṇendra, "Indra (lord, foremost) of the Gaṇas, a class of demigods"; epithet of Ganeśa, who, along with Kārttikeya, is a son of Śiva and Durgā.

Ganges, the most holy river in northern India flowing from the Himālayas (out of the cave named Gomukhī, "cow-mouthed") to the Bay of Bengal. Because she (goddess Gaṅgā, the Ganges) was caught first in Śiva's matted hair, which protected the earth from the impact of her descent from heaven to the mortal world, she is said to be Śiva's second wife. Auspicious Ganges water is used in purification rituals and *pūjās* of all sorts.

Garuḍa, a gigantic warrior bird and eternal enemy of snakes; the vehicle or transport for Viṣṇu. Garuḍa is referred to in *The Slaying of Meghanāda* as the father of Jaṭāyu; by other accounts he is Jaṭāyu's uncle; see Vinatā.

Gauḍa (also spelled Gaur in English), archaic name for the land of Bengal.

Gaurī, "she who has a fair complexion"; epithet of Durgā.

Gavākṣa, "he whose eyes are like those of a bull"; name of a warrior from the southern kingdom of Kiṣkindhyā, allied with Rāma against the Rākṣasas.

Ghaṭotkaca, an enormous warrior born from the union of Bhīmasena and the Rākṣasī Hiḍimbā. After Ghaṭotkaca's birth, Bhīma returned to the company of his Pāṇḍava brothers; his son, raised by Hiḍimbā, promised to come to his father's side when called to mind. In the midst of the internecine Bhārata war, Ghaṭotkaca reappeared to fight for his father's cause on the side of the Pāṇḍavas and, after decimating the Kaurava ranks, was slain by Karṇa with the Śakti missile designated "single-slayer" (see Ekāghnī) discharged from the bow "black-back" (see Kālapṛṣṭha).

Giriśa, "lord of the mountain"; epithet of Śiva.

Godāvarī, name of a river in southern India.

Gokula, "cow herd"; name of the village where Kṛṣṇa was raised, somewhat distant from the city of Mathurā wherein he was born; also called Vraja, it encompasses Vṛndāvana, where Kṛṣṇa sported with Rādhā and the other Gopīs or cowherd women; situated beside the Yamunā River.

Gomukhī, "whose mouth (or face) looks like that of a cow"; name of a sacred cave in the Himālayas from which emanates the holy Ganges River.

Haimavatī, "of the Himālayas"; epithet of Durgā/Gaurī, "mother" of Kārttikeya; see Kārttikeya.

halāhala, a particular poison, also known as *kālakūṭa*. Along with *amṛta* or the elixir of immortality, the poison *halāhala* (*kālakūṭa*) was one of the many products that came out of the primordial ocean when churned by the Suras (gods) and the Asuras (antigods). The poison would have destroyed the world had not that virulent substance been swallowed by Śiva, whose neck thus turned blue, which accounts for one of Śiva's epithets, Nīlakaṇṭha ("he whose throat is blue").

Hanumān (also spelled Hanūmān), "having a pronounced mandible"; name of a powerful warrior from the southern kingdom of Kiṣkindhyā, allied with Rāma against the Rākṣasas. Hanumān is "the son of the wind," the son of Prabhañjana, and able to traverse vast distances quickly.

Hara, "destroyer"; epithet of Śiva.

Hari, a name of Viṣṇu.

Hastinā (also Hastināpura and Hāstinapura), city of the Kauravas and their patriarch, the blind Dhṛtarāṣṭra; following the Bhārata war, the Pāṇḍavas' capital city; located on a bank of the Ganges.

Hemakūṭa, "gold-peaked"; name of a mythical mountain located in the northern reaches of the Himālayas; identified with Mount Meru.

Hiḍimbā, a Rākṣasī enamored of Bhīmasena, with whom she conceived a son, Ghaṭotkaca.

Himādri, "the mountain of snow"; another name for Himālaya ("abode of snow"), the mountain range who is considered the father of Pārvatī, also known as Durgā.

Hiraṇyakaśipu, name of a Daitya king, slain by Viṣṇu in his Narasiṃha *avatāra*, the fourth of Viṣṇu's ten *avatāra* forms. Hiraṇyakaśipu had obtained a boon from Brahmā by which he, Hiraṇyakaśipu, could not be killed by god, man, or beast. He then established an oppressive sovereignty over all the three worlds—heaven, earth, and Pātāla, the netherworld. At the request of Hiraṇyakaśipu's son Prahlāda, who was a devotee of Viṣṇu, Viṣṇu assumed the form of neither god nor man nor beast but of a half man (*nara*), half beast (*siṃha*, the lion), and slew Hiraṇyakaśipu.

hotṛ, a Brahmin priest who performs Vedic sacrifices, some of which consist of offerings of ghee (drawn butter) into the sacrificial fire.

Hṛṣīkeśa, "he who is master of the senses"; epithet of Viṣṇu.

Hutāśana, "who eats the offering of ghee"; epithet of Agni, the god of fire or fire itself.

Ikṣvāku, founder of the "solar" dynasty in Ayodhyā, from which Rāma is descended; term used to designate any descendant from within that lineage.

Indirā, name of Lakṣmī.

Indra, lord of the gods; lord of the skies; also, a superlative suffix: for example, "Indra among sons" means "best of sons." Indra wields the thunderbolt. The rainbow is said to be Indra's bow (in modern Bangla, it is called Rāma's bow). In post-Vedic Hinduism, Indra is less powerful and could be defeated; see Indrajit ("victor over Indra") and Tāraka.

Indrajit, "victor over Indra"; epithet of Meghanāda, who by the power of *rudra* overcame Indra in battle.

Indrāṇī, wife of Indra; analogous to the superlative use of "Indra" meaning "best of . . . (feminine)."

Indraprastha, a city given to the Pāṇḍavas by the Kuru patriarch Dhṛtarāṣṭra, and located on a bank of the Yamunā River.

Indumatī, paternal grandmother of Rāma.

Īśāna, name of Śiva; associated with him as lord of the northeast direction.

Īśānī, name of Durgā.

Īśvarī, goddess, feminine of Īśvara (god, lord); indicates Durgā in *The Slaying of Meghanāda.*

Jagadambā, "mother of the world"; epithet of various forms of the goddess. It designates Durgā (cantos 2 and 5) and Lakṣmī (cantos 6 and 7).

Jāhnavī, epithet of Gaṅgā, the Ganges; patronymic from the sage Jahnu; see Ganges.

Jāmbuvāna (also spelled Jāmbuvat), name of a warrior from the southern kingdom of Kiṣkindhyā who is allied with Rāma against the Rākṣasas.

Janaka, king of Videha/Mithilā and father of Sītā.

Jānakī, epithet of Sītā; patronymic from Janaka, king of Videha/Mithilā.

Jaṭādhara, "he who holds upon his head the *jaṭā* (a pile of matted hair)"; epithet of Śiva.

Jaṭāyu, a warrior who perishes while attempting to prevent Rāvaṇa from transporting the kidnapped Sītā back to Laṅkā. Referred to in *The Slaying of Meghanāda* as the son of Garuḍa, he is by other accounts Garuḍa's nephew; see Vinatā.

jāṭi, a weapon of some sort.

jāti (also spelled *jātī*), a white flower associated with the spices mace and nutmeg.

Jayā, one of the two female attendants of Durgā, Vijayā being the other.

Jiṣṇu, "victorious"; epithet of a number of gods and also Arjuna, but designates Indra in *The Slaying of Meghanāda.*

Kabandha, name of a headless Rākṣasa. By a strike from one of Indra's thunderbolts, Kabandha's skull and thighs were pushed into his body, leaving him with no visible head, a large barrel-shaped torso, a mouth in the middle of his belly, and exceedingly long arms.

kadamba, a variety of tree with fragrant orange blossoms, beneath which Kṛṣṇa dallies with the cowherd maids.

kādambā, the female of a variety of waterfowl, similar to the teal, whose call is soft and melodious.

Kaikeyī, Daśaratha's second of three wives; Kauśalyā (Rāma's mother) and Sumitrā (Lakṣmaṇa and Śatrughna's mother) are the other two. On the advice of Mantharā, her personal serving woman, Kaikeyī took advantage of her position as her husband's favorite wife and asked him for two boons, which he, consumed by passion for her, granted. One was that when he vacated the throne, his eldest son, Rāma, would be exiled from Ayodhyā for fourteen years; the other was that her own son, Bharata, would be installed as crown prince, in line to succeed his father. Later, when reminded of this by Kaikeyī, Daśaratha agonized over what he had earlier promised. Rāma, that most righteous of sons, kept his father honest by willingly and most dutifully choosing on his own to go into exile. Daśaratha, out of grief for his departed son, died soon thereafter.

Kailāsa, the mountain in the Himālayas on the peak of which Śiva and Durgā reside; also, the city there in which live Śiva and Durgā.

kālakūṭa, a particular poison, also known as *halāhala* (see *halāhala*); used in *The Slaying of Meghanāda* specifically to designate snake venom.

Kālanemi, name of a Rākṣasa warrior. In the Bangla *Rāmāyaṇa* by Kṛttivāsa, he becomes identified as a maternal uncle of Rāvaṇa to whom Rāvaṇa promises half of the kingdom of Laṅkā if he, Kālanemi, will slay Hanumān before the latter can secure the life-restoring herb by which fallen Lakṣmaṇa is to be revived from (near) death. While on this fool's errand, Kālanemi fantasizes about his presumed half of the kingdom, including, in this fantasy, his half of Rāvaṇa's many wives—Mandodarī, his nephew's chief wife, among them. Hanumān defeats Kālanemi, and so the fulsome daydream goes unrealized. The expression "Kālanemi's half of Laṅkā (*Kālanemir Laṅkābhāga*)" in Bangla is comparable to "counting one's chickens before they are hatched; building castles in the air." The term "Uncle Kālanemi (*Kālanemi māmā*)" refers to an esteemed person who aids and abets in nefarious activities. Datta makes this very recognizable Rākṣasa into the father of Pramīlā, a female character whom Datta has created, drawing selectively from several sources. In other Hindu mythology, the name Kālanemi is associated with Kaṃsa, the wicked king of Mathurā who is slain by Kṛṣṇa.

Kālapṛṣṭha, "black-back"; name of Karṇa's bow.

Kali, a personification of wickedness; the one-spot on a pair of dice (the losing mark); and the name of the fourth and most degenerate era (see *yuga*). Kali coveted Damayantī, the gorgeous princess who had chosen Nala as her husband (see Nala [2]). Angered, and concluding that Nala had reneged on his promise to the gods, which the gods assured him Nala had not, Kali vindictively sought and gained the opportunity to enter Nala's body and, through his evil influence, to cause Nala to engage in dice gaming and to lose everything, his kingdom and all his possessions, except for his faithful wife Damayantī.

Kālī, the goddess in her most horrific aspect. The iconography of Kālī shows her as of black complexion, essentially naked though wearing a garland of human heads and a belt of human hands, and often holding in one of her four hands a bloody human head and in another a sword of some sort. She frequents execution and cremation grounds and battlefields wherein slaughter occurs; she is also seen standing naked upon the chest of her supine husband, Śiva.

Kālidāsa, classical Sanskrit's most famous poet. Best known as the author of the poem entitled *Meghadūta* (The cloud messenger) and the eponymously titled drama *Śakuntalā*, Kālidāsa also composed the celebrated verse narrative by the name of *Raghuvaṃśa* (The Raghu lineage). It is Kālidāsa as author of *Raghuvaṃśa* that Datta claims as one of his ancestors in a long and illustrious line of poets who have over the centuries composed literature on the theme of Rāma and the *Rāmāyaṇa*.

Kāma, "passion, love, carnal desire"; the disembodied god of love; husband of Rati ("passion, coitus"). When Indra had been defeated by the Asura Tāraka and the enemies of the gods had occupied heaven, Indra with his divines went to Brahmā seeking help. Brahmā told them that a son born of Śiva's seed would in time vanquish Tāraka. But Śiva was meditating, unconcerned with the world and oblivious to women—one of whom, Gaurī (Durgā, Haimavatī), waited on him and was destined to be his bride. In order to rouse Śiva from his trance and put him in the right frame of mind for the task at hand, Indra engaged the services of Kāma. Accompanied by his followers—the spring breezes—and serenaded by the cuckoo and honeybees, Kāma, armed with his flower-bow and five blossom-arrows, went to Śiva. As Kāma drew back the bowstring fitted with his arrow called *sammohana* ("beguilement"; the other four arrows, all pertaining to mental or physical states associated with being in love, are *unmādana* [stupefaction], *śoṣaṇa* [desiccation], *tāpana* [burning], and *stambhana* [paralysis]), Śiva became slightly restless, then stirred from his meditation. When he looked about, he saw before him Kāma, bow in hand. Śiva was incensed by this intrusion upon his yogic exercise. The third eye, located in Śiva's forehead, opened and fire poured out, reducing Kāma on the spot to ashes. Kāma's wife Rati continues to accompany her husband, who is now without a body. Śiva, his trance broken by Kāma, eventually marries Haimavatī and spills his seed in excitement while with her. From that seed is born Kārttikeya, the future slayer of Tāraka; see Kārttikeya and Tāraka.

Kamalā, "lotus-lady"; epithet of Lakṣmī.

kamaṇḍalu, a gourd or vessel made of wood or earth in which to hold water, carried by ascetics and religious students.

Kandarpa, one of the names for Kāma, god of love. The etymology of the name is in doubt but could have meant originally "inflamer of a god."

Kapardī, "he who has a mass of matted hair"; epithet of Śiva.

kāṛā, a relatively small, single-headed drum.

Karbūra (also spelled Karbura), another name for Rākṣasa; often considered synonymous with Asura, Daitya, and Dānava.

Karṇa, a half brother of the Pāṇḍavas (fathered by the sun on Kuntī before her marriage to Pāṇḍu) but one who fought on the side of the Kauravas. Karṇa, born wearing earrings and impregnable armor, relinquished them to Indra in exchange for that god's Śakti missile with which he planned to slay Arjuna. Indra had stipulated that the missile could be used by Karṇa to kill but one enemy. As Ghaṭotkaca, seemingly invincible, set about laying waste the Kaurava forces, Karṇa was prevailed upon to expend his "single-slayer" (see Ekāghnī) weapon. This Karṇa did, killing Ghaṭotkaca, though knowing full well that he, Karṇa, would be leaving himself vulnerable to Arjuna—by whom he was subsequently slain.

Kārttikeya (also known as Kārttika), god of war; general of the gods and known for his good looks; matronymic from Kṛttikā, who is technically not his mother but his sixfold wet nurse. He was born of the seed spilled from Śiva, who had been excited by Gaurī (Durgā, Haimavatī, Pārvatī). The myth is common knowledge, but details of his birth vary among texts. In one most popular Bangla narrative, Śiva ejaculates while dallying with Gaurī. Gaurī, unable to hold his semen, casts it into the fire who, in turn, immerses it in the Jāhnavī (Ganges) who deposits it among the reeds upon the shore where the six Kṛttikās (the Pleiades personified) found and nursed the child, who has six heads from having six wet nurses. The birth of Kārttikeya and his slaying of Tāraka are celebrated in the famous Sanskrit artful "great narrative poem" (*mahākāvya*) by Kālidāsa, *Kumārasambhava* (The birth of Kumāra [a name for the war god]); see Kāma and Tāraka.

Kātyāyanī, epithet of Durgā. The name is derived from the fact that the sage Kātyāyana, one of the authors of the *dharma śāstras* (treatises on *dharma*), worshiped Durgā.

kaunta, a lancelike weapon.

Kaurava, refers to Dhṛtarāṣṭra's one hundred sons, who fought and were slain in the great Bhārata war; patronymic from Kuru, famed king in the "lunar" dynasty. Pāṇḍu and Dhṛtarāṣṭra are brothers and descendants of Bharata within that same "lunar" lineage. Kaurava, technically, can refer to an ancestor of either Pāṇḍu or

Dhṛtarāṣṭra; the epithet, however, has come to designate Dhṛtarāṣṭra's one hundred sons exclusively, in contradistinction to their cousins, the Pāṇḍavas, and is used in this way in *The Slaying of Meghanāda.*

Kauśalyā, mother of Rāma; Daśaratha's first of three wives, Kaikeyī and Sumitrā being the other two.

Kaustubha, a wondrous mythical gem, produced from the churning of the ocean and worn suspended from a cord around Viṣṇu's neck.

Keśarī, "he who has the mane of a lion or of a stallion"; name of a warrior from the southern kingdom of Kiṣkindhyā, allied with Rāma against the Rākṣasas.

Keśava, "having much hair"; epithet of Viṣṇu.

Khara, "sharp, keen"; name of a Rākṣasa warrior and considered to be a half-brother to Rāvaṇa. Along with a Rākṣasa named Dūṣaṇa, Khara is slain by Rāma and Lakṣmaṇa in the Pañcavaṭī Forest well before the battle on Laṇkā. Both Khara and Dūṣaṇa were sent against Rāma and Lakṣmaṇa by Sūrpaṇakhā to avenge the humiliation to her from Lakṣmaṇa; see Sūrpaṇakhā.

Kīcaka, an army general in the kingdom of Virāṭa where the Pāṇḍavas and Draupadī spent the thirteenth and final year of their exile, incognito. Kīcaka took a liking to the beautiful Draupadī, was publicly abusive to her and kicked her, but also wanted to make love to her. Yudhiṣṭhira had placed his brothers under strict orders not to break with their disguises, and thus the public insults of their collective wife had to be tolerated. It was a mere thirty days before the thirteen long years were to be concluded, but Kīcaka had been strongly importuning Draupadī. In desperation, she went to Bhīmasena. Bhīma devised a plan whereby she would seemingly agree to meet Kīcaka in the dance practice hall, after dark when it was empty. But there in place of Draupadī that night sat Bhīma, unrecognizable by Kīcaka in the darkness. Following a bit of foreplay, Kīcaka, to assuage her wounded pride that seemed to be lingering due to the previous public abuse and to get her more in the mood for love-making, invited "Draupadī" to kick him in the head, for which he bowed down before her. Bhīma then proceeded to give Kīcaka three solid kicks to the head. Kīcaka, stunned momentarily, eventually got to his feet, and a horrendous fight ensued—including, specifically, biting and scratching and rolling about on the floor and punching and more kicking—ending in the death of Kīcaka.

kiṃśuka, a tree bearing beautiful blood-red flowers.

Kinnara, a class of celestial demigods with a head like a horse and a body like that of a human, known for their exceptional singing voice.

Kinnarī, a class of celestial demigoddesses with a head like a horse and a body like that of a human, known for their exceptional singing voice.

Kirāta, a particular community of forest dwellers who lived by hunting.

Kirīṭī, "he who wears a diadem"; epithet of Arjuna.

Kiṣkindhyā, name of a kingdom, and of its capital city, in the southern part of the South Asian subcontinent. When Rāma and Lakṣmaṇa arrived there, searching for Sītā, Kiṣkindhyā's ruler was Vāli; following the death of Vāli, brought about by Rāma himself, Sugrīva became king in his elder brother's stead and formed an alliance with Rāma.

koṣā, a small, shallow, elongated copper vessel for holding Ganges water used during a *pūjā*.

koṣī, a small copper ladle for spooning water out of a *koṣā*.

Kṛṣṇa, an *avatāra* form of Viṣṇu and the most popular form of Viṣṇu among Bengali Vaiṣṇavas. He is known best to Bengalis as the lover of Rādhā and the other Gopīs—cowherd maidens—with whom he sports in Vṛndāvana, a forested grove in the district of Vraja, near Madhupura. He wears a yellow *dhuti*, plays the flute, and is of blue-black complexion. So attractive is he that he charms even the god of love, Madana himself; in turn, Kṛṣṇa/Viṣṇu can be charmed by his own (Viṣṇu's own) lovely consort, Lakṣmī. The oppressive King Kaṃsa of Madhupura, warned that a son of his cousin Devakī and her husband Vasudeva would bring about his death, had the couple imprisoned and slew their first six children. The seventh, Balarāma, was transferred into the womb of Vasudeva's other wife, Rohiṇī, prior to birth. Vasudeva spirited away in the dead of night his eighth child, Kṛṣṇa, to the village of Gokula in Vraja across the Yamunā River and left him in the care of a cowherd named Nanda and his wife Yaśodā, there to be raised out of harm's way. It is from Vraja that the adult Kṛṣṇa is summoned to Madhupura by another of his uncles, Akrūra, to carry out the task of removing from this world the wicked Kaṃsa, thus fulfilling his function as an *avatāra* to rid the world of some great threat to mankind and the gods.

Kṛtānta, "he who terminates, he who brings about an end"; epithet of Yama, god of death.

Kṛttikā, one of the twenty-seven stars (*nakṣatra*: a constellation or lunar "house" through which the moon passes), all twenty-seven of which are considered beautiful wives of Candra, the moon; the Pleiades constellation (the six visible stars) deified. She/They served as six wet nurses for Kārttikeya, who therefore has six heads with which to nurse the sixfold Kṛttikā.

Kṛttivāsa, author of the most well-known *Rāmāyaṇa* in Bangla.

Kṣatriya, the warrior class; the second social class in Hindu society's *varṇa* hierarchy, consisting of, in presumed order of rank, Brāhman, Kṣatriya, Vaiśya, and Sūdra.

Kṣemaṅkarī, "she who bestows auspiciousness"; epithet of various goddesses, referring in *The Slaying of Meghanāda* to Durgā (cantos 2 and 9) and to the goddess known specifically as Māyā (canto 8).

Kuliśī, "he who has the thunderbolt"; epithet of Indra.

Kumāra, name for Kārttikeya; see Kārttikeya.

Kumbhakarṇa, "he who has jug-ears"; one of Rāvaṇa's three brothers, along with Vibhīṣaṇa and elder half-brother Kubera. Rāvaṇa, Kumbhakarṇa, and Vibhīṣaṇa all practiced austerities for which Brahmā was obliged to grant the brothers individually a boon. Each expected to ask for immortality, but only Vibhīṣaṇa's request would be honored. In the case of Rāvaṇa, Brahmā allowed instead that he need not fear Yakṣas, Rākṣasas, gods, or Gandharvas. Since Rāvaṇa considered men and animals of no threat, he was pleased to accept Brahmā's offer of virtual immortality, unaware that the god Viṣṇu would incarnate as the human being Rāma and be his undoing. The gods, frightened that Kumbhakarṇa might become indestructible, implored Sarasvatī, goddess of speech, to go and sit upon Kumbhakarṇa's tongue. When Brahmā asked Kumbhakarṇa what boon he wished, his tongue spoke, requesting perpetual sleep. Brahmā declared it so. Rāvaṇa, realizing what had happened, weeping, begged Brahmā to alter his edict. Obligingly, Brahmā modified the boon to be that Kumbhakarṇa would sleep for six months at a stretch and then awake for a day, at which time he would eat gluttonously. If, however, Kumbhakarṇa were awakened before the completion of the full six months, he would be slain that very day.

Kumbhīpāka, name of one of the numerous hell holes or punishment pits in Naraka, "hell." (Naraka is not the same as Pātāla, "the netherworld"; see Pātāla.)

Kumuda, "red lotus blossom"; name of a warrior from the southern kingdom of Kiṣkindhyā, allied with Rāma against the Rākṣasas.

Kuru, famed king in the "lunar" dynasty. Kuru—like the patronymic made from it, Kaurava—is used to refer to the descendants of Dhṛtarāṣṭra, as opposed to the Pāṇḍavas.

Kurukṣetra, "Kuru-field"; the field on which was waged the major battle between the Pāṇḍavas and their cousins, the Kauravas, the central event related in the *Mahābhārata.*

kuśa, a particular grass, used as an auspicious seat, not exclusively but particularly at the time of performing a religious ritual.

Kusumeṣu, "he whose arrows are flowers"; epithet of Kāma, god of love.

Lakṣmaṇa, one of Rāma's three younger half brothers; Bharata and Śatrughna are the other two.

Lakṣmī, goddess of luck or good fortune as well as of beauty (also called Śrī), identified as the wife of Viṣṇu. She was produced from the ocean at the time of the churning—along with the elixir of immortality, Viṣṇu's Kaustubha gem, and so on—and thus can be thought of as the daughter of the ocean. The Bangla *Mahābhārata* explains her presence in the ocean (instead of seated at Viṣṇu's side or with head resting on Viṣṇu's chest) as the result of a curse by the irascible sage Dūrvāsā. She is said to have appeared from a lotus or on a lotus from within the sea, or with a lotus in her hand—thus the association with lotuses; see Kamalā. She, as good fortune, is associated with wealth; anyone who possesses wealth and fortune possesses her—until and unless he loses such, at which time Lakṣmī is said to desert him. As a king's fortune or majesty, she is often called Rājalakṣmī. Since Rāma is considered an *avatāra* or incarnation of Viṣṇu, Sītā becomes associated with his wife Lakṣmī. And, in the Bangla Hindu mythology related to the annual Durgā Pūjā festival, Lakṣmī and goddess Sarasvatī join Ganeśa and Kārttikeya as the four children of Śiva and Durgā.

Laṅkā, Rāvaṇa's island kingdom; refers both to the island and to the walled city on the island; associated with modern Śrī Laṅkā.

lāṭhi, a stick or staff, a common weapon for law-enforcement personnel.

līlā, "sport, godly diversion"; what transpires on earth is all divine play, inexplicable and incomprehensible to man.

Madana, "the maddener"; epithet of Kāma, the god of love whose wife is Rati; see Rati. Kāma is sexual desire and thereby maddens or inflames; on the other hand, he was driven to distraction by Viṣṇu, in his Kṛṣṇa incarnation, hence the epithet of Kṛṣṇa as Madanamohana or "maddener of Madana" and "he who inflames Madana" in cantos 1 and 6, respectively.

Mādhava, another name for Viṣṇu, but also for Kṛṣṇa. Of course, the two are one, and the same appellation for both tends to emphasize this unity. In *The Slaying of*

Meghanāda, Mādhava refers to Kṛṣṇa in cantos 2 and 5, and to Viṣṇu, husband of Lakṣmī, elsewhere.

Madhupura, a city kingdom, also known as Mathurā, ruled by the wicked Kaṃsa, Kṛṣṇa's uncle (Kṛṣṇa's mother, Devakī, and Kaṃsa are cousins) whom Kṛṣṇa slays. Madhupura lies on one side of the Yamunā River; on the other side of that river is Vraja (containing the village of Gokula and the forested area known as Vṛndāvana) wherein Kṛṣṇa grows up and dallies with the cowherd womenfolk, the Gopīs, Rādhā prominent among them. Another uncle, Akrūra, summons Kṛṣṇa to Madhupura in order to rid that city-kingdom of its horrid tyrant Kaṃsa. Kṛṣṇa obliges and goes off to Madhupura, leaving Vraja never to return; see Kṛṣṇa.

Mahābhārata, "the great Bhārata [war]"; one of the two major Hindu Indian epics, the *Rāmāyaṇa* being the other. In eighteen *parvas* or books, the *Mahābhārata* recounts the events leading up to the war; the war itself between the descendants of Bharata, specifically the five sons of Pāṇḍu (the Pāṇḍavas—Yudhiṣṭhira, Bhīmasena, Arjuna, Sahadeva, and Nakula) and the one hundred sons of Pāṇḍu's brother, the blind Dhṛtarāṣṭra, known collectively as the Kauravas, Duryodhana chief among them; and the aftermath of the war.

Mahāśakti, "the great Śakti"; *śakti* means "power" but also is the name by which the mother goddess is known. She is "power" deified. All Hindu goddesses are, in some sense, an aspect of the one "mother goddess" or Śakti or goddess Durgā.

Mahendra, "the great Indra"; epithet of Indra.

Maheśa, "the great Īśvara or god"; epithet of Śiva.

Maheśī, "the great goddess"; feminine form of Maheśa; epithet of Durgā.

Maheśvarī, "the great goddess"; feminine form of Maheśvara ("the great god"); epithet of Durgā.

Mahiṣāsura, the buffalo Asura, slain by Durgā. The iconic representation of Durgā slaying Mahiṣāsura is found in every public display of the goddess during the autumnal Durgā Pūjā, the major annual Hindu festival in Bengal—an event in mythic time that corresponds with Rāma's slaying of Rāvaṇa.

Maināka, a mythical mountain with wings. All mountains used to be able to fly, but some abused the privilege by falling on cities and villages. So, Indra, with his thunderbolt, clipped their wings. Only Maināka escaped—Indra in hot pursuit—and received sanctuary in the ocean. When Hanumān was leaping/flying across the ocean to search for Sītā on Laṅkā, the ocean requested Maināka to elevate half of his body out of the water in order to provide Hanumān with an intermediate resting spot. Maināka obeyed; Hanumān thanked him; and Indra, pleased with this mountain's good behavior, gave him *abhaya*—assurances that he need not fear, that is, he could keep his wings.

Maithilī, epithet of Sītā, derived from the place name Mithilā, the capital of Sītā's home kingdom, Videha.

mākāla, a lovely reddish golden fruit with an inedible and foul-smelling pulp (used figuratively in Bangla for a very handsome but worthless person).

makara, a mythical sea creature, sometimes translated as dolphin, crocodile, seal, or fish. In the Zodiac, the *makara* corresponds to the equally mythical beast Capricorn. The god of love's banner bears the *makara* insignia.

Makarākṣa, "*makara*-eyed"; name of a Rākṣasa warrior.

Mānasa, "mind"; name of a mythical lake located in the Himālayas, near Mount Kailāsa.

Manasija, "he who is born of the mind or heart"; epithet of Kāma, god of love.

Mandākinī, name for the Ganges River as it flows in the heavens.

Mandara, name of a mythological mountain. All mountains in mythic times had wings and were able to fly—and were thus in motion—until Indra, with his thunderbolt, clipped their wings and made them stationary. The mountain called Mandara, moreover, was turned upside down and used by the Suras (gods) and Asuras (antigods) as a rod to churn the cosmic ocean; the serpent Vāsuki, also known as Ananta, served as the cord wrapped around Mandara by which that "mountain peak as churning rod" was spun in a back-and-forth motion. The poetic conceit of a woman's breasts putting to shame a mountain is a fairly common one.

mandāra, a celestial flowering tree and its blossom.

Māndhātā, a king of the "solar" dynasty. The expression "during the reign of Māndhātā" conveys the sense of "in very ancient times."

Mandodarī, Rāvaṇa's chief queen, mother of Meghanāda, and daughter of the Dānava architect Maya.

Manmatha, "he who churns the mind or heart"; epithet of Kāma, god of love.

Mantharā, Kaikeyī's personal serving woman. Mantharā advised her mistress to get Daśaratha to promise that Kaikeyī's son Bharata be installed as the crown prince and that Rāma be sent into exile for fourteen years.

mantra, formulaic speech, ritualistic speech, meant to effect something.

Mārīca, a Rākṣasa requested by Rāvaṇa to assume the guise of a golden stag in order to tempt Sītā and thereby lead Rāma and Lakṣmaṇa away from her so that Rāvaṇa could approach and abduct her. (The word for "mirage" is *marīcikā* and, though not cognate with Mārīca, it is suggestive of this elusive Rākṣasa.)

Mātali, Indra's chariot driver.

Maya, a notable Dānava, father of Rāvaṇa's chief queen Mandodarī and a master builder. He escaped the burning Khāṇḍava Forest and was protected by Arjuna. In gratitude, Maya constructed for the Pāṇḍavas an exquisite assembly hall at Indraprastha on the bank of the Yamunā River, one that rivaled the Kauravas' court in Hāstinapura (also Hastinā/Hastināpura) on the bank of the Ganges.

māyā, "illusion"; theologically speaking, *māyā* is what humans think to be the real world but what is in fact all illusion. The material world is a manifestation of a god's/goddess' power of *māyā.*

Māyā, a quasi-separate goddess in *The Slaying of Meghanāda,* though all goddesses are in a sense an aspect of one and the same mother goddess. Māyā is referred to at times as Mahāmāyā (the great or grand Māyā), a name that can apply to any number of goddesses. (Bhāratacandra's *Annadā Maṅgala,* probably the best-known and most popular Bangla text at the time when Datta was writing *The Slaying of Meghanāda,* refers to goddesses Lakṣmī, Sarasvatī, and the eponym Annapurṇā/Annadā all as Mahāmāyā.)

Meghanāda, "cloud-noise" or "thunder"; epithet of Rāvaṇa's most illustrious son, also known as Indrajit.

Meghavāhana, "whose transport is the clouds"; epithet of Indra, lord of the skies.

Menakā, name of one of the class of celestial demigoddesses called Apsarās, known for their exceptional beauty and their dancing ability.

Meru, name of a mythical mountain located in the northern reaches of the Himālayas, considered to be the North Pole; also called Sumeru.

Mīnadhvaja, "he whose banner displays a fish"; epithet of Kāma, god of love.

Miśrakeśī, name of one of the class of celestial demigoddesses called Apsarās, known for their exceptional beauty and their dancing ability.

Mohana, "he who enchants"; epithet of Śiva.

Mohinī, "she who enchants"; the persona, that of an exceedingly beautiful woman, assumed by Viṣṇu to enchant the Asuras and thereby steal away from them the *amṛta* that had been churned from the primordial ocean.

mṛdaṅga, a percussive musical instrument.

Mṛtyuñjaya, "he who is victorious over death"; epithet of Śiva.

mudgara, a cudgel or short club.

Mura, a Daitya slain by Kṛṣṇa/Viṣṇu.

muraja, a percussive musical instrument.

Muralā, attendant of Vāruṇī, who is the wife of the god of the oceans; name of a river in southern India that empties into the Bay of Bengal.

Murāri, "he who is the enemy of Mura (a Daitya slain by Kṛṣṇa)"; (1) epithet of Kṛṣṇa, and of Viṣṇu; also, (2) name of a famed Sanskrit poet, author of *Anargharāghava* (The priceless Rāghava), a drama centered on Rāma.

muṣala, a pestle-like bludgeon.

Nāga, snake; demigods who occupy the nether realm of Pātāla.

nāgapāśa, a noose resembling a snake; a weapon used to immobilize one's opponent.

Nagendra, "the Indra (lord, foremost) of mountains"; epithet of Himālaya, father of Pārvatī/Durgā.

Nahuṣa, a king in ancient times. Once, when Indra after slaying Vṛtra went off to do purifying penance, all the sages got together and persuaded Nahuṣa to occupy the throne of the king of the gods, vacated by Indra.

Naikaṣeya, epithet of Rāvaṇa (also applied to two of his brothers, Kumbhakarṇa and Vibhīṣaṇa); matronymic from Nikaṣā.

Nala, (1) name of a warrior from the southern kingdom of Kiṣkindhyā, allied with Rāma against the Rākṣasas (cantos 6, 7, and 8). Also, (2) name of a king, both handsome and good, whom the beautiful princess Damayantī chose for her husband at the *svayamvara* (see *svayamvara*) attended by a number of the gods (canto 6). Previously, those gods, having learned of her good qualities, had asked Nala to intercede on their behalf to ask Damayantī to marry one of them, not Nala. Nala, ever obliging, relayed the proposal to Damayantī, who, however, affirmed her love for only Nala. She suggested a *svayamvara* at which she would choose Nala, thereby absolving Nala of any responsibility for advancing his own suit personally over that of the gods. Being told of Damayantī's intentions by Nala, the gods decided to come disguised as Nala. Only after she begged them to evince godly attributes (no perspiration, casting no shadow, feet not touching the ground, eyes not blinking) could she determine who was the real Nala, whom she then chose to be her husband.

Namuci, "he who lets no one escape"; name of an Asura slain by Indra.

Nandana, "gladdening"; Indra's paradisiacal garden.

Nandī, Śiva's main attendant.

nārāca, a kind of missile made of iron, shot from a bow.

Narāntaka, "he who destroys men"; one of Rāvaṇa's sons.

Nikaṣā, mother of Rāvaṇa, Kumbhakarṇa, and Vibhīṣaṇa.

Nikumbhilā, (1) a temple on Laṅkā or (2) the name of a ritual performed at a particular place. According to some, it is a grove at Laṅkā city's western gate for the performance of sacrificial rites; according to others, it is a cave located in the western part of Laṅkā; according to one editor of the Bangla *Rāmāyaṇa*, it—whatever it is—is located "twenty *krośa* [one *krośa* equals approximately two miles] from Sri Lanka's Colombo" (Nayanacandra Mukhopadhyay, *Sacitra Kṛttivāsī Rāmāyaṇa*, app. I, s.v. *nikumbhilā*).

Nīla, name of a warrior from the southern kingdom of Kiṣkindhyā, allied with Rāma against the Rākṣasas.

Nīlakaṇṭha, "he whose throat is blue"; epithet of Śiva, who drank the poison produced at the time of the churning of the cosmic ocean in order to save creation. The poison darkened his throat, but Śiva survived.

Niśācara, "he who moves at night"; another name for a Rākṣasa.

Niśācarī, "she who moves at night"; another name for a Rākṣasī.

Niṣāda, a hunter; the name of a particular caste of low status. The first occurrence of this word, in canto 4, in a simile describing Sītā succumbing to grief as she relates, in essence, a portion of the *Rāmāyaṇa*, is evocative of the manner in which Vālmīki—who grieved over the killing of a bird by a Niṣāda hunter—is said to have discovered the meter, *śloka*, used to compose the Sanskrit *Rāmāyaṇa*; see Vālmīki.

Nistāriṇī, "she who saves"; epithet of Durgā.

Niśumbha, younger brother of the Asura Śumbha, both slain by Durgā.

Nṛmuṇḍamālinī, "she who wears a necklace of human heads"; epithet of the goddess Kālī but also the name of Pramīlā's maid servant.

pā, the cuckoo's call. A wonderful songbird and so recognized as such in South Asia, the cuckoo is said to sing the fifth note of the scale as its very own, "quintessential" song. The names of the tones—"do, re, mi, fa, sol, la, ti," of a Western diatonic scale—are in the classical Indian musical system "sā, re, gā, mā, pā, dhā, ni," with "pā" being the fifth interval. A gloss for the word "fifth" in premodern Bangla is "fine, charming." Writes Sukumar Sen, "The peculiar meaning comes from the popular idea of the fifth note (the cuckoo's cry) being the sweetest of the septet"; *An Etymological Dictionary of Bengali: c. 1000–1800 A.D.* (Kolkata: Eastern Publishers, 1971).

Padmayoni, "he who originates from a lotus"; epithet of Brahmā.

Pañcamukha, "he who has five faces"; epithet of Śiva, whose iconographic representation sometimes, but not always, shows him with five faces facing in five directions; see Sahasrākṣa for a tale of how Śiva got his five faces.

Pañcaśara, "he who has five arrows"; epithet of Kāma, god of love, whose five arrows are made of the blossoms of the mango, *aśoka*, jasmine, *bakula*, and myrtle, and induce beguilement, burning, desiccation, paralysis, and stupefaction.

Pañcatantra, "the five lessons"; a Sanskrit text of moral tales teaching princes how to behave.

Pañcavaṭī, a tract of forest through which flows the Godāvarī River, located within the larger Daṇḍaka Forest in southern India; the locale where Sītā, Rāma, and Lakṣmaṇa were spending some of their days in exile.

Pāṇḍava, patronymic from Pāṇḍu, who had five sons, Yudhiṣṭhira, Bhīmasena, Arjuna, Sahadeva, and Nakula. Pāṇḍu's sons and those of Pāṇḍu's brother, the blind Dhṛtarāṣṭra, fought against each other in the great war narrated in the *Mahābhārata*.

pārijāta, a mythical heavenly flowering tree and its blossom, extracted from the cosmic ocean when churned by the Suras (gods) and Asuras (antigods).

Pārtha, epithet of Arjuna; matronymic from Pṛthā (also known as Kuntī), mother of Yudhiṣṭhira, Bhīma, and Arjuna. Although the name could apply to all three of Kuntī's children, it most commonly designates Arjuna.

Pārvatī, "daughter of the mountain"; epithet of Durgā; patronymic from Parvata (literally, "mountain"), also known as Himālaya.

Pāśī, "possessing a noose"; epithet of Varuṇa, god of the sea.

Pāśupata, "related to Paśupati"; a wondrous weapon bestowed upon Arjuna by Paśupati (Śiva, in the guise of a Kirāta hunter); it is the missile that will be discharged by Śiva (Paśupati) at the time of the destruction of the universe.

Paśupati, "lord of the animals"; epithet of Śiva.

Pātāla, one of the three worlds comprising the universe—the other two being the earth (*martya*) and the heavens (*svarga*). Pātāla is quite separate from, and should not be confused with, Naraka or "hell," where punishment is meted out to those who have transgressed *dharma*.

paṭṭiśa, a large, double-edged battle-ax mounted on a shaft as long as a man is tall.

Paulastya, epithet of Rāvaṇa; patronymic from the sage Pulastya, ancestor of Kubera, Rāvaṇa, Kumbhakarṇa, and Vibhīṣaṇa; it designates Rāvaṇa only in *The Slaying of Meghanāda*.

Paulomī, epithet of Śacī, wife of Indra; patronymic from the Dānava Puloma, who cursed Indra for violating his daughter and then was slain by Indra.

Paurava, epithet of the Pāṇḍavas; patronymic from Puru, distant ancestor of the Pāṇḍavas (and Kauravas).

Pavana, god of the winds; the wind deified. Pavana is the father of Hanumān, ally of Rāma. In *The Slaying of Meghanāda*, the wind is cast in the role of one hostile to the sea, a characterization that comes from Datta's reading of the Homeric epics, not from the Indic epic tradition.

phiṅgā, a rather common black-colored songbird.

Phuladhanu, "he whose bow is made of flowers"; epithet of Kāma, god of love.

Pināka, name of Śiva's bow. It was the bow used as a test at Sītā's *svayamvara* (see *svayamvara*); only the suitor who had the strength to string Pināka would be considered a fit spouse. Rāma's strength was such that he not merely bent the bow enough to string it but in fact broke that most powerful of bows.

Pinākī, "he who wields the bow named Pināka"; epithet of Śiva.

Pītāmbara, "he who wears the yellow garment"; epithet of Kṛṣṇa and Viṣṇu, referring to the latter in *The Slaying of Meghanāda*.

Prabhā, "radiance"; name of the wife of Sūrya, who is both god of the sun and the sun deified.

Prabhañjana, "breaker"; epithet of Pavana, who is both god of the winds and the wind itself deified; father of Hanumān.

Prabhāṣā, "well-spoken lady"; Meghanāda's wet nurse.

Pracetas, name of Varuṇa, god of the sea.

praharaṇa, a *lāṭhi* or stave or club of some sort.

prakṣveḍana, a spear made of iron.

Pralaya, the time of and the act of the destruction of the universe, following the fourth and most degenerate *yuga*, the Kali *yuga*, after which the universe will be created anew; see *yuga*. It is Śiva who destroys the world. At this time of universal dissolution, fires and storms rage, and the world is inundated.

Pramatta, "besotted"; name of a Rākṣasa warrior.

Pramīlā, the one and only wife of Meghanāda and daughter of a Dānava by the name of Kālanemi. Meghanāda has no wife in Vālmīki's Sanskrit *Rāmāyaṇa* or any named spouse in Kṛttivāsa's Bangla version—though the number of his wives is given in that latter text as 9,000.

Pramoda, "gladness"; name of a pleasant retreat on the isle of Laṅkā, some distance from the walled city.

Providence, a translation throughout *The Slaying of Meghanāda* of the word Vidhātā; see Vidhātā.

pūjā, an act of ritual worship.

Puloma, father of Indra's wife Śacī. The Dānava Puloma was slain by his son-in-law, Indra, whom Puloma had cursed for violating his daughter.

Puṇḍarīkākṣa, "he who has lotus-blossom-like eyes"; epithet of Kṛṣṇa and Viṣṇu, referring to the latter in *The Slaying of Meghanāda*.

Purāṇa, "old"; the texts containing ancient lore, the Puranas.

Purandara, "destroyer of cities"; epithet of Indra.

purohit, a Hindu priest.

Puṣpaka, name of Kubera's wondrous flying chariot, the original commandeered by his half-brother Rāvaṇa and used by the latter for, among other things, transporting the kidnapped Sītā from the Pañcavaṭī Forest on the mainland of India to his island kingdom on Laṅkā.

rabāb, a stringed musical instrument, cognate with the European rebec or rebeck.

rāga, principal mode or scale in Indian classical music, of which there are six.

Rāghava, epithet of Rāma; patronymic from Raghu, great-grandfather of Rāma, Bharata, Lakṣmaṇa, and Śatrughna; designates Rāma only in *The Slaying of Meghanāda*.

Rāghavacandra, epithet of Rāma; see Rāghava. Though "candra" literally means moon, Rāma is of the "solar" dynasty of kings, not of the other major royal line, the "lunar" lineage, which includes the Pāṇḍavas and the Kauravas.

Rāghavānuja, "the one born after Rāghava (Rāma)"; can apply to Bharata, Lakṣmaṇa, and Śatrughna, the three younger brothers of Rāma, but designates Lakṣmaṇa only in *The Slaying of Meghanāda*.

Rāghavendra, "an Indra (lord, foremost) among Rāghavas"; epithet of Rāma.

Raghu, a patriarch within Rāma's lineage; great-grandfather of Rāma; see Dilīpa.

rāgiṇī, secondary mode or scale in Indian classical music, of which there are thirty-six.

Rāhu, an Asura identified with the eclipse. An eclipse of the moon, which is made of ambrosia (called *amṛta*, also *soma*), occurs when the moon is swallowed by Rāhu. During the churning of the primordial ocean by the Suras (gods) and Asuras (antigods), the Asuras initially captured the *amṛta* extracted from the ocean. At one point Rāhu tried to make himself immortal by drinking that *amṛta,* but Viṣṇu decapitated him. Since the *amṛta* touched his mouth and started down his gullet only, it is only that part of him, the head and upper throat, that became immortal and continued to exist as a separate entity. Rāhu still lusts after the *amṛta* of immortality and manages to swallow the moon from time to time. Since Rāhu has no body, the moon passes through his mouth and reappears out of his gullet, never to be consumed and digested by that Asura.

Rājalakṣmī, "Lakṣmī of the king"; epithet of goddess Lakṣmī; as Rājalakṣmī, she is royal fortune personified, present when the raja and the rajadom are prosperous, absent when their fortunes are reversed.

Rākṣasa, an antigod or opposer of the gods; the name, ironically, derives from *rakṣ*, "to protect," and is interpreted to mean something to be protected from; often considered synonymous with Asura, Daitya, Dānava, and Karbūra.

Rākṣasī, the feminine of Rākṣasa, a female Rākṣasa.

Raktabīja, "drop(s) of blood"; name of a particular Asura who served as general in the army of the two Asura brothers Śumbha and Niśumbha. He was a particularly difficult adversary for Durgā to overcome, for whenever a drop of his blood would fall to the ground, another Raktabīja would spring forth to continue the fight.

Raktākṣa, "he whose eyes are blood red"; name of a warrior from the southern kingdom of Kiṣkindhyā, allied with Rāma against the Rākṣasas.

Ramā, "pleasing lady"; epithet of Lakṣmī.

Rāma, name of the warrior prince, eldest son of Daśaratha, husband of Sītā; immortalized in the epic tale, *Rāmāyaṇa*. In later Hinduism, Rāma was elevated from mortal to god, becoming known as an *avatāra* or incarnation of Viṣṇu.

Rāmabhadra, name of Rāma. The "bhadra" is an honorific suffix meaning blessed or fortunate. Rāmabhadra is also a name for Kṛṣṇa's elder brother, Balarāma, though not used in this sense in *The Slaying of Meghanāda.*

Rāmacandra, name of Rāma. Though "candra" literally means moon, Rāma is of the "solar" dynasty of kings, not of the other major royal line, the "lunar" lineage, which includes the Pāṇḍavas and the Kauravas.

Rāmānuja, "the one born after Rāma"; can apply to Bharata, Lakṣmaṇa, and Śatrughna, the three younger brothers of Rāma, but designates only Lakṣmaṇa in *The Slaying of Meghanāda.*

Rāmāyaṇa, "the wanderings of Rāma"; one of the two major Hindu Indian epics, the *Mahābhārata* being the other. In seven *kāṇḍas* or books, the *Rāmāyaṇa* tells of the self-imposed exile of Rāma, Lakṣmaṇa, and Sītā; Sītā's abduction by the Rākṣasa king, Rāvaṇa; the war on Laṅkā between the Rākṣasa forces and Rāma's, with his southern allies including Hanumān; and the rescue of Sītā.

Rambhā, name of one of the members of the class of celestial demigoddesses called Apsarās, known for their exceptional beauty and their dancing ability.

rasa, "juice"; the quintessence of something; the prevailing sentiment or emotion in a work of literature. This pregnant and salient term of Indian aesthetics stands for, on one level, the eight (or sometimes nine or ten) dominant sentiments present in literature: *śṛṅgāra* (erotic love) (also called *ādirasa*, "the original *rasa*"), *vīra* (heroism, virility), *karuṇa* (pathos), *adbhuta* (wonder), *hāsya* (mirth), *bhayānaka* (terror), *bībhatsa* (disgust), and *raudra* (fury)—and sometimes *śānta* (contentment) and *vātsalya* (parental affection). An individual piece of literature is to have one of these *rasas* dominant, though others may be present. On another level, *rasa* has been interpreted by aestheticians to mean an almost metaphysical quality of good literature that is produced by the work of literature and experienced or tasted by the literary connoisseur; such a *rasa* is transitory, lasting only as long as the literature is being experienced.

Rasātala, lowest level of the seven-tiered netherworld called Pātāla; often metonymically used for Pātāla collectively.

Rati, "passion, coitus"; wife of Kāma, god of love.

Ratnākara, "gem quarry" or "ocean"; the name of the poet Vālmīki when he was still a murderous thief; see Vālmīki.

Raurava, name of one of the many hell holes or pits of punishment in Naraka, "hell." (Naraka is not the same as Pātāla, "the netherworld"; see Pātāla.)

Rāvaṇa, lord of the Rākṣasas and ruler of Laṅkā.

Rāvaṇānuja, "the one born after Rāvaṇa"; can apply to Kumbhakarṇa and Vibhīṣaṇa, younger brothers of Rāvaṇa, but designates only Vibhīṣaṇa in *The Slaying of Meghanāda*.

Rāvaṇi, epithet of Meghanāda; patronymic from Rāvaṇa.

Rohiṇī, one of the twenty-seven stars (*nakṣatra*: a constellation or lunar "house" through which the moon passes), all twenty-seven of which are considered beautiful wives of Candra, the moon. Rohiṇī, among those twenty-seven, is most often named as the moon's favorite wife. (Rohiṇī is also the name of Vasudeva's second wife, mother of Balarāma; see Kṛṣṇa.)

Rudra, "furious"; epithet of Śiva. Also, the Rudras, plural and collectively, are considered the progeny of Rudra and are associated with the (furious) winds.

rudra tejas, Śiva's [Rudra's] power [*tejas*] objectified.

Śacī, wife of Indra, lord of the gods.

Ṣaḍānana, "he who has six faces"; epithet of Kārttikeya, god of war, general of the gods.

Sadānanda, "he who is always pleased"; epithet of Śiva.

Sahasrākṣa, "he who has 1,000 eyes"; epithet of Indra. Indra became infatuated with the sage Gautama's wife, Ahalyā. In Gautama's absence, Indra disguised himself as Gautama and had sex with Ahalyā. Gautama happened upon the cuckolding Indra and cursed him to have 1,000 vaginas all over his body, vaginas which in time metamorphosed into eyes. Ahalyā, for her part, was cursed to become a stone for 1,000 years, only to be released from that curse by the touch of Rāma's foot, which occurred soon after Rāma, Lakṣmaṇa, and Sītā wandered off into exile. A different tale is told in the Bangla *Mahābhārata* to account for this epithet of Indra. In order to defeat the two Asura brothers, Sunda and Upasanda, who had been given a boon by Brahmā that each could be killed by no one except his own brother, Viśvakarmā, the gods' architect and master builder, fashioned an exceedingly gorgeous woman from the most handsome bits of the supremely beautiful beings in all the three worlds, thereby creating Tilottamā ("she of the best [*uttamā*] of bits [*tila*]"). Tilottamā incited jealousy between the two brothers, who fell to fighting and eventually killed each other; see Sunda. Prior to appearing before those brothers, however, Tilottamā stood in front of the gods. Her glamor so riveted Śiva that his face(s) became five, pointing in all directions so that wherever his face looked, she was there. Those four (new, directional) faces, plus the one he had before Tilottamā appeared, account for the five faces of Śiva and also for his epithet, Pañcamukha, "he who has five faces." Indra, also, reacted somatically to Tilottamā's stunning beauty. When Indra saw Tilottamā, more eyes developed in and of themselves all over his body, the better for Indra to gaze at pretty Tilottamā.

Śaiva, a devotee of Śiva.

Śakra, "he who supports; mighty"; epithet of Indra, lord of the skies.

Śākta, a devotee of Śakti, of the mother goddess, of goddesses Durgā and Kālī, in particular.

Śakti, "power, force, strength" ; (1) a name by which the mother goddess is known. All Hindu goddesses are, in some sense, an aspect of the one "mother goddess" or Śakti or, in other words, goddess Durgā. Also, (2) name of the special missile by which Lakṣmaṇa is seemingly slain; see Ekāghnī.

Śaktidhara, "wielder of power"; epithet of Kārttikeya, god of war, general of the gods.

śāla, a variety of tree, particularly tall, the lumber from which is strong.

śālmalī, a variety of tree, the seed pods of which produce a kapoklike substance.

Śamana, "he who calms or quells"; epithet of Yama, god of death.

Śambara, name of an Asura in Vedic times associated with and slain by Indra, then later, in the time of the epics, associated with and slain by Kāma, god of love.

Śambhu, "helpful"; epithet of Śiva.

śamī, a variety of tree. High up in such a tree the Pāṇḍavas deposited their battle gear before approaching, in disguise, King Virāṭa at the start of their thirteenth year in exile.

Samīra, the wind deified.

Sañjaya, personal warrior manservant of Dhṛtarāṣṭra. It is he who tells the blind king of the results of the great Bhārata war, including the deaths of Dhṛtarāṣṭra's one hundred sons.

Sañjīvanī, "life-instilling, life-restoring"; a name for the realm of Yama, the god of death.

Śaṅkara, name of Śiva.

Śaṅkarī, name of Durgā.

sapharī, a variety of fish with silvery scales.

saptasvarā, a musical instrument consisting of seven vessels filled with water and played by striking their rims.

Śarabha, a mythological animal with eight legs, stronger than both the lion and the elephant; name of a warrior from the southern kingdom of Kiṣkindhyā, allied with Rāma against the Rākṣasas.

Saramā, wife of Rāvaṇa's brother Vibhīṣaṇa.

Sāraṇa, Rāvaṇa's prime minister.

Sarasvatī, goddess of speech, the arts, and learning.

Sarayū, a river in northern India on which was located Rāma's capital of Ayodhyā.

Sarvabhuk, "eater of everything"; epithet of Agni, god of fire and fire itself and Meghanāda's chosen deity.

Sarvaśuci, "he who is all pure"; epithet of Agni, god of fire and fire itself and Meghanāda's chosen deity.

Śaśāṅkadhāriṇī, "wife of him who holds the hare-marked moon [on his head]"; epithet of Durgā.

Satī, "she who is true"; epithet of Durgā; see Dakṣa (2).

Śatrughna, the youngest of Rāma's three half-brothers, Bharata and Lakṣmaṇa being the others.

Satya, "truth"; name of the first of four eras (see *yuga*) in the Hindu cosmological cycle.

Saumitri, epithet of Lakṣmaṇa; matronymic from Sumitrā, youngest of Daśaratha's three wives.

Sauri (also spelled Śauri), "he who is heroic"; epithet of Viṣṇu.

śela, a sharp-pointed missile.

seṃuti, a white roselike flower.

Senā, name of the wife of Kārttikeya. The word *senā* also means army, and Kārttikeya is the general of the gods.

Śeṣa, a mythological snake, also known as Ananta; sometimes identified as king of the Nāgas (the great snakes); represented at times as forming the canopy with his hoods over Viṣṇu and at other times as supporting the entire world on his many heads, usually given as a thousand, but increased to 10,000 (*ayuta*) by Datta.

Śikhidhvaja, "he whose banner displays a peacock"; epithet of Kārttikeya, whose vehicle is the peacock.

śimula, another name for the *śālmalī* tree; see *śālmalī*.

Sītā, wife of Rāma. She was found as a baby by King Janaka in a plowed furrow (*sita*), hence the name.

Śiva, the great lord; the god who presides over the destruction of the universe at the end of the four-*yuga* cycle, concluding with the Kali *yuga*; husband of Durgā; chosen deity of Rāvaṇa. Śiva is also known as Rudra, "the furious one," whose abstracted power is called *rudra* and is at one point bestowed upon Rāvaṇa. Śiva is the greatest of yogis; he holds a trident, has on his head the *jaṭā* (a pile of matted hair), wears snakes upon his body, and has a third eye in the middle of his forehead which, when open, spews fire and once incinerated the god of love, Anaṅga; the Ganges River, also called Tripathagā, falls from heaven to earth, landing in his hair (canto 9).

Skanda, name of Kārttikeya.

Smara, "memory"; epithet of Kāma, god of love.

Śrī, (1) an honorific title for men, comparable to "Mr." or "the honorable"; also, (2) name of Lakṣmī, goddess of beauty and good fortune, and spouse of Viṣṇu.

Śrīkaṇṭha, "he whose voice is that of Śrī, goddess of beauty"; epithet of the famed Sanskrit poet and scholar Bhavabhūti, who composed the drama *Uttararāmacarita* (The later history of Rāma).

Sthāṇu, "stationary, firm, immovable"; epithet of Śiva, alluding to his condition while deep within a yogic trance.

Subāhu, "he who has good (strong) arms"; name of a warrior from the southern kingdom of Kiṣkindhyā, allied with Rāma against the Rākṣasas.

Sudakṣiṇā, wife of Dilīpa, one of Rāma's predecessors in the "solar" dynasty.

Sugrīva, king of the southern kingdom of Kiṣkindhyā and ally of Rāma. With Rāma's active help, Sugrīva slew his elder brother Vāli (Rāma did the actual killing), laid claim to the Kiṣkindhyā throne, and married his brother's wife Tārā; in exchange for Rāma's assistance, Sugrīva committed his troops to aid Rāma in recovering Sītā.

Śūlapāṇi, "he whose hand holds a trident"; epithet of Śiva.

Śūlī, "he who has a trident"; epithet of Śiva.

Sumālī, name of a warrior from the southern kingdom of Kiṣkindhyā, allied with Rāma against the Rākṣasas.

Śumbha, elder brother of the Asura Niśumbha, both slain by Durgā.

Sumitrā, mother of Lakṣmaṇa and Śatrughna and the youngest of Daśaratha's three wives, Kauśalyā and Kaikeyī being the other two.

Sunāsīra, name of Indra; the name itself may derive from the names of two rural deities favorable to the growth of grain.

Sunda, an Asura and elder brother of Upasunda. The brothers were totally unified in thought and deed and decided to gain control of the three worlds by virtue of the power they would accumulate through performing austerities. For years they fasted, living on air alone. Brahmā, noting their austerities, summoned them and offered them a boon. They chose immortality. Brahmā balked, unwilling to accede to such a request. The brothers responded by saying they would continue their austerities (and thereby continue to accumulate power) until and unless they were bestowed the boon they sought. Brahmā explained to them that birth inevitably implied death. He asked them to make some provision for death. The brothers answered by proposing that they were not to be killed at the hands of another; only if and when they themselves were to turn on one another would they be slain by their own hands. Brahmā said "be it so," and the brothers proceeded to conquer and oppress all the three worlds. The holy sages and gods, now displaced from their heavens, approached Brahmā, seeking a solution to the obvious problem. Brahmā called upon Viśvakarmā, the gods' builder, and directed him to fashion the most gorgeous woman in the entire three worlds. For this, Viśvakarmā collected the most handsome bits of the most stunningly beautiful beings in all the three worlds and created Tilottamā ("she of the best [*uttamā*] of bits [*tila*]"). When the brothers, who had been dallying atop the Vindhya mountains with their numerous Asura wives and Vidyādharī demigoddesses, saw Tilottamā, they were utterly infatuated. Sunda took hold of her right hand; Upasunda grasped her left. Sunda then told Upasunda to let go of her hand, that he saw her first, that she was his wife, and that she should be respected as such by Upasunda. Upasunda claimed she married him and that Sunda ought not touch the wife of his younger brother. The two brothers insult each other and eventually come to blows, whereby each kills the other.

Sūrpaṇakhā (also spelled Śūrpaṇakhā), sister of Rāvaṇa. Upon seeing Rāma in the Pañcavaṭī Forest, this Rākṣasī was smitten with desire. By wizardry, she assumed the form of a beautiful woman, approached Rāma, and proposed marriage. Rāma, in jest but mock concern, told her that he did not want her to become a mere co-wife (to Sītā), suggesting instead that she proposition Lakṣmaṇa who looked the bachelor, though he was actually already married; see Ūrmilā. This, Sūrpaṇakhā did, but Lakṣmaṇa encouraged her, facetiously, to press her case with Rāma. And she readily did that also, by trying to eat her competition, Sītā. Seeing his wife in danger, Rāma directed Lakṣmaṇa to protect Sītā, which Lakṣmaṇa accomplished by discharging a missile that lopped off Sūrpaṇakhā's nose and ears. Defaced and humiliated, she retreated to the side of the Rākṣasas Khara and Dūṣaṇa. They and their legions attacked but were defeated by Rāma and Lakṣmaṇa. Sūrpaṇakhā then returned to Laṅkā, where she incited Rāvaṇa to punish Rāma by kidnapping Sītā, arguing that Rāma would die out of sorrow for his lost wife. Rāvaṇa, hearing the description of pretty Sītā and being himself lustful by nature, agreed to do so. He enlisted the help of the Rākṣasa Mārīca, who first tried to talk Rāvaṇa out of this foolhardy venture but ended up assisting him by turning himself into a golden stag that Rāma and then Lakṣmaṇa followed into the forest—giving Rāvaṇa the chance to abduct the unprotected Sītā, thereby touching off the great battle in Laṅkā and bringing about Rāvaṇa's eventual downfall. Vālmīki's Sanskrit version of the *Rāmāyaṇa* had extended this scene somewhat by having first the sole surviving Rākṣasa return to tell Rāvaṇa of the deaths of Khara and Dūṣaṇa. Rāvaṇa approaches Mārīca with his scheme for kidnapping Sītā only to have Mārīca talk him out of it, for Mārīca had previously met up with Rāma and been defeated. Then Sūrpaṇakhā returns, disfigured. She both titillates (with a description of Sītā's beauty) and shames her brother into action. The results are the same. Rāvaṇa steals away Sītā and by so doing sets in motion the course of events that lead to his own destruction.

Suvacanī, "she who is well spoken"; name of a goddess invoked by women in distress; a goddess whose words come to fruition.

Svātī, one of the twenty-seven stars (*nakṣatra*: a constellation or lunar "house" through which the moon passes), all twenty-seven of which are considered beautiful wives of Candra, the moon. Pearls are said to form when and only when it rains while the star Svātī is in the night sky; it is then that oysters suck in those particular raindrops, turning them into pearls. Also, Svātī is identified with the star Arcturus and as a wife of the sun.

svayamvara, a ceremony by which the bride-to-be chooses from prospective grooms the one whom she will marry. Along with such a ceremony, the prospective grooms may be put to a test to determine who is the fittest and proper husband; see Pināka and Nala (2).

Śyāma, "dark colored, dark blue or green or black"; epithet of Kṛṣṇa, the dark lord, whose complexion is usually depicted as dark blue or blue-black.

tāla, a variety of palm tree.

Tālajaṅghā, "having shanks like palm trees"; name of a Rākṣasa warrior.

tamas, "ignorance, darkness"; one of the three qualities that is constitutive of everything in differing portions, the other two being *sattva* (truth, goodness) and *rajas* (passion, spiritedness).

Tāpasendra, "Indra (lord, foremost) of the ascetics"; epithet of Śiva.

Tārā, wife of Vāli, king of Kiṣkindhyā. Following the death of Vāli, Tārā becomes the wife of Sugrīva, Vāli's younger brother. Tārā's name is homonymic with the word for "star, astral body."

Tāraka, an Asura who captured heaven and was eventually defeated by Kārttikeya. Indra, vanquished by Tāraka, had gone with the other gods to seek Brahmā's counsel. Brahmā declared that only a son (named Ṣaḍānana, "the six-headed," also called Kārttikeya) born of Śiva's seed could slay Tāraka. Śiva at that time was unmarried and deep in yogic meditation. He had to be aroused from his trance. For that purpose, Indra sought the services of Kāma, the god of love, who awakened Śiva but was burned to ashes by Śiva for his effort. Later Śiva spilled his semen while dallying with Gaurī (Durgā, Haimavatī), which resulted in the birth of Kārttikeya, who eventually led the gods against the Asuras and personally slew Tāraka; see Kāma and Kārttikeya.

Tārakāri, "enemy of Tāraka (name of an Asura)"; epithet of Kārttikeya.

Tāriṇī, "she who rescues"; epithet of Durgā.

tomara, a lance of sorts.

Trijaṭā, "she who wears three piles of matted hair"; serving woman for Rāvaṇa and his chief queen, Mandodarī.

Tripathagā, "she who flows in three paths"; epithet of Gaṅgā, the Ganges River, who falls from the heavens onto Śiva's matted hair. The three paths refers to the Ganges as she flows in heaven, on the earth, and through Pātāla's netherworld.

Tripura, "three cities"; name of an Asura, defeated by Śiva. The three cities, collectively personified as an Asura, were built by Maya in the heavens (of gold), in the space between heaven and earth (of silver), and on earth (of iron). When the Asuras were about to destroy the three worlds, the gods importuned Śiva, who responded by burning the three cities and putting to death all the Asuras who lived there.

Tripurāri, "foe of the Three Cities (Tripura)"; epithet of Śiva.

Triśūlī, "he who has a trident"; epithet of Śiva.

Tryambaka, "he who has three eyes"; epithet of Śiva.

tulasī, name of a holy tree, especially sacred to Vaiṣṇavas, that is, devotees of Kṛṣṇa and of Rāma.

turi, a battle horn made of brass.

Tviṣāmpati, "lord of a mass of brilliance"; epithet of Sūrya, the sun god.

Udagra, "haughty, monstrous"; name of a Rākṣasa.

Ugracaṇḍā, "she who is wrathful and violent"; epithet of Durgā in her more violent and wrathful aspect.

ululu, the sound "ulululululu . . . ," made by women at auspicious times or festive occasions; it is a sound of joy, as opposed to the howl or keening denoted by the Latinate English word "ululation."

Umā, name of Durgā, wife of Śiva; often used to imply the goddess as the young wife of Śiva, as opposed to the goddess in her more powerful, warriorlike mien.

Upasunda, an Asura and younger brother of Sunda; see Sunda.

Upendra, "born subsequent to Indra"; epithet of Viṣṇu.

Ūrmilā, wife of Lakṣmaṇa, and also younger sister of Sītā.

Urvaśī, name of one member of the class of celestial demigoddesses called Apsarās, known for their exceptional beauty and their dancing ability.

Vaḍabā, name of Pramīlā's horse. Vaḍabā is also the name of a horse head that resides within the ocean. The "fire of Vaḍabā," known too as Vāḍaba or "the mare's fire," spews from her mouth and burns forever underwater in the depths of the Indian Ocean; see Vāḍaba.

Vāḍaba, "the mare's fire." It burns beneath the sea, at the South Pole by some accounts.

A couple of stories relate its coming into existence. One speaks of the sage Aurva, born of the Bhṛgu lineage. Kṣatriya forces were slaying the Brāhman Bhārgavas, even destroying children in the womb. One Bhārgava woman, to preserve her embryo, hid it in her thigh (*ūru*, hence the derivative name Aurva). Aurva burst forth from her thigh, blinded the enemy with his brilliance, and from his anger produced a flame that threatened to burn the three worlds. The Bhārgavas prevailed upon him to spare the world and cast his flaming rage into the ocean. Another tale tells of the sage Ūrva (alternative name for Aurva) who, desiring a son not born of woman's womb, churned fire in his own chest and brought forth a fiery son who then took his place in the southern seas and was known as Vaḍabā.

Vaidehī, epithet of Sītā; derived from Videha, name of a kingdom whose main city was Mithilā, ruled over by Sītā's father, Janaka.

Vaijayanta, name of Indra's palace in his heaven, which is called Amarāvatī or just Amarā.

Vaikuṇṭha, name of Viṣṇu's heavenly city.

Vainateya, the great bird Garuḍa, vehicle for and attendant of Viṣṇu; matronymic from Vinatā.

Vaiśvānara, "belonging to all men"; epithet of Agni, the god of fire and fire itself; Meghanāda's chosen deity.

Vaitaraṇī, the river that separates Naraka, "hell," from the other three worlds of heaven (*svarga*), earth (*martya*), and Pātāla.

Vajrapāṇi, "he whose hand holds a thunderbolt"; epithet of Indra.

Vajrī, "he who has a thunderbolt"; epithet of Indra.

Vāli, ruler of the southern kingdom of Kiṣkindhyā, slain by Rāma; elder brother of Sugrīva.

Vālmīki, composer of the Sanskrit *Rāmāyaṇa*. Ratnākara, son of a sage, was during the first part of his life a dacoit, robbing and murdering for a living. God Brahmā and the sage Nārada approached him one day and successfully persuaded him to change his ways by suggesting the sinner ask his father, mother, wife, and son whether they, who lived off his illicit earnings, would be willing to bear the burden of his sins. None of the ingrates was, which moved Ratnākara to reform. Brahmā directed him to repeat Rāma's name and thereby absolve himself of all his sins. Ratnākara, however, feeling unworthy, could not bring himself to utter Rāma's sacred name, so Brahmā had him pronounce the word which describes a man who has died. Death and a dead person being polluting, Ratnākara felt fit to utter such an unworthy word. The word "dead" is pronounced *marā* in Bangla. As Ratnākara chanted *marā marā marā*, he eventually, with the words running together (*marā marā marā marāmarāmarā*), was saying Rāma's name (*ma/rāma/rāma/rāma rāma rāma rāma rāma*). Ratnākara then sat in one spot and chanted that holy name for 60,000 years during which time his body was devoured by ants. But still he continued to chant Rāma's name, from within the ant hill. After 60,000 years Brahmā returned, saw the ant hill, and heard the words "Rāma, Rāma, Rāma" coming from within. He had Indra cause rain to fall for seven days, washing away all of Ratnākara but his bones. Then Brahmā, the creator, summoned Ratnākara back to life, gave him the name Vālmīki, a patronymic from *valmīka* (ant hill), and instructed him to compose the *Rāmāyaṇa*. Vālmīki (alias Ratnākara) protested that he knew not poetry nor meter, to which Brahmā replied: "Sarasvatī shall dwell upon your tongue / Much poetry shall issue from your mouth." As the passage proceeds, we find Vālmīki seated beneath a tree, beside a lake, chanting Rāma's efficacious name. At such time, a hunter (Niṣāda) happens by and fells with his arrow one of two herons perched upon a branch above Vālmīki. Those herons were making love when the one was hit, falling into Vālmīki's lap. Horrified by this senseless violence against innocent birds, Vālmīki cursed the fowler. The curse itself, emanating from a profound sense of grief (*śoka*), came out as though spontaneously in a new metrical pattern called *śloka*: a Sanskrit couplet meter (unrhymed) of sixteen syllables per line divided into hemistiches of eight units each. And so, we have the origin (out of *śoka*) of *śloka*, the prevalent epic meter in Sanskrit literature. (Bangla relies predominantly upon *payār*—see Introduction—in its epics.) Vālmīki then proceeded to compose the *Rāmāyaṇa* in his newly found *śloka* meter.

Vāma, name of Śiva.

Vāmana, the fifth *avatāra* of Viṣṇu when he descended to earth in the form of a dwarf to humble the Daitya Bali; see Bali.

Vanadevī, "forest goddess"; a goddess presiding over the forest.

Varadā, "she who grants boons"; epithet of goddesses, Sarasvatī, and others.

Varānanā, "she whose face is beautiful"; name of an Apsarā, demigoddesses renowned for their beauty; in *The Slaying of Meghanāda* the epithet applies to Rati, wife of Kāma, god of love.

Vāruṇī, wife of Varuṇa, god of the sea. Her name (feminine of Varuṇa) is spelled several ways.

Vāsantī, "she who is like the springtime"; "the jasmine"; "a light orange color"; name of the confidante to Meghanāda's wife Pramīlā.

Vāsava, epithet of Indra as lord of the Vasus, "the good ones," that is, the gods; "Indra's bow/Vāsava's bow" is the rainbow.

Vāsavajit, "victor over Vāsava"; epithet of Meghanāda.

Vāskala, name of a Rākṣasa warrior.

Vibhāvasu, "he whose wealth is brilliance"; epithet of Agni, god of fire and fire itself; Meghanāda's chosen deity.

Vibhīṣaṇa, younger brother of Rāvaṇa and husband of Saramā. He advises his brother to return Sītā, is kicked for his counsel, and defects to become one of Rāma's trusted allies.

Vidhātā, "providence"; often identified with Brahmā. The term "Providence" in this translation of *The Slaying of Meghanāda* is always a rendering of the word *vidhātā*.

Vidhi, "fate"; often identified with Brahmā. The term "Fate" in this translation of *The Slaying of Meghanāda* is always a rendering of the word *vidhi*.

Vidyādhara, a class of celestial demigods, known for their skills in the arts.

Vidyādharī, a class of celestial demigoddesses, known for their skills in the arts and for their beauty.

Vijayā, one of the two female attendants of Durgā, Jayā being the other.

vīṇā, a stringed musical instrument.

Vinatā, mother of Garuḍa and five other sons, including her eldest son Aruṇa, who in turn had two sons, one of them being Jaṭāyu.

Vindhya, the mountain range in central India which, in a sense, divides northern from southern India.

Vīrabāhu, "virile-armed"; a son of Rāvaṇa and Citrāṅgadā. He is a character created by Kṛttivāsa.

Vīrabhadra, name of a warrior and factotum for Śiva.

Virāṭa, name of a king in whose realm the Pāṇḍavas lived in disguise during their thirteenth year of exile; also, name of the kingdom itself.

Virūpākṣa, "odd-eyed"; (1) name of a Rākṣasa warrior; also, (2) an epithet of Śiva, referring to the third eye in the middle of his forehead.

Viśalyakaraṇī, the restorative herb that grows upon Mount Gandhamādana on the Indian mainland, and is needed to revive Lakṣmaṇa. In more traditional *Rāmāyaṇas*, Hanumān leaps or flies to the mountain and, after some adventures, manages to bring back to Laṅkā the entire mountain, including the herb. In *The Slaying of Meghanāda*, where Hanumān is no flying monkey, the mountain, according to Rāvaṇa's prime minister, would appear to have come of its own accord.

Viśvanātha, "lord of the universe"; epithet of Śiva.

Vītihotra, "he by whom the *soma* offering is eaten"; epithet of Agni, who is both the god of fire and fire itself; Meghanāda's chosen deity.

Vraja, the land where Kṛṣṇa grew up and played with the Gopīs or cowherd maidens, Rādhā in particular. Vraja, wherein is found the village of Gokula and the Vṛndāvana Forest, is located on one bank of the Yamunā River; across that river a little bit away lies Madhupura, where the adult Kṛṣṇa goes to slay King Kaṃsa, never to return to Vraja; see Kṛṣṇa and Madhupura.

Vṛṣabhadhvaja, "he whose banner displays a bull"; epithet of Śiva.

Vṛṣadhvaja, "he whose banner displays a bull"; epithet of Śiva.

Vṛtra, name of an Asura whom Indra slew with his thunderbolt. An ancient malevolent force from Vedic times, Vṛtra was associated with darkness and drought and considered in perpetual conflict with Indra, lord of the skies.

Vyomakeśa, "he whose hair is in the sky"; epithet of Śiva.

Yakṣa, a class of supernatural beings related to the Rākṣasas, though usually not malevolent. Their lord, Kubera, is the elder half brother of Rāvaṇa and presides over riches; see Dhanada.

Yama, god of death. He carries a staff (*daṇḍa*) with which to punish (*daṇḍa* also means punishment); see Daṇḍadhara.

Yamunā, a major river in northern India; flows from the Himālayas past Hastinā (first the Kauravas' and later the Pāṇḍavas' capital), past Madhupura and Vraja (where Kṛṣṇa was born and where he grew up, respectively), and joins the Ganges River at Prayāga, now called Allahabad, on their collective way to the Bay of Bengal. Yamunā is considered to be the daughter of the sun (canto 1); one of the many tales illustrating Kṛṣṇa's powers tells of him subduing (actually dancing on the multiple heads of) the poisonous water serpent Kāliya, who threatened those from Vraja bathing in the Yamunā River (canto 3).

Yogāsana, "a posture or sitting position for yogic meditation"; name of a plateau at the very top of Mount Kailāsa where Śiva meditates.

Yogīndra, "Indra (lord, foremost) of yogis"; epithet of Śiva as well as, quite literally, "the greatest of yogis." In *The Slaying of Meghanāda,* Yogīndra is said to possess a "mind-lake." Mānasa means "the mind, thought, desire, the heart" and is the name of a particular lake in the Himālayas to which swans (*haṃsa*) retreat with the advent of the monsoon season, according to a well-established poetic conceit. Moreover, a *mānasa-putra* is a son created from one's mind or heart or desire, a "son of the mind or heart." Extending this to the image in canto 7, the *mānasa-haṃsa* is both a "swan of the mind" and a "swan upon lake Mānasa." Cintāmaṇi (literally, "gem of thought," epithet of Viṣṇu) is likened here to the swans (thought personified) upon the lake-cum-mind of the greatest of yogis, Śiva, deep in meditation; see Cintāmaṇi.

Yoginī, a female yogi. Along with Ḍākinīs, who are female goblinlike demigoddesses, Yoginīs also attend upon Śiva and Durgā.

yuga, each of the four "ages" which, taken together, form a complete cycle (*kalpa*) in Hindu cosmological time. In descending order (temporally and morally), they are the Satya (also called Kṛta) *yuga,* sometimes characterized as "the golden age," the Tretā *yuga*, the Dvāpara *yuga*, and the Kali *yuga* or the present era, known as the most degenerate of all. At the conclusion of the Kali *yuga* comes Pralaya or the destruction of the world, following which a new cycle will begin.

CPSIA information can be obtained
at www.ICGtesting.com
Printed in the USA
BVHW040304040919
557490BV00002B/3/P

9 780195 167993